The Twentieth-Century Performance Reader

For the first time it is possible to compare major writings on all types of performance – dance, music, theatre, live art – in one volume. In this pioneering selection of seminal texts, written by over forty international practitioners, the editors encourage performance to be considered across and between disciplines, rather than presenting merely an historical survey.

Sections are organised not chronologically or according to art form, but alphabetically, therefore allowing the reader freedom to cross-refer and compare without restraint. The contributors – not only performers, composers, choreographers, directors and playwrights, but also key critics and theorists – all seek to affirm performance as a discipline in its own right. The writing is fully supplemented with contextual summaries, cross-references and suggested further reading, and features a definitive new bibliography. Artaud, Bausch, Brecht, Cage, Cunningham, Duncan, Glass, Hijikata, Kantor, Marinetti, Rainer, Schechner and Soyinka are just some of the writers included in this volume.

This reader will be an essential sourcebook for researchers, practitioners and all students of dance, music, theatre, drama and performance studies. It will also be of interest to anyone who enjoys innovative live performance.

Michael Huxley teaches and researches dance and performance history at De Montfort University. **Noel Witts** is Professor of Performing Arts at De Montfort University and also writes and broadcasts for the BBC.

The Twentieth-Century Performance Reader

The

Twentieth-Century

Performance

Reader

Edited, with an introduction and
contextual summaries, by

Michael Huxley

and

Noel Witts

ROUTLEDGE

First published 1996
by Routledge
11 New Fetter Lane, London EC4P 4EE

Simultaneously published in the USA
and Canada by Routledge
29 West 35th Street, New York,
NY 10001

Reprinted 1997

© 1996 Michael Huxley and Noel Witts

Typeset in Bell Gothic and Perpetua by
Florencetype Ltd, Stoodleigh, Devon

Printed and bound in Great Britain by
Biddles Ltd, Guildford and King's Lynn

British Library Cataloguing in Publication Data

A catalogue record for this book is available
from the British Library

Library of Congress Cataloguing in Publication Data

A catalogue record for this book is available
from the Library of Congress

ISBN 0–415–11627–9 (hbk)
ISBN 0–415–11628–7 (pbk)

To our students – past, present and future

Contents

CONTENTS

CONTENTS

Preface

THIS BOOK CONTAINS selected twentieth-century texts
on performance that, together, help define the field. The selec-
tions are primarily statements or writings by practitioners about
performance itself; these are supplemented by key critical and
theoretical texts that have helped to define or codify what artists
themselves have produced. It is a book for all those interested in
performance in the twentieth century – a celebration of those who
have led the way and who have been prime innovators. It contains
writings by directors, choreographers, composers, devisers, writers
and critics, as well as performers, that show how the field of
performance has developed through our time. The texts speak for
themselves and the ideas that they contain can be seen in relation
to each other. There are both resonances and dissonances, though
these may not necessarily come in the places you might expect.

All the work chosen has as its focus the practice of performance – its skills, concerns, techniques, viewpoints, philosophy. It covers all aspects of live performance (theatre, dance, opera, music,
performance, live art) which are compared with other performance
media where appropriate.

Many major twentieth-century figures have written little
about their work or, if they have, have done so in a way that is
not immediately and readily comparable with the ideas of others.
In compiling this book, we have therefore not included a number

of people who, nevertheless, are central to defining performance as a historical phenomenon. To understand the work of these figures it would be necessary to experience it or to read what the critics have written about it. The only critical descriptions that we have included are those that refer to general issues, rather than the work of one specific artist. You will therefore not find texts by, nor specifically dealing with, artists such as Martha Graham, although some of their work is referred to in drawing the wider context of twentieth-century performance.

However, we are fortunate that many twentieth-century performance innovators have committed their ideas to paper. This book, unsurprisingly, contains familiar texts from Bertolt Brecht, Jerzy Grotowski and Konstantin Stanislavski. It also contains many less familiar texts from practitioners such as Laurie Anderson, Tatsumi Hijikata and Tadeusz Kantor. The ideas that they deal with in performance and that they have written about can now be compared. There are also key statements from theorists that give both a historical and a critical context to these writings, for instance in the texts by Sally Banes and Raymond Williams.

It is immediately apparent that the artists included here did not write for each other, or for an anthology such as this. This is evident in the way they have often tended to use different terminology to describe similar activities. Terms such as 'performance', 'actor', 'director', locate their writing historically, geographically, and culturally. The language used changes with the innovations that this book documents, and the introduction that follows explores this phenomenon.

This book allows the reader choice in the ways in which it can be used. It is not prescriptive, and therefore is not organised according to either chronological or thematic categories. After each text there is a brief summary that anchors it historically. There then follow some brief suggestions as to immediate connections with other authors and texts. Some of these connections are purely historical (who else was working then); some are conceptual (wherein are found development, argument and debate). In other cases the links are direct, through people working together or commenting on each other's work. There are some suggestions that are serendipitous and, finally, those that we did not see until we put this book together.

The texts are deliberately organised alphabetically rather than chronologically but we have included a chronological list at the end, for interest. We wish to avoid spurious intimations that artists, simply by following each other chronologically, develop the idea of performance or, even worse, are part of a cultural 'evolution'.

We have been reluctant to group texts according to themes as many of them contain more than one. Placing a text within a thematic category tends to ossify its position and implies that it is resistant to further examination, or indeed to critical examination that might turn up a new theme that was not apparent at the time of writing. We have, however, identified four themes on which to focus. These themes emerge from the central focus of the book, the act of performance. They are touched on by each author and are described in the introduction, Twentieth-Century Performance: The Case for a New Approach. This is supported by notes that develop some of the topics arising from consideration of this book's texts. They refer to wider issues, particularly those relating to modernism and postmodernism.

Each text is followed by a contextual summary. Each summary gives some key facts about the author and an introduction to the writing in its context. This is followed by cross-references to other authors within this book. Suggestions for further reading about either the specific topic or the author are also given.

The cross references are a key feature. They allow the reader to begin to work through the network of ideas and historical connections that are to be found in this collection of writings. They are intended as an open system. Thus, the reader might wish to make comparisons with other historical figures and ideas.

The general bibliography is designed to support the introduction and includes an extensive selection of those texts which refer to the wider issues of the nature of performance.

Everyone will find ways of working through this book. Wherever you begin you will find help, but not prescribed patterns, to lead you further into the debate. What you will not find are one-way streets labelled dance, music, drama. The thinking behind this book is unashamedly multidisciplinary, which, of course, reflects a major concern of performance in the twentieth century.

The idea for this book came from our BA (Hons.) Performing Arts course at the then Leicester Polytechnic, and particularly from one of its contributory lecture series, 'Perspectives in the Performing Arts'. For many years we looked for a sourcebook that would encompass all aspects of performance; one that would be relevant to students of dance, music, theatre and the visual arts. Our first thanks, therefore, must go to our students for demanding more than we could give them at the time.

Secondly, we would like to thank Julia Hall at Routledge for recognising that this need was reflected in similar courses throughout the world and for having the confidence in the idea and in us.

Thirdly, thanks go to our colleagues at De Montfort University variously for their help, advice, reading, corrections, time and support – Nicholas Arnold, Teresa Brayshaw, Gavin Bryars, Ramsay Burt, Andrew Hugill, Martin Leach, Michael Patterson, Michael Scott and Wray Vamplew.

Last, but not least, thanks to Jayne Huxley and Krys Witts, whose continuing support and patience allowed this book to be completed.

Acknowledgements

WE GRATEFULLY ACKNOWLEDGE permission to publish extracts as follows:

Cover photograph of Wuppertal Dance Theater by Ulli Weiss. Reproduced by permission of the photographer.

'The Speed of Change: Interview with Tom Stromberg'. Reproduced by permission of Tom Stromberg.

'Actor, Space, Light, Painting' by Adolph Appia from *Adolph Appia: Texts on Theater* edited by Richard Beacham, published by Routledge. Reproduced by permission of Routledge.

'Theatre and Cruelty' from *The Theater and Its Double* by Antonin Artaud, translated by Victor Corti, published by Calder Publications Limited. Copyright English translation © John Calder (Publishers) Ltd 1970, 1974, 1977, 1981, 1985, 1989 and Calder Publications © 1993. Reproduced by permission of the Calder Educational Trust, London.

Sally Banes, *Terpsichore in Sneakers: Post-Modern Dance*, © by Sally Banes, Wesleyan University Press. By permission of University Press of New England.

ACKNOWLEDGEMENTS

Eugenio Barba: 'Words or Presence' from *The Floating Islands: Reflections with Odin Teatret*, © Eugenio Barba. Reproduced with permission of the author.

'The Grain of the Voice', from *Image, Music, Text* by Roland Barthes, published by HarperCollins Publishers Limited and by Farrar, Straus & Giroux, Inc. Book Publishers. Reproduced by permission of HarperCollins Publishers for the world excluding North America and the Philippines and by permission of Farrar, Straus and Giroux for North America and the Philippines.

'What is Epic Theatre?' from *Illuminations* by Walter Benjamin, copyright © 1955 by Suhrkamp Verlag, Frankfurt a.M., English translation copyright © 1968 by Harcourt Brace & Company, reprinted by permission of the publisher for America. Reproduced by permission of Random House UK Limited for UK and the Commonwealth (excluding Canada).

'Notes on the Invention of Tradition' from *Theatre and the World: Performance and the Politics of Culture* by Rustom Bharucha, published by Routledge. Reproduced by permission of Routledge.

Bertolt Brecht, 'Short Description of a New Technique in Acting which Produces an Alienation Effect', reproduced by permission of Methuen (UK) and Farrar, Straus and Giroux (US).

'The Deadly Theatre' from *The Empty Space* by Peter Brook reproduced by permission of the publishers, HarperCollins Publishers Limited.

John Cage, 'Four Statements on the Dance', reprinted from *Silence* © by John Cage, Wesleyan University Press. Reproduced by permission of University Press of New England.

'Some Remarks on the Situation of the Modern Composer' by Hanns Eisler from *Hanns Eisler: A Rebel in Music*. Original German text © Deutscher Verlag für Musik, Leipzig. English translation © Seven Seas Books/Verlag Volk & Welt, Berlin 1978. Reproduced by permission of Deutscher Verlag für Musik.

'Notes on "Einstein on the Beach"' by Philip Glass. Copyright © 1976 Philip Glass. Used by Permission. All Rights Reserved.

'Foreword' to *Performance Art from Futurism to the Present* by RoseLee Goldberg, © 1979 RoseLee Goldberg. Originally published in large format as *Performance: Live Art 1909 to the Present*. First published in the World of Art series 1988. This Edition © 1988 RoseLee Goldberg. Published by Thames and Hudson Ltd. Reproduced with permission of the publisher.

Jerzy Grotowski (1968, 1969), 'Statement of Principles', from *Towards a Poor Theatre*, translated by M. Buszewicz and J. Barba, edited by Eugenio Barba. © Jerzy Grotowski. Reproduced with permission of the author.

'The Theatre of Death: A Manifesto' by Tadeusz Kantor, translated by Vog T. and Margaret Stelmasznski, from *Twentieth Century Polish Theatre* edited by Bohdan Drozdowski and published by John Calder (Publishers) Ltd, London. Copyright this translation © John Calder (Publishers) Ltd 1979. Reproduced by permission of the Calder Educational Trust, London.

'Interview with Elizabeth LeCompte', reproduced by permission of Nick Kaye.

'Robert LePage in Discussion with Richard Eyre', *Platform Papers 3: Directors*, London, Royal National Theatre. Reproduced by permission of the Royal National Theatre.

F. T. Marinetti 'The Founding and Manifesto of Futurism' reproduced by permission of Farrar, Straus and Giroux (world rights).

Vsevolod Meyerhold, 'First Attempts at a Stylised Theatre' from *Meyerhold on Theatre* edited by E. Braun and published by Methuen. Permission granted by Reed Consumer Books Ltd.

Müller, Heiner. *Hamletmachine and other Texts for the Stage*. Carl Weber, ed. The Johns Hopkins University Press, Baltimore/London, 1984, for Performing Arts Journal Publications.

'A Quasi Survey of Some "Minimalist" Tendencies in the Quantitatively Minimal Dance Activity Midst the Plethora, or an Analysis of Trio A' by Yvonne Rainer. Reproduced by permission of the author.

'How Did Dada Begin?' by Richter, Hans from *Dada: Art and Anti-Art*, 1965 published by Thames and Hudson Ltd. Reproduced by permission of the publisher.

'The five avant gardes or . . . Or none?' from *The Future of Ritual: Writings on Culture and Performance* by Richard Schechner, © 1993 Richard Schechner, published by Routledge. Reproduced by permission of Routledge.

Oskar Schlemmer 'Man and Art Figure' in Walter Gropius & Arthur Wensinger, eds, *The Theater of the Bauhaus*, pp. 17–32. © 1961 Wesleyan University Press. By permission of University Press of New England.

ACKNOWLEDGEMENTS

'Theatre in African Traditional Cultures: Survival Patterns' by Wole Soyinka in *Art, Dialogue and Outrage* by Wole Soyinka, published by Methuen London. Reproduced by permission of Reed Consumer Books Ltd.

Konstantin Stanislavski 'Intonations and Pauses' from *Building a Character*. Reproduced by permission of Reinhardt Books.

Every effort has been made to trace and contact known copyright holders before publication. If any copyright holders have any queries they are invited to contact the publishers in the first instance.

Twentieth-Century Performance:

The Case for a New Approach

■ Michael Huxley

■ Noel Witts

T HERE HAVE BEEN MANY ATTEMPTS to characterise aspects of performance in the twentieth century, all of which have in some way been partial. Some have been art-form specific, some period specific and yet others specific to a particular and stated philosophical or aesthetic concern. Thus we find histories of dance, of theatre, of the avant-garde, of modern music, of performance art, etc.;[1] some of these do address an overarching concern for performance,[2] while others address the multidisciplinary nature of performance. However, none has addressed all forms of performance and none has addressed performance as a discipline in its own right, nor the ways in which this has changed with the century. In the analysis that follows we have attempted a characterisation of the practice of performance in the twentieth century that encompasses and accounts for the range of different voices represented in this book.

In compiling this collection of readings we have taken it as axiomatic that the central concern of any study of performance must be the act of performance itself. Therefore, the main issue for this analysis is the very nature of this act. It is an approach that differentiates this field from, for example, aesthetics or semiotics. Those involved in the making of performance – actors, dancers, musicians, directors, composers, choreographers, designers, devisers – take this for granted, but those who write about it often treat performance as merely another artefact. Whilst many writers will refer to the particularity of specific performances, few refer to the particularity of performance itself. Some writers on performance have used it as a major subject of cultural or political exploration, and in doing so have added it to the sum of possible academic approaches.[3] However, there have been comparatively few attempts to address critically the 'live' nature of the phenomenon: that its uniqueness lies in its ephemerality and in the practical processes that produce it. We have attempted to characterise the practical nature of performance by selecting particular practitioners' writings, and by appending contextual remarks to them.

Most live performance leaves only a 'trace' of itself. This alone makes the act of searching for the roots, methods and reasons behind its creation a crucial one. To understand the diversity of performance one must consider the practice and the practical concerns that have engaged its creators. Performance means process as well as final artefact, and an engagement with process is essential to any full understanding of the form. This fact has eluded many historians of performance: it is easier simply to consider the traces – the drawings, photographs, videotapes. Engagement with an artist's creative process is more problematic and, with performance, much more wide-ranging.

It is striking that this century's performance work is both wide in its compass and constantly changing with the technology and politics of the times. It is partly the necessity to represent ourselves to ourselves at different times that has accounted for the diversity which performance practitioners have given us. Equally, writers on performance are constantly mining its rich historical seams and finding new insights from the past. It is a phenomenon that is open-ended in its manifestations and boundless in the opportunities it offers both for interpretation and for future practice.[4] It is this richness that is celebrated here.

How then does one write about such a broad-based phenomenon? How does one mark out a territory that is so wide; territory that not only encompasses the literary text on the one hand and the visual on the other, but also the seeming disparities of ritual, theatre and entertainment?[5]

It is all too easy to eschew the traditional disciplinary categories – dance, music, drama, theatre, live art – but in so doing there is a danger of ending up without any focus. A focus is necessary to keep on reminding ourselves that all the practitioners included here have been concerned with the nature of performance. If we look more closely at what twentieth-century artists have said about performance, it becomes possible to identify a range of concerns, or reasons, or purposes to their explorations, even if that reason is nothing more than experiment for the sake of experiment. However, artists' concerns and purposes are rarely singular and often change through time.

For example, it is not only the stylistic features of Pina Bausch's dance theatre work that have changed, but the nature and purpose of her performance. She has concerned herself not only with the formal qualities of theatricality but also with the technical means of achieving these, and with an underlying personal exploration of the social and political purpose of dance. This helps explain why her work has changed from the recognisable choreographic form of *The Rite of Spring* (1975) through the reminiscence of *Café Müller* (1978) to the questioning of *1980: A Piece by Pina Bausch* (1980) and *On the Mountain a Cry Was Heard* (1984). For those fortunate enough to have seen her work live, the lasting impression is of someone working with the very stuff of performance in every way.[6] Equally, anyone watching the various phases of Peter Brook's work cannot but help notice that the changing nature of the work is a manifestation of the changing nature of the explorations that he and his performers have made. These in turn have been affected by Brook's personal and political agenda. He has moved from what may be regarded as mainstream Shakespearean work to the great experiment of the 1970 *A Midsummer Night's Dream*; then by way of *The Ik* (1975) to the more formal and spiritual concerns of *The Mahabharata* (1985) and *The Man Who* (1993). Trisha Brown's work has also shown massive changes in the way it looks from *Trillium* (1962) and *Rule Game 5* (1964) through *Man Walking Down the Side of a Building* (1969) to *Set and Reset* (1983) on to *Astral Convertible* (1989). However, what has changed is the extent and complexity of her experiments, not her willingness to experiment.

The difficulty in trying to characterise performance as a whole is that there are already seemingly more than enough ways of doing so. However, we would contend that either historical, geographical or disciplinary limits lead to constraints. There seems to be virtually no conceptual overlap between the disciplines in 'discipline-based histories'. Thus modern dance is usually described through the generations of the choreographers who have made it, or, at best, in formal comparison of modern dance with ballet. Similarly, modern theatre is defined by types of theatre that are often discipline specific, such as 'theatre of cruelty', 'directors' theatre', etc. Modern music is defined in formal terms such as 'serialism'. Performance art is related to art movements within which its ideas originated – for example 'Dada'.[7] It is comparatively rare that one finds in texts about specific disciplines mentions of artists from other disciplines.[8]

There have been attempts to deal with a wider notion of 'theatre' which also includes dance, such as those of Kirby and Kostelanetz.[9] It is also notable that more recent writers, such as Hewison (1990) in the UK, and Sayre (1989) in the

US, manage to treat the recent avant-garde as a multidisciplinary and boundless phenomenon. In particular, Sayre, in his history of the recent American avant-garde, uses an analysis that is inclusive rather than exclusive – thus identifying themes such as feminism, collaboration, narrative. Feminism and gender studies have led to a further redefining of how we look at aspects of performance.[10] Each of these, however, only applies to a particularly defined area.

For a broad perspective on performance as a whole none of these types of characterisation is wholly helpful. What is needed is a way of focusing on themes that cross disciplines – but one that does not invalidate approaches that are part of both the practical and critical traditions. The pluralism of performance asks for a similar analytical approach.

Four main themes of twentieth-century performance practice

One way of looking at the evidence presented in this book is to see the nature of performance as being focused on a number of interlinked themes. We have identified four, which are:

1   the processes of making performance
2   the formal possibilities of performance
3   the technical possibilities of performance
4   the social, political and/or spiritual purposes of performance

The very diversity of performance means that there is usually no single explanation for why it has a particular nature. There seems to be a constant shifting of emphasis between any two or more of these themes. It is, however, useful to identify them at the outset as reference points. These can anchor a particular performance, an artist, a period, or work, or make comparisons in drawing a broad picture of the century's achievements.

The processes of making performance

In this book, and indeed in practice, we tend to speak of 'devising' or 'making' works, as earlier terms such as 'playwriting', 'choreography', or even 'composition', seem inadequate. The task of describing the work of say Robert Wilson or the Wooster Group requires a new terminology that acknowledges the way the text of performance has changed. Indeed, it is artists themselves who have recently eschewed such terms, not least Yvonne Rainer and Elizabeth LeCompte.[11] Even the term 'writer' has come under scrutiny as the writer contributes but one part of the total performance 'text'. Indeed, with performance, writers have ceased to be 'authors', with all the implications of 'authority' that the term implies, and have tended towards becoming providers of the text.[12]

All the texts contained in this book are about and by people who take the act of performance as a point of investigation, rather than a given, whatever their place on the spectrum from the traditional to the avant-garde. This applies as much to Konstantin Stanislavski as it does to Robert Lepage. The similarities of concern for the whole messy business of making work suggest that LeCompte, Bausch, Brown and Rainer have more in common than, say, Rainer and Humphrey. It is not so much their discipline or country of origin that links them but their concern for a particular, late twentieth-century approach to the process; one that emphasises uncertainty. The earlier attempts by artists in various disciplines to impose an order, an adherence to rules through method, have been replaced by a recognition that it is precisely the lack of rules, the lack of order, that demands a new type of rigour, a new search for truth and honesty.

By taking a broad view of performance it becomes essential to include composers who have worked within a broadly theatrical context, since music has been the spring for many twentieth-century developments. Bertolt Brecht's use of Hanns Eisler's music gave a whole new vision of music as part of political theatre. John Cage's collaborations with Merce Cunningham have helped redefine the possible relationships between music and dance. Philip Glass's approaches to music theatre show that his concern for a total theatre begins with the process of devising the work.

The formal possibilities of performance

One of the things thrown into relief by focusing on these four stated concerns of performance is the negotiation between the traditional and the avant-garde. There are many examples to show that the avant-garde in its time later became part of the orthodoxy. A fine example would be Brecht's experimental theatrical form in the 1930s. Paradoxically, his plays became part of an orthodox approach in British theatre education in the 1980s. Equally, the formal concerns, taken out of context, of dancers such as Rainer, are as open to pastiche as the compositional techniques of Doris Humphrey. They thus lose their original intention. There does seem to be a continuing tension created whereby artists have either sought to maintain an avant-garde stance or retreated from it.[13] These tensions and debates have changed through the century as different performers have sought to make progress either by questioning tradition, or reinventing it, or by sliding from radicalism into orthodoxy. In doing so they have been addressing one or more of the themes we identify.

These formal considerations seem to apply to the visual arts too. This leads into a main sub-theme that runs through this selection – the increasing ability to talk of performance and 'live art' in comparable terms, because of the shared concerns and ideas of performers and visual artists. This has been extensively demonstrated by Roselee Goldberg.[14] We can see how performative elements in three-dimensional creation have informed the more traditional performance forms. This stream has come from the visual arts, and in the work of Edward Gordon Craig, Adolph Appia, Robert Wilson and Robert Lepage we have seen the promotion of the visual as the crucial performative statement. Similarly, we find the choreographer Merce Cunningham and the composer John Cage working together with visual artists on an equal footing, collaborating at the level of ideas.

In theatre, in particular, form has frequently been discussed by reference to the playwright. Only three playwrights are included in this book, one of these for his remarks on performance practice and another for his writing as a cultural historian. Bertolt Brecht and Heiner Müller are remarkable for the radical approaches to performance practice that their texts demand. They therefore fall within the context that has been established here. Each, by their writing, has contributed to the advance of performance practice in ways that few other twentieth-century playwrights have done.

The traditional play focuses on the spoken word and the actor; but to talk of the actor or performer as being the prime constituent of performance limits the definition of what is performance. Many of the essentials of late twentieth-century life are as much abstract and visual as textual.

The technical possibilities of performance

Clearly many of the main technical theatrical innovations during the twentieth century have been concerned with the visual and physical, rather than the textual. The play – the written text interpreted by actors – is but one of the possible theatrical forms of our time, although this is an idea that evidently seems to confound many Western theatre critics. Most recent textual innovation has been concerned with the interpretation, or positioning of the text with other media or symbols of performance. Thus the theatre of Heiner Müller, for example, is concerned above all with forcing the actors and director to make physical or visual decisions about possible meanings, and works against a straightforward delivery of a play text according to written instructions. The meaning of Müller's texts lies as often as not with the performer.

Other artists have made technical and formal innovations which in a philosophical and political sense have expanded the possibilities for performance. Vysevolod Meyerhold, Merce Cunningham and Eugenio Barba have all in their different ways extended the technical vocabularies of their disciplines so that new performance statements could be made, to be taken up and adapted by others.

Technology has created a new vision of the world, and theatre can now be expected to deal with the complex treatment of complex subjects, and of complex responses to twentieth-century life. Many of the technological innovations that we take for granted were developed by those involved with live performance. From Adolph Appia's early proposals for *The Ring* (1891–95), through Erwin Piscator's early experiments with film and live performance, to Robert Wilson's expanded use of stage space in *Einstein on the Beach* (1976), we see new stage visions of the world created by technological advance.

Some significant recent performance work has been concerned with the re-interpretation of classical texts – Robert Wilson's *Faust* and Robert Lepage's *Coriolan* – or with the invention of new visual and verbal worlds that owe little to the tradition of the theatrical world defined by text. One way of looking at the twentieth century's contribution to performance is, from our perspective as editors, to see it as the collapsing of orthodox forms. This is comparable to the historical processes of the century which first revolutionised the idea of Europe, and then collapsed the idea of two Europes, with all the attendant problems that now face us. Indeed it may be that one of the crucial characteristics of a live performance in our time is that, because of its 'present' nature, it must constantly search for forms that represent society in times of change, as if paralleling the way that novelists seek for new subjects. It therefore has different functions from those of the past.

The social and/or political purposes of performance

It is through performance that many artists have attempted to find their place in the world. This century has seen some of the greatest conflagrations of history – two world wars, the Vietnam war, the rise and collapse of communism in eastern Europe. These have thrown into sharp focus the attempts of performance practitioners to give their work a role and a contemporary meaning. Some of the figures included in this book are well known for political focuses throughout their lives – Bertolt Brecht, Augusto Boal, Hanns Eisler, Julian

Beck. The political orientations of other artists are perhaps less well known, and may not have constituted a main focus to their work. These can nevertheless be seen to be significant, for example, in the more recent polemics of Laurie Anderson in the USA. At the same time events have controlled society's view of a possible role for performance. For example, the artists of the east European countries often used theatre both as an expression of national and political identity and, as in Poland, as an escape valve, necessary for an intellectual class that needed to be appeased by their rulers. For many of the nations under communism the act of performance became a source of national identity, and, for example, the theatre pieces of Tadeusz Kantor and the plays of Heiner Müller encapsulated a whole nation's experience of history. Quite different ideas of national identity are evident in the Japanese Butoh of Tatsumi Hijikata or in the traditional theatre forms that Wole Soyinka and Rustom Bharucha describe. In the UK, with its comparatively settled democracy, it is arguable that performance has rarely taken for itself a direct political role, but for a brief period in the 1960s and early 1970s when world political concerns were controlled by attitudes taken towards the war in Vietnam. Equally, those in authority in a society frequently give indications of how they are treating people covertly by the way they treat their performers overtly – be it Brecht, Benjamin, Eisler, Schlemmer and Wigman in Germany in the 1930s or Soyinka in Nigeria during the 1960s and again in the 1990s.[15]

Many of the artists here represented have seen themselves, in both a political and a spiritual sense, as paving the way for a better world. Antonin Artaud, Bertolt Brecht, Isadora Duncan, Jerzy Grotowski, the Living Theatre, Erwin Piscator and Mary Wigman all saw their art as a focus for changing their audiences' perceptions. The stream of 'holy theatre' that Christopher Innes[16] has examined, stemming from Artaud, has created a constant spiritual thrust for performance.

For many performers the personal commitment to their work and to what it said at a particular time was considerably greater than a simple individual statement. For dancers in the 1910–30 period, particularly Duncan and Wigman, the personal was political. It led the former to her allegiance to the new Soviet state and, following her impassioned stage performances and proclamations of her faith in the new system, to her exile from her birthplace, the USA. For Wigman in the 1920s, her performances were the embodiment of what she saw as a personal statement of her commitment as a woman to the new modern dance, a form that would express and reveal herself. It was precisely this aspect of herself that the National Socialists in Germany in the 1930s vilified. Nonetheless, because of the personal commitment to the new form and to the country from which, for her, it sprang, she remained and worked under a hostile regime.[17]

The place of theory

The four themes serve as markers to establish the place of particular artists' performance work during the twentieth century. Different groupings of artists can be found, often leading to surprising comparisons. Moreover, they also serve as a way of defining what is particular about the diversity and changes of performance; they help to define its pluralism. The same criteria might be applied to those writing about performance from a theoretical perspective.

Thus in Walter Benjamin's and Roland Barthes' writings on theatre there is a concern not only for the formal and technical but also the political. Despite the different social situation, described above, Raymond Williams's perspective is broadly similar. Contrariwise, in John Martin's analysis of modern dance it is mainly the formal and technical features to which he alludes. However, Sally Banes's later analysis of postmodern dance clearly lays out the relationships between process, form, technical innovation, the political and the personal. The most recent of the theorists included here, Richard Schechner, identifies the themes of past avant-gardes whilst making a case for a particular, personal, spiritual, political framework.

It is evident then that theorists do not just have different stances; that is to be expected. They also rely on a different basis for their characterisation of performance, or the particular performance type with which they are involved. There is therefore a need to discuss the role of theory and how it too has a diversity and is subject to change.

The act of live performance has crossed the borders between disciplines. At the same time, new ways of talking and writing about performance have crossed the boundaries of analytical approaches. Recent performance theory, critical theory, semiotics, psychoanalysis and feminist theory have produced debates among theorists and performers that have contributed to a perceptible shift in the new work being created in the postmodernist context. Indeed it is in the realm of theory that the main debates about terminology occur.

There is some considerable debate about when modern performance might be said to have begun.[18] It is variously defined as either a late nineteenth-century phenomenon or an early twentieth-century one. Literary and musical definitions favour the former; theatrical, artistic and dance definitions the latter. There is also a chronological difference between European and American modernism. However, there is a broad consensus that modernism as a twentieth-century movement was well established by the time of the First World War. Indeed, many artists and performers responded to this terrible era in a modernist way.

All the writings representing the early chronological period in this book, from Alfred Jarry in 1896 to Hans Richter in 1964, can be said to be dealing with modern ideas. Those who attempted to set out specific theories or philosophies are quite clear that this is what they were doing, for example F. T.

Marinetti (1909) and Oskar Schlemmer (1924). Mary Wigman (1933) and Hanns Eisler (1935) refer to their modern points of view in their titles. The theorists John Martin (1933) and Walter Benjamin (1939), though ideologically quite different, emphasise the new modern era that has dawned, and the ramifications this has for art and for performance.

The later term, postmodernism, engenders even greater debate.[19] It now has a radically different connotation for performance as a whole from the meaning ascribed to it by dancers such as Yvonne Rainer in the early 1960s. Her historic statement juxtaposes a 'minimalist' manifesto against the concerns of the modernism found in writings such as Martin's (1933). The confusions wrought by the term are neatly and concisely stated for dance in Sally Banes's characterisation of 1987. Moreover, she points up the relation of the term to practitioners on the one hand and theorists on the other in a way that is applicable to other areas of performance. She suggests that in dance 'post-modern began as a choreographer's term but it has since become a critic's term that most choreographers now find either constricting or inexact.'[20] In this collection we have included other theorists who have made significant contributions to the debate about postmodernism, notably Roland Barthes (1972) and Richard Schechner (1993). These are juxtaposed with exemplars of its practice, such as Trisha Brown (1978), Heiner Müller (1984), Laurie Anderson (1992) and Elizabeth LeCompte (1993).

We are now in a period when it is possible to look critically and historically at earlier modernist experiments. Indeed part of postmodernist performance has been precisely a practitioner's critique of modernist ideas. In this selection both these and other approaches are allowed to speak for themselves, and, by comparison, to each other as well.

Writers as diverse as Roland Barthes, Walter Benjamin, Bertolt Brecht and Richard Schechner have seen the necessity of talking of performance as a means of de-coding the world. Each, from a different perspective, pioneered modes of writing about performance practice that still show a clarity that stands out beside the often obscure and difficult prose of those who do not have as firm a grasp of the nature of performance. It is not surprising, however, to find directors, choreographers and composers writing about a new social and aesthetic role for their art, and major theorists with a deep understanding of the nature of performance, such as Barthes, writing lucidly about its performative aspects.[21] The case that has been argued here is not so much for a particular theoretical standpoint but for a plurality of standpoints that will complement the performance that is being theorised about. What is asked for is a concern for performance as an activity in its own right, an acknowledgement of its processes and concerns, as well as the product, and a clarity in describing it.

Conclusion

Much of the material of this book shows practitioners – actors, dancers, musicians, directors, composers, choreographers, designers, devisers – questioning past attitudes, and doing so in print. At the same time we can see that many of the ideas of one era often come to haunt another, as ghosts of past reflections often visit us as dimly recognised friends. Martin Esslin, in a memorable phrase, once described theatre as 'the one place where society debates with itself in public'.[22] This collection shows the continuing force with which performance practitioners have sought to fuel debate, and the practices that they have evolved to make those debates important and memorable. This is not a history of twentieth-century performance. We hope it is a modest contribution to redefining the way such a history of the discipline will be written; but that's another book!

Notes

1   For example, Christopher Innes, whilst covering a wide historical period (1892–1992) defines his sphere as 'avant-garde theatre' and then goes on to further define this as having as its hallmark 'an aspiration to transcendence, to the spiritual in its widest sense' (1993:3). Usually, there is an art-form specific definition built in, with many histories of dance, music, theatre, but hardly any that include all three. Extant readers follow the same pattern, e.g. J.M. Brown (1980), Cohen (1974, 1992) and Steinberg (1980) for dance; Drain (1995) for theatre.

2   For example, Roselee Goldberg, despite constraining her field in her 1988 title, *Performance Art*, in fact gives a broad definition of what she regards as performance. She says it 'has provided a presence for the artist in society. This presence, depending on the nature of the performance can be esoteric, shamanistic, instructive, provocative or entertaining' (1988:8). Her overview of the twentieth century in terms of art historical movements therefore includes a wide range of performance forms from live art through dance to theatre and music.

3   For instance Reinelt and Roach (1992).

4   Goldberg makes the point about 'performance' in a more limited sense, as live art, when she says that it is a 'history of a permissive, open-ended medium with endless variables' (1988:9).

5   The distinction between ritual, theatre and entertainment is made as early as 1924 by Schlemmer. In doing so he celebrates the diversity of types of performance thereby encompassed. It is still discussed in the 1990s, for example by Schechner (1993) as a means of defining his stance.

6   Often a rare opportunity. Her company, Wuppertal Tanztheater, has, for instance, at the time of writing, only visited London once, in 1982.

7   For instance, comparing four acknowledged histories of dance, theatre, music and performance art respectively we find the following: Au (1988) on dance has chapters on 'first steps towards a new form', 'truly modern', 'the decentralization of ballet',

'the metamorphosis of form', etc.; Innes (1993) on theatre has 'therapy and sub-liminal theatre', 'Antonin Artaud and the theatre of cruelty', 'ritual and acts of communion', 'black masses and ceremonies of negation', 'myth and theatre labora-tories', 'secular religions and physical spirituality'; Griffiths (1978) on music has 'new harmony', 'neoclassicism', 'serialism', etc.; Goldberg (1988) on performance art (but with many direct references to dance and music) refers to 'Futurism', 'Russian Futurism and Constructivism', 'Dada', 'Surrealism', 'Bauhaus', etc.

8   Interestingly, when this does happen, the same names tend to occur, notably John Cage, Merce Cunningham and Oskar Schlemmer.

9   Kirby (1969) collects a diversity of performance texts under the umbrella *Total Theatre*, and Kostelanetz (1968, 1980) attempts a definition of *The Theatre of Mixed Means*, which he restates as 'my epithet . . . for performances that de-emphasize speech in the course of using a variety of means, including human bodies, lights, film, objects, and stagecraft' (1993:148).

10   In dance, for instance, there have been contributions by Adair (1992), Burt (1995), Thomas (1993); in theatre by Case (1988).

11   David Gordon, for instance, says that he will use 'constructed' or any word other than 'choreographed'. Quoted in the film *Making Dances*, WGBH Boston (1980).

12   The questioning of the role of the 'author' could be traced to Benjamin's pivotal work 'The Author as Producer' (in Benjamin 1973b). The crucial statement on the 'authority' of the 'author' can be located in Barthes's famous article (1968, 1977) 'The Death of the Author'.

13   Richard Schechner gives one view of the avant-garde and its role in the article that is included in this book. However, the term's application has changed radically since it was first employed to describe art by Bakunin's followers in the late nineteenth century. The current debate about its meaning is encapsulated by the diverse view-points of, for instance, Schechner (1993), Innes (1993) and Kostelanetz (1993).

14   In *Performance Art From Futurism to the Present* (1988) Goldberg ably incorporates a range of performers and performances into her history by virtue of concerns and interests shared between them and by those coming more strictly from a visual arts background.

15   Brecht, Benjamin, and many others fled fascist Germany in 1933 after having been vilified by the regime. Sixty years later, at the time of writing, Soyinka had just fled Nigeria because the regime's attitude to his work had become intolerable.

16   Innes's (1993) *Avant-Garde Theatre 1892–1992* is a revised version of his (1981) *Holy Theatre*.

17   More recent examples might include Richard Schechner, whose personal journey into theatre anthropology led him to Hinduism in 1976 (1993:1–4).

18   The modern period in music, according to Griffiths (1978), had a definite begin-ning, being the flute melody in Debussy's *Prélude à 'L'après-midi d'un faune'*, composed between 1892 and 1894. In theatre it depends on whether you approach the question from a literary or a performance standpoint. Literary critics Bradbury and McFarlane (1976) give their anthology of writings on modernism in European literature a historical period of 1890–1930. They therefore include Ibsen, Strindberg, Yeats, Pirandello and Chekhov. From this perspective, many modern plays might be

placed in the late nineteenth century, whereas, from a theatrical perspective, modernism begins in the expressionist era of European theatre. In dance, it depends on which side of the Atlantic you consider. From the European perspective, the establishment of Rudolf Laban's first studio in Munich was contemporaneous with the work of those such as Kandinsky and the Expressionists who came to define modernism in the visual arts around 1912. But then again, there is a case for beginning with Matisse and 'Les Fauves' and the period 1904–07. From an American point of view, despite the early work of Duncan, St Denis and Fuller which is considered contemporaneously with the Europeans, most American writers do not consider American early modern dance to have been 'truly modern' until the 1920s with the advent of the solo careers of Graham, Humphrey and Weidman. (Au 1988:119). Modernism in the visual arts in the United States starts with the Armory Show in 1913 ('The International Exhibition of Modern Art' at the 69th Regiment Armory, New York); see M.W. Brown (1988).

19 See Banes (1987) *Terpsichore in Sneakers: Post-Modern Dance*; Foster (1983) *Postmodern Culture*; Garvin (1980) *Romanticism, Modernism, Postmodernism*; Huyssen (1986) *After the Great Divide: Modernism, Mass Culture, Postmodernism*; Jencks (1987) *What is Post-Modernism?*; Kaye (1994) *Postmodernism and Performance*.

20 Banes (1987:xv). She goes on to define it very carefully in terms of choreographers' practice from the 1960s through the 1980s.

21 In Barthes's case the selection in this book is concerned with music but he has also written with great clarity on other forms of performance, notably the music hall and striptease (Barthes 1972:84–7).

22 Esslin (1976), unpublished address to National Student Drama Festival, Edinburgh, 1976.

Chapter 1

Laurie Anderson

THE SPEED OF CHANGE

After your 'Home of the Brave' tour you released a new record, 'Strange Angels.' A new performance 'Halcion Days' for Sevilla Expo '92 is in the pipeline. This performance will also be given later in Berlin (Hebbel-Theater) and Frankfurt (Theater am Turm). You have also started to give talks at a number of universities in America. Can you tell me more about this series of events?

Instead of doing a music video for the album 'Strange Angels,' I chose to do a series of public service announcements about various political situations. During the last year I have been presenting a long talk entitled 'Voices From The Beyond' which is the most overtly political work I have ever done. I'm not even sure it's art anymore. It goes back and forth between story-telling and advocacy. So far I have given more than 20 such talks. A number of universities have invited me to talk to their students. During these events I don't sing and I don't show videos. All I do is project one slide and talk. The subjects I talk about deal with time going backwards. People believe in a kind of countdown ending in the year 2000. They all stare at the three zeros at the end of this number. I have more and more doubts directly connected with this countdown. Sometimes people need important signs because so many things have happened during the past two years. You have to realize that in the United States there are a lot of 'fundamentalists' who believe that in the year 2000 they will all be joining Jesus Christ. The holy city of Jeruzalem, all the Americans flying out of their cars at midnight, as it were, to join Jesus Christ straight off. Sixty million people in the United States are fascinated by the idea that at the end of this century God will come down to earth to drag all Christians away, to take them with him on the spot, whether they are busy telephoning or doing I don't know what. And even more people believe in hell and punishment.

Well, all this sounds as though you are making tirades, which also has a negative ring to it.

Yes, they are tirades, but I try to be realistic, not negative. However, it is interesting to see how people react to my talks. For example, I try and talk about the fact that ever since the Gulf War the United States has only had one news broadcasting service. What happened to ABC and all the other broadcasting stations? They have all been supplanted by CNN. The whole world is filtered for us by CNN.

Have you been very preoccupied with the Gulf War and the discussions surrounding it?

Yes. There have been so many arrangements with the American military. Just like in every war the military pursue a well-defined aim. Part of it consists in dictating to broadcasting stations how the war is to be reported, what language to use when and where. Therefore, the whole world has been listening to news broadcasts straight out of the Pentagon.

During the Gulf War it was almost impossible for anyone to object to policy or tactics. The war was presented of course as a drama, an advertisement, a show complete with super graphics and a thunderous patriotic soundtrack. It was already in post-production while it was still happening. Nobody complained for the same reason that moviegoers don't jump up during a movie and shout things like, 'Lousy plot!' If you complained you had to disguise it as yet another form of entertainment, like the musicians who got together to record 'Give Peace A Chance' and then announced that maybe they were for the war, maybe not, but they just felt like singing the song anyway. Now that the patriotic frenzy and the victory parades are history, the war can be discussed. It is now seen by many people as a cynical attempt to draw attention away from pressing economic problems. This does not mean that this kind of hysteria couldn't happen again. Far from it. As the hearings on sexual harassment proved, Americans love televised sex and power soap operas especially if they are happening in real time.

That's where your tirades start?

No, it's not that I beat people over the head saying: 'Look, didn't you realize, didn't you ask?' Actually I am a patriot. I believe that Americans are basically compassionate people.

You are moving away from huge pop concerts and gigantic shows?

Yes. At the moment I am working on a different level. That's why I'm more interested in working with small theatres and in small halls. At the universities I only project a single slide and talk and talk. People expect music and high-tech visuals. I think they're surprised that I'm asking them to think so much instead. As a storyteller, I find this really exhilarating. I can make lots of quick jump-cuts . . . move things around.

In Kurt Vonnegut's latest book one of the protagonists watches a video showing the Second World War backwards. To watch the Second World War forwards drives people to despair. But this character watches the film backwards. And backwards it is a vision of Utopia. An aircraft flies backwards, backwards over Germany. Bombs fly from the ground to the aircraft as if attracted by a magnet and then they return to America. The things I am working on have got this kind of dynamic. The speed of change. In another book I have read the author claims that terrorists are the only true artists. They are the only people capable of changing anything. Interesting theory.

Do you now intend to change the world?

I try to **look** at things well, not to change them. That's not my job. In the late '60s and early '70s I worked as a political cartoonist for a publication called 'The Street Wall Journal.' I also published pamphlets of my drawings – cartoons about men, women, and power – and handed them out on the street. At the same time, I was working as a sculptor and I saw this as quite separate from my political work.

Gradually politics and art coincided in a series of photo works such as 'Object/Objectivity' (in which I shot photographs of men who approached me – 'Hey, baby!' – on the street) and concerts such as a duet between the United States and Canada performed on the border. Much of my work has been about authority and reactions to authority.

How do you now integrate your thoughts into your artwork?

17

In America freedom of expression is being threatened. I think there is no point in making rules about whether artists should deal directly with these issues or use distance and filters. Both are certainly valid and it depends on the circumstances. In the last couple of years, the world has changed so quickly that it's impossible to absorb the shocks. At the same time, it's been very difficult for me to ignore them and I decided to use this information in performances, like thinking out loud. I didn't feel the need to translate them into songs or images. This would have been impossible. On the other hand, the most dangerous aspect of work that is political is the potential for advocacy and propaganda. I don't think that the purpose of art is to make this a nicer, more civilized world. I think the purpose of art is the free expression of the artist, whatever that might mean.

My idea of form is often an argument or a conversation so I don't have to abandon this dialectic to deal with the shifts between politics and art or between one political idea versus another. In fact, this form is deeply appropriate for the material.

In Vienna, not too long ago, I met the Czechoslovakian minister of Education and the Arts. And he made a suggestion. He had discovered some prehistoric wall-paintings in one of the caves in Czechoslovakia. He invited me to visit this cave and to transcribe these drawings into music. He suggested that I organize a concert in this cave. What makes it so special is the fact that the concert will have to take place in complete darkness because prehistoric men did the paintings in complete darkness. Yes, and I love this project.

What is the situation like for artists in New York?

For many artists it is impossible to survive the media offensive. Increasingly, avant-garde artists are being absorbed by it. New York is drained of money. We can't afford to show the new Robert Wilson piece. The avant-garde is the first to go.

Are you an avant-garde artist?

Fortunately, I don't have to think about this question. Why don't **you** tell people what I am? I don't even think that people want artists to be defined. But since I've been working on this new project I think that it has more to do with backwards than with forwards. Avant-garde has always been based on speed. And I'm interested in this theme.

In America, there are a number of artists who use their success and the money they earn from commercial activities to help small theatre groups etc. Willem Dafoe, for example, the famous film actor, plays each night theatre for an audience of 99 people as a member of the Wooster Group.

I think he's a good example. I really appreciate his loyalty to downtown theatre.

You once said that art is for people who want to use it. Do you still believe that?

Yes, I do. There is always a kind of search going on and of course this is expressed in the work of the artist.

We have talked so much about politics and so little about your art. Now, be honest! If I ask you which you consider to be more important: form or content?

Inseparable.

(The interviewer was Tom Stromberg, New York, autumn 1991)

■ ■ ■

Source

Anderson, L. (1991, 1992). 'The Speed of Change: Interview with Tom Stromberg', *Theatreschrift* 1(1): 119–130.

Laurie Anderson (1947–)

American multimedia performance artist. She has worked in many disciplines (including) as performer, musician, singer, photographer, film maker, recording artist, and as a polemicist. Her stage works include *United States Part I–IV* (1983), a seven-hour performance at the Brooklyn Academy Opera House, *Home of the Brave*, which toured the world and was produced as a video of the same name, and, latterly, *Voices from Beyond* (1991) and *Halcyon Days* (1992). She has recorded her work as *Big Science* (1982), *United States Live* (1983), *Mister Heartbreak* (1984), *Home of the Brave* (1986), *Strange Angels* (1989) and *Big Red* (1994). Her music has been used for live dance – Trisha Brown's *Set and Reset* (1983) – and film – Spalding Gray's film *Monster in a Box* (1991).

Anderson's music and her performances embrace both live art and rock music, using the anti-theatrical understatement of the former and the full-blown stage theatricality of the latter to make memorable audio-visual statements. Her work is multireferential and multilayered and there is a complexity of reference at the level of ideas. *O Superman* (1982) is dedicated to the French composer, Massenet, and pastiches lines in his opera *Le Cid*. In *Strange Angels* (1989) she paraphrases Walter Benjamin's (1940) *Theses on the Philosophy of History* – 'history is an angel being blown backwards into the future'.

In this interview she talks about the use of narrative as polemic. The presentation of her work has been simplified, recalling her earlier work, before her large-scale tours. She discusses her place as a US artist and how she uses her position as an artist to comment on her country.

Reader cross-references

Benjamin – on whom she draws, and to whom political comparison can be made
Brown – with whom she collaborated
Schlemmer – comparison with early visual theatre
Wilson and **Lepage** – contemporary North American theatre directors who make visual theatre

Further reading and listening

Anderson, L. (1982) 'Big Science', New York: Warner Bros.
Anderson, L. (1983) 'United States Live', New York: Warner Bros.
Anderson, L. (1989) 'Strange Angels', New York: Warner Bros.
Sayre, H.M. (1989) 'Three Performances', *The Object of Performance: The American Avant-Garde since 1970*, Chicago: University of Chicago Press: 145–155.

Chapter 2

Adolph Appia

ACTOR, SPACE, LIGHT, PAINTING

THE ART OF STAGE PRODUCTION is the art of projecting into Space what the original author was only able to project in Time. The temporal element is implicit within any text, with or without music . . . The first factor in staging is the interpreter: the actor himself. The actor carries the action. Without him there can be no action and hence no drama . . . The body is alive, mobile and plastic; it exists in three dimensions. Space and the objects used by the body must most carefully take this fact into account. The overall arrangement of the setting comes just after the actor in importance; it is through it that the actor makes contact with and assumes reality within the scenic space.

Thus we already have two essential elements: the actor and the spatial arrangement of the setting, which must conform to his plastic form and his three-dimensionality.

What else is there?

Light!

Light, just like the actor, must become active; and in order to grant to it the status of a medium of dramatic expression it must be placed in the service of . . . the actor who is above it in the production hierarchy, and in the service of the dramatic and plastic expression of the actor.

. . . Light has an almost miraculous flexibility . . . it can create shadows, make them living, and spread the harmony of their vibrations in space just as music does. In light we possess a most powerful means of expression through space, if this space is placed in the service of the actor.

So here we have our normal established hierarchy:

the *actor* presenting the drama;
space in three dimensions, in the service of the actor's plastic form;
light giving life to each.

But — as you have inferred, there is a but — what about painting? What do we understand about painting in terms of scenic art?

A collection of painted backcloths and flats arranged vertically on the stage, more or less parallel to one another, and extending upstage. These are covered with painted light, painted shadow, painted forms, objects and architecture; all of it, of course, on a flat surface since that is the nature of painting . . .

Our staging practice has reversed the hierarchical order: on the pretext of providing us with elements which are difficult or impossible to realize in solid form, it has developed painted décor to an absurd degree, and disgracefully subordinated the living body of the actor to it. Thus light illuminates the backcloths (which have to be seen), without a care for the actor, who endures the ultimate humiliation of moving between painted flats, standing on a horizontal floor.

All modern attempts at scenic reform touch upon this essential problem; namely, on how to give to light its fullest power, and through it, integral plastic value to the actor and the scenic space.

Our stage directors have, for a long time, sacrificed the physical and living presence of the actor to the dead illusion of painting. Under such a tyranny, it is obvious that the human body could never develop in any normal way its means of expression. This marvellous instrument, instead of sounding in freedom, exists only under severe constraints.

Everyone knows today that the return to the human body as an expressive element of the first rank is an idea that captures the mind, stimulates the imagination, and opens the way for experiments which may be diverse and no doubt of unequal value, but are all directed towards the same reform . . . Yet our contemporary productions have forced us into such a despicably passive state that we conceal it carefully in the darkness of the house. But now, with the current attempt by the human body to rediscover itself, our feeling almost leads to the beginning of fraternal collaboration; we wish that we were ourselves the body that we observe: the social instinct awakens within us, though in the past we coldly suppressed it, and the division separating the stage and the auditorium becomes simply a distressing barbarism arising from our selfishness.

We have arrived at the crucial point for dramatic reform . . . which must be boldly announced: the dramatic author will never liberate his vision so long as he believes it yoked by necessity to a barrier separating the action from the spectator . . . The inevitable conclusion is that the usual arrangement of our theatres must evolve gradually towards a more liberal conception of dramatic art . . .

We shall arrive, eventually, at what will simply be called the *House*: a sort of cathedral of the future, which in a vast, open and changeable space will welcome the most varied expressions of our social and artistic life, and will be the ideal place for dramatic art to flourish, *with or without spectators.*

■　■　■

Source

Appia, A. (1919, 1954, 1993) 'Actor, Space, Light, Painting', *Adolphe Appia: Texts on Theatre*, ed. R.C. Beacham, London: Routledge: 114–115.[1]

Adolph Appia (1862–1928)

Swiss designer and philosopher of theatre; the first to write about theatre as a visual art form, where light and shadow, form and space, are as important, if not sometimes more so, than the physical performer. Appia's life was spent writing about, and experimenting with, the technical properties of light and shadow, primarily because of the profound influence of Richard Wagner's cycle of music dramas, *Der Ring Des Nibelungen* (*The Ring of the Nibelung*), for which he prepared detailed scenic and lighting scenarios which were summarily rejected by Wagner's family after the death of the composer in 1883. He wrote three books on theatre – *Music and the Stage* (1897), *The Staging of Wagnerian Drama* (1895), and *The Work of Living Art* (1921) – as well as numerous articles.

Appia's work has had a profound influence on modern stage design, and his stark blocks of shadow and light were instrumental in helping Wieland Wagner, Wagner's grandson, revive his grandfather's work at the theatre in Bayreuth following the profound and damaging embarrassments of the Nazi canonisation of the composer in the Second World War. Appia's collaboration with the Swiss choreographer Jaques-Dalcroze at Hellerau in the 1910s produced and initiated

a whole new approach to movement and scenography, culminating in his production of Gluck's *Orpheus and Euridice* (1913).[2]

This essay represents a good summary of his thinking, concentrating as it
does on principles of staging which emphasise the actor within the stage space.

Reader cross-references

Craig – similar concerns and explorations in England and Russia
Meyerhold – a concern to see the actor within a scenic frame
Piscator – contemporary European view on the aesthetics of staging
Schlemmer – theatre spatial experiments at the Bauhaus
Wilson and **Lepage** – late twentieth-century examples of visual theatre

Further reading

Beacham, R.C. (1987) *Adolphe Appia*, Cambridge: Cambridge University Press.
Brockett, O.G. and Findlay, R.R. (1973) *Century of Innovation*, Englewood Cliffs,
N.J.: Prentice-Hall.
Volbach, W. (1968) *Adolph Appia*, Middletown, Conn.: Weslyan University Press.

Notes

1   Beacham (1993: 239): 'This is excerpted from an untitled manuscript Appia
     prepared for presentation on 3 April 1919 at the Olympic Institute in
     Lausanne, accompanied by slides illustrating his designs. The conference
     was entitled "the future of drama and stage production"; the title "Actor,
     space, light, painting" was given to an abbreviated version of Appia's essay
     after his death.'
2   David Thomas, at Warwick University in 1991, produced a reconstruction
     of Appia's work.

Chapter 3

Antonin Artaud

THEATRE AND CRUELTY

W E HAVE LOST THE IDEA of theatre. And in as much as theatre restricts itself to probing the intimacy of a few puppets, thereby transforming the audience into Peeping Toms, one understands why the elite have turned away from it or why the masses go to the cinema, music-hall and circus to find violent to gratification whose intention does not disappoint them.

Our sensibility has reached the point where we surely need theatre that wakes us up heart and nerves.

The damage wrought by psychological theatre, derived from Racine, has rendered us unaccustomed to the direct, violent action theatre must have. Cinema in its turn, murders us with reflected, filtered and projected images that no longer *connect* with our sensibility, and for ten years has maintained us and all our faculties in an intellectual stupor.

In the anguished, catastrophic times we live in, we feel an urgent need for theatre that is not overshadowed by events, but arouses deep echoes within us and predominates over our unsettled period.

Our longstanding habit of seeking diversions has made us forget the slightest idea of serious theatre which upsets all our preconceptions, inspiring us with fiery, magnetic imagery and finally reacting on us after the manner of unforgettable soul therapy.

Everything that acts is cruelty. Theatre must rebuild itself on a concept of this drastic action pushed to the limit.

Infused with the idea that the masses think with their senses first and foremost and that it is ridiculous to appeal primarily to our understanding as we do in everyday psychological theatre, the Theatre of Cruelty proposes to resort to mass theatre, thereby rediscovering a little of the poetry in the ferment of great, agitated crowds hurled against one another, sensations only too rare nowadays, when masses of holiday crowds throng the streets.

If theatre wants to find itself needed once more, it must present everything in love, crime, war and madness.

Everyday love, personal ambition and daily worries are worthless except in relation to the kind of awful lyricism that exists in those Myths to which the great mass of men have consented.

This is why we will try to centre our show around famous personalities, horrible crimes and superhuman self-sacrifices, demonstrating that it can draw out the powers struggling within them, without resorting to the dead imagery of ancient Myths.

In a word, we believe there are living powers in what is called poetry, and that the picture of a crime presented in the right stage conditions is something infinitely more dangerous to the mind than if the same crime were committed in life.

We want to make theatre a believable reality inflicting this kind of tangible laceration, contained in all true feeling, on the heart and senses. In the same way as our dreams react on us and reality reacts on our dreams, so we believe ourselves able to associate mental pictures with dreams, effective in so far as they are projected with the required violence. And the audience will believe in the illusion of theatre on condition they really take it for a dream, nor for a servile imitation of reality. On condition it releases the magic freedom of daydreams, only recognisable when imprinted with terror and cruelty.

Hence this full scale invocation of cruelty and terror, its scope testing our entire vitality, confronting us with all our potential.

And in order to affect every facet of the spectator's sensibility, we advocate a revolving show, which instead of making stage and auditorium into two closed worlds without any possible communication between them, will extend its visual and oral outbursts over the whole mass of spectators.

Furthermore, leaving the field of analysible emotional feelings aside, we intend using the actor's lyricism to reveal external powers, and by this means to bring the whole of nature into the kind of theatre we would like to evoke.

However extensive a programme of this kind may be, it does not over-reach theatre itself, which all in all seems to us to be associated with ancient magic powers.

Practically speaking, we want to bring back the idea of total theatre, where theatre will recapture from cinema, music-hall, the circus and life itself, those things that always belonged to it. This division between analytical theatre and a world of movement seems stupid to us. One cannot separate body and mind, nor the senses from the intellect, particularly in a field where the unendingly repeated jading of our organs calls for sudden shocks to revive our understanding.

Thus on the one hand we have the magnitude and scale of a show aimed at the whole anatomy, and on the other an intensive mustering of objects, gestures and signs used in a new spirit. The reduced role given to understanding leads to drastic curtailment of the script, while the active role given to dark poetic feeling necessitates tangible signs. Words mean little to the mind; expanded areas and objects speak out. New imagery speaks, even if composed in words. But spatial, thundering images replete with sound also speak, if we become versed in arranging a sufficient interjection of spatial areas furnished with silence and stillness.

We expect to stage a show based on these principles, where these direct active means are wholly used. Therefore such a show, unafraid of exploring the limits of our nervous sensibility, uses rhythm, sound, words, resounding with song, whose nature and startling combinations are part of an unrevealed technique.

Moreover, to speak clearly, the imagery in some paintings by Grunewald or Hieronymus Bosch gives us a good enough idea of what a show can be, where things in outside nature appear as temptations just as they would in a Saint's mind.

Theatre must rediscover its true meaning in this spectacle of a temptation, where life stands to lose everything and the mind to gain everything.

Besides we have put forward a programme which permits pure production methods discovered on the spot to be organised around historic or cosmic themes familiar to all.

And we insist that the first Theatre of Cruelty show will hinge on these mass concerns, more urgent and disturbing than any personal ones.

We must find out whether sufficient production means, financial or otherwise, can be found in Paris, before the cataclysm occurs, to allow such theatre (which must remain because it is the future) to come to life. Or whether real blood is needed right now to reveal this cruelty.

■　■　■

Source

Artaud, A. (1938, 1964, 1970) 'Theatre and Cruelty', *The Theatre and Its Double*, trans. V. Corti, London: Calder & Boyars: 64–67.

Written in 1933, first published in 1938 in *Le Théâtre et son double* by Editions Gallimard and then in *Antonin Artaud: Œuvres Complètes, Tome IV* by Editions Gallimard (1964), from which text this 1970 English translation was made.[1]

Antonin Artaud (1896–1948)

French actor and writer who, through his life experience, has had a profound influence on notions of theatre in our time. While not himself producing a tangible system he nevertheless, through the publication of the English translations of his collection of essays, *The Theatre and Its Double* (1958 and 1970), acted as a catalyst for generations of theatre makers by opening up new modes of perception. Artaud promoted a way of thinking which rejected logic and reason as 'the chains that bind us', and wanted the theatre, through its immediacy, to embrace the non-verbal elements of consciousness, and to arouse powerful therapeutic emotions in the audience. He wanted the theatre, through its power, to create a complete physical, mental and moral upheaval in the population, which would lead to enlarged and revolutionary perceptions, from which one can understand his attraction for the generation of the 1960s in Europe and the USA.

In this essay Artaud attacks psychological theatre, advocating instead a form of total theatre which will engage the spectator in creating his own power to change, not only himself, but society as whole. He thus, like many of the artists in this book, was constantly in conflict with established theatre forms, advocating instead the search for man's instinctive impulsive life. Much influenced by Freud's *Interpretation of Dreams*, Artaud's life became an emblem of man's search for consciousness, proposing in the process that the theatre abandon naturalistic set, space and language to create a new order.

Reader cross-references

Beck – later, messianic claims for the purpose of theatre
Brook – who acknowledges him as an early influence
Grotowski – for a similar, contemporary, messianic role for theatre
Hijikata – for later Japanese celebrations of the irrational
Jarry and **Richter** – who wished theatre would stir audiences from their apathy

Marinetti – who wished to sweep away logic and embrace physicality and sensuality

Soyinka – a West African perspective on ritual

Stanislavski – a contemporary, contrasting view of theatre

Wigman – a contemporary, modern dance viewpoint

Further reading

Artaud, A. (1971) *Artaud on Theatre*, ed. C. Schumacher, London: Methuen.

Esslin, M. (1976) *Artaud*, London: Fontana/Collins.

Innes, C. (1993) *Avant Garde Theatre* 1892–1992, London: Routledge.

Note

1   1938 edition published in *Collection Métamorphoses no. IV.* See also M.C. Richard's first English translation (1958), New York: Grove.

Chapter 4

Sally Banes

TERPSICHORE IN
SNEAKERS:
POST-MODERN DANCE

WHEN YVONNE RAINER started using the term 'postmodern' in the early 1960s to categorize the work she and her peers were doing at Judson Church and other places, she meant it in a primarily chronological sense. Theirs was the generation that came after modern dance, which was itself originally an inclusive term applied to nearly any theatrical dance that departed from ballet or popular entertainment. By the late 1950s, modern dance had refined its styles and its theories, and had emerged as a recognizable dance genre. It used stylized movements and energy levels in legible structures (theme and variations, ABA, and so on) to convey feeling tones and social messages. The choreography was buttressed by expressive elements of theater such as music, props, special lighting and costumes. The aspirations of modern dance, anti-academic from the first, were simultaneously primitivist and modernist. Gravity, dissonance, and a potent horizontality of the body were means to describe the stridency of modern life, as choreographers kept one eye on the future while casting the other to the ritual dances of non-Western culture.[1] Though they were especially conscious of their oppositional role to modern dance, the early post-modern choreographers, possessed of an acute awareness of a historical crisis in dance as well as in the other arts, recognized that they were both bearers and critics of two separate dance traditions. One was the uniquely twentieth-century phenomenon of modern dance; the other was the balletic, academic *danse de l'école*, with its strict canons of beauty, grace, harmony, and the equally potent, regal verticality of the body extending back to the Renaissance courts of Europe. Rainer, Simone Forti, Steve Paxton, and other post-modern choreographers of the sixties were not united in terms of their aesthetic. Rather, they were united by their radical approach to choreography, their urge to reconceive the medium of dance.

By the early 1970s, a new style with its own aesthetic canons seems to have emerged. In 1975, Michael Kirby published an issue of *The Drama Review* devoted to post-modern dance, using the term in print for one of the first times in regard to dance and proposing a definition of the new genre:

> In the theory of post-modern dance, the choreographer does not apply visual standards to the work. The view is an interior one: movement is not preselected for its characteristics but results from certain decisions, goals, plans, schemes, rules, concepts, or problems. Whatever actual movement occurs during the performance is acceptable as long as the limiting and controlling principles are adhered to.[2]

According to Kirby, post-modern dance rejects musicality, meaning, characterization, mood, and atmosphere; it uses costume, lighting, and objects in purely functional ways. At present, Kirby's definition seems far too limited. It refers to only one of several stages – analytic post-modern dance – in the development of post-modern dance, which I intend to trace here.

The term 'post-modern' means something different in every art form, as well as in culture in general. In 1975, the same year the post-modern dance issue of *The Drama Review* appeared, Charles Jencks used the term to refer to a new trend in architecture that had also begun to emerge in the early sixties. According to Jencks, post-modernism in architecture is a doubly-coded aesthetic that has popular appeal, on the one hand, and esoteric historical significance for the cognoscenti, on the other.[3] In the dance world, perhaps only Twyla Tharp could have fitted such a definition at the time, but her work was not commonly considered post-modern dance. (Much 'new dance' of the eighties could also fit such a definition, but at this point it would be revisionist to call only eighties dance post-modern. It is, rather, as I discuss below, post-modern*ist*.) In the visual-art world and in theater, a number of critics have

31

used the term to refer to artworks that are copies of or comments on other artworks, challenging values of originality, authenticity, and the masterpiece and provoking Derridean theories of simulacra. This notion fits some post-modern dances, but not all.

In dance, the confusion the term 'post-modern' creates is further complicated by the fact that historical modern dance was never really *modernist*. Often it has been precisely in the arena of post-modern dance that issues of modernism in the other arts have arisen: the acknowledgment of the medium's materials, the revealing of dance's essential qualities as an art form, the separation of formal elements, the abstraction of forms, and the elimination of external references as subjects. Thus in many respects it is post-modern dance that functions as *modernist* art. That is, post-modern dance came after modern dance (hence, post-) and, like the post-modernism of the other arts, was anti-modern dance. But since 'modern' in dance did not mean modernist, to be anti-modern dance was not at all to be anti-modernist. In fact, quite the opposite. The analytic post-modern dance of the seventies in particular displayed these modernist preoccupations, and it aligned itself with that consummately modernist visual art, minimalist sculpture.[4] And yet, there are also aspects of post-modern dance that do fit with post-modernist notions (in the other arts) of pastiche, irony, playfulness, historical reference, the use of vernacular materials, the continuity of cultures, an interest in process over product, breakdowns of boundaries between art forms and between art and life, and new relationships between artist and audience.[5] Some of the new directions of dance in the eighties are even more closely allied to the concerns and techniques, especially that of pastiche, of post-modernism in the other arts. But if we were to call sixties and seventies post-modern dance *post-modern* and dub eighties new dance *post-modernist*, the confusion would probably not be worth the scrupulous accuracy. Further, as I argue in the section on the eighties below, I believe the avant-garde dance of all three decades is united and can be embraced by a single term. And I continue to recommend the term 'post-modern'. The use of the word, however, deserves yet another caveat. Although in dance 'post-modern' began as a choreographer's term, it has since become a critic's term that most choreographers now find either constricting or inexact. By now, many writers on dance use the term so loosely it can mean anything or nothing. However, since the term has been used widely for almost a decade, it seems to me that, rather than avoid it, we should define it and use it discriminately.

Notes

1   For an explication of traditional modern dance structures, see the three bibles of modern dance composition: Louis Horst, *Pre-Classic Dance Forms* (New York: The Dance Observer, 1937; reprint ed., Dance Horizons, 1972); Louis Horst and Carroll Russell, *Modern Dance Forms* (San Francisco: Impulse Publications, 1961); and Doris Humphrey, *The Art of Making Dances* (New York: Rinehart, 1959; reprint ed., Grove Press, 1962); see also the many reviews and histories of modern dance, including those cited in notes to the introduction to the first edition of this book.

2   Michael Kirby, 'Introduction,' *The Drama Review* 19 (T-65; March 1975): 3.

3   Charles Jencks, *The Language of Post-Modern Architecture* (New York: Rizzoli, 1977).

4   Nöel Carroll unravelled some of these complexities with particular clarity in his lecture on post-modernism in the arts and in culture generally at Jacob's Pillow, Becket, Massachusetts, 16 July 1985.

5   Jerome Rothenberg discusses some of these aspects of post-modernism in 'New Models, New Visions: Some Notes Toward a Poetics of Performance,' in Michel Benamou and Charles Caramello, eds., *Performance in Postmodern Culture* (Madison, WI: Coda Press, 1977). In 'Postmodern Dance and the Repudiation of Primitivism,' *Partisan Review* 50 (1983): 101–121, Roger Copeland argues that modern dance strove for synthesis in terms of form and unity in terms of the audience's experience of the work. A mistrust of language underlies the primitivist longings of the modern dancers. Here and in a second article, 'Postmodern Dance/Postmodern Architecture/Postmodernism,' *Performing Arts Journal* 19 (1983): 27–43, Copeland makes some useful observations about post-modern dance. However, his definition is much more narrow than the one I propose here, although he does suggest the possibility of two different camps of post-modern dance (in 'Postmodern Dance/Postmodern Architecture/Postmodernism,' p. 33).

■   ■   ■

Source

Banes, S. (1987) Introduction to the Wesleyan paperback edition, *Terpsichore in Sneakers: Post-Modern Dance,* 2nd edition, Middletown, Conn.: Wesleyan University Press: xiii–xv.

First published (1980) by Houghton Mifflin.

Sally Banes (1951–)

American dance historian and critic. Her research into the seminal Judson Dance Theatre (1962–64) developed into the works not only on this period but also the period of what came to be known as American Post Modern Dance. Formerly performance art critic for the *Village Voice* and editor of *Dance Research Journal*, she has written on other aspects both of dance and of avant-garde art in America in the 1960s. Currently, she is Professor of Dance and Theatre and Chair of the Dance Program at University of Wisconsin-Madison.

In the first edition of *Terpsichore in Sneakers: Post-Modern Dance* (1980) she wrote an extensive introduction which became a definitive statement on the origins and historical phases of post-modern dance in America. In the introduction to the second edition she revises that definition and provides the explanation of how the term post-modern came to be used to describe certain approaches to dance in the 1960s and subsequently.[1]

The extract included here precisely delineates the term post-modern dance as a preface to her categorisation of the four phases of American post-modern dance as follows: The 1960s: Breakaway Post-Modern Dance; The 1970s: Analytic Post-Modern Dance; The 1980s: The Rebirth of Content. She also includes a coda – Outside New York.

This is an essential reference for placing Brown, Cunningham and Rainer. The definition also provides direct comparison with Martin's (1933) definition of modern dance and with the writings of Wigman and Humphrey, who fall within that genre.

Reader cross-references

Brown – detailed example of choreographer's process of postmodern dance
Cunningham – whose concerns are at the interface between modern/postmodern dance
Martin – comparison with earlier characterisation of modern dance
Rainer – conceptual analysis of postmodern dance by a choreographer
Schechner – an alternative view of postmodernism

Further reading

Banes, S. (1981) *Democracy's Body: Judson Dance Theatre 1962–1964*, Ann Arbor, Mich.: UMI Research Press.
Banes, S. (1994) *Greenwich Village 1963: Avant-Garde Performance and the Effervescent Body*, Durham, N.C.: Duke University Press.

Banes, S. (1994) *Writing Dancing in the Age of Postmodernism*, Middletown, Conn.: Wesleyan University Press.

Note

1   Banes originally uses the term 'post-modern' (with a hyphen), whereas later writers use 'postmodern' (one word). There is an interesting correspondence between Banes and Susan Manning in *The Drama Review* on the use of 'modern' and 'postmodern'. Manning, S. (1988) 'Modernist Dogma and Postmodern Rhetoric: A Response to Sally Banes' Terpsichore in Sneakers', *The Drama Review* 32 (4) T120, Winter 1988:32–39; Banes, S. 'Terpsichore in Combat Boots', *The Drama Review* 33 (1) T121, Spring 1989:13–15; and Manning, S. 'Terpsichore in Combat Boots', *The Drama Review* 33 (1) T121, Spring 1989:15–16.

Chapter 5

Eugenio Barba

WORDS OR PRESENCE

T RAINING DOES NOT teach how to act, how to be clever, does not prepare one for creation. Training is a process of self-definition, a process of self-discipline which manifests itself indissolubly through physical reactions. It is not the exercise in itself that counts – for example, bending or somer-saults – but the individual's justification for his own work, a justification which although perhaps banal or difficult to explain through words, is physio-logically perceptible, evident to the observer. This approach, this personal justification decides the meaning of the training, the surpassing of the partic-ular exercises which, in reality, are stereotyped gymnastic movements.

This inner necessity determines the quality of the energy which allows work without a pause, without noticing tiredness, continuing even when exhausted and at that very moment going forward without surrendering. This is the self-discipline of which I spoke.

Let us understand each other, however: it is not by killing oneself with exhaustion that one becomes creative. It is not on command, by forcing, that one opens oneself to others. Training is not a form of personal asceticism, a malevolent harshness against oneself, a persecution of the body. Training puts one's own intentions to the test, how far one is prepared to pay with one's own person for all that one believes and declares. It is the possibility of bridging the gap between intention and realization. This daily task, obsti-nate, patient, often in darkness, sometimes even searching for a meaning for it, is a concrete factor in the transformation of the actor as a man and as a member of the group. This imperceptible daily transformation of one's own way of seeing, approaching and judging the problems of one's own existence and of that of others, this sifting of one's own prejudices, one's own doubts – not through gestures and grandiloquent phrases but through the silent daily activity – is reflected in one's work which finds new justifications, new reactions: thus one's north is displaced.

■

In the beginning, we had a programme of set exercises that we taught everybody and that everybody had to follow. These were exercises of every kind, taken from ballet, mime, pure gymnastics, Hatha-Yoga and acrobatics. We worked out a whole series of physical actions and called this 'biomechanics' after the term used by Meyerhold. We defined biomechanics as a very dynamic reaction to an external stimulus. The exercises were of an acrobatic nature and very violent. However, they had been transformed by our imaginations around what we thought to be the training of the oriental actor. Starting from this training as it existed in our fantasy, we wanted to achieve a rhythm of work that was intense yet had the same precision, the same economy of movement, the same suggestiveness and power that we attribute to the oriental actor. For us, bio-mechanics was not a technically exact and historical reconstruction of the exercises elaborated by Meyerhold, who had a particular aim in view: namely, the creation of a social *emploi* for the actor. We used this term to set in motion our imagination, to stimulate us. What could it be like, this biomechanics? We attempted to re-invent it, to rediscover it in our bodies according to our own justifications. It was the actors who, individually or in collaboration, worked out the map of this territory. Within it were also the 'battles', the fights, the exercises for the reflexes in which the actor must immediately adapt himself to a situation, think with his whole body, react with all of it.

■

In spite of my experience in oriental theatre, especially Indian Kathakali, I haven't drawn directly from it. I tried to make my actors imagine this theatre of colors and exoticism, acrobatics and religiosity, by appealing to their subjectivity and their fantasy.

Kathakali, like all oriental theatre, cannot be copied or transplanted. It can only serve as a stimulus, a point of departure. The actor in oriental theatre is immersed in a tradition that he must wholly respect. He is merely executing a role whose minutest detail has, as in a musical score, been elaborated by some master in a more or less distant past. As with a pianist or a classical ballet dancer, his evolution cannot be separated from virtuosity. In Western theatre, however, the actor is – or should be – a creator. His clash with the text, through his own sensibility and his own historical experience, opens up a unique and personal universe to his spectators.

This essential difference also determines one's approach to the profession, the preparation, that which is now usually called training. Even today, the Kathakali or Kabuki actor begins his training at the same age as a European child who wishes to devote himself to ballet. The psychological and also physiological consequences are evident. It is meaningless to go to Japan or India and take exercises from Kabuki or Kathakali in order to adapt them passively to the European pedagogical tradition, in the hope that our actors too might become 'virtuosi' like their oriental colleagues. Let me repeat, it is not the exercises in themselves that are decisive, but one's personal attitude, that inner necessity which incites and justifies on an emotional level and with a logic that will not allow itself to be trapped by words, the choice of one's own profession.

This attitude determines the creation of norms that become almost an artistic or ethical super-ego in the actor. Similar norms are also to be found in theatre forms based on a purely technical apprenticeship. Here the historical circumstances and the environmental conditions in which the theatre work evolves, influence the elaboration of these norms which are reflected in the technique. For example, the entire training of a young actor wishing to devote himself to Kabuki takes place in a rarefied atmosphere, without the possibility of contact with actors from other theatrical forms, either Noh or modern theatre, in a strict professional hierarchy petrified in family dynasties whose mentality contrasts with the efficient industrial vocation revealed by contemporary Japan.

The same applies to the Kathakali actor. While the Kabuki actor is owned by a large impresario firm which places him in various theatres, the Kathakali actor works on religious ground, the temple courtyard, dedicates his work and his performance to divinities, lives in a very modest way without the prospect ever of becoming a star like his Japanese colleague. These socio-historical circumstances, together with a particular professional tradition which still has great value and prestige for the young would-be actor, are decisive factors in the conception and elaboration of that expressiveness which is codified and so transformed into technique.

■

In the beginning of our activity we too believed in the 'myth of technique', something which it was possible to acquire, to possess, and which would have allowed the actor to master his own body, to become conscious of it. So, at this stage, we practised exercises to develop the dilation of the eyes in order to increase their expressiveness. They were exercises which I had taken from India while studying the training of Kathakali actors. The expressiveness of the eyes is essential in Kathakali and the control of their musculature demands several hours of hard training daily for many years. The different nuances each have a precise significance; the way of frowning, the direction of a glance, the degree of opening or closing the lids are codified by tradition and are in fact concepts and images which are immediately comprehensible to the spectator. Such control in a European actor would only restrain the organic reactions of the face and transform it into a lifeless mask.

Like a melting pot in which the most disparate metals fuse, so inside me at the outset I tried to blend together the most diverse influences, the impressions which for me had been the most fertile: oriental theatre, the experiments of the Great Reform, my personal experience from my stay in Poland and with Grotowski. I wanted to adapt all this to my ideal of technical perfection even in the part of the artistic work which we called composition, a word which had arrived in our theatre through the Russian and French terminology and Grotowski's interpretation of it. I believed that composition was the capacity of the actor to create signs, to consciously mould his own body into a deformation which was rich in suggestiveness and power of association: the body of the actor as a Rosetta stone and the spectator in the role of Champollion. The aim was on a conscious level, by cold calculation, to attain that which is warm and which obliges us to believe with all our senses. But I often felt this composition to be imposed, something external which functioned on a theatrical level but lacked the drilling force that could perforate the crust of all too obvious significations. The composition might be rich, striking, throwing the actor into relief, yet it was like a veil which hid from me something that I felt inside myself but which I didn't have the courage to face, to reveal to myself — or rather to reveal to others.

In the first period of our existence all the actors did the same exercises together in a common collective rhythm. Then we realized that the rhythm varied for each individual. Some have a faster vital rhythm, others a slower one. We began to talk about organic rhythm, not in the sense of a regular beat but of variation, pulsation like that of our heart as shown by a cardiogram. This perpetual variation, however minute, revealed the existence of a wave of organic reactions which engaged the entire body. Training could only be individual.

This faith in technique as a sort of magic power which could render the actor invulnerable, guided us also in the domain of the voice. At the start, we followed the practices of oriental theatre: straightforward imitations of certain timbres of the voice. Using Grotowski's terminology, we called the different tones of voice 'resonators'. In oriental theatre training, the young actor learns entire roles mechanically with all their vocal nuances, timbres, intonations, exclamations – a complete fabric of sounds perfected through tradition and which the actor must repeat precisely in order to gain the appreciation of a critical audience. We too began coldly to find a series of timbres, tones, intonations, and exercised them daily.

This period of calculated work, of pure 'technicity', seemed to confirm that the hypothesis of the actor-virtuoso was right. The effects produced were interesting. But during their work a few actors managed to reach the territory of their own 'vocal flora'. This opened up to stimuli that were striking in their suggestiveness, in their emotional charge, and were not based on logic or a certain intellectuality: enter the ghost of your father and you, Hamlet, cry out because you are afraid or because you are glad. And out comes a strangled, flat, impersonal, cliché of a cry.

So we discovered the value of personal images for engaging the voice, in order to attain one's individual sound universe. No more calculated effects or mechanically placed voice. Simply reactions, responses to the image which served as a stimulus. We began to talk of vocal actions. That which for us had once been a postulate – the voice as a physiological process – now became a tangible reality which engaged the entire organism and projected it in space. The voice was a prolongation of the body which, through space, hit, touched, caressed, encircled, pushed, searched far away or close by; an invisible hand which stretched out from the body to act in space or renounce action. And even this renunciation was spoken by the invisible hand. But in order that the voice might act, it must know *where* the point was toward which it was directed, *who* that point was and *why* it was addressing him.

From that moment I ceased to speak of resonators. The whole body of the actor resounded, the room resounded, as well as something inside me as I listened, provided the actor really addressed this point in space which, although invisible to my eyes, was concrete to him, perceptible to all his senses, present with physical features.

■

For a long time the 'myth of technique' nourished our work. Then gradually it brought me to a situation of doubt. I had to admit that the argument for technique was a rationalization, a pragmatic blackmail – if you do this, you obtain that – which I used to make the others accept my way of working, to give it a useful and logical justification. On a personal level – dimly, full of shadows – I felt that under the alibi of work which the others defined as theatre I was trying to annihilate the actor in my companion, wash him of the character, destroy the theatre in our relationship so that we might meet one another as men, as companions in arms who have no need to defend themselves, bound closer than brothers by the doubts and illusions of years passed patiently together: not the actor, not the character, but the companion of a long period of my life.

It was no longer a matter of teaching or learning something, of tracing a personal method, of discovering a new technique, of finding an original language, of demystifying oneself or others. Only of not being afraid of one another. Having the courage to approach one another until one becomes transparent and allowing glimpses of the well of one's own experience. From here stems that 'pudeur' which refuses the presence of strangers during the work. And when the time comes for others to be present – spectators – these are witnesses of this human situation that we continue to call theatre. Because we have no name for this new frontier beyond which there is little we can say to one another in a theatrical language, even if its phrases are said with perfection. Virtuosity does not lead to situations of new human relationships which are the decisive ferment for a reorientation, a new way of defining oneself vis-à-vis others and of overcoming the facile self-complacency.

Thus the training transformed itself into a process of self-definition, far removed from any utilitarian justification and guided by individual subjectivity. Everyone decides for himself on its meaning. Once again: the exterior forms of the exercises are of no importance. But self-discipline remains.

■

During training one often runs the risk of a sclerosis. This is caused either by the ingenuous attitude which leads one to believe that with training comes creativity, or by the lack of personal justification which brings about the repetition of exercises as gymnastics. We too have gone through similar periods. Then I succumbed to the temptation to explain, to come up with a sort of training philosophy, Ariadne's thread for my companions lost in the labyrinth of uncertainty. With great loyalty my companions tried to motivate their own work with my words, my explanations. But something was wrong, something didn't ring true, and in the end a sort of split became apparent between what they were doing and what they wanted to do or believed they were doing to satisfy me, to meet me. When I realized this, I gave up all explanation.

After working together many hours a day for many years, it is not my words but perhaps only my presence that can say something.

■   ■   ■

Source

Barba, E. (1979) 'Words or Presence', *The Floating Islands: Reflections with Odin Teatret*, trans. J. Barba, F. Pardeilhan, J.C. Rodesch, S. Shapiro and J. Varley, Denmark: Thomsens Bogtrykheri 73–79.

First published (1972) in *The Drama Review* 53.

Eugenio Barba (1936–)

Born in southern Italy, emigrated to Norway in 1954. He is now, as a theatre director, theorist, and founder of Odin Teatret (1964), one of this century's major innovators and a focus for much contemporary experimental work. He studied in Poland with Jerzy Grotowski, and published the first book about him, *Towards a Poor Theatre* (1968). In 1966 Odin Teatret moved to Holstebro in Denmark, from where its fame spread as a performing company, and as a source for theatre training. Odin's performances range from the processional and celebratory to the intensely mythic and personal, and include *Kaspariana* (1967), *The Million* (1979), *Judith* (1987), and *The Castle of Holstebro* (1990), which have been performed across Europe. Barba is also a major and unique theorist of theatre practice, and in 1979 in Denmark founded ISTA (International School of Theatre Anthropology), a peripatetic meeting of theatre scholars and practitioners, with the aim of comparing both Eastern and Western methods of theatre practice. The major publication arising from this work has been *The Secret Art of the Performer* (1991), a dictionary of theatre anthropology.

This essay is from Barba's first Odin book and stresses his major and enduring theme, that the training of the performer is an individual and personal responsibility. Barba's work explores alternatives to psychological assumptions about performance, and with his use and examination of terms such as the performer's 'presence' or 'energy', provides a training philosophy which is practised and studied in several European schools and universities as a major twentieth-century technique. Not to accept character as a unit of the measure of performance links him with many major practitioners featured in this book.

Reader cross-references

Boal – a contemporary approach to theatre games and exercises
Brecht – an anti-psychological attitude to theatre
Grotowski – the roots of Barba's theory of performance energy
Hijikata – a contemporary Japanese approach
Soyinka – a West African perspective on ritual

Further reading

Barba, E. and Savarese, N. (1991) *A Dictionary of Theatre Anthropology: The Secret Art of the Performer*, London: Routledge.
Watson, I. (1995) *Towards a Third Theatre*, London: Routledge.

Chapter 6

Roland Barthes

THE GRAIN
OF THE VOICE

LANGUAGE, ACCORDING TO Benveniste, is the only semiotic system capable of *interpreting* another semiotic system (though undoubtedly there exist limit works in the course of which a system feigns self-interpretation – *The Art of the Fugue*). How, then, does language manage when it has to interpret music? Alas, it seems, very badly. If one looks at the normal practice of music criticism (or, which is often the same thing, of conversations 'on' music), it can readily be seen that a work (or its performance) is only ever translated into the poorest of linguistic categories: the adjective. Music, by natural bent, is that which at once receives an adjective. The adjective is inevitable: this music is *this*, this execution is *that*. No doubt the moment we turn an art into a subject (for an article, for a conversation) there is nothing left but to give it predicates; in the case of music, however, such predication unfailingly takes the most facile and trivial form, that of the epithet. Naturally, this epithet, to which we are constantly led by weakness or fascination (little parlour game: talk about a piece of music without using a single adjective), has an economic function: the predicate is always the bulwark with which the subject's imaginary protects itself from the loss which threatens it. The man who provides himself or is provided with an adjective is now hurt, now pleased, but always *constituted*. There is an imaginary in music whose function is to reassure, to constitute the subject hearing it (would it be that music is dangerous – the old Platonic idea? that music is an access to *jouissance*, to loss, as numerous ethnographic and popular examples would tend to show?) and this imaginary immediately comes to language via the adjective. A historical dossier ought to be assembled here, for adjectival criticism (or predicative interpretation) has taken on over the centuries certain institutional aspects. The musical adjective becomes legal whenever an *ethos* of music is postulated, each time, that is, that music is attributed a regular – natural or magical – mode of signification. Thus with the ancient Greeks, for whom it was the musical *language* (and not the contingent work) in its denotative structure which was immediately adjectival, each mode being linked to a coded expression (rude, austere, proud, virile, solemn, majestic, warlike, educative, noble, sumptuous, doleful, modest, dissolute, voluptuous); thus with the Romantics, from Schumann to Debussy, who substitute for, or add to, the simple indication of tempo (*allegro*, *presto*, *andante*) poetic, emotive predicates which are increasingly re-fined and which are given in the national language so as to diminish the mark of the code and develop the 'free' character of the predication (*sehr kräftig*, *sehr präcts*, *spirituel et discret*, etc.).

Are we condemned to the adjective? Are we reduced to the dilemma of either the predicable or the ineffable? To ascertain whether there are (verbal) means for talking about music without adjectives, it would be necessary to look at more or less the whole of music criticism, something which I believe has never been done and which, nevertheless, I have neither the intention nor the means of doing here. This much, however, can be said: it is not by struggling against the adjective (diverting the adjective you find on the tip of the tongue towards some substantive or verbal periphrasis) that one stands a chance of exorcising music commentary and liberating it from the fatality of predication; rather than trying to change directly the language on music, it would be better to change the musical object itself, as it presents itself to discourse, better to alter its level of perception or intellection, to displace the fringe of contact between music and language.

It is this displacement that I want to outline, not with regard to the whole of music but simply to a part of vocal music (*lied* or *mélodie*): the very precise space (genre) of *the encounter between a language and a voice*. I shall straightaway give a name to this signifier at the level of which, I believe, the temptation of ethos can be liquidated (and thus the adjective banished): the *grain*, the grain of the voice when the latter is in a dual posture, a dual production – of language and of music.

What I shall attempt to say of the 'grain' will, of course, be only the apparently abstract side, the impossible account of an individual thrill that I constantly experience in listening to singing. In order to disengage this 'grain' from the acknowledged values of vocal music, I shall use a twofold opposition: theoretical, between the pheno-text and the geno-text (borrowing from Julia Kristeva), and paradigmatic, between two singers, one of whom I like very much (although he is no longer heard), the other very little (although one hears no one but him), Panzera and Fischer-Dieskau (here merely ciphers: I am not deifying the first nor attacking the second).

Listen to a Russian bass (a church bass – opera is a genre in which the voice has gone over in its entirety to dramatic expressivity, a voice with a grain which little signifies): something is there, manifest and stubborn (one hears only *that*), beyond (or before) the meaning of the words, their form (the litany), the melisma, and even the style of execution: something which is directly the cantor's body, brought to your ears in one and the same movement from deep down in the cavities, the muscles, the membranes, the cartilages, and from deep down in the Slavonic language, as though a single skin lined the inner flesh of the performer and the music he sings. The voice is not personal: it expresses nothing of the cantor, of his soul; it is not original (all Russian cantors have roughly the same voice), and at the same time it is individual: it has us hear a body which has no civil identity, no 'personality', but which is nevertheless a separate body. Above all, this voice bears along *directly* the symbolic, over the intelligible, the expressive: here, thrown in front of us like a packet, is the Father, his phallic stature. The 'grain' is that: the materiality of the body speaking its mother tongue; perhaps the letter, almost certainly *signifiance*.

Thus we can see in song (pending the extension of this distinction to the whole of music) the two texts described by Julia Kristeva. The *pheno-song* (if the transposition be allowed) covers all the phenomena, all the features which belong to the structure of the language being sung, the rules of the genre, the coded form of the melisma, the composer's idiolect, the style of the interpretation: in short, everything in the performance which is in the service of communication, representation, expression, everything which it is customary to talk about, which forms the tissue of cultural values (the matter of acknowledged tastes, of fashions, of critical commentaries), which takes its bearing directly on the ideological alibis of a period ('subjectivity', 'expressivity', 'dramaticism', 'personality' of the artist). The *geno-song* is the volume of the singing and speaking voice, the space where significations germinate 'from within language and in its very materiality'; it forms a signifying play having nothing to do with communication, representation (of feelings), expression; it is that apex (or that depth) of production where the melody really works at the language – not at what it says, but the voluptuousness of its sounds-signifiers, of its letters – where melody explores how the language works and identifies with that work. It is, in a very simple word but which must be taken seriously, the *diction* of the language.

From the point of view of the pheno-song, Fischer-Dieskau is assuredly an artist beyond reproach: everything in the (semantic and lyrical) structure is respected and yet nothing seduces, nothing sways us to *jouissance*. His art is inordinately expressive (the diction is dramatic, the pauses, the checkings and releasings of breath, occur like shudders of passion) and hence never exceeds culture: here it is the soul which accompanies the song, not the body. What is difficult is for the body to accompany the musical diction not with a movement of emotion but with a 'gesture-support';[1] all the more so since the whole of musical pedagogy teaches not the culture of the 'grain' of the voice but the emotive modes of its delivery – the myth of respiration. How many singing teachers have we not heard prophesying that the art of vocal music rested entirely on the mastery, the correct discipline of breathing! The breath is the *pneuma*, the soul swelling or breaking, and any exclusive art of breathing is likely to be a secretly mystical art (a mysticism levelled down to the measure of the long-playing record). The lung, a stupid organ (lights for cats!), swells but gets no erection; it is in the throat, place where the phonic metal hardens and is segmented, in the mask that *signifiance* explodes, bringing not the soul but *jouissance*. With FD, I seem only to hear the lungs, never the tongue, the glottis, the teeth, the mucous membranes, the nose. All of Panzera's art, on the contrary, was in the letters, not in the bellows (simple technical feature: you never heard him *breathe* but only divide up the phrase). An extreme rigour of thought regulated the prosody of the enunciation and the phonic economy of the French language; prejudices (generally stemming from oratorical and ecclesiastical diction) were over-thrown. With regard to the consonants, too readily thought to constitute the very armature of our language (which is not, however, a Semitic one) and always prescribed as needing to be 'articulated', detached, emphasized *in order to fulfil the clarity of meaning*, Panzera recommended that in many cases they be *patinated*, given the wear of a language that had been living, func-tioning, and working for ages past, that they be made simply the springboard for the admirable vowels. There lay the 'truth' of language – not its func-tionality (clarity, expressivity, communication) – and the range of vowels received all the *signifiance* (which is meaning in its potential voluptuousness): the opposition of *é* and *è* (so necessary in conjugation), the purity – almost *electronic*, so much was its sound tightened, raised, exposed, held – of the most French of vowels, the *ü* (a vowel not derived by French from Latin). Similarly, Panzera carried his *r*'s beyond the norms of the singer – without denying those norms. His *r* was of course rolled, as in every classic art of singing, but the roll had nothing peasant-like or Canadian about it; it was an artificial roll, the paradoxical state of a letter-sound at once totally abstract (by its metallic brevity of vibration) and totally material (by its manifest deep-rootedness in the action of the throat). This phonetics – am I alone in perceiving it? am I hearing voices within the voice? but isn't it the truth of the voice to be hallucinated? isn't the entire space of the voice an infinite one? which was doubtless the meaning of Saussure's work on anagrams – does not exhaust *signifiance* (which is inexhaustible) but it does at least hold in check the attempts at *expressive reduction* operated by a whole culture against the poem and its melody.

It would not be too difficult to date that culture, to define it histori-cally. FD now reigns more or less unchallenged over the recording of vocal music; he has recorded everything. If you like Schubert but not FD, then Schubert is today *forbidden* you – an example of that positive censorship (censorship by repletion) which characterizes mass culture though it is never criticized. His art – expressive, dramatic, *sentimentally clear*, borne by a voice lacking in any 'grain', in signifying weight, fits well with the demands of an *average* culture. Such a culture, defined by the growth of the number of listeners and the disappearance of practitioners (no more amateurs), wants art, wants music, provided they be clear, that they 'translate' an emotion and represent a signified (the 'meaning' of a poem); an art that innoculates pleasure (by reducing it to a known, coded emotion) and reconciles the subject to what in music *can be said*: what is said about it, predicatively, by Institution, Criticism, Opinion. Panzera does not belong to this culture (he could not have done, having sung before the coming of the microgroove record; moreover I doubt whether, were he singing today, his art would be recognized or even simply *perceived*); his reign, very great between the wars, was that of an exclusively bourgeois art (an art, that is, in no way petit-bour-geois) nearing the end of its inner development and, by a familiar distortion, separated from History. It is perhaps, precisely and less paradoxically than it seems, because this art was *already* marginal, mandarin, that it was able to bear traces of *signifiance*, to escape the tyranny of meaning.

The 'grain' of the voice is not – or is not merely – its timbre; the *signifiance* it opens cannot better be defined, indeed, than by the very friction between the music and something else, which something else is the particular language (and nowise the message). The song must speak, must *write* – for what is produced at the level of the geno-song is finally writing. This sung writing of language is, as I see it, what the French *mélodie* sometimes tried to accom-plish. I am well aware that the German *lied* was intimately bound up with the German language via the Romantic poem, that the poetical culture of Schumann was immense and that this same Schumann used to say of Schubert that had he lived into old age he would have set the whole of German literature to music, but I think nevertheless that the historical meaning of the *lied* must be sought in the music (if only because of its popular origins). By contrast, the historical meaning of the *mélodie* is a certain culture of the French language. As we know, the Romantic poetry of France is more oratorical than textual; what the poetry could not accomplish on its own, however, the *mélodie* has occasionally accomplished with it, working at the language through the poem. Such a work (in the specificity here acknowledged it) is not to be seen in the general run of the *mélodies* produced which are too accommodating towards minor poets, the model of the petit-bourgeois romance, and salon usages, but in some few pieces it is indisputable – anthologically (a little by chance) in certain songs by Fauré and Duparc, massively in the later (prosodic) Fauré and the vocal work of Debussy (even if *Pelléas* is often sung badly – dramatically). What is engaged in these works is, much more than a musical style, a practical reflection (if one may put it like that) on the language; there is a progressive movement from the language to the poem, from the poem to the song and from the song to its performance. Which means that the *mélodie* has little to do with the history of music and much with the theory of the text. Here again, the signifier must be redistributed.

Compare two sung deaths, both of them famous: that of Boris and that of Mélisande. Whatever Mussorgsky's intentions, the death of Boris is *expressive* or, if preferred, *hysterical*; it is overloaded with historical, affective contents. Performances of the death cannot be but dramatic: it is the triumph of the pheno-text, the smothering of *signifiance* under the soul as signified. Mélisande, on the contrary, only dies *prosodically*. Two extremes are joined, woven together: the perfect intelligibility of the denotation and the pure prosodic segmentation of the enunciation; between the two a salutary gap (filled out in Boris) – the *pathos*, that is to say, according to Aristotle (why not?), passion *such as men speak and imagine it*, the accepted idea of death, *endoxical* death. Mélisande dies *without any noise* (understanding the term in its cybernetic sense): nothing occurs to interfere with the signifier and there is thus no compulsion to redundance; simply, the production of a music-language with the function of preventing the singer from being expressive. As with the Russian bass, the symbolic (the death) is thrown immediately (without mediation) before us (this to forestall the stock idea which has it that what is not expressive can only be cold and intellectual; Mélisande's death is 'moving', which means that it shifts something in the chain of the signifier).

The *mélodie* disappeared – sank to the bottom – for a good many reasons, or at least the disappearance took on a good many aspects. Doubtless it succumbed to its salon image, this being a little the ridiculous form of its class origin. Mass 'good' music (records, radio) has left it behind, preferring either the more pathetic orchestra (success of Mahler) or less bourgeois instruments than the piano (harpsichord, trumpet). Above all, however, the death of the *mélodie* goes along with a much wider historical phenomenon to a large extent unconnected to the history of music or of musical taste: the French are abandoning their language, not, assuredly, as a normative set of noble values (clarity, elegance, correctness) – or at least this does not bother me very much for these are institutional values – but as a space of pleasure, of thrill, a site where language works *for nothing*, that is, in perversion (remember here the singularity – the solitude – of *Lois* by Philippe Sollers, theatre of the return of the prosodic and metrical work of the language).

The 'grain' is the body in the voice as it sings, the hand as it writes, the limb as it performs. If I perceive the 'grain' in a piece of music and accord this 'grain' a theoretical value (the emergence of the text in the work), I inevitably set up a new scheme of evaluation which will certainly be individual – I am determined to listen to my relation with the body of the man or woman singing or playing and that relation is erotic – but in no way 'subjective' (it is not the psychological 'subject' in me who is listening; the climactic pleasure hoped for is not going to reinforce – to express – that subject but, on the contrary, to lose it). The evaluation will be made outside of any law, outplaying not only the law of culture but equally that of anti-culture, developing beyond the subject all the value hidden behind 'I like' or 'I don't like'. Singers especially will be ranged in what may be called, since it is a matter of my choosing without there being any reciprocal choice of me, two prostitutional categories. Thus I shall freely extol such and such a performer, little-known, minor, forgotten, dead perhaps, and turn away from such another, an acknowledged star (let us refrain from examples, no doubt of merely biographical significance); I shall extend my choice across all the genres of vocal music including popular music, where I shall have no difficulty in rediscovering the distinction between the pheno-song and the geno-song (some popular singers have a 'grain' while others, however famous, do not). What is more, leaving aside the voice, the 'grain' – or the lack of it – persists in instrumental music; if the latter no longer has language to lay open *signifiance* in all its volume at least there is the performer's body which again forces me to evaluation. I shall not judge a performance according to the rules of interpretation, the constraints of style (anyway highly illusory), which almost all belong to the pheno-song (I shall not wax lyrical concerning the 'rigour', the 'brilliance', the 'warmth', the 'respect for what is written', etc.), but according to the image of the body (the figure) given me. I can hear with certainty – the certainty of the body, of thrill – that the harpsichord playing of Wanda Landowska comes from her inner body and not from the petty digital scramble of so many harpsichordists (so much so that it is a different instrument). As for piano music, I know at once which part of the body is playing – if it is the arm, too often, alas, muscled like a dancer's calves, the clutch of the finger-tips (despite the sweeping flourishes of the wrists), or if on the contrary it is the only erotic part of a pianist's body, the pad of the fingers whose 'grain' is so rarely heard (it is hardly necessary to recall that today, under the pressure of the mass long-playing record, there seems to be a flattening out of technique; which is paradoxical in that the various manners of playing are all flattened out *into perfection*: nothing is left but pheno-text).

This discussion has been limited to 'classical music'. It goes without saying, however, that the simple consideration of 'grain' in music could lead to a different history of music from the one we know now (which is purely pheno-textual). Were we to succeed in refining a certain 'aesthetics' of musical pleasure, then doubtless we would attach less importance to the formidable break in tonality accomplished by modernity.

Note

1   'Which is why the best way to read me is to accompany the reading with certain appropriate bodily movements. Against non-spoken writing, against non-written speech. For the gesture-support.' Philippe Sollers, *Lois*, Paris 1972, p. 108.

■ ■ ■

Source

Barthes, R. (1972, 1977) 'The Grain of the Voice', *Image–Music–Text*, trans. and ed. S. Heath, London: Fontana: 179–189.
      Originally published in *Musique en jeu* 9.

Roland Barthes (1915–80)

French theorist, philosopher, writer and critic; one of the main exponents of the development of structuralism as semiotics. He studied at the University of Paris, and taught French in Romania and Egypt before becoming Professor at the Collège de France, Paris, and subsequently at the Centre National de la Recherche

Scientifique. His critical work began in 1953 with his first book, *La Degré Zéro de l'Écriture* (*Writing Degree Zero*) (1953) and developed in Paris, where he became one of the central figures in the development of European postmodernism. Many subsequent European theorists, including Baudrillard, Derrida and Kristeva have acknowledged his influence. There has followed a whole genre of theatre analysis based on semiotics, notably, and exemplified by, Elam (1980).

The application of his theories gained attention through his collection of essays *Mythologies* (1957, 1972). Here he analysed a variety of cultural 'myths' exposing the reality behind, amongst other things, striptease and detergents, by decoding them. His work frequently analyses or alludes to performance and sets it in a wider context. His range encompasses all manner of cultural products and he is especially strong on cinema, photography and music. He contributed a major late twentieth-century idea, the death of the author, which has had a profound effect on thinking about authorship in general and performance in particular (1968). Here, famously, he says 'a text is made of multiple writings, drawn from many cultures. ... A text's unity lies not in its origin but in its destination. ... The birth of the reader must be at the cost of the death of the Author' (1968, 1977:148).

In this article Barthes applies his analysis to music. By 'grain' he means the embodiment of what has produced, in this case, the musical sound. His conclusions are applicable to all forms of performance and indeed he goes on here to say that '"the grain" is the body in the voice as it sings, the hand as it writes, the limb as it performs.'

Reader cross-references

Benjamin – an earlier European theoretical position
Brecht – another consideration of 'distance' in performance
Cage – another view of the quality of music
Cunningham – a view of the act of dancing that is worth comparison
Soyinka – disputes his theoretical stance
Williams – contemporary, British critical viewpoint

Further reading

Barthes, R. (1957, 1972) *Mythologies*, trans. A. Lavers, London: Jonathan Cape.
Elam, K. (1980) *The Semiotics of Theatre and Drama*, London: Methuen.

Chapter 7

Pina Bausch

NOT HOW PEOPLE MOVE
BUT WHAT MOVES THEM

Pina Bausch, when you left the Folkwang Dance Institute in 1973 and came here to Wuppertal, you said that you were afraid of being devoured by the machinery, the theater machinery that is. Do you still have that feeling nowadays?

Things are a lot different from what I had imagined they would be. In those days, I thought it might not be possible to do anything individual at all. I imagined the routine and the regulations and all the rest of it. I thought that the theater would have to go on running as usual. I was very afraid of that in those days.

And what are you afraid of nowadays?

At the moment . . . well, yes, perhaps I'm a little scared by the situation I've got myself into, that I just don't have the time to say, 'Can't I just take off somewhere for two weeks?' I don't mean holidays – well, yes, holidays then, simply to relax, to get away from this pressure and this load for a moment. It just never stops . . . Sometimes I wonder just how long I can take it . . . but the problem takes care of itself usually. If things are giving you pleasure, if they're fun – I mean work in general – then one . . . what's the word again? . . . one regenerates on one's own. That's nice in a way . . . yes, actually it has been great up until

now. Really, I'm surprised I have so much energy. Where else can it come from?

Could you say roughly how many hours you have to work in a week?

One couldn't count it, because . . . well, one can't divide it. Actually . . . actually I'm always working. Every hour is a working hour and then again it's not. It depends what one means by the word.

Is it a strain on you, the fact that audiences and critics now have such a tremendously high level of expectation?

I don't know. Perhaps it has never really changed. Actually, the feeling has always been the same. There always comes a moment where one is so unsure about what one has done because one lacks the necessary distance – and then there's this fear which is always there anyhow and always has been. And it's absolutely no help at all saying, 'Yes, it's going to work. I've done other things before'. The fear remains the same.

Would you say that this fear enters the pieces as a theme?

No, I don't think so.

Do you have themes? Specific themes? Or does this change?

Well, I'd say they sort of move in a circle. It's always the same things or similar things. Actually the themes are always to do with man-woman relationships, the way we behave or our longing or our inability, only sometimes the color changes. I *have* noticed that. Nowadays I often find supposedly cheerful things a lot sadder. In some ways, I've changed a bit, too.

You once said that basically you aren't interested in how people move, that you are more interested in what moves people. How does someone who holds that maxim come to be in dance theater?

Well, why do we do it? Why do we dance in the first place? There is a great danger in the way things are developing at the moment and have been developing in the last few years. Everything has become routine and no one knows any longer why they're using these movements. All that's left is just a strange sort of vanity which is becoming more and more removed from actual people. And I believe that we ought to be getting closer to one another again.

When you say 'we', you mean dance, choreography?

Yes, and the dancers too.

Where are you from and how did you first start to dance?

My father ran a public house and initially I was taken along to a ballet school for children.

That means you started off actually learning ballet as opposed to having seen it performed somewhere, which might have been a decisive experience for you?

Yes, I had never seen any ballet before.

And did you enjoy dancing right from the start?

Well, I went along and I tried to do what the others were doing. Somehow I recall us having to lie on our stomachs and touch our heads with our legs, and then there was this woman who said, 'She's a real contortionist!' That sounds really stupid now, but somehow I was terribly pleased that somebody had praised me. When your father has a public house you're sort of always just tagging along; basically one is always on one's own. You have no family life either. I was always up till midnight or one o'clock, or sitting under a table somewhere in the public house. We never took our meals together either. That's why I never really had any. . . . My parents never had the time to look after me very much.

Still, we're still a long way from this little girl actually making the decision that she wants to become a dancer.

Oh, it was nothing like that at all. I simply went along and then they started taking me for small children's parts, the lift boy in some operetta or . . . oh, I don't know . . . the Moor in the harem who had to wave the fan, or a newspaper boy. Things like that. And I was always terribly scared.

But you still had no plans to work in theater at that point?

I didn't really think about it. That's probably something that just simply happened. I really was always very scared about doing anything, but I enjoyed it terribly. And by the time I was ready to leave school, which is when one really started to think, or had to think about what one was going to do, because one knew that school was over – by that time it was basically clear.

And so you went straight from school to the Folkwang Dance Institute? Or was there a period in between?

That's basically what I did. I went to the Folkwang School.

And when did the dancer turn choreographer?

In those days at the Folkwang School, they had a great interest in – what did they call it then? – in improvisation classes. Much more than nowadays. . . . But they weren't improvisation classes at all. We did a bit of composition work, worked on a few little dances and study pieces. Anyway, I was one of the more active students in this respect. But it wasn't until I returned from America and I found there was nothing really happening in the group I was in and I was feeling very dissatisfied as a dancer. . . . I would have liked to express myself in a totally different way, but we just didn't have the opportunity. We didn't have very much to do either. There was nothing new happening and actually it was frustration which made me think of maybe trying to do something for myself. But it wasn't because I wanted to choreograph. The sole reason was because I wanted to dance. Yes, the reason I wanted to do something for myself was because I simply wanted to dance.

Something you just very briefly mentioned there: America. You studied dance for several years in New York. Was this episode in your life without any real significance or was it important for your development?

I think it was very important. The mere fact of having lived in a city like that was very important to me. The people, the city – which to me embodies something of 'today' and where literally everything is mixed, be it nationality, interests, or fashionable things – all right next to one another. Somehow I find that incredibly important.

But you wouldn't want to live there now?

I relate very strongly to New York. You see, when I think about New York, I have this kind of feeling which is normally quite alien to me otherwise – it's a bit like it were home . . . homesickness in other words. It's very strange.

One basically thinks of you as being a typical child of this countryside. Pina Bausch without the Bergisches Land or without the Ruhrgebiet, without Essen and Wuppertal – one somehow feels it wouldn't be possible. Could you imagine yourself, Pina Bausch, as ballet director at the Bavarian State Opera in Munich?

If I were offered the chance, or if someone thought it right for me to go to one particular theater, be it in Munich or somewhere else, then really it's simply only a question of how strongly I feel that it's right for me to go. But I could only ever do the things I feel I must do, I think. If someone were to say, 'You can come and work here but you have to do this, this and this' – then I don't think I'd be able to.

It would be impossible for you to do a traditional production of The Sleeping Beauty, *for example?*

I wouldn't want to.

You said that basically you live twenty-four hours a day for choreography and ballet . . .

Well, I'm not so sure about choreography . . .

Alright, but it occupies you around the clock, twice around the clock to be precise. How does this translate into practice? How do you approach a piece?

I live from hand to mouth. That's the way it is. Yes, that's actually how it works too. . . . When we're working on a piece, I have absolutely no time to start thinking about the next piece – either that or I'm simply unable to divide my time. . . . It just isn't possible. I first have to finish the one I'm doing and then I go straight on to the next one. I can feel what I'm looking for but often I'm unable to say rationally just what it is. I cannot put it into words, perhaps I don't even want to put it into words sometimes. Sometimes you come across things quite by accident, something you read. But basically I do look for them.

And where does the material come from, by and large?

The material which appears on stage? Oh, that's a much later stage in the process. I always panic before I start on a piece. I really am very frightened of starting, of saying categorically, 'Alright, we're going to rehearse today.' And I shirk it. I keep pushing it away from me as long as I can and then I'll start on it around the corner, so to speak. Sometimes I might ask to see one of the dancers and I'll say, 'Could we maybe try something out?' Or I talk to them about it a bit. But basically I find it incredibly difficult taking the first step because . . . because I know they, the dancers, are then going to expect me to tell them what I want. And then I panic. I'm scared of having to tell them because what I have is often so vague. It's true, I know I can always say, 'Here I am – there are one or two particular things in my head at the moment,' and I might even find some kind of word to describe it and then I'll say, 'Right. Well, here's where we start from. Let's see where it takes us.' It's great that I'm even able to put this into words nowadays. Two years ago I couldn't. I just didn't have those kind of words. I found it so damned difficult because anything one said was suddenly . . . well, you were so pinned down. Then, all of a sudden, you would say something and hope that the other person would pick up the clue because what I meant was actually something else. Anything I said was just an aid to making myself understood. Sometimes it's just an idea or a thought. . . . I suddenly get the feeling that if I talk about it too much then I've dirtied it already. I can't say why that is. And then I always have this feeling that I must protect it. I must talk round it so that it remains untouched, at least to begin with. Basically I want the group to use their imagination. We're still not doing what we really want to do.

And what do you really want to do?

Well I think we're all still holding back. It's quite natural because after all we want to be loved and liked. And I think there is something that holds you back somewhere. You think that there's this point and if you go beyond that then there's no exact telling where it will lead.

I always felt that this need to be loved was in fact something which made you want to produce, not something which held you back.

Right, right . . . but then it's both. Because it's a process, you see. Wanting to be loved; that's definitely our motor. I don't know. It might be different if I were on my own, but there are always other people involved. I don't want to force people and say, 'Now you've got to do this.' What I'd like – and this was the actual aim – is to try and get somewhere as a group. I'd like the others in the group to feel that the things which occupy me are also of importance to them. Maybe that's something I can't do at the present because we haven't reached that stage as a group yet.

You mentioned the word process. Process means development. You yourself have developed considerably. For example you've developed further and further away from the classical form of modern dance towards drama, although I know that this is only a very superficial description of the process. Do you have any idea where the process is leading you or where you yourself are going? Could you imagine retiring from dance completely and becoming a theater director, for example?

That's possible. I don't know. I'm always trying. I keep desperately trying to dance. I'm always hoping I'm going to find new ways of relating to movement. I can't go on working in the previous way. It would be like repeating something, something strange.

Might it also be that movement simply no longer suffices for what you want to say – that you also require words?

Words? I can't say exactly. But then again, on the contrary . . . it might be a movement. It is simply a question of when is it dance, when is it not. Where does it start? When do we call it dance? It does in fact have something to do with consciousness, with bodily consciousness, and the way we form things. But then it needn't have this kind of aesthetic form. It can have a quite different form and still be dance. Basically one wants to say something which cannot be said, so what one has done is to make a poem where one can feel what is meant. And so words, I find, are a means – a means to an end. But words are not the true aim.

What would you describe the true aim as being? Communication, or is it art?

I don't know. I don't know.

(The interviewer was Jochen Schmidt, 1978)

■　■　■

Source

Bausch, P. and Schmidt, J. (1978, 1984) 'Not How People Move But What Moves Them', *Pina Bausch–Wuppertal Dance Theater or The Art of Training a Goldfish*, trans. P. Stadie, ed. N. Servos Köln: Ballett-Bühnen Verlag: 227–230.

Pina Bausch (1940–)

German choreographer and director of Wuppertal Dance Theater. She began her career as a dancer after training first with Kurt Jooss at the Folkwang School in Essen and then in New York at the Juilliard School. From 1962 to 1968 she danced with the Folkwang Ballet, where she began her choreographic career. She became Director of Wuppertal Dance Theater for the 1973–74 season and has remained there. Her works for the company have included *Bluebeard* (1977),

Café Müller (1978), and *1980: A Piece by Pina Bausch* (1980). The company has toured Europe, the Americas and extensively elsewhere, but has only visited London once (1982).

Bausch's work is remarkable in both the scale and detail of her theatricality. She uses the smallest nuances of her dancers' attributes on stage and, at the same time, magnifies them into full-scale works which can last hours. Her dance theatre emphasises how people behave, presenting them in real time, as real people, yet writ large. The choreography appears deceptively simple, yet it is highly complex. The staging of her work has frequently transformed the stage area with hyperrealistic sets or with natural materials such as earth, water, turf, flowers.

This interview is one of four with Jochen Schmidt and published in Servos's definitive study of her early works. It was conducted in November 1978, shortly before the premiere of *Kontakthof*. She talks straightforwardly and frankly about aspects of her working method. Her observations are realistic, rather than codified, reflecting her attitude towards the making of her work.

Reader cross-references

Brown, Cunningham and **Rainer** – comparison with modern and postmodern American dance

Humphrey – an earlier, modern, systematised approach to choreography

LeCompte – another confrontational approach

Lepage – a theatrical contemporary

Müller – who acknowledges his admiration for her work

Wigman – to whom Bausch and other exponents of Tanztheater looked for their roots

Wilson – the use of non-linear theatrical juxtapositions

Further reading

Ballett International for the most extensive collection of articles and reviews on Bausch's work.

Servos, N. (ed.) (1984) *Pina Bausch-Wuppertal Dance Theater or The Art of Training a Goldfish*, trans. P. Stadie, Köln: Ballett-Bühnen Verlag.

Chapter 8

Beck

Julian Beck

ACTING EXERCISES

Acting Exercises:

Notes for a Primary Lesson (1)

Not to submit to an acting lesson unless its graphic purpose is clear. The body, if not stimulated by an inspiring impetus, does not react with interest. The movements, consequently the expression, are empty because they are empty of meaning.

The Living Theatre works something like this: we find an idea that we want to express physically. Then we do what is necessary to realize it. If it requires special exercises, then we do them.

Whenever we work physically we find things that we never could find if we did nothing but think.

We have rarely been able to find sufficient time simply to exercise. There is hardly enough time to do the necessary. Emergency.

All the time knowing that without living physically the powers of the mind diminish.

Therefore we are always individually doing Yoga, as we go thru the day doing other things we check our breathing, our posture, our movement, regularly. And the body's awareness of what's around it, and the space.

To train the body to extend its ordinary capacities. To extend imagination and intellect. Exercise should not be used to train the body to express the banal. We want things not yet known to the controlled consciousness which is ruining us. If sensitivity is not heightened by the exercise, and only the banal is expressed, we remain what we are, frustrated, unfulfilled, crippled.

Aimless exercise reinforces the accessibility of the banal.

At the same time it is important to nourish the body with use. The body understands that; but exercise without objective confuses the mind.

■　■　■

Source

Beck, J. (1972) 'Acting Exercises: Notes for a Primary Lesson (1)', *The Life of the Theatre: The Relation of the Artist to the Struggle of the People*, San Francisco: City Lights Books.

Julian Beck (1925–85)

Performer and director. With Judith Malina he created the Living Theatre, whose view of theatre as a rite of purgation via contact with a collective of performers owed much to the ideas of both Artaud and Grotowski. Throughout the 1960s the Living Theatre became famous as New York and the USA's most revolutionary theatre company, creating large-scale and lengthy performance rituals, often based on archetypal subjects, such as *Frankenstein* (1965), or *Paradise Now* (1968).

In their performances character and plot were replaced by physical and collective imagery often demanding participation on the part of the audience, which was often gladly given. As in the work of Artaud and the Dadaists, the group presented the audience with a rejection of contemporary, war-torn civilisation – this was the period of the Vietnam War in America – in favour of individual spiritual change through the rites of theatre. The group – actors from all persuasions – often pursued their politics in performance to an extent which disturbed the authorities – the group's intention. In 1970 this culminated in a declaration to 'abandon theatre and ... create circumstances which will lead to action'. The work included ceremonies of initiation and communion as a direct response to the 'machines' of a mechanistic and psychologically tortured outside world. The group became nomadic, moving from country to country for refuge.

'Acting Exercises' emphasises the attack on bourgeois values by proposing an essentially poetic approach to the world and to theatre, echoing the words of Artaud, a potent and compelling combination for the student generation of 1968, for whom the Living Theatre became representatives of a powerful artistic credo.

Reader cross-references

Artaud, **Grotowski** and **Jarry** – messianic/revolutionary claims for theatre
Boal – a contemporary South American view of theatre as a force for change
Brook – a collective collaborative ethic
Brown and **Rainer** – contemporary, contrasting, response to the times
Lepage – an oppositional view of the function of performance
Schechner – North American theatre contemporary
Stanislavski – earlier, contrasting view of the actor's training

Further reading

Biner, P. (1972) *The Living Theatre*, New York: Avon Books.
The Living Theatre (1971) *Paradise Now*, New York: Random House.
Silvestro, C. (ed.) (1971) *The Living Book of the Living Theatre*, Greenwich, Conn.: New York Graphic Society.

Chapter 9

Walter Benjamin

WHAT IS EPIC THEATER?

The relaxed audience

'There is nothing more pleasant than to lie on a sofa and read a novel,' wrote a nineteenth-century narrator, indicating the great extent to which a work of fiction can relax the reader who is enjoying it. The common image of a man attending a theatrical performance is the opposite: one pictures a man who follows the action with every fiber of his being at rapt attention. The concept of the epic theater, originated by Brecht as the theoretician of his poetic practice, indicates above all that this theater desires an audience that is relaxed and follows the action without strain. This audience, to be sure, always appears as a collective, and this differentiates it from the reader, who is alone with his text. Also, this audience, being a collective, will usually feel impelled to react promptly. This reaction, according to Brecht, ought to be a well-considered and therefore a relaxed one – in short, the reaction of people who have an interest in the matter. Two objects are provided for this interest. The first is the action; it has to be such that the audience can keep a check on it at crucial places on the basis of its own experience. The second is the performance; it should be mounted artistically in a pellucid manner. (This manner of presentation is anything but artless; actually, it presupposes artistic sophistication and acumen on the part of the director.) Epic theater appeals to an interest group who 'do not think without reason.' Brecht does not lose sight of the masses, whose limited practice of thinking is probably described by this phrase. In the endeavor to interest the audience in the theater expertly, but definitely not by way of mere cultural involvement, a political will has prevailed.

The plot

The epic theater purposes to 'deprive the stage of its sensation derived from subject matter.' Thus an old story will often do more for it than a new one. Brecht has considered the question of whether the incidents that are presented by the epic theater should not already be familiar. The theater would have the same relationship to the plot as a ballet teacher has to his pupil: his first task would be to loosen her joints to the greatest possible extent. This is how the Chinese theater actually proceeds. In his essay 'The Fourth Wall of China' (*Life and Letters Today*, Vol. XV, No. 6, 1936), Brecht states what he owes to this theater. If the theater is to cast about for familiar events, 'historical incidents would be the most suitable.' Their epic extension through the style of acting, the placards and captions, is intended to purge them of the sensational.

In this vein Brecht takes the life of Galileo as the subject of his latest play. Brecht presents Galileo primarily as a great teacher who not only teaches a new physics, but does so in a new way. In his hands, experiments are not only an achievement of science, but a tool of pedagogy as well. The main emphasis of this play is not on Galileo's recantation; rather, the truly epic process must be sought in what is evident from the labeling of the penultimate scene: '1633 to 1642. As a prisoner of the Inquisition, Galileo continues his scientific work until his death. He succeeds in smuggling his main works out of Italy.'

Epic theater is in league with the course of time in an entirely different way from that of the tragic theater. Because suspense belongs less to the outcome than to the individual events, this theater can cover the greatest spans of time. (The same is true of the earlier mystery plays. The dramaturgy of *Oedipus* or *The Wild Duck* constitutes the counterpole of epic dramaturgy.)

The untragic hero

The French classical theater made room in the midst of the players for persons of rank, who had their armchairs on the open stage. To us this seems inappropriate. According to the concept of the 'dramatic element' with which we are familiar, it seemed inappropriate to attach to the action on the stage a nonparticipating third party as a dispassionate observer or 'thinker.' Yet Brecht often had something like that in mind. One can go even further and say that Brecht made an attempt to make the thinker, or even the wise man, the hero of the drama. From this very point of view one can define his theater as epic theater. This attempt is taken furthest in the character of Galy Gay, the packer. Galy Gay, the protagonist of the play *A Man's a Man*, is nothing but an exhibit of the contradictions which make up our society. It may not be too bold to regard the wise man in the Brechtian sense as the perfect showcase of its dialectics. In any case, Galy Gay is a wise man. Plato already recognized the undramatic quality of that most excellent man, the sage. In his Dialogues he took him to the threshold of the drama; in his *Phaidon*, to the threshold of the passion play. The medieval Christ, who also repre-sented the wise man (we find this in the Early Fathers), is the untragic hero *par excellence*. But in the secular drama of the West, too, the search for the untragic hero has never ceased. In always new ways, and frequently in conflict with its theoreticians, this drama has differed from the authentic – that is, the Greek – form of tragedy. This important but poorly marked road, which may here serve as the image of a tradition, went via Roswitha and the mystery plays in the Middle Ages, via Gryphius and Calderón in the Baroque age; later we may trace it in Lenz and Grabbe, and finally in Strindberg. Scenes in Shakespeare are its roadside monuments, and Goethe crosses it in the second part of *Faust*. It is a European road, but a German one as well-provided that we may speak of a road and not of a secret smugglers' path by which the legacy of the medieval and the Baroque drama has reached us. It is this mule track, neglected and overgrown, which comes to light today in the dramas of Brecht.

The interruption

Brecht differentiates his epic theater from the dramatic theater in the narrower sense, whose theory was formulated by Aristotle. Appropriately, Brecht intro-duces his art of the drama as non-Aristotelian, just as Riemann introduced a non-Euclidian geometry. This analogy may bring out the fact that it is not a matter of competition between the theatrical forms in question. Riemann eliminated the parallel postulate; Brecht's drama eliminated the Aristotelian catharsis, the purging of the emotions through empathy with the stirring fate of the hero.

The special character of the relaxed interest of the audience for which the performances of the epic theater are intended is the fact that hardly any appeal is made to the empathy of the spectators. Instead, the art of the epic theater consists in producing astonishment rather than empathy. To put it succinctly: instead of identifying with the characters, the audience should be educated to be astonished at the circumstances under which they function.

The task of the epic theater, according to Brecht, is not so much the development of actions as the representation of conditions. This presentation does not mean reproduction as the theoreticians of Naturalism understood it. Rather, the truly important thing is to discover the conditions of life. (One might say just as well: to alienate [*verfremden*] them.) This discovery (alienation) of conditions takes place through the interruption of happenings. The most primitive example would be a family scene. Suddenly a stranger enters. The mother was just about to seize a bronze bust and hurl it at her daughter; the father was in the act of opening the window in order to call a policeman. At that moment the stranger appears in the doorway. This means that the stranger is confronted with the situation as with a startling picture: troubled faces, an open window, the furniture in disarray. But there are eyes to which even more ordinary scenes of middle-class life look almost equally startling.

The quotable gesture

In one of his didactic poems on dramatic art Brecht says: 'The effect of every sentence was waited for and laid bare. And the waiting lasted until the crowd had carefully weighed our sentence.' In short, the play was interrupted. One can go even further and remember that interruption is one of the funda-mental devices of all structuring. It goes far beyond the sphere of art. To give only one example, it is the basis of quotation. To quote a text involves the interruption of its context. It is therefore understandable that the epic theater, being based on interruption, is, in a specific sense, a quotable one. There is nothing special about the quotability of its texts. It is different with the gestures which fit into the course of the play.

'Making gestures quotable' is one of the substantial achievements of the epic theater. An actor must be able to space his gestures the way a typesetter produces spaced type. This effect may be achieved, for instance, by an actor's quoting his own gesture on the stage. Thus we saw in *Happy End* how Carola Neher, acting a sergeant in the Salvation Army, sang, by way of proselytizing, a song in a sailors' tavern that was more appropriate there than it would have been in a church, and then had to quote this song and act out the gestures before a council of the Salvation Army. Similarly, in *The Measure Taken* the party tribunal is given not only the report of the comrades, but also the acting out of some of the gestures of the comrade they are accusing. What is a device of the subtlest kind in the epic theater generally becomes an immediate purpose in the specific case of the didactic play. Epic theater is by definition a gestic theater. For the more frequently we interrupt someone in the act of acting, the more gestures result.

The didactic play

In every instance, the epic theater is meant for the actors as much as for the spectators. The didactic play is a special case largely because it facilitates and suggests the interchange between audience and actors and vice versa through the extreme paucity of the mechanical equipment. Every spectator is enabled to become a participant. And it is indeed easier to play the 'teacher' than the 'hero.'

In the first version of *Lindberghflug* (Lindbergh's Flight), which appeared in a periodical, the flier was still presented as a hero. That version was intended as his glorification. The second version – and this is revealing – owes its origin to the fact that Brecht revised himself. What enthusiasm there was on both continents on the days following this flight! But this enthusiasm petered out as a mere sensation. In *The Flight of the Lindberghs* Brecht endeavors to refract the spectrum of the 'thrill' (*Erlebnis*) in order to derive from it the hues of 'experience' (*Erfahrung*) – the experience that could be obtained only from Lindbergh's effort, not from the excitement of the public, and which was to be conveyed to 'the Lindberghs.'

T.E. Lawrence, the author of *Seven Pillars of Wisdom*, wrote to Robert Graves when he joined the air force that such a step was for modern man what entering a monastery was for medieval man. In this remark we perceive the same tension that we find in *The Flight of the Lindberghs* and the later didactic plays. A clerical sternness is applied to instruction in a modern technique – here, that of aviation; later, that of the class struggle. This second application may be seen most fully in *Mother*. It was a particularly daring undertaking to keep a social drama free of the effects which empathy produces and which the audience was accustomed to. Brecht knew this and expressed it in an epistolary poem that he sent to a New York workingmen's theater when *Mother* was produced there. 'We have been asked: Will a worker understand this? Will he be able to do without his accustomed opiate, his mental participation in someone else's uprising, the rise of others; the illusion which whips him up for a few hours and leaves him all the more exhausted, filled with vague memories and even vaguer hopes?'

The actor

Like the pictures in a film, epic theater moves in spurts. Its basic form is that of the shock with which the single, well-defined situations of the play collide. The songs, the captions, the lifeless conventions set off one situation from another. This brings about intervals which, if anything, impair the illusion of the audience and paralyze its readiness for empathy. These intervals are reserved for the spectators' critical reaction – to the actions of the players and to the way in which they are presented. As to the manner of presentation, the actor's task in the epic theater is to demonstrate through his acting that he is cool and relaxed. He too has hardly any use for empathy. For this kind of acting the 'player' of the dramatic theater is not always fully prepared. Perhaps the most open-minded approach to epic theater is to think of it in terms of 'putting on a show.'

Brecht wrote: 'The actor must show his subject, and he must show himself. Of course, he shows his subject by showing himself, and he shows himself by showing his subject. Although the two coincide, they must not coincide in such a way that the difference between the two tasks disappears.' In other words: an actor should reserve for himself the possibility of stepping out of character artistically. At the proper moment he should insist on portraying a man who reflects about his part. It would be erroneous to think at such a moment of Romantic Irony, as employed by Tieck in his *Puss in Boots*. This irony has no didactic aim. Basically, it demonstrates only the philosophic sophistication of the author who, in writing his plays, always remembers that in the end the world may turn out to be a theater.

To what extent artistic and political interests coincide on the scene of epic theater will become manifest in the style of acting appropriate to this genre. A case in point is Brecht's cycle *The Private Life of the Master Race*. It is easy to see that if a German actor in exile were assigned the part of an SS man or a member of the People's Court, his feelings about it would be quite different from those of a devoted father and husband asked to portray Molière's Don Juan. For the former, empathy can hardly be regarded as an appropriate method, since he presumably cannot identify with the murderers of his fellow fighters. Another mode of performance, which calls for detachment, would in such cases be right and fitting and particularly successful. This is the epic stagecraft.

Theater on a dais

The aims of the epic theater can be defined more easily in terms of the stage than of a new drama. Epic theater allows for a circumstance which has been too little noticed. It may be called the filling in of the orchestra pit. The abyss which separates the players from the audience as it does the dead from the living; the abyss whose silence in a play heightens the sublimity, whose resonance in an opera heightens the intoxication – this abyss, of all elements of the theater the one that bears the most indelible traces of its ritual origin, has steadily decreased in significance. The stage is still raised, but it no longer rises from an unfathomable depth; it has become a dais. The didactic play and the epic theater are attempts to sit down on a dais.

■   ■   ■

Source

Benjamin, W. (1973) 'What is Epic Theater?', *Illuminations*, trans. H. Zohn, London: Fontana: 149–156.

First published in 1939 in *Mass und Wert* 2; in 1955 in *Schriften* by Suhrkamp Verlag, Frankfurt-am-Main; first English translation 1968 and first published in Great Britain 1970.[1]

Walter Benjamin (1892–1940)

German Marxist literary critic. He was a central figure, along with Adorno, Horkheimer and Marcuse, of the Frankfurt School, based on the Institute for Social Research that was founded in 1923. Benjamin and the early Frankfurt School were originators of Marxist critical theory, whereby cultural aspects of social change were acknowledged, as well as material ones. He had a considerable influence on the thinking of radical 1960s' cultural movements.

Benjamin contributed a number of highly influential ideas to both the study of performance and its practice. Introduced to Brecht in the 1920s, they worked together, first in Germany and then during Benjamin's visits to Brecht in exile. They continued an extensive correspondence throughout the 1930s. Benjamin fled the Gestapo in 1940 and committed suicide whilst trying to cross into Spain.

Benjamin's key contributions include the idea that the function of art in the twentieth century has changed from the ritual to the political,[2] and the idea that the author is not a special person but a producer[3] and therefore in a position to be on the side of the proletariat in the fight against capitalism and fascism.

Benjamin writes about Brecht's work in many of his central political essays. In 'What is Epic Theater?', he praises Brecht's new form of theatre as one that corresponds to the new technology of the twentieth century. He goes on to describe precisely how this form of theatre differs from the old, bourgeois forms and how it therefore establishes a new and relevant relationship with its audience.

Reader cross-references

Anderson – an oblique but telling acknowledgement of his ideas
Barthes – a later European perspective on the 'author'
Brecht – intellectual collaborator, correspondent and friend
Brook – a critique of the dead hand of bourgeois theatre
Cage – a contemporary, contrary view of the purpose of art
Eisler – musical contemporary, fellow Marxist
Martin – a contemporary, contrasting American critic
Soyinka – an intellectual stance that acknowledges West African roots
Williams – a perspective from the later British left tradition

Further reading

Benjamin, W. (1973a) *Illuminations*, trans. H. Zohn, London: Fontana.
Benjamin, W. (1973b) *Understanding Brecht*, trans. A. Bostock, London: NLB.

Notes

1   See also A. Bostock's translations in (1973b) *Understanding Brecht:* 1–22.
2   Described in his essay (1973a) 'The Work of Art in the Age of Mechanical Reproduction', *Illuminations*.
3   See (1973b) 'The Author as Producer', *Understanding Brecht*.

Chapter 10

Rustom Bharucha

NOTES ON THE INVENTION
OF TRADITION

L ET ME SHARE some thoughts with you on that worn-out, inexhaustible subject – tradition. Instead of attempting to define it in a pan-Indian context, I would like to situate it within its multiple uses in the contemporary Indian theatre. To what extent has 'tradition' (which originates from the Latin word – *tradere* – to 'hand over' or 'deliver') been used in the context of 'handing down knowledge' or 'passing on a doctrine?' And to what extent has it been 'invented' (to use Eric Hobsbawm's valuable term) in response to larger political, economic and social factors?

As I demonstrate in this essay, tradition can be invented in any number of ways, even though we may not be aware of it. The most conspicuous of 'inventions' are 'fabrications', such as the Republic Day Parade, where the diverse cultures of India are 'unified' through a carefully choreographed spectacle. In recent years, this kind of 'invention' has become increasingly virtuosic as is evident in the Festivals of India and the Utsavs of New Delhi. Here, through a conglomeration of effects, which could include songs, dances, tableaux, symbols, floats, fireworks, informal minglings between 'native' performers and 'foreign' spectators, selling of Indian food and other 'indigenous' activities, an atmosphere is constructed whereby 'the Indian tradition' is affirmed, not necessarily as people in India would understand it, but as our government would like to represent it to the world.

In this essay, I will not deal with this ubiquitous phenomenon but focus instead on the more seemingly 'creative' inventions of tradition that have been implemented by our own artists, directors and 'experts' in the Indian theatre. Much of the discussion will focus on the *discourse* of theatre, in which concepts of the 'folk' and the 'theatre of roots' will be examined as inventions of the urban intelligentsia. More often than not, when people 'invent' tradition ('authentic' or 'spurious', through acts of 'cultural preservation' or 'subversion'), they unavoidably imply that they are no longer in touch with its immediacies. Yet an illusion is often maintained whereby the 'invention' is placed within the mainstream of tradition itself.

Mediations of technology

At a very basic level, one could say that 'inventions' develop from an urge to 'find out or produce something new'. They are not 'discoveries' of things which already exist but need to be 'exposed', 'made known'. Inventions uphold a different sense of the unknown. Instead of 'exposure', they are concerned with *making* new artefacts. Very often, these artefacts emerge through the mediations of a new technology and machinery that precipitate an alteration of forms. In the following section let us examine some of these mediations through the intervention and assimilation of 'foreign' structures of representation.

It is well known that our tradition has always provided us with a surfeit of narratives in the theatre. Our 'professional theatre' in the late nineteenth century scored some of its most spectacular successes with theatrical renderings from the *Mahabharata* and the *Ramayana*. That all-Indian phenomenon, the Parsee theatre, funded and administered by the Parsees, but acted, directed, designed and most important, seen by a wide range of communities all over India, invariably had a stock of 'traditional' plays. Invariably, they were mythological in content, providing a direct stimulus to the religious block-busters of the early Indian cinema.

The point to be stressed here is that our 'tradition' had already been mediated by the colonial machinery of the nineteenth-century theatre, the conventions and stage tricks derived from the pantomimes and historical extravaganzas of the English Victorian stage. However, it should also be emphasized that these derivations had been thoroughly 'Indianized' through music, song, colour, pathos, melodrama and the histrionic delivery of lines that are intrinsically a part of the popular theatrical tradition in India.

At a very elemental level, 'tradition' in the nineteenth-century commercial theatre meant 'spectacle'. It provided audiences with new possibilities of adoring gods and mythological heroes in kinetic, technicolour settings. In its importation of theatre technology, there were trapdoors that facilitated supernatural ascents and descents, a 'fly system' that enabled *apsaras* to float rather precariously into the wings and, at a later stage, the novelties of the revolving stage, cloud machines and the cyclorama.

So alluring were these derivations of an essentially foreign theatre tradition, and so widespread their influence, that even today one can trace their remnants in a number of 'traditional' performances. In Yakshagana, for instance, or of what remains of it, traces of the popular Gubbi theatre tradition still linger in painted backdrops and histrionic acting styles that are anathema to the purists. I have even seen a Krishnalila performance in a village where a very belligerent female impersonator upstaged Krishna in a sequinned costume and a wig that looked like relics from *Shirin Farhad*.

At one level, these commercial interventions are 'perversions', but nonetheless, they have been absorbed within traditional performance structures in deference to 'popular taste'. It needs to be emphasized that the clear-cut distinctions between 'popular culture' (which is the category in which 'company theatre' or 'Parsee theatre' could be placed) and 'folk culture' (to which Yakshagana ostensibly belongs), cannot be regarded as absolute or mutually exclusive. Nor can we assume that it is 'folk forms' which invariably influence popular entertainment, because they happen to be older and 'rooted' in the cultural psyche of the people. Very often, it is the other way around, when, for example, the 'perversions' of commercial Bengali theatre, notably cabaret, have directly influenced the 'folk' theatre tradition of Jatra.

In fact, if there is one 'indigenous' source of influence that has played a fertile role in promoting new genres, it would not be the 'folk theatre' (which is struggling to hold on to its identity), but the 'company theatre' tradition, which no longer exists, but whose idiom has been absorbed in the commercial Hindi cinema, and more recently, in the representation of myth on Doordarshan serials. If one had to trace the origins of mass appeal embedded in Ramanand Sagar's *Ramayana*, one would have to turn to its use of Parsee theatre conventions, which are barely recognizable, yet perceptible, submerged under layers of conventions from other traditions. Apart from the obvious influence of mythological films, there are traces of science fiction, advertising, high tech, cartoons and even through some convoluted process of unconscious assimilation, the visuals of Monty Python.

Whatever one may think of its artistic merits, one cannot deny that Sagar's *Ramayana* has been sufficiently convincing to millions of people to serve as a source of *darshan*. What may seem bizarre and mindlessly eclectic has been intensely familiar to the masses. The eternal fiction of the *Ramayana* has not merely survived its 'invention' on the idiot box, it may even have stimulated a form of Hindu revivalism, whose manipulative possibilities by fundamentalists and politicians need not be stressed. One can despair about the absence of historicity in representations like Sagar's *Ramayana*, but they also reveal very decisively that people are prepared to accept new 'inventions' of tradition so long as their faith in dominant myths is substantiated and enriched.

In this regard, in reflecting on the mediation of new technologies to project myths, what needs to be stressed is not so much the technology itself, but how it is viewed. The *Ramayana* has been seen within the proscenium framework of the Parsee theatre tradition, which in turn has been miniaturized on the two-dimensional rectangular television screen. It has also been seen for many years in numerous stagings of the Ramlila held in many parts of India, most notably in Ramnagar, where the *lila* extends over the entire town for a month. The fact that the *Ramayana* has survived its diverse 'inventions' testifies not only to the innate richness of the epic and its deep significance to most Indians, but it also reveals the phenomenal viewing capacities of the Indian spectators, who are capable of seeing the illusion of an image with or without its technological mediation. Sometimes, if they feel inclined, they may focus only on the technology, such as a 'special effect' in the Ramayana serial, and applaud its sheer virtuosity. But at other moments, all that matters to them is the 'vision' that they alone see, which is precipitated by the representation, and yet detached from it.

Darshan is capable of subverting technology. Even if an Indian spectator may not be fully conscious of his seeing capacities, there is nothing quite like his ability to see God within an actor's frame. Nor can one undernate his capacity to tune in and out of an image. While avant-garde circles in America and Europe may cultivate the faculty of 'selective inattention', it seems to me that this comes very naturally to our spectators. Particularly in our rural and *mofussil* audiences, one finds an almost collective concentration and dispersal of energies. One moment could be totally rapt, as the spectators see a divine presence on stage. This could be followed by a very candid, and frequently, critical response to the representation on the level of pure theatricality. At still other moments, the play could be seen in a state of collective somnolence. But then, at just the appropriate moment in the narrative, everyone could be awake and totally absorbed in the action on stage.

I dwell on this enormously flexible seeing process because it may be one of the contributing factors to our 'invention' of tradition. Certainly, it would be wrong to say that it is only 'artists' who are capable of invention. What seems more pertinent (though harder to substantiate) is that there is a collusion between the artist and the people regarding the nature and limits of invention. At this point in time, one can say that technology has not yet coopted the 'visionary' possibilities of seeing assumed by our spectators in their viewing of myths. But in time to come, as these performances get increasingly commodified and the onslaught of the media becomes more fierce, it will be critical to see how the viewing capacities of our spectators will be altered. Will they still be able to see what they choose to see and are willed to see, or will they be numbed into total passivity? Will the 'inventions' of tradition on the media create new myths, or will they simply reduce myth to the level of commercials?

Environmental changes

Apart from the mediation of technology in determining 'inventions' of tradition, there are more practical matters that affect the changes in 'traditional forms'. A year ago, I attended a Ramlila performance in the village of Amaur near Kanpur to find a permanent Ravana made out of stone. I could scarcely conceal my disappointment that the principle of burning the demon-god, so essential for the celebration of the *lila*, had been ignored for economic reasons. 'It is too expensive to burn Ravana every year', I was told. 'After all, this is a small village, not Ramnagar.' Only later did I realize that Ravana had been burned, but symbolically, through his headgear and weapon, which were made out of paper and wood. The rest of his body remained indomitably cast in stone, but nonetheless, he had already been 'burned'.

These paradoxes of faith reveal the acute consciousness of our people, both to everyday matters of survival and the endurance of faith. For them, it is not a matter of 'using' tradition (as it is for us in the so-called contemporary theatre); it is a question of *living* tradition and making the necessary adjustments to keep it going. If a traditional performance dies, then maybe it was meant to, because it could no longer be sustained either economically or socially.

About the worst attitude to tradition is to incarcerate it within an immutable form that ostensibly never changes. If tradition lives today, it is because it has always changed in the course of its history. How it changes within its own performative and cultural context is frequently undocumented and even forgotten, because the change occurs slowly, organically, in deference to the larger needs of its community.

It is only in recent years through interventions like tourism, film documentation and interculturalism that the changes in 'traditional' performances have become at once more visible and swift. It could also be that we have developed a new awareness, a post-colonial consciousness, of what was previously taken for granted. In this context, I believe that one must differentiate between those changes which are intrinsic to growth of a traditional performance, and those which are imposed on it through external intervention, though I must acknowledge that it is sometimes difficult to differentiate between them.

When I hear, for instance, of how a Theyyam performer has of his own accord incorporated a flashing electric bulb into his headgear to enhance his sense of the demoniac, this seems like a perfectly valid response to electricity, an intervention in the rural performer's world. The change in the costume is intrinsic insofar as it comes from the performer's response to his changing environment. On the other hand, can I deny that I am disturbed to see neon lights in a *koothambalam*, where, ideally, the *koodiyattam* performer should be watched in the glow of the *vilakku*, his eyes illuminated by the fire in the lamp? The problem with this use of electricity is that it does not seem to bother the performers themselves. It is my 'aesthetic' sense that is jarred, revealing my own 'taste' and cultural conditioning.

Still more problematic is the transportation of a traditional performance from its own environment to a proscenium-bound, air-conditioned theatre in New Delhi or a *mela* in Paris. This environmental change alters the very context of the performance. In some extravaganzas, the performers are merely 'slotted' into a spectacle over which they have no control. Reduced to exotica, they resemble spots of colour without mind, body or soul.

How does one accept these changes in performances resulting from altered environments?

1   In the case of the Theyyam performer, one cannot but appreciate the sheer ingenuity of the performer in incorporating a historical change (electricity) within the framework of his costume. Here one senses an organic relationship between the environment and the performer.

2   In the case of the neon lights in the *koothambalam*, one can accept these lights as useful even though they fail to enhance the energy of the performance. At best, one could say that the performer learns to accept them, and then forget them, not unlike classical singers who have adjusted to the sound of the harmonium. In the long run, the use of 'conveniences' like neon lights and harmoniums is, perhaps, best accepted as a compromise – useful, but not particularly creative.

3   In the case of the altered environments provided by proscenium theatres and spectacles, it is difficult to accept their impositions on the choices of the performers. Inadequate exposure to these spaces, and more specifically, to the power relationships embodied in them, create an imbalance between what the performers are ready to give and what is expected of them from a foreign clientele.

In such spaces, the performers invariably fail to represent themselves. Rather, they are represented by the environments themselves, and by all the values – political, social, commercial – embodied in them. This does not mean that traditional performers should not perform in these 'alien' spaces, but new mechanisms and relationships need to be explored whereby performers have more time and power to control their representations.

Inventing the 'folk'

Expertise plays an important role in determining categories in which 'tradition' can be placed. One such category is the 'folk', which received an official sanction at the First Drama Seminar organized by the Sangeet Natak Akademi in 1956. Inaugurated by Dr S. Radhakrishnan, who was then the Vice-President of India, the Seminar was part of a series that was intended to serve as a cultural counterpart to Nehru's Five-Year Plans. The intention of the Akademi was to hold 'one seminar every four years for each of the arts of dance, drama, music, and film'.

Predictably, in the immediate wave of post-Independence nationalism, there was a definite drive among the participants to uphold the 'Indianness' of Indian culture. Some of our most prominent artists and cultural figures, including Mulk Raj Anand, Kamaladevi Chattopadhyay, Balraj Sahni, Sombhu Mitra and V. Raghavan, pondered a wide spectrum of immediate problems. They included the ownership of theatres, censorship laws, the Dramatic Performances Control Act, entertainment tax and almost as a secondary issue, the state of 'folk drama'.

One should remember that 'folk theatre' had not yet become fashionable and that the models of 'professionalism' in theatre continued to be European. Nonetheless, there was a fervent attempt in the Seminar to confront 'traditional' sources for the rejuvenation of our theatre. The most animated discussion in this regard was the one relating to *bhavai*, where the conflicting views of the participants reveal some of the deeply entrenched premises and problems underlying the urban construction and use of 'folk theatre' in India today.

First of all, it becomes very clear from the discussion on *bhavai* (as from the Seminar in general) that the Indian theatre had already become regionalized, with 'experts' representing each state. The 'folk drama' as a category had also been regionalized. No attempt was made in the Seminar to situate the concept of the 'folk' in a larger historical perspective – to see, for instance, how 'folk forms' became vehicles for contemporary political content during the IPTA days, thereby revealing the innate urban assumption that the 'folk' is not contemporary. Like a vessel, it has to be 'filled' with new ideas and political content. Instead of questioning such assumptions, the participants of the Seminar seemed to accept totally the validity of 'folk drama' as an adequate category in which to confront the specificities of rural cultures in India.

Before proceeding with the discussion on *bhavai*, I believe it would be useful to reflect on the morphology of the term 'folk' in the Indian theatre. Since the participants in the Seminar did not question their use of this deceptively simple term, it is necessary for us to do so here.

It is not clear when the term 'folk' entered the vocabulary of the Indian theatre worker. Certainly, it became popular during the IPTA movement when urban artists were compelled to discover their 'roots' in rural cultures. What needs to be emphasized is that the 'folk' has become an established category in the Indian theatre today. Actors and directors use it freely without questioning its obvious, yet diffused links to the word 'people'. Nor is it assumed to be a 'foreign' word, any more so than 'tradition', which is used more readily than the Indian equivalents of *parampara* or *sampradaya*.

Even in the academic world of folklore studies, it is significant that Indian equivalents for 'folklore' have been established only in recent years (Claus and Korom 1988, p. 32). The diffused use of the term 'folk' in Indian contexts could be related to the fact that our established culture refused to accept it as a respectable object of study. As late as 1932 the Indian folklorist, Sarat Chandra Roy, had lamented the fact that 'folklore' had not received the attention in India that 'tradition' was beginning to receive in discussions conducted by the Indian Science Congress, the Oriental Conference, and the Bombay Historical Congress (ibid., p. 31). Four years later, in 1936, when Dr Chelnat Achyutha Menon published *Ballads of North Malabar*, we are told that it was the first book of its kind in Kerala that 'raised the subject in public estimation' by 'persuading' the 'educated Malyalee' that folk studies had a 'place in the cultural life of the country' (Raghavan 1945, p. ii).

In the context of the class and caste consciousness of the educated Indians, it is not surprising that the 'folk' were associated not just with 'people', but 'common people'. Perhaps 'peasant' was one of the closest associations with the word 'folk' in its early history. Countering this history of prejudice, the IPTA movement glorified the 'folk' in the context of the freedom struggle. The 'folk' became emblematic of our 'lost heritage' and 'authentic history' that we were determined to reclaim from the British.

Along with the patriotic aura surrounding the 'folk' in IPTA, there is also an inner tension underlying this word with specific reference to 'people'. In the initial phase of the IPTA movement, when it was only too easy for artists with vastly different economic and political backgrounds to subsume their differences under the immediate pressures and lure of patriotism, one could say that the 'folk' and the 'people' embraced each other's needs. But there was also an unspoken assumption that it was the 'folk' who performed for the 'people', not the other way around. We don't speak of the 'folk' watching a 'people's performance', it is 'people' who watch a 'folk performance'.

Unavoidably, it was 'people' who were viewed in a more corporal light; they were 'flesh-and-blood' figures who constitute the 'mass'. The 'folk', on the other hand, were inextricably linked to *forms* – burrakatha, tamasha, nautanki. Even today, I would argue that in the nebulous vocabulary of the Indian theatre artist, and his even vaguer social consciousness of his means of production, the 'folk' has been disembodied from the needs of the 'people'. Quite literally, it has become a nomenclature for a wide range of supposedly non-urban performance traditions, that are primarily enjoyed by urban audiences.

Significantly, for those IPTA artists with a more politically active ideology (inevitably Marxist), who favoured a realist intervention in the arts modelled on Bijon Bhattacharya's *Nabanna*, it was the rhetoric of 'the people' that dominated over the 'folk'. Not surprisingly, this group can be most strongly identified with the Bengal front of the IPTA movement. If it is not too much of a witticism, I should emphasize that after Independence, the 'people' stayed on in West Bengal, while the 'folk' eventually gravitated in the direction of New Delhi, which is the centre for all folk-related activities, including the handicrafts and the cottage industries. This is the centre where tradition is 'invented', 'manufactured', and 'exported' with an increasingly efficient and centralized system. It is also the centre where definitions of 'Indian culture' are made and disseminated.

To return to the Drama seminar in New Delhi, one notes that 'folk drama' was defined not so much through an analysis of the term (which was taken for granted), but through a debate as to how one should intervene in 'folk culture'. The underlying thrust of Dina Gandhi's address on *bhavai*, which provided the source of the debate on 'folk drama', was not 'Why should we intervene?' but rather, 'We must intervene now. How do we go about it?' Part of the problem with her suggestions, as with most urban recommendations for the 'folk arts', is that she assumed an empathy with the folk artists, and then proceeded to represent them as if she were speaking on their behalf. In the process, her own use of these 'folk forms' became confused with their 'indigenous' state of being, which she lamented was in a state of decay, if not total extinction.

From Gandhi's address, it becomes obvious that her concern was not only for the 'folk form' and its 'extraordinary life-force', but for its artists, who were going to be 'wiped off due to neglect, unemployment, and actual starvation' ('Discussion on *Bhavai*', p. 114). Instead of confronting this crisis through active involvement, however, Gandhi recommended 'researches and studies' which could confirm that *bhavai* had 'a definite contribution to make to our culture' (ibid.). In retrospect, this priority given to research is problematic since it almost seems like a precondition before the *bhavai* artists can be 'saved' Gandhi seems oblivious of the ironies involved in conflating the economic necessities of the *bhavai* performers with the need to develop their artistic potential. For her, the 'sacred duty' of 'emancipating' the folk artists could come about only through the organization of a research centre, a training school for the traditional performers, and a careful study of *bhavai* texts, so that 'spurious interpolations can be eliminated' (ibid.).

Countering Gandhi's advocacy of intervention, the extremely sophisticated and westernized Alkazi then spoke up in the Seminar for the people. 'We want to educate the Bhavai artists', he said. 'But we do not for a moment consider that the nearer they reach us, the quicker would they discard the arts of their forefathers' (ibid., p. 120). Then also, in response to the 'so-called crudities and vulgarities' entering the *bhavai* form, he asked: 'Should we be so prude and puritanic as to evaluate every art in the light of our own moral code?' (ibid., pp. 120–1). More prosaically, he affirmed that 'we should not poke our noses in this affair because we do not really know what would exactly be good for this form and for its exponents' (ibid., p. 121). The job should be left to anthropologists.

Though, predictably, there was a resistance to this suggestion – an anthropological intervention is scarcely less 'neutral' than an artistic one – the debate between Gandhi and Alkazi does resonate even today, despite a sense of *déjà vu*. We have heard their positions before in other post-Independence contexts, and we continue to hear them even now. While Alkazi seemed to accept the inherent distance, culturally and socially, between the 'urban' and the 'folk' artist, thereby upholding his innate elitism, Gandhi wanted to bridge the gap in some meaningful way. Yet, this 'bridging' could scarcely be seen as altruistic. As Balraj Sahni pointed out, with reference to Gandhi's production of *Mena Gurjari*, which 'contemporized' the folk form (notably by eliminating the male impersonation of women), these experiments in folk drama were a valuable source of growth for 'our own [urban] theatre'. All Gandhi wanted to do, according to Sahni, was to 'revitalize her own art', and to retain as much of *bhavai*'s 'indigenous' qualities as 'a sophisticated audience would be able to appreciate' (ibid., p. 122).

This is about the most honest statement that one could hope to find about the urban use of folk forms. Let us acknowledge that this 'use' is more useful to the urban artist than to the 'folk' who inspired the creation. 'Folk drama' is essentially an urban construct that cannot claim to be entirely 'indigenous' (and therefore, 'authentic'). It is a simulation of the 'folk form', sufficiently 'indigenous' (yet not entirely *desi*) to win the approval of urban audiences. The clientele of 'folk drama' is not the 'folk', but city people who need to be reminded of their 'roots and native places' from which they are irrevocably displaced. . . .

Beginnings

There are two images from our mythological tradition that seem relevant to this discussion, or rather, my need to intervene in its history. At one level, the images are quite unrelated, separated by narrative and time – one is from the *Mahabharata*, the other from the Punjabi legend of Puran Bhagat. And yet, at a subterranean level, these images are united through their advocacy of what I must call 'violence'. Today, we could do with some of this 'violence' in our suffocatingly safe theatre.

In the *Mahabharata*, there is that memorable moment when Yudhisthira receives permission from Bhishma to kill him. The 'father' legitimizes his own death at the hands of his 'son'. Violence receives a paternalistic, if not divine sanction. It is now Yudhisthira's *dharma* to kill Bhishma.

There is a different kind of violence in the story of Puran Bhagat, which does not involve killing, but, rather, a rejection of the father and whatever he represents – family, kingdom, state, authority, love. After being incarcerated in a dungeon for the first twelve years of his life, then exiled, and later imprisoned, Puran Bhagat goes through many trials and humiliations before he acquires the self-realization of a *yogi*. In the final episode, when his father begs him to take over the kingdom, Puran rejects the offer: 'If you cannot govern your kingdom, let it go to the dogs. . . . I will have none of you and your belongings. I am a *yogi*. I must go' (Gill 1986, p. 146). And he *leaves* without any attempt to reconcile differences or to affirm traditional ties.

In Puran's exit, one finds a paradigm of rejection. I do not believe that there is a single artist in the Indian theatre today who is prepared to 'reject' tradition as resolutely as Puran turns away from his father and inheritance. Perhaps, this is a totally unfair demand on my part. Maybe our artists are still too close to 'tradition' (or whatever they make of it) to dissociate themselves from its hold in order to pursue their own journeys in theatre.

At the same time, they do not believe that they have the right to 'kill' tradition with as much respect and fervour as Yudhisthira kills Bhishma. Perhaps, they have not yet received the inner sanction to fulfil this necessary task. It is safer, therefore, for them to fold their hands and deify tradition, perpetuating deference and cowardice.

Unable to 'reject' or 'kill' (which, in artistic terms, would involve a subversion of the 'traditional form'), our theatre artists remain in limbo.

They don't know how to free themselves from tradition or live with it without compromising on their own truth. In the meantime, they 'invent' tradition not so much from an inner necessity, but in deference to larger cultural and political factors that favour a sanctification or dressing-up of the past.

It is time to end this facile use of our tradition. Instead of bothering with the minutiae of hand-held curtains, masks, make-believe *poorvarangas*, and stirring exits and entrances to throbbing drums, we need to ask ourselves some crucial questions: *What is our sacrifice in theatre today? Who are we performing for in the absence of gods? How can we transform ourselves through theatre? What are we celebrating on stage?*

I ask these questions not because I have the answers, but because they seem necessary to begin a confrontation with tradition that could transcend its 'inventions' in our theatre today.

References

Awasthi, Suresh (1985), 'In Defence of the "Theatre of Roots"', *Sangeet Natak*, Nos. 77–8.

Bhatt, Haridasa (n.d.), 'Theatre for all – Folk Performing Arts of Karnataka', typewritten manuscript.

Claus, Peter and Korom, Frank (1988), Folk, Folklore, and Folkoristics', *Folkoristics and Indian Folklore,* Haywatrd: WRC Consulting, April 1988.

Eliot, T.S. (1969), 'Tradition and the Individual Talent', *The Sacred Wood*, London: Methuen.

Gill, Harjeet Singh (1986), 'The Human Condition in Puran Bhagat', *The Word and the World*, New Delhi: Sage Publications.

Kambar, Chandrasekhar (n.d.), 'Yakshagana As I See', typewritten manuscript.

Kapur, Anuradha (1988), 'Thinking about Tradition: The Ramlila at Ramnagar', *Journal of Arts and Ideas*, No. 16.

Raghavan, M.D. (1945), *Folk Plays and Dances of Kerala*, Trichur: Mangalodyam Press

Rea, Kenneth (1978), 'The Tradition and the Innovation', in *Theatre in India: The Old and the New, Theatre Quarterly*, Vol. VIII, No. 31, Autumn 1978.

Williams, Raymond (1981), *Culture*, Glasgow: Fontana Press.

—— (1985), *Keywords*, London: Flamingo Books.

All references to the First Drama Seminar organized by the Sangeet Natak Akademi, including 'Discussion on *Bhavai*', are taken from a printed documentation of the entire Seminar, which unfortunately does not identify either the publisher or the date of publication.

■　■　■

Source

Bharucha, R. (1993) 'Notes on the Invention of Tradition', *Theatre and the World*, London: Routledge: 192–200, 208–210.

Rustom Bharucha (1946–)

Writer, director and dramaturg, who lives and works in India. Bharucha's writings include those from the period when he was working in New York (1981–84) and subsequently in India. Of his theatre projects, the most renowned is *Request Concert* (1986–88), with Franz Xaver Kroetz, which was seen in India, Indonesia, Korea, Germany and Japan.

In his book *Theatre and the World* Bharucha analyses and takes issue with many Western ideas of interculturalism, beginning historically with Craig, Artaud and Grotowski. He writes extensively on more recent intercultural projects in the theatre and in writing. He gives a detailed analysis of Schechner and of Peter Brook's *Mahabharata* from this perspective. He is critical of Western artists and theorists who either simply appropriate other cultures or suggest that culture is a matter of choice.

This essay, in contrast, explores ideas of the development of an indigenous cultural tradition. He says that much of what passes for 'tradition' in Indian theatre has in fact been mediated by imperialism. Hence the need to invent tradition in the new age of technology. His view seems in sharp contrast to European and African ideas of tradition.

Reader cross-references

Artaud, Craig and **Grotowski** – who, in *Theatre and the World*, he identifies as early 'interculturalists'

Brook – a different view on the idea of tradition, with whom Bharucha takes issue

Hijikata – a contrasting, Japanese view of the use of tradition in contemporary times

Schechner – a contrasting stance on tradition and on intercultural experiment

Soyinka – a different stance on tradition, and also, elsewhere, on interculturalism

Further reading

Bharucha, R. (1993) *Theatre and the World*, London: Routledge.

Chapter 11

Augusto Boal

THE THEATRE AS DISCOURSE

G EORGE IKISHAWA used to say that the bourgeois theater is the finished theater. The bourgeoisie already knows what the world is like, *their* world, and is able to present images of this complete, finished world. The bourgeoisie presents the spectacle. On the other hand, the proletariat and the oppressed classes do not know yet what their world will be like; consequently their theater will be the rehearsal, not the finished spectacle. This is quite true, though it is equally true that the theater can present images of transition.

I have been able to observe the truth of this view during all my activities in the people's theater of so many and such different countries of Latin America. Popular audiences are interested in experimenting, in rehearsing, and they abhor the 'closed' spectacles. In those cases they try to enter into a dialogue with the actors, to interrupt the action, to ask for explanations without waiting politely for the end of the play. Contrary to the bourgeois code of manners, the people's code allows and encourages the spectator to ask questions, to dialogue, to participate.

All the methods that I have discussed are forms of a rehearsal-theater, and not a spectacle-theater. One knows how these experiments will begin but not how they will end, because the spectator is freed from his chains, finally acts, and

85

becomes a protagonist. Because they respond to the real needs of a popular audience they are practiced with success and joy.

But nothing in this prohibits a popular audience from practicing also more 'finished' forms of theater. In Peru many forms previously developed in other countries, especially Brazil and Argentina, were also utilized and with great success. Some of these forms were:

1 *Newspaper theater:* It was initially developed by the Nucleus Group of the Arena Theater of Sao Paulo, of which I was the artistic director until forced to leave Brazil.[1] It consists of several simple techniques for transforming daily news items, or any other non-dramatic material, into theatrical performances.

(a) Simple reading: the news item is read detaching it from the context of the newspaper, from the format which makes it false or tendentious.

(b) Crossed reading: two news items are read in crossed (alternating) form, one throwing light on the other, explaining it, giving it a new dimension.

(c) Complementary reading: data and information generally omitted by the newspapers of the ruling classes are added to the news.

(d) Rhythmical reading: as a musical commentary, the news is read to the rhythm of the samba, tango, Gregorian chant, etc., so that the rhythm functions as a critical 'filter' of the news, revealing its true content, which is obscured in the newspaper.

(e) Parallel action: the actors mime parallel actions while the news is read, showing the context in which the reported event really occurred; one hears the news and sees something else that complements it visually.

(f) Improvisation: the news is improvised on stage to exploit all its variants and possibilities.

(g) Historical: data or scenes showing the same event in other historical moments, in other countries, or in other social systems, are added to the news.

(h) Reinforcement: the news is read or sung with the aid or accompaniment of slides, jingles, songs, or publicity materials.

(i) Concretion of the abstract: that which the news often hides in its purely abstract information is made concrete on the stage: torture, hunger, unemployment, etc., are shown concretely, using graphic images, real or symbolic.

(j) Text out of context: the news is presented out of the context in which it was published; for example, an actor gives the speech about austerity previously delivered by the Minister of Economics while he devours an enormous dinner: the real truth behind the minister's words becomes demystified – he wants austerity for the people but not for himself.

2 *Invisible theater:* It consists of the presentation of a scene in an environment other than the theater, before people who are not spectators. The place can be a restaurant, a sidewalk, a market, a train, a line of people, etc. The people who witness the scene are those who are there by chance. During the spectacle, these people must not have the slightest idea that it is a 'spectacle,' for this would make them 'spectators.'

The invisible theater calls for the detailed preparation of a skit with a complete text or a simple script; but it is necessary to rehearse the scene sufficiently so that the actors are able to incorporate into their acting and their actions the intervention of the spectators. During the rehearsal it is also necessary to include every imaginable intervention from the spectators; these possibilities will form a kind of optional text.

The invisible theater erupts in a location chosen as a place where the public congregates. All the people who are near become involved in the eruption and the effects of it last long after the skit is ended.

A small example shows how the invisible theater works. In the enormous restaurant of a hotel in Chiclayo, where the literacy agents of ALFIN were staying, together with 400 other people, the 'actors' sit at separate tables. The waiters start to serve. The 'protagonist' in a more or less loud voice (to attract the attention of other diners, but not in a too obvious way) informs the waiter that he cannot go on eating the food served in that hotel, because in his opinion it is too bad. The waiter does not like the remark but tells the customer that he can choose something *à la carte*, which he may like better. The actor chooses a dish called 'Barbecue a la pauper.' The waiter points out that it will cost him 70 *soles*, to which the actor answers, always in a reasonably loud voice, that there is no problem. Minutes later the waiter brings him the barbecue, the protagonist eats it rapidly and gets ready to get up and leave the restaurant, when the waiter brings the bill. The actor shows a worried expression and tells the people at the next table that his barbecue was much better than the food they are eating, but the pity is that one has to pay for it. . . .

'I'm going to pay for it; don't have any doubts. I ate the "barbecue a la pauper" and I'm going to pay for it. But there is a problem: I'm broke.'

'And how are you going to pay?' asks the indignant waiter. 'You knew the price before ordering the barbecue. And now, how are you going to pay for it?'

The diners nearby are, of course, closely following the dialogue – much more attentively than they would if they were witnessing the scene on a stage. The actor continues:

'Don't worry, because I *am* going to pay you. But since I'm broke I will pay you with labor-power.'

'With what?' asks the waiter, astonished. 'What kind of power?'

'With labor-power, just as I said. I am broke but I can rent you my labor-power. So I'll work doing something for as long as it's necessary to pay for my "barbecue a la pauper," which, to tell the truth, was really delicious – much better than the food you serve to those poor souls. . . .'

By this time some of the customers intervene and make remarks among themselves at their tables, about the price of food, the quality of the service in the hotel, etc. The waiter calls the headwaiter to decide the matter. The actor explains again to the latter the business of renting his labor-power and adds:

'And besides, there is another problem: I'll rent my labor-power but the truth is that I don't know how to do anything, or very little. You will have to give me a very simple job to do. For example, I can take out the hotel's garbage. What's the salary of the garbage man who works for you?'

The headwaiter does not want to give any information about salaries, but a second actor at another table is already prepared and explains that he and the garbage man have gotten to be friends and that the latter has told him his salary: seven *soles* per hour. The two actors make some calculations and the 'protagonist' exclaims:

'How is this possible! If I work as a garbage man I'll have to work ten hours to pay for this barbecue that it took me ten minutes to eat? It can't be! Either you increase the salary of the garbage man or reduce the price of the barbecue! . . . But I can do something more specialized; for example, I can take care of the hotel gardens, which are so beautiful, so well cared for. One can see that a very talented person is in charge of the gardens. How much does the gardener of this hotel make? I'll work as a gardener! How many hours work in the garden are necessary to pay for the "barbecue a la pauper"?'

A third actor, at another table, explains his friendship with the gardener, who is an immigrant from the same village as he; for this reason he knows that the gardener makes ten *soles* per hour. Again the 'protagonist' becomes indignant:

'How is this possible? So the man who takes care of these beautiful gardens, who spends his days out there exposed to the wind, the rain, and the sun, has to work seven long hours to be able to eat the barbecue in ten minutes? How can this be, Mr. Headwaiter? Explain it to me!'

The headwaiter is already in despair; he dashes back and forth, gives orders to the waiters in a loud voice to divert the attention of the other customers, alternately laughs and becomes serious, while the restaurant is transformed into a public forum. The 'protagonist' asks the waiter how much he is paid to serve the barbecue and offers to replace him for the necessary number of hours. Another actor, originally from a small village in the interior, gets up and declares that nobody in his village makes 70 *soles* per day; therefore nobody in his village can eat the 'barbecue a la pauper.' (The sincerity of this actor, who was, besides, telling the truth, moved those who were near his table.)

Finally, to conclude the scene, another actor intervenes with the following proposition:

'Friends, it looks as if we are against the waiter and the headwaiter and this does not make sense. They are our brothers. They work like us, and they are not to blame for the prices charged here. I suggest we take up a collection. We at this table are going to ask you to contribute whatever you can, one *sol*, two *soles*, five *soles*, whatever you can afford. And with that money we are going to pay for the barbecue. And be generous, because what is left over will go as a tip for the waiter, who is our brother and a working man.'

Immediately those who are with him at the table start collecting money to pay the bill. Some customers willingly give one or two *soles*. Others furiously comment:

'He says that the food we're eating is junk, and now he wants us to pay for his barbecue! . . . And am I going to eat this junk? Hell no! I wouldn't give him a peanut, so he'll learn a lesson! Let him wash dishes. . . .'

The collection reached 100 *soles* and the discussion went on through the night. It is always very important that the actors do not reveal themselves to be actors! On this rests the *invisible* nature of this form of theater. And it is precisely this invisible quality that will make the spectator act freely and fully, as if he were living a real situation – and, after all, it is a real situation!

It is necessary to emphasize that the invisible theater is not the same thing as a 'happening' or the so-called 'guerrilla theater.' In the latter we are clearly talking about 'theater,' and therefore the wall that separates actors from spectators immediately arises, reducing the spectator to impotence: a spectator is always less than a man! In the invisible theater the theatrical rituals are abolished; only the theater exists, without its old, worn-out patterns. The theatrical energy is completely liberated, and the impact produced by this free theater is much more powerful and longer lasting.

Several presentations of invisible theater were made in different locations in Peru. Particularly interesting is what happened at the Carmen

Market, in the *barrio* of Comas, some 14 kilometers away from downtown Lima. Two actresses were protagonists in a scene enacted at a vegetable stand. One of them, who was pretending to be illiterate, insisted that the vendor was cheating her, taking advantage of the fact that she did not know how to read; the other actress checked the figures, finding them to be correct, and advised the 'illiterate' one to register in one of ALFIN's literacy courses. After some discussion about the best age to start one's studies, about what to study and with whom, the first actress kept on insisting that she was too old for those things. It was then that a little old woman, leaning on her cane, very indignantly shouted:

'My dears, that's not true? For learning and making love one is never too old!'

Everyone witnessing the scene broke into laughter at the old woman's amorous outburst, and the actresses were unable to continue the scene.

3 Photo-romance: In many Latin-American countries there is a genuine epidemic of photo-romances, sub-literature on the lowest imaginable level, which furthermore always serves as a vehicle for the ruling classes' ideology. The technique here consists in reading to the participants the general lines in the plot of a photo-romance without telling them the source of this plot. The participants are asked to act out the story. Finally, the acted-out story is compared to the story as it is told in the photo-romance, and the differences are discussed.

For example: a rather stupid story taken from Corín Tellado, the worst author of this brutalizing genre, started like this:

A woman is waiting for her husband in the company of another woman who is helping her with the housework. . . .

The participants acted according to their customs: a woman at home expecting her husband will naturally be preparing the meal; the one helping her is a neighbor, who comes to chat about various things; the husband comes home tired after a long day's work; the house is a one-room shack, etc., etc. In Corín Tellado, on the contrary, the woman is dressed in a long evening gown, with pearl necklaces, etc.; the woman who is helping her is a black maid who says no more than 'Yes, ma'am'; 'The dinner is served, ma'am'; 'Very well, ma'am'; 'Here comes Mr. X, ma'am'; and nothing else. The house is a marble palace; the husband comes home after a day's work in his factory, where he had an argument with the workers because they, 'not understanding the crisis we are all living through, wanted an increase in salaries . . .,' and continuing in this vein.

This particular story was sheer trash, but at the same time it served as a magnificent example of ideological insight. The well-dressed woman received a letter from an unknown woman, went to visit her, and discovered her to be a former mistress of her husband; the mistress stated that the husband had left her because he wanted to marry the factory owner's daughter, that is, the well-dressed woman. To top it all, the mistress exclaimed:

'Yes, he betrayed me, deceived me. But I forgive him because, after all, he has always been very ambitious, and he knew very well that with me he could not climb very high. On the other hand, with you he can go very far indeed!'

That is to say, the former mistress forgave her lover because he had in the highest degree that capitalistic eagerness to possess everything. The desire to be a factory owner is presented as something so noble that even a few betrayals on the way up are to be forgiven. . . .

And the young wife, not to be outdone, pretends to be ill so that he will have to remain at her side, and so that, as a result of this trick, he will finally fall in love with her. What an ideology! This love story is crowned with a happy ending rotten to the core. Of course the story, when told without the dialogues and acted out by peasants, takes on an entirely different meaning. When at the end of the performance, the participants are told the origin of the plot they have just acted out, they experience a shock. And this must be understood: when they read Corín Tellado they immediately assume the passive role of 'spectators'; but if they first of all have to act out a story themselves, afterwards, when they do read Corín Tellado's version, they will no longer assume a passive, expectant attitude, but instead a critical, comparative one. They will look at the lady's house, and compare it to their own, at the husband's or wife's attitudes and compare them with those of their own spouses, etc. And they will be prepared to detect the poison infiltrating the pages of those photo-stories, or the comics and other forms of cultural and ideological domination.

I was overjoyed when, months after the experiments with the educators, back in Lima, I was informed that the residents of several *barrios* were using that same technique to analyze television programs, an endless source of poison directed against the people.

4 *Breaking of repression:* The dominant classes crush the dominated ones through repression; the old crush the young through repression; certain races subjugate certain others through repression. Never through a cordial understanding, through an honest interchange of ideas, through criticism and autocriticism. No. The ruling classes, the old, the 'superior' races, or the masculine sex, have their sets of values and impose them by force, by unilateral violence, upon the oppressed classes, the young, the races they consider inferior, or women.

The capitalist does not ask the working man if he agrees that the capital should belong to one and the labor to another; he simply places an armed policeman at the factory door and that is that – private property is decreed.

The dominated class, race, sex, or age group suffers the most constant, daily, and omnipresent repression. The ideology becomes concrete in the figure of the dominated person. The proletariat is exploited through the domination that is exerted on all proletarians. Sociology becomes psychology. There is not an oppression by the masculine sex in general of the feminine sex in general: what exists is the concrete oppression that men (individuals) direct against women (individuals).

The technique of breaking repression consists in asking a participant to remember a particular moment when he felt especially repressed, accepted that repression, and began to act in a manner contrary to his own desires. That moment must have a deep personal meaning: I, a proletarian, am oppressed; we proletarians are oppressed; therefore the proletariat is oppressed. It is necessary to pass from the particular to the general, not vice versa, and to deal with something that has happened to someone in particular, but which at the same time is typical of what happens to others.

The person who tells the story also chooses from among the rest of the participants all the other characters who will participate in the reconstruction of the incident. Then, after receiving the information and directions provided by the protagonist, the participants and the protagonist act out the incident just as it happened in reality – recreating the same scene, the same circumstances, and the same original feelings.

Once the 'reproduction' of the actual event is over, the protagonist is asked to repeat the scene, but this time without accepting the repression, fighting to impose his will, his ideas, his wishes. The other participants are urged to maintain the repression as in the first performance. The clash that results helps to measure the possibility one often has to resist and yet fails to do so; it helps to measure the true strength of the enemy. It also gives the protagonist the opportunity of trying once more and carrying out, in fiction, what he had not been able to do in reality. But we have already seen that this is not cathartic: the fact of having rehearsed a resistance to oppression will prepare him to resist effectively in a future reality, when the occasion presents itself once more.

On the other hand, it is necessary to take care that the generic nature of the particular case under study be understood. In this type of theatrical experiment the particular instance must serve as the point of departure, but it is indispensable to reach the general. The process to be realized, during the actual performance or afterward during the discussion, is one that ascends from the *phenomenon* toward the *law*; from the phenomena presented in the plot toward the social laws that govern those phenomena. The spectator-participants must come out of this experience enriched with the knowledge of those laws, obtained through analysis of the phenomena.

5 *Myth theater:* It is simply a question of discovering the obvious behind the myth: to logically tell a story, revealing its evident truths.

In a place called Motupe there was a hill, almost a mountain, with a narrow road that led through the trees to the top; halfway to the top stood a cross. One could go as far as that cross: to go beyond it was dangerous; it inspired fear, and the few who had tried had never returned. It was believed that some sanguinary ghosts inhabited the top of the mountain. But the story is also told of a brave young man who armed himself and climbed to the top, where he found the 'ghosts.' They were in reality some Americans who owned a gold mine located precisely on the top of that mountain.

Another legend is that of the lagoon of Cheken. It is said that there was no water there and that all the peasants, having to travel for several kilometers to get a glass of water, were dying of thirst. Today a lagoon exists there, the property of a local landowner. How did that lagoon spring up and how did it become the property of one man? The legend explains it. When there was still no water, on a day of intense heat all the villagers were lamenting and praying to God to grant them even a tiny stream of water. But God did not have pity on that arid village. At midnight of the same day, however, a man dressed in a long black poncho and riding a black horse arrived and addressed the landowner, who was then only a poor peasant like the others:

'I will give a lagoon for all of you, but *you*, friend, must give me your most precious possession.'

The poor man, very distressed, moaned:

'But I have nothing; I am very poor. We all here suffer from the lack of water, live in miserable shacks, suffer from the most terrible hunger. We have nothing precious, not even our lives. And myself in particular, my only precious possession is my three daughters, nothing else.'

'And of the three,' responded the stranger, 'the oldest is the most beautiful. I will give you a lagoon filled with the freshest water of all Peru; but in exchange you will give me your oldest daughter so that I may marry her.'

The future landlord thought for a long while, cried a lot, and asked his frightened eldest daughter if she would accept such an unusual marriage proposal. The obedient daughter expressed herself in this way:

'If it is for the salvation of all, so that the thirst and hunger of all the peasants will come to an end, if it is so that you may have a lagoon with the freshest water of all Peru, if it is so that that lagoon will belong to you alone and bring you personal prosperity and riches – for you will be able to sell this wonderful water to the peasants, who will find it cheaper to buy from you than to travel so many kilometers – if it is for all this, tell the gentleman in the black poncho, astride his black horse, that I will go with him, even if in my heart I am suspicious of his true identity and of the places he will take me.'

Happy and contented, and of course somewhat tearful, the kind father went to inform the man in black of the decision, meanwhile asking the daughter to make some little signs showing the price of a liter of water, in order to expedite the work. The man in black undressed the girl, for he did not want to take anything from that house besides the girl herself, and placed her on his horse, which set off at a gallop toward a great depression in the plains. Then an enormous explosion was heard, and a large cloud of smoke remained in the very place where the horse, horseman, and naked girl had disappeared. From the huge hole that had been made in the ground, a spring started to flow and formed the lagoon with the freshest water of all Peru.

This myth no doubt hides a truth: the landlord took possession of what did not belong to him. If formerly the noblemen attributed to God the granting of their property and rights, today explanations no less magical are still used. In this case, the property of the lagoon was explained by the loss of the eldest daughter, the landlord's most precious possession – a transaction took place! And serving as a reminder of that, the legend said that on the nights of the new moon one could hear the girl singing at the bottom of the lagoon, still naked and combing her long hair with a beautiful golden comb. . . . Yes, the truth is that for the landlord the lagoon was like gold.

The myths told by the people should be studied and analyzed and their hidden truths revealed. In this task the theater can be extraordinarily useful.

6 *Analytical theater:* A story is told by one of the participants and immediately the actors improvise it. Afterward each character is broken down into all his social roles and the participants are asked to choose a physical object to symbolize each role. For example, a policeman killed a chicken thief. The policeman is analyzed:

(a) he is a worker because he rents his labor-power; symbol: a pair of overalls;
(b) He is a bourgeois because he protects private property and values it more than human life; symbol: a necktie, or a top hat, etc.;
(c) he is a repressive agent because he is a policeman; symbol: a revolver.

This is continued until the participants have analyzed all his roles: head of a family (symbol: the wallet, for example), member of a fraternal order, etc., etc. It is important that the symbols be chosen by the participants present and that they not be imposed 'from above.' For a particular community the symbol for the head of the family might be a wallet, because he is the person who controls the household finances, and in this way controls the family. For another community this symbol may not communicate anything, that is, it may not be a symbol; then an armchair may be chosen. . . .

Having analyzed the character, or characters (it is advisable to limit this operation to the central characters only, for the sake of simplicity and clarity), a fresh attempt to tell the story is made, but taking away some of the symbols from each character, and consequently some social roles as well. Would the story be exactly the same if:

(a) the policeman did not have the top hat or the necktie?
(b) the robber had a top hat or necktie?
(c) the robber had a revolver?
(d) the policeman and the robber both had the same symbol for the fraternal order?

The participants are asked to make varying combinations and the proposed combinations must be performed by the actors and criticized by all those present. In this way they will realize that human actions are not the exclusive and primordial result of individual psychology: almost always, through the individual speaks his class!

7   *Rituals and masks:*   The relations of production (infrastructure) determine the culture of a society (superstructure).

Sometimes the infrastructure changes but the superstructure for a while remains the same. In Brazil the landlords would not allow the peasants to look them in the face while talking with them: this would mean lack of respect. The peasants were accustomed to talking with the landlords only while staring at the ground and murmuring: 'yes, sir; yes, sir; yes, sir.' When the government decreed an agrarian reform (before 1964, date of the fascist *coup d'état*) its emissaries went to the fields to tell the peasants that now they could become landowners. The peasants, staring at the ground, murmured: 'yes, friend; yes, friend; yes, friend.' A feudalistic culture had totally permeated their lives. The relationships of the peasant with the landlord were entirely different from those with the agent of the Institute of Agrarian Reform, but the ritual remained unchanged.

This particular technique of a people's theater ('Rituals and masks') consists precisely in revealing the superstructures, the rituals which reify all human relationships, and the masks of behavior that those rituals impose on each person according to the roles he plays in society and the rituals he must perform.

A very simple example: a man goes to a priest to confess his sins. How will he do it? Of course, he will kneel, confess his sins, hear the penitence, cross himself, and leave. But do all men confess always in the same way before all priests? Who is the man, and who is the priest?

In this case we need two versatile actors to stage the same confession four times:

First scene: the priest and the parishioner are landlords;
Second scene: the priest is a landlord and the parishioner is a peasant;
Third scene: the priest is a peasant and the parishioner is a landlord;
Fourth scene: the priest and the parishioner are peasants.

The ritual is the same in each instance, but the different social masks will cause the four scenes to be different also.

This is an extraordinarily rich technique which has countless variants: the same ritual changing masks; the same ritual performed by people of one social class, and later by people of another class; exchange of masks within the same ritual; etc., etc.

Conclusion: 'Spectator,' a Bad Word!

Yes, this is without a doubt the conclusion: 'Spectator' is a bad word! The spectator is less than a man and it is necessary to humanize him, to restore to him his capacity of action in all its fullness. He too must be a subject, an actor on an equal plane with those generally accepted as actors, who must also be spectators. All these experiments of a people's theater have the same objective – the liberation of the spectator, on whom the theater has imposed finished visions of the world. And since those responsible for theatrical performances are in general people who belong directly or indirectly to the ruling classes, obviously their finished images will be reflections of themselves. The spectators in the people's theater (i.e., the people themselves) cannot go on being the passive victims of those images.

As we have seen in the first essay of this book, the poetics of Aristotle is the *poetics of oppression*: the world is known, perfect or about to be perfected, and all its values are imposed on the spectators, who passively delegate power to the characters to act and think in their place. In so doing the spectators purge themselves of their tragic flaw – that is, of something capable of changing society. A catharsis of the revolutionary impetus is produced! Dramatic action substitutes for real action.

Brecht's poetics is that of the enlightened vanguard: the world is revealed as subject to change, and the change starts in the theater itself, for the spectator does not delegate power to the characters to think in his place, although he continues to delegate power to them to act in his place. The experience is revealing on the level of consciousness, but not globally on the level of the action. Dramatic action throws light upon real action. The spectacle is a preparation for action.

The *poetics of the oppressed* is essentially the poetics of liberation: the spectator no longer delegates power to the characters either to think or to act in his place. The spectator frees himself; he thinks and acts for himself! Theater is action!

Perhaps the theater is not revolutionary in itself; but have no doubts, it is a rehearsal of revolution!

Note

1   Under the author's leadership the Arena Theater developed into one of Brazil's – indeed, one of Latin America's – most outstanding theaters. After 1964, when military rule was established in that country, Boal's work continued, though hampered by censorship and other restrictions imposed by the government. His outspoken position against the authoritarian regime led to his imprisonment and torture in 1971. Released after three months and acquitted of all charges, he was nevertheless compelled to leave Brazil in order to insure the safety of himself and his family. After political circumstances also forced him to leave Buenes Aires, Argentina, he took up residence in Portugal.

■ ■ ■

Source

Boal, A. (1974, 1979) 'Poetics of the Oppressed: Fourth stage: The Theatre as Discourse', *Theatre of the Oppressed*, trans. C.A. and M.O.L. McBride, London: Pluto: 142–156.

Originally published as *Teatro de Oprimido*.

Augusto Boal (1934–)

Brazilian director and political activist turned politician, who developed a series of theatrical strategies to effect change in the lives of individuals on a personal, social, and political level. His work has become a system known as Theatre of the Oppressed, which makes use of a composite series of games and exercises, published as *Games for Actors and Non-Actors* (1992). Boal began to develop his thinking while director of the Arena Theatre in São Paolo (1956–71). He moved to Argentina in 1971, where he devised the techniques of invisible theatre as a way to stimulate debate on current political issues. Invited to participate in a Peruvian literacy campaign in 1973, he developed image theatre, which promotes physical expression over the spoken word. Boal's work has been influential among theatre practitioners in Europe as an alternative means of training and of restoring theatre to a meaningful role in society outside theatres; a democratic forum for potential change in people's lives. The rainbow of desire is the name given to a new series of exercises which examine individual and internalised oppressions in more detail, and which places the work more in the field of psychotherapy. Boal is currently Member of Parliament of Rio de Janiero's Workers Party (PT), where he is developing his most recent theatre form – the legislative theatre – which involves using theatre techniques to enable communities to propose laws which they would like the Council (Chambre de Vereadores) to formalise.

This section from Boal's first book describes in some detail strategies used among the poor and dispossessed of Peru in 1973. It proposes theatre as a universal language, which explains its attraction for Western directors and actors looking for a renewed role for theatre in the second half of the century.

Reader cross-references

Barba – contemporary approach to theatre games and exercises
Beck – a contemporary North American view of theatre
Brecht – another, European, political role for theatre to which Boal refers
Brown – comparison with a dancer working with non-theatrical processes and spaces
Grotowski and **Stanislavski** – acting exercises
Rainer – whose work in a North American context stressed the democracy of the body

Further reading

Boal, A. (1992) *Games for Actors and Non-Actors*, trans. A. Jackson, London: Routledge.
Boal, A. (1995) *The Rainbow of Desire*, trans. A. Jackson, London: Routledge.
Schutzman, M. and Cohen-Cruz, J. (eds) (1993) *Playing Boal*, London: Routledge.

Chapter 12

Bertolt Brecht

SHORT DESCRIPTION OF A NEW TECHNIQUE OF ACTING WHICH PRODUCES AN ALIENATION EFFECT

W HAT FOLLOWS REPRESENTS an attempt to describe a technique of acting which was applied in certain theatres (1) with a view to taking the incidents portrayed and alienating them from the spectator. The aim of this technique, known as the alienation effect, was to make the spectator adopt an attitude of inquiry and criticism in his approach to the incident. The means were artistic.

The first condition for the A-effect's application to this end is that stage and auditorium must be purged of everything 'magical' and that no 'hypnotic tensions' should be set up. This ruled out any attempt to make the stage convey the flavour of a particular place (a room at evening, a road in the autumn), or to create atmosphere by relaxing the tempo of the conversation. The audience was not 'worked up' by a display of temperament or 'swept away' by acting with tauntened muscles; in short, no attempt was made to put it in a trance and give it the illusion of watching an ordinary unrehearsed event. As will be seen presently, the audience's tendency to plunge into such illusions has to be checked by specific artistic means (3).

The first condition for the achievement of the A-effect is that the actor must invest what he has to show with a definite gest of showing. It is of course necessary to drop the assumption that there is a fourth wall cutting the audience off from the stage and the consequent illusion that the stage action is taking place in reality and without an audience. That being so, it is possible for the actor in principle to address the audience direct.

It is well known that contact between audience and stage is normally made on the basis of empathy. Conventional actors devote their efforts so exclusively to bringing about this psychological operation that they may be said to see it as the principal aim of their art (5). Our introductory remarks will already have made it clear that the technique which produces an A-effect is the exact opposite of that which aims at empathy. The actor applying it is bound not to try to bring about the empathy operation.

Yet in his efforts to reproduce particular characters and show their behaviour he need not renounce the means of empathy entirely. He uses these means just as any normal person with no particular acting talent would use them if he wanted to portray someone else, i.e. show how he behaves. This showing of other people's behaviour happens time and again in ordinary life (witnesses of an accident demonstrating to newcomers how the victim behaved, a facetious person imitating a friend's walk, etc.), without those involved making the least effort to subject their spectators to an illusion. At the same time they do feel their way into their characters' skins with a view to acquiring their characteristics.

As has already been said, the actor too will make use of this psychological operation. But whereas the usual practice in acting is to execute it during the actual performance, in the hope of stimulating the spectator into a similar operation, he will achieve it only at an earlier stage, at some time during rehearsals.

To safeguard against an unduly 'impulsive', frictionless and un-critical creation of characters and incidents, more reading rehearsals can be held than usual. The actor should refrain from living himself into the part prematurely in any way, and should go on functioning as long as possible as a reader (which does not mean a reader-aloud). An important step is memorizing one's first impressions.

When reading his part the actor's attitude should be one of a man who is astounded and contradicts. Not only the occurrence of the incidents, as he reads about them, but the conduct of the man he is playing, as he experiences it, must be weighed up by him and their peculiarities understood; none can be taken as given, as something that 'was bound to turn out that way', that was 'only to be expected from a character like that'. Before memorizing the words he must memorize what he felt astounded at and where he felt impelled to contradict. For these are dynamic forces that he must preserve in creating his performance.

When he appears on the stage, besides what he actually is doing he will at all essential points discover, specify, imply what he is not doing; that is to say he will act in such a way that the alternative emerges as clearly as possible, that his acting allows the other possibilities to be inferred and only represents one out of the possible variants. He will say for instance 'You'll pay for that', and not say 'I forgive you'. He detests his children; it is not the case that he loves them. He moves down stage left and not up stage right. Whatever he doesn't do must be contained and conserved in what he does. In this way every sentence and every gesture signifies a decision; the character remains under observation and is tested. The technical term for this procedure is 'fixing the "not . . . but"'.

The actor does not allow himself to become completely transformed on the stage into the character he is portraying. He is not Lear, Harpagon, Schweik; he shows them. He reproduces their remarks as authentically as he can; he puts forward their way of behaving to the best of his abilities and knowledge of men; but he never tries to persuade himself (and thereby others) that this amounts to a complete transformation. Actors will know what it means if I say that a typical kind of acting without this complete transformation takes place when a producer or colleague shows one how to play a particular passage. It is not his own part, so he is not completely transformed; he underlines the technical aspect and retains the attitude of someone just making suggestions.

Once the idea of total transformation is abandoned the actor speaks his part not as if he were improvising it himself but like a quotation (7). At the same time he obviously has to render all the quotation's overtones, the remark's full human and concrete shape; similarly the gesture he makes must have the full substance of a human gesture even though it now represents a copy.

Given this absence of total transformation in the acting there are three aids which may help to alienate the actions and remarks of the characters being portrayed:

1 Transposition into the third person.
2 Transposition into the past.
3 Speaking the stage directions out loud.

Using the third person and the past tense allows the actor to adopt the right attitude of detachment. In addition he will look for stage directions and remarks that comment on his lines, and speak them aloud at rehearsal ('He stood up and exclaimed angrily, not having eaten: . . .', or 'He had never been told so before, and didn't know if it was true or not', or 'He smiled, and said with forced nonchalance: . . .'). Speaking the stage directions out loud in the third person results in a clash between two tones of voice, alienating the second of them, the text proper. This style of acting is further alienated by taking place on the stage after having already been outlined and announced in words. Transposing it into the past gives the speaker a stand-point from which he can look back at his sentence. The sentence too is thereby alienated without the speaker adopting an unreal point of view; unlike the spectator, he has read the play right through and is better placed to judge the sentence in accordance with the ending, with its consequences, than the former, who knows less and is more of a stranger to the sentence.

This composite process leads to an alienation of the text in the rehearsals which generally persists in the performance too (9). The directness of the relationship with the audience allows and indeed forces the actual speech delivery to be varied in accordance with the greater or smaller significance attaching to the sentences. Take the case of witnesses addressing a court. The underlinings, the characters' insistence on their remarks, must be developed as a piece of effective virtuosity. If the actor turns to the audience it must be a whole-hearted turn rather than the asides and soliloquizing technique of the old-fashioned theatre. To get the full A-effect from the poetic medium the actor should start at rehearsal by paraphrasing the verse's content in vulgar prose, possibly accompanying this by the gestures designed for the verse. A daring and beautiful handling of verbal media will alienate the text. (Prose can be alienated by translation into the actor's native dialect.)

Gesture will be dealt with below, but it can at once be said that everything to do with the emotions has to be externalized; that is to say, it must be developed into a gesture. The actor has to find a sensibly percep-tible outward expression for his character's emotions, preferably some action that gives away what is going on inside him. The emotion in question must be brought out, must lose all its restrictions so that it can be treated on a big scale. Special elegance, power and grace of gesture bring about the A-effect.

A masterly use of gesture can be seen in Chinese acting. The Chinese actor achieves the A-effect by being seen to observe his own movements.

Whatever the actor offers in the way of gesture, verse structure, etc., must be finished and bear the hallmarks of something rehearsed and rounded-off. The impression to be given is one of ease, which is at the same time one of difficulties overcome. The actor must make it possible for the audience to take his own art, his mastery of technique, lightly too. He puts an incident before the spectator with perfection and as he thinks it really happened or might have happened. He does not conceal the fact that he has rehearsed it, any more than an acrobat conceals his training, and he emphasizes that it is his own (actor's) account, view, version of the incident.

Because he doesn't identify himself with him he can pick a definite attitude to adopt towards the character whom he portrays, can show what he thinks of him and invite the spectator, who is likewise not asked to identify himself, to criticize the character portrayed.

The attitude which he adopts is a socially critical one. In his exposition of the incidents and in his characterization of the person he tries to bring out those features which comes within society's sphere. In this way his performance becomes a discussion (about social conditions) with the audience he is addressing. He prompts the spectator to justify or abolish these conditions according to what class he belongs to (13).

The object of the A-effect is to alienate the social gest underlying every incident. By social gest is meant the mimetic and gestural expression of the social relationships prevailing between people of a given period (14).

It helps to formulate the incident for society, and to put it across in such a way that society is given the key, if titles are thought up for the scenes. These titles must have a historical quality.

This brings us to a crucial technical device: historicization.

The actor must play the incidents as historical ones. Historical incidents are unique, transitory incidents associated with particular periods. The conduct of the persons involved in them is not fixed and 'universally human'; it includes elements that have been or may be overtaken by the course of history, and is subject to criticism from the immediately following period's point of view. The conduct of those born before us is alienated [*Entfremdet*] from us by an incessant evolution.

It is up to the actor to treat present-day events and modes of behaviour with the same detachment as the historian adopts with regard to those of the past. He must alienate these characters and incidents from us.

Characters and incidents from ordinary life, from our immediate surroundings, being familiar, strike us as more or less natural. Alienating them helps to make them seem remarkable to us. Science has carefully developed a technique of getting irritated with the everyday, 'self-evident', universally accepted occurrence, and there is no reason why this infinitely useful attitude should not be taken over by art (17). It is an attitude which arose in science as a result of the growth in human productive powers. In art the same motive applies.

As for the emotions, the experimental use of the A-effect in the epic theatre's German productions indicated that this way of acting too can stimulate them, though possibly a different class of emotion is involved from those of the orthodox theatre (18). A critical attitude on the audience's part is a thoroughly artistic one (19). Nor does the actual practice of the A-effect seem anything like so unnatural as its description. Of course it is a way of acting that has nothing to do with stylization as commonly practised. The main advantage of the epic theatre with its A-effect, intended purely to show the world in such a way that it becomes manageable, is precisely its quality of being natural and earthly, its humour and its renunciation of all the mystical elements that have stuck to the orthodox theatre from the old days.

Appendix: selected notes

1   *Edward II* after Marlowe (Munich Kammerspiele).
    Trommeln in der Nacht (Deutsches Theater, Berlin).
    The Threepenny Opera (Theater am Schiffbauerdamm, Berlin).
    Die Pioniere von Ingolstadt (Theater am Schiffbauerdamm).
    Aufstieg und Fall der Stadt Mahagonny, opera (Aufricht's Kurfürstendammtheater, Berlin).
    Mann ist Mann (Staatstheater, Berlin).
    Die Massnahme (Grosses Schauspielhaus, Berlin).
    The Adventures of the Good Soldier Schweik (Piscator's Theater am Nollendorfplatz, Berlin).
    Die Plattköpfe und die Spitzköpfe (Riddersalen, Copenhagen).
    Señora Carrar's Rifles (Copenhagen, Paris).
    Furcht und Elend des Dritten Reiches (Paris).

3   E.g. such mechanical means as very brilliant illumination of the stage (since a half-lit stage plus a completely darkened auditorium makes the spectator less level-headed by preventing him from observing his neighbour and in turn hiding him from his neighbour's eyes) and also *making visible the sources of light*.

Making visible the sources of light

There is a point in showing the lighting apparatus openly, as it is one of the means of preventing an unwanted element of illusion; it scarcely disturbs the necessary concentration. If we light the actors and their performance in such a way that the lights themselves are within the spectator's field of vision we destroy part of his illusion of being present at a spontaneous, transitory, authentic, unrehearsed event. He sees that arrangements have been made to show something; something is being repeated here under special conditions, for instance in a very brilliant light. Displaying the actual lights is meant to be a counter to the old-fashioned theatre's efforts to hide them. No one would expect the lighting to be hidden at a sporting event, a boxing match for instance.

Whatever the points of difference between the modern theatre's presentations and those of a sporting promoter, they do not include the same concealment of the sources of light as the old theatre found necessary.
(Brecht: 'Der Bühnenbau des epischen Theaters')

5   Cf. these remarks by Poul Reumert, the best-known Danish actor:

> . . . If I feel I am *dying*, and if I *really* feel it, then so does everybody else; if I act as though I had a dagger in my hand, and am entirely filled by the one idea of killing the child, then everybody shudders. . . . The whole business is a matter of mental activity being communicated by emotions, or the other way round if you prefer it: a feeling so strong as to be an obsession, which is translated into thoughts. If it comes off it is the most infectious thing in the world; anything external is then a matter of complete indifference. . . .

And Rapaport, 'The Work of the Actor', *Theater Workshop*, October 1936:

> . . . On the stage the actor is surrounded entirely by fictions. . . . The actor must be able to regard all this as though it were true, as though he were convinced that all that surrounds him on the stage is a living reality and, along with himself, he must convince the audience as well. This is the central feature of our method of work on the part. . . . Take any object, a cap for example; lay it on the table or on the floor and try to regard it as though it were a rat; make believe that it is a rat, and not a cap. . . . Picture what sort of a rat it is; what size, colour? . . . We thus commit ourselves to believe quite naïvely that the object before us is something other than it is and, at the same time, learn to compel the audience to believe. . . .

This might be thought to be a course of instruction for conjurers, but in fact it is a course of acting, supposedly according to Stanislavsky's method. One wonders if a technique that equips an actor to make the audience see rats where there aren't any can really be all that suitable for disseminating the truth. Given enough alcohol it doesn't take acting to persuade almost anybody that he is seeing rats: pink ones.

7   *Quotation*

Standing in a free and direct relationship to it, the actor allows his character to speak and move; he presents a report. He does not have to make us forget that the text isn't spontaneous, but has been memorized, is a fixed quantity; the fact doesn't matter, as we anyway assume that the report is not about himself but about others. His attitude would be the same if he were simply speaking from his own memory.[. . .]

8   The epic actor has to accumulate far more material than has been the case till now. What he has to represent is no longer himself as king, himself as scholar, himself as gravedigger, etc., but just kings, scholars, gravediggers, which means that he has to look around him in the world of reality. Again, he has to learn how to imitate: something that is discouraged in modern acting on the ground that it destroys his individuality.

9   The theatre can create the corresponding A-effect in the performance in a number of ways. The Munich production of *Edward II* for the first time had titles preceding the scenes, announcing the contents. The Berlin production of *The Threepenny Opera* had the titles of the songs projected while they were sung. The Berlin production of *Mann ist Mann* had the actors' figures projected on big screens during the action.

13   Another thing that makes for freedom in the actor's relationship with his audience is that he does not treat it as an undifferentiated mass. He doesn't boil it down to a shapeless dumpling in the stockpot of the emotions. He does not address himself to everybody alike; he allows the existing divisions within the audience to continue, in fact he widens them. He has friends and enemies in the audience; he is friendly to the one group and hostile to the other. He takes sides, not necessarily with his character but if not with it then against it. (At least, that is his basic attitude, though it too must be variable and change according to what the character may say at different stages. There may, however, also be points at which everything is in the balance and the actor must withhold judgment, though this again must be expressly shown in his acting.)

14   If King Lear (in Act I, scene 1) tears up a map when he divides his kingdom between his daughters, then the act of division is alienated. Not only does it draw our attention to his kingdom, but by treating the kingdom so plainly as his own private property he throws some light on the basis of the feudal idea of the family. In *Julius Caesar* the tyrant's murder by Brutus is alienated if during one of his monologues accusing Caesar of tyrannical motives he himself maltreats a slave waiting on him. Weigel as *Maria Stuart* suddenly took the crucifix hanging round her neck and used it coquettishly as a fan, to give herself air. (See too Brecht: 'Übungsstücke für Schauspieler' in *Versuche II*, p. 107.)

17   *The A-effect as a procedure in everyday life*

The achievement of the A-effect constitutes something utterly ordinary, recurrent; it is just as widely-practised way of drawing one's own or someone else's attention to a thing, and it can be seen in education as also in business conferences of one sort or another. The A-effect consists in turning the object of which one is to be made aware, to which one's attention is to be drawn, from something ordinary, familiar, immediately accessible, into something peculiar, striking and unexpected. What is obvious is in a certain sense made incomprehensible, but this is only in order that it may then be made all the easier to comprehend. Before familiarity can turn into awareness the familiar must be stripped of its inconspicuousness; we must give up assuming that the object in question needs no explanation. However frequently recurrent, modest, vulgar it may be it will now be labelled as something unusual.

A common use of the A-effect is when someone says: 'Have you ever really looked carefully at your watch?' The questioner knows that I've looked at it often enough, and now his question deprives me of the sight which I've grown used to and which accordingly has nothing more to say to me. I used to look at it to see the time, and now when he askes me in this importunate way I realize that I have given up seeing the watch itself with an astonished eye; and it is in many ways an astonishing piece of machinery. Similarly it is an alienation effect of the simplest sort if a business discussion starts off with the sentence: 'Have you ever thought what happens to the waste from your factory which is pumped into the river twenty-four hours a day?' This waste wasn't just swept down the river unobserved; it was carefully channelled into the river; men and machines have worked on it; the river has changed colour, the waste has flowed away most conspicuously, but just as waste. It was superfluous to the process of manufacture, and now it is to become material for manufacture; our eye turns to it with interest. The asking of the question has alienated it, and intentionally so. The very simplest sentences that apply in the A-effect are those with 'Not . . . But': (He didn't say 'come in' but 'keep moving'. He was not pleased but amazed). They include an expectation which is justified by experience but, in the event, disappointed. One might have thought that . . . but one oughtn't to have thought it. There was not just one possibility but two; both are introduced, then the second one is alienated, then the first as well. To see one's mother as a man's wife one needs an A-effect; this is provided, for instance, when one acquires a stepfather. If one sees one's teacher hounded by the bailiffs an A-effect occurs: one is jerked out of a relationship in which the teacher seems big into one where he seems small. An alienation of the motor-car takes place if after driving a modern car for a long while we drive an old model T Ford. Suddenly we hear explosions once more; the motor works on the principle of explosion. We start feeling amazed that such a vehicle, indeed any vehicle not drawn by animal-power, can move; in short, we understand cars, by looking at them as something strange, new, as a triumph of engineering and to that extent something unnatural. Nature, which certainly embraces the motor-car, is suddenly imbued with an element of unnaturalness, and from now on this is an indelible part of the concept of nature.

The expression 'in fact' can likewise certify or alienate. (He wasn't in fact at home; he said he would be, but we didn't believe him and had a look; or again, we didn't think it possible for him not to be at home, but it was a fact.) The term 'actually' is just as conducive to alienation. ('I don't actually agree'.) Similarly the Eskimo definition 'A car is a wingless aircraft that crawls along the ground' is a way of alienating the car.

In a sense the alienation effect itself has been alienated by the above explanation; we have taken a common, recurrent, universally-practised operation and tried to draw attention to it by illuminating its peculiarity. But we have achieved the effect only with those people who have truly ('in fact') grasped that it does 'not' result from every representation 'but' from certain ones: only 'actually' is it familiar.

18   About rational and emotional points of view

The rejection of empathy is not the result of a rejection of the emotions, nor does it lead to such. The crude aesthetic thesis that emotions can only be stimulated by means of empathy is wrong. None the less a non-aristotelian dramaturgy has to apply a cautious criticism to the emotions which it aims at and incorporates. Certain artistic tendencies like the provocative behaviour of Futurists and Dadaists and the icing-up of music point to a crisis of the emotions. Already in the closing years of the Weimar Republic the post-war German drama took a decisively rationalistic turn. Fascism's grotesque emphasizing of the emotions, together perhaps with the no less important threat to the rational element in Marxist aesthetics, led us to lay particular stress on the rational. Nevertheless there are many contemporary works of art where one can speak of a decline in emotional effectiveness due to their isolation from reason, or its revival thanks to a stronger rationalist message. This will surprise no one who has not got a completely conventional idea of the emotions.

The emotions always have a quite definite class basis; the form they take at any time is historical, restricted and limited in specific ways. The emotions are in no sense universally human and timeless.

The linking of particular emotions with particular interests is not unduly difficult so long as one simply looks for the interests corresponding to the emotional effects of works of art. Anyone can see the colonial adventures of the Second Empire looming behind Delacroix's paintings and Rimbaud's 'Bateau Ivre'.

If one compares the 'Bateau Ivre' say, with Kipling's 'Ballad of East and West', one can see the difference between French mid-nineteenth century colonialism and British colonialism at the beginning of the twentieth. It is less easy to explain the effect that such poems have on ourselves, as Marx already noticed. Apparently emotions accompanying social progress will long survive in the human mind as emotions linked with interests, and in the case of works of art will do so more strongly than might have been expected, given that in the meantime contrary interests will have made themselves felt. Every step forward means the end of the previous step forward, because that is where it starts and goes on from. At the same time it makes use of this previous step, which in a sense survives in men's consciousness as a step forward, just as it survives in its effects in real life. This involves a most interesting type of generalization, a continual process of abstraction. Whenever the works of art handed down to us allow us to share the emotions of other men, of men of a bygone period, different social classes, etc., we have to conclude that we are partaking in interests which really were universally human. These men now dead represented the interests of classes that gave a lead to progress. It is a very different matter when Fascism today conjures up on the grandest scale emotions which for most of the people who succumb to them are not determined by interest.

19 Is the critical attitude an inartistic one?

An old tradition leads people to treat a critical attitude as a predominantly negative one. Many see the difference between the scientific and artistic attitudes as lying precisely in their attitude to criticism. People cannot conceive of contradiction and detachment as being part of artistic appreciation. Of course such appreciation normally includes a higher level, which appreciates critically, but the criticism here only applies to matters of technique; it is quite a different matter from being required to observe not a representation of the world but the world itself in a critical, contradictory, detached manner.

To introduce this critical attitude into art, the negative element which it doubtless includes must be shown from its positive side: this criticism of the world is active, practical, positive. Criticizing the course of a river means improving it, correcting it. Criticism of society is ultimately revolution; there you have criticism taken to its logical conclusion and playing an active part. A critical attitude of this type is an operative factor of productivity; it is deeply enjoyable as such, and if we commonly use the term 'arts' for enterprises that improve people's lives why should art proper remain aloof from arts of this sort?

['Kurze Beschreibung einer neuen Technik der Schauspielkunst, die einen Verfremdungseffekt hervorbringt', from *Versuche* II, 1951, less notes 2, 4, 6, 10, 11, 15, 16 and part of 7]

■   ■   ■

Source

Brecht, B. (1940, 1964) 'Short Description of a New Technique of Acting which Produces an Alienation Effect', *Brecht on Theatre: the Development of an Aesthetic*, trans. and ed. J. Willett, New York: Hill & Wang: 136–147.

Bertolt Brecht (1898–1956)

German dramatist, poet and theatre director. Brecht worked as assistant to the great German director, Max Reinhardt, before establishing himself as a writer-director in the 1920s. He collaborated extensively with three composers – Kurt Weill, Hanns Eisler and Paul Dessau – on works which have changed the ways in which theatre can be of use in changing an audience's perception of society. In his major works, *The Threepenny Opera* (1928), *The Caucasian Chalk Circle* (1945) and *Mother Courage* (1949), as well as in his more overtly political experiments such as *The Mother* (1932), he pioneered new techniques of both acting and staging, as well as of using music with text.

Brecht wanted actors to evolve a 'Verfremdunseffekt', which has been misleadingly translated as 'alienation'. The German means simply 'to make strange', and the technique he describes is intended to make an audience attend to the contradictions in society which his plays present, with greater concentration.

After going into exile in Europe at the start of the Second World War, Brecht went to America, where he was eventually called to trial for his alleged communist sympathies. After returning to the new state of East Germany at the end of the war, he established his own company, The Berliner Ensemble, to perform his plays. Over the period of six years before his early death in 1956, he developed one of the greatest acting ensembles of Europe, which was to have a profound effect on much subsequent theatre performance.

His major concern is clear – that of the role of the actor in the twentieth century. Modern times, according to Brecht, demand new techniques – theatrical as well as industrial – and his attempt to revolutionise theatre is one of the most significant contributions to both theory and practice.

Reader cross-references

Barba – a later anti-psychological attitude to theatre
Benjamin – friend and comrade, developed a Marxist theoretical approach
Boal – another, South American, political role for theatre
Eisler – longstanding musical collaborator
Grotowski and **Stanislavski** – different European approaches to actor training
LeCompte – a later non-psychological approach
Meyerhold and **Piscator** – contemporary, European views of political theatre
Müller – a later German director
Wigman – a contemporary compatriot in modern dance
Williams – a later, British, position
Wilson – comparison with a later director

Further reading

Esslin, M. (1964) *Brecht: A Choice of Evils*, London: Methuen.
Thomson, P. and Sachs, G. (eds) (1994) *Cambridge Companion to Brecht*, Cambridge: Cambridge University Press.
Willett, J. (ed.) (1940, 1964) *Brecht on Theatre: The Development of an Aesthetic*, New York: Hill & Wang.

Chapter 13

Peter Brook

THE DEADLY THEATRE

I CAN TAKE ANY EMPTY SPACE and call it a barestage. A man walks across this empty space whilst someone else is watching him, and this is all that is needed for an act of theatre to be engaged. Yet when we talk about theatre this is not quite what we mean. Red curtains, spotlights, blank verse, laughter, darkness, these are all confusedly superimposed in a messy image covered by one all-purpose word. We talk of the cinema killing the theatre, and in that phrase we refer to the theatre as it was when the cinema was born, a theatre of box office, foyer, tip-up seats, footlights, scene changes, intervals, music, as though the theatre was by very definition these and little more.

I will try to split the word four ways and distinguish four different meanings – and so will talk about a Deadly Theatre, a Holy Theatre, a Rough Theatre and an Immediate Theatre. Sometimes these four theatres really exist, standing side by side, in the West End of London, or in New York off Times Square. Sometimes they are hundreds of miles apart, the Holy in Warsaw and the Rough in Prague, and sometimes they are metaphoric: two of them mixing together within one evening, within one act. Sometimes within one single moment, the four of them, Holy, Rough, Immediate and Deadly inter-twine.

The Deadly Theatre can at first sight be taken for granted, because it means bad theatre. As this is the form of theatre we see most often, and as it is most closely linked to the despised, much-attacked commercial theatre it might seem a waste of time to criticize it further. But it is only if we see

that deadliness is deceptive and can appear anywhere, that we will become aware of the size of the problem.

The condition of the Deadly Theatre at least is fairly obvious. All through the world theatre audiences are dwindling. There are occasional new movements, good new writers and so on, but as a whole, the theatre not only fails to elevate or instruct, it hardly even entertains. The theatre has often been called a whore, meaning its art is impure, but today this is true in another sense — whores take the money and then go short on the pleasure. The Broadway crisis, the Paris crisis, the West End crisis are the same: we do not need the ticket agents to tell us that the theatre has become a deadly business and the public is smelling it out. In fact, were the public ever really to demand the true entertainment it talks about so often, we would almost all be hard put to know where to begin. A true theatre of joy is non-existent and it is not just the trivial comedy and the bad musical that fail to give us our money's worth — the Deadly Theatre finds its deadly way into grand opera and tragedy, into the plays of Molière and the plays of Brecht. Of course nowhere does the Deadly Theatre install itself so securely, so comfortably and so slyly as in the works of William Shakespeare. The Deadly Theatre takes easily to Shakespeare. We see his plays done by good actors in what seems like the proper way — they look lively and colourful, there is music and everyone is all dressed up, just as they are supposed to be in the best of classical theatres. Yet secretly we find it excruciatingly boring — and in our hearts we either blame Shakespeare, or theatre as such, or even ourselves. To make matters worse there is always a deadly spectator, who for special reasons enjoys a lack of intensity and even a lack of entertainment, such as the scholar who emerges from routine performances of the classics smiling because nothing has distracted him from trying over and confirming his pet theories to himself, whilst reciting his favourite lines under his breath. In his heart he sincerely wants a theatre that is nobler-than-life and he confuses a sort of intellectual satisfaction with the true experience for which he craves. Unfortunately, he lends the weight of his authority to dullness and so the Deadly Theatre goes on its way.

Anyone who watches the real successes as they appear each year will see a very curious phenomenon. We expect the so-called hit to be livelier, faster, brighter than the flop — but this is not always the case. Almost every season in most theatre-loving towns, there is one great success that defies these rules; one play that succeeds not despite but because of dullness. After all, one associates culture with a certain sense of duty, historical costumes and long speeches with the sensation of being bored; so, conversely, just the right degree of boringness is a reassuring guarantee of a worthwhile event. Of course, the dosage is so subtle that it is impossible to establish the exact formula – too much and the audience is driven out of its seats, too little and it may find the theme too disagreeably intense. However, mediocre authors seem to feel their way unerringly to the perfect mixture – and they perpetuate the Deadly Theatre with dull successes, universally praised. Audiences crave for something in the theatre that they can term 'better' than life and for this reason are open to confuse culture, or the trappings of culture, with something they do not know, but sense obscurely could exist – so, tragically, in elevating something bad into a success they are only cheating themselves.

If we talk of deadly, let us note that the difference between life and death, so crystal clear in man, is somewhat veiled in other fields. A doctor can tell at once between the trace of life and the useless bag of bones that life has left; but we are less practised in observing how an idea, an attitude or a form can pass from the lively to the moribund. It is difficult to define but a child can smell it out. Let me give an example. In France there are two deadly ways of playing classical tragedy. One is traditional, and this involves using a special voice, a special manner, a noble look and an elevated musical delivery. The other way is no more than a half-hearted version of the same thing. Imperial gestures and royal values are fast disappearing from everyday life, so each new generation finds the grand manner more and more hollow, more and more meaningless. This leads the young actor to an angry and impatient search for what he calls truth. He wants to play his verse more realistically, to get it to sound like honest-to-God real speech, but he finds that the formality of the writing is so rigid that it resists this treatment. He is forced to an uneasy compromise that is neither refreshing, like ordinary talk, nor defiantly histrionic, like what we call ham. So his acting is weak and because ham is strong, it is remembered with a certain nostalgia. Inevitably, someone calls for tragedy to be played once again 'the way it is written'. This is fair enough, but unfortunately all the printed word can tell us is what was written on paper, not how it was once brought to life. There are no records, no tapes – only experts, but not one of them, of course, has firsthand knowledge. The real antiques have all gone – only some imitations have survived, in the shape of traditional actors, who continue to play in a traditional way, drawing their inspiration not from real sources, but from imaginary ones, such as the memory of the sound an older actor once made – a sound that in turn was a memory of a predecessor's way.

I once saw a rehearsal at the Comédie Française – a very young actor stood in front of a very old one and spoke and mimed the role with him like a reflection in a glass. This must not be confused with the great tradition, say, of the Noh actors passing knowledge orally from father to son. There it is meaning that is communicated – and meaning never belongs to the past. It can be checked in each man's own present experience. But to imitate the externals of acting only perpetuates manner – a manner hard to relate to anything at all.

Again with Shakespeare we hear or read the same advice – 'Play what is written'. But what is written? Certain ciphers on paper. Shakespeare's words are records of the words that he wanted to be spoken, words issuing as sounds from people's mouths, with pitch, pause, rhythm and gesture as part of their meaning. A word does not start as a word – it is an end product which begins as an impulse, stimulated by attitude and behaviour which dictates the need for expression. This process occurs inside the dramatist; it is repeated inside the actor. Both may only be conscious of the words, but both for the author and then for the actor the word is a small visible portion of a gigantic unseen formation. Some writers attempt to nail down their meaning and intentions in stage directions and explanations, yet we cannot help being struck by the fact that the best dramatists explain themselves the least. They recognize that further indications will most probably be useless. They recognize that the only way to find the true path to the speaking of a word is through a process that parallels the original creative one. This can neither be by-passed nor simplified. Unfortunately, the moment a lover speaks, or a king utters, we rush to give them a label: the lover is 'romantic', the king is 'noble' – and before we know it we are speaking of romantic love and kingly nobility or princeliness as though they are things we can hold in our hand and expect the actors to observe. But these are not substances and they do not exist. If we search for them, the best we can do is to make guesswork reconstructions from books and paintings. If you ask an actor to play in a 'romantic style' he will valiantly have a go, thinking he knows what you mean. What actually can he draw on? Hunch, imagination and a scrap book of theatrical memories, all of which will give him a vague 'romanticness' that he will mix up with a disguised imitation of whatever older actor he happens to admire. If he digs into his own experiences the result may not marry with the text; if he just plays what he thinks is the text, it will be imitative and conventional. Either way the result is a compromise: at most times unconvincing.

It is vain to pretend that the words we apply to classical plays like 'musical', 'poetic', 'larger than life', 'noble', 'heroic', 'romantic', have any absolute meaning. They are the reflections of a critical attitude of a particular period, and to attempt to build a performance today to conform to these canons is the most certain road to deadly theatre – deadly theatre of a respectability that makes it pass as living truth.

Once, when giving a lecture on this theme, I was able to put it to a practical test. By luck, there was a woman in the audience who had neither read nor seen *King Lear*. I gave her Goneril's first speech and asked her to recite it as best she could for whatever values she found in it. She read it very simply – and the speech itself emerged full of eloquence and charm. I then explained that it was supposed to be the speech of a wicked woman and suggested her reading every word for hypocrisy. She tried to do so, and the audience saw what a hard unnatural wrestling with the simple music of the words was involved when she sought to act to a definition:

Sir, I love you more than words can wield the matter;
Dearer than eyesight, space, and liberty;
Beyond that can be valued, rich or rare;
No less than life, with grace, health, beauty, honour;
As much as child e'er loved, or father found;
A love that makes breath poor, and speech unable;
Beyond all manner of so much I love you.

Anyone can try this for himself. Taste it on the tongue. The words are those of a lady of style and breeding accustomed to expressing herself in public, someone with ease and social aplomb. As for clues to her character, only the façade is presented and this, we see, is elegant and attractive. Yet if one thinks of the performances where Goneril speaks these first lines as a macabre villainess, and looks at the speech again, one is at a loss to know what suggests this – other than preconceptions of Shakespeare's moral attitudes. In fact, if Goneril in her first appearance does not play a 'monster', but merely what her given words suggest, then all the balance of the play changes – and in the subsequent scenes her villainy and Lear's martyrdom are neither as crude nor as simplified as they might appear. Of course, by the end of the play we learn that Goneril's actions make her what we call a monster – but a real monster, both complex and compelling.

In a living theatre, we would each day approach the rehearsal putting yesterday's discoveries to the test, ready to believe that the true play has once again escaped us. But the Deadly Theatre approaches the classics from the viewpoint that somewhere, someone has found out and defined how the play should be done.

■　■　■

Source

Brook, P. (1968, 1990) 'The Deadly Theatre', *The Empty Space*, Harmondsworth: Penguin: 1–17.

   First published (1968) by McGibbon & Kee.

Peter Brook (1925–)

European theatre director, who studied at Oxford, and established himself by directing relatively conventional Shakespearean productions, alongside opera at London's Covent Garden. Notable productions included *Titus Andronicus* (1955, with Laurence Olivier), *King Lear* (1962, with Paul Scofield), and *Oedipus* (1968). In the early 1960s he read Artaud's *Theatre and Its Double*, newly available in English translation, and staged his famous 1964 Theatre of Cruelty Season, which included Artaud's *Spurt of Blood*. There followed a series of productions which have now achieved the status of classics – Peter Weiss's *Marat/Sade* (1964), *US* (1966), and *A Midsummer Night's Dream* (1970). In 1970 Brook left the UK to found the International Centre for Performance Research in Paris, with the help of a million-dollar grant from the Ford Foundation. This international company of performers, whose 'disunity is their unity', went on to develop *Orghast at Persepolis* (1971), played in the classical ruins in Iran, the *Ik* (1975), and others, culminating in a performance of the Indian epic *Mahabharata* (1985), which toured the world. His latest piece of theatrical research has been *The Man Who* (1993), based on the neurological discoveries of Oliver Sacks.

   Brook's restless eclecticism has meant that he cannot easily be classified, but he shares with the Polish director Grotowski a continual search for some form of universal understanding based on theatre. In spite of criticism from some non-Western sources he remains the major British director of our time, and one of the few whose work is always an occasion for celebration, and a source of inspiration to others.

   This essay introduces his concept of deadly theatre, or the theatre of which we see most, against which all Brook's variety is juxtaposed.

Reader cross-references

Artaud – an early inspiration, for a search for universal meaning
Beck – North American notion of collective collaboration
Benjamin – another critique of the dead hand of bourgeois theatre
Bharucha – a contrary view of the purpose of tradition, who also takes issue
   with Brook

Grotowski – a contemporary explorer of theatre whom Brook acknowledged as unique

Schechner – for another, North America, view of intercultural experiment

Further reading

Reeves, G. and Hunt, A. (1993) *Peter Brook*, Cambridge: Cambridge University Press.

Selbourne, D. (1982) *The Making of A Midsummer Night's Dream*, London: Methuen.

Williams, D. (1988) *Peter Brook, a Theatrical Casebook*, London: Methuen.

Williams, D. (ed.) (1991) *Peter Brook and the Mahabharata*, London: Routledge.

Chapter 14

Trisha Brown

TRISHA BROWN:
AN INTERVIEW

M Y DANCE TRAINING began in Aberdeen, Washington, when I studied with a teacher, Marion Hageage, whose background was primarily musical. I studied acrobatics — that was my long suit — tap, ballet and jazz dance. I was in my early teens at this time and my class was at the end of the day when the instructor was tired and, sharing her privacy with me, would dance around in a slow jazzy manner punctuated with meaningful silences and high kicks. I tagged along as fast as I could go, memorizing the outflow. These dances, which could best be categorized as Hollywood style dance routines, were performed in local recitals and hospitals. Later I attended Mills College and became a dance major by the end of the first year. The training incorporated Martha Graham technique and Louis Horst composition which culminated in a senior recital. I also spent a couple of summers at Connecticut College studying with Louis Horst, José Limón and Merce Cunningham. Doris Humphrey was there also, but I was not advanced enough to be in her classes. After graduation from Mills College I went to Reed College to teach and started the dance department. I stayed there two years, but exhausted conventional teaching methods after the first few months and then became involved with improvisational teaching. During this period I began developing my own dance vocabulary.

In the summer of 1959, I joined Simone Forti, Yvonne Rainer and other dancers at Anna Halprin's six week workshop in Marin County, California. Anna was working with the choreographic idea of task, such as sweeping with a broom – an ordinary action, organized by an ordinary activity and performed as if you were not performing but off alone somewhere, sweeping up. There was also experimentation with sound – verbalization and singing as a material, and beyond that, defined or wide open improvisations night and day by very talented people. Improvisation has been a rich and continuous involvement for me. If you stand back and think about what you are going to do before you do it, there is likely to be a strenuous editing process that stymies the action. On the other hand, if you set yourself loose in an improvisational form, you have to make solutions very quickly and you learn how to. That is the excitement of improvisation. If, however, you just turn the lights out and go gah-gah in circles, that would be therapy or catharsis or your happy hour, but if in the beginning you set a structure and decide to deal with X, Y and Z materials in a certain way, nail it down even further and say you can only walk forward, you cannot use your voice or you have to do 195 gestures before you hit the wall at the other end of the room, that is an improvisation within set boundaries. That is the principle, for example, behind jazz. The musicians may improvise but they have a limitation in the structure just as improvisation in dance does. This is what I would call structured improvisation because it locates you in time and place with content. The workshop was invaluable because Anna Halprin has a rampant imagination and puts a high priority on originality and self-exposition.

Six months or a year later I had pretty much burned up everything on the West Coast and Simone Forti urged me to come to New York. When I got there I continued to improvise with Simone and Dick Levine, and began taking Robert Dunn's class at Merce Cunningham's studio. Robert Dunn was applying the Cagian concepts of chance and indeterminacy to dance. One of Bob's most important contributions was the method of analysis of the work shown. After presenting a dance, each choreographer was asked, 'How did you make that dance?' The students were inventing forms rather than using the traditional theme and development or narrative, and the discussion that followed applied nonevaluative criticism to the movement itself and the choreographic structure as well as investigating the disparity between the two simultaneous experiences, what the artist was making and what the audience saw. This procedure illuminated the interworkings of the dances and minimized value judgements of the choreographer, which for me meant permission, permission to go ahead and do what I wanted to do or had to do – to try out an idea of borderline acceptability. I remember his giving an assignment to make a three-minute dance and that was the whole assignment. This assignment was totally nonspecific except for duration, and the ambiguity provoked days of sorting through possibilities trying to figure out what time meant, was 60 seconds the only difference between three minutes and four minutes, how do you stop something, why, what relation does time have to movement, and on and on. Dick Levine taught himself to cry and did so for the full time period while I held a stopwatch instructed by him to shout just before the time elapsed, 'Stop it! Stop it! Cut it out!' both of us ending at exactly three minutes. That dance is a good example of the practice of substituting one medium, in this case acting/crying, to solve a dance problem.

I definitely do want my audiences to understand my work although I have done my share of dances that were difficult for the general public. In the 1960's, my audiences were small but consistent and knowledgeable. We grew up together. Now my audiences are larger, informed through literature and aware that some dance is not entertainment.

There was improvisation in 1969 where I asked the audience to yell 'yellowbelly' which means 'coward' in Aberdeen, Washington; I performed the piece twice. The first time they were very sweet about it so I stopped and I asked them to yell in a nasty way and they did. They started jeering and yelling. I was improvising and absolutely frozen and I have not any idea what I did, although I had a few amorphous possibilities prepared. When I stopped, they really jeered at me, so I started up again and finally we both stopped. It was terrifying because it was confronting the performer's fear that you will get up before an audience and forget what you are doing. The point was to set up precisely that situation and it certainly tested both me and the audience. The second time I performed it in Rome and had them yell in Italian. It was a more sophisticated audience and they just would not yell. When they sat back and refused to yell, I refused to move. Then when someone would yell, I would start and stop moving when they stopped yelling. It was the most amazing relationship until they got very angry and all began to yell. Then I performed my dance which was an improvisation, for this time I had absolutely nothing prepared, nothing at all. I started spinning and continued until I was totally dizzy, then I stopped and tried to do a beautiful articulate dance, but without any success. That relationship to the audience was certainly rough and symbiotic.

The first performance of *Accumulation* (1971) was four and a half minutes long and accompanied by the Grateful Dead's *Uncle John's Band*. Movement one, rotation of the fist with the thumb extended, was begun and repeated seven or eight times. Movement two was added and one and two were repeated eight times. Then movement three was added and one, two and three were repeated, eventually bringing into play the entire body. At first the additions were in numerical sequence but later movements got wedged in between earlier additions and the piece grew in several directions, expanding rather than lengthening. The second performance was in silence and 55 minutes long. I worked in performance to keep the separateness and clarity of each move against the blurring effect of relentless repetition. What went through my mind was, 'This is all there is.' By then another move would be active and 'This is all there is.' The tempo was mainly constant but fluctuated in relation to biological changes of temperature, fatigue and second winds. Since I did not use music, these delicate changes in time could occur. Both the dance and its structure were visible and bare-bone simple. None of the movements had any significance beyond what they were. And I never felt more alive, more expressive or more exposed in performance.

The result of choreography that goes beyond what the audience is familiar with is that you find out what you can do, what your own personal limitation edges are. In that arises the possibility of doing that which is not interesting to your audience, not up until now thought of as acceptable to an audience. There is also a question of tension in the relationships between an audience and a performer. In dances of this sort it seems that you are stretching or pushing or rather raising the level of tension considerably. In *Primary Accumulation* (1972) a supine solo figure systematically accumulates 30 moves in eighteen minutes. The figure rotates 45 degrees each on the last two moves, making a 90 degree turn with the completion of the phrase. The phrase is repeated until a 360 degree turn is achieved, revealing all sides of the dance/dancer in the last two minutes of the dance.

This object-like dance became the material for other dances. In *Group Primary Accumulation*, four dancers placed equidistant from each other in a line from downstage to upstage perform the piece in unison. After the 360 degree turn, two movers enter and transport the performers to new positions that relate to the physical space and also to each other. The movement unavoidably changed in an unconscious theme and variations as the dancers were carried, stacked, stood and separated.

Two dancers lying side by side eighteen inches apart performed *Split Solo*. All of the movements of *Primary Accumulation* that occur on the right side of the body were done by the person on the right and all the movements on the left side of the body by the person on the left. The dance went in and out of looking like one huge fat person or two people having one dance, shifting their roles of doing and waiting. The final version of *Group Primary Accumulation* was for four dancers on four rafts on a lake. The dance/dancers were set free to drift and spin in a continuously changing spatial relationship and inaccurate unison.

My involvement with Judson Memorial Church came out of Dunn's classes and the compositions we were making. Judson was the only place to perform then and that is how it began. The first piece that I showed at Judson was called *Trillium*, a structured improvisation of very high energy movements involving a curious timing and with dumb silences like stopping dead in your tracks. It was a kinesthetic piece, a serial composition where I involved myself in one movement after another accompanied by a tape by Simone Forti. In thinking of the opening section of *Trillium*, I am reminded of working in a studio on a movement exploration of transversing the three positions sitting, standing and lying. I broke those actions down into their basic mechanical structure, finding the places of rest, power, momentum and peculiarity. I went over and over the material, eventually accelerating and mixing it up to the degree that lying down was done in the air.

In *Rulegame 5* (1964) there were seven rows of masking tape laid down in an area approximately 21 feet by 21 feet. Five performers proceed along the above prescribed path, changing height in equal amounts, from highest (erect) on row one to lowest (prone) on row seven. The performers may pass other performers parallel to themselves only if the relationship of high, middle and low is correct, and if not, they speak to each other and make the proper adjustments. The scheme served as a structure for movement and language improvisation, but could have been performed as a task if the element of time had been dictated.

There is a performance quality that appears in improvisation that did not in memorized dance as it was known up to that date. If you are improvising with a structure your senses are heightened; you are using your wits, thinking, everything is working at once to find the best solution to a given problem under pressure of a viewing audience. In contrast, at that time, modern dancers glazed over their eyes, knuckling down behind that glaze to concentrate and deliver their best performance – an understandable habit but unfortunately resulting in the robot-look. At Judson, the performers looked at each other and the audience, they breathed audibly, ran out of breath, sweated, talked things over. They began behaving more like human beings, revealing what was thought of as deficiencies as well as their skills.

Another piece I made at this time, *A String*, was composed of three parts. To make the third section titled *Inside* (1966), I stood facing a wall in my studio at a distance of about twelve feet and, beginning at the extreme left, I read the wall as a score while moving across the room to the far right. Any question that arose about the speed, shape, duration or quality of a move was determined by the visual information on the wall. An odd distribution of actions and gestures emanated from the architectural collection of alcove, door, peeling paint and pipes. After finishing the first wall, I repositioned myself in the same way for the second wall and repeated the procedure for the third and fourth. Therefore, in performance, I moved along the edge of the room, facing out, on the knee caps of the audience, who were placed in a rectangular seating formation duplicating the interior of my studio. I was marking the edge of the space, leaving the center of the room empty, the movement concretely specific to me, abstract to the audience. And I looked at them. I added the problem of looking at the audience, not 'with meaning,' but with eyes open and seeing.

In these early works, I used trained dancers as well as non-trained dancers. My own style of movement in, say, *Trillium* was too personal and difficult to teach to others and therefore remained solo material. In group pieces centering around tasks, I used untrained dancers – ordinary people who were well aligned and physically alert. Some trained dancers, in an effort to appear bigger than life and project across those footlights, puffed themselves up with tension and a dramatic delivery which stylized the movement, making it impossible for them to do an ordinary activity like walking. I am using trained dancers now because my work has become technically so demanding that a non-dancer could not do it.

Ordinary movement includes climbing, falling, leaning and balancing. In *Planes* (1968), the first of a series of dances that came to be known as equipment pieces, I built a thirteen foot by eighteen foot wall with holes cut out at equal intervals across its surface which functioned as hand and footholds, enabling three dancers to continuously turn, spin and climb in slow motion and all directions while appearing to be free-falling. The audience's perspective was altered. The back wall of the stage became like the floor of the auditorium.

I continued to find or construct the environment as well as the dance. *Man Walking Down the Side of a Building* was exactly like the title – seven stories. A natural activity under the stress of an unnatural setting. Gravity reneged. Vast scale. Clear order. You start at the top, walk straight down, stop at the bottom. All those soupy questions that arise in the process of selecting abstract movement according to the modern dance tradition – what, when, where and how – are solved in collaboration between choreographer and place. If you eliminate all those eccentric possibilities that the choreographic imagination can conjure and just have a person walk down an aisle, then you see the movement as the activity. The paradox of one action working against another is very interesting to me, and is illustrated by *Walking Down the Side of a Building* where you have gravity working one way on the body and my intention to have a naturally walking person working in another way.

Floor of the Forest (1969) was performed in a twelve foot by fourteen foot pipe frame across which were tied ropes densely threaded with clothes – sleeves were woven beneath pant legs forming a solid rectangular surface. The frame was suspended horizontally at eye level in the center of an empty room. Two people dressed and undressed their way through it. It was done as naturally as it could be done. A normally vertical activity performed horizontally and reshaped by the vertical pull of gravity. It was strenuous. Great strain and effort to support the body weight while negotiating buttons and zippers. We rested at times and when we rested hanging down, an article of clothing became a hammock. The audience ducked down to see the performers suspended or climbing below the frame or stretched upward to see the activity above. They had to choose which part of the dance to look at. The second time *Floor of the Forest* was performed (1969), the frame was suspended overhead and a full-scale rummage sale took place below. The audience trying on clothes below is added to the horizontal dressing and undressing of the performers above. The audience had to choose between looking up at the dance or down at a bargain or drop back to the outside edge of the room in order to take it all in. The clothes were familiar to me, I had collected them from friends. The piece, therefore, continues to this day through my seeing or being told of one of those bargains.

Pure movement is a movement that has no other connotations. It is not functional or pantomimic. Mechanical body actions like bending, straightening or rotating would qualify as pure movement providing the context was neutral. I use pure movements, a kind of breakdown of the body's capabilities. I also use quirky, personal gestures, things that have specific meaning to me but probably appear abstract to others. I may perform an everyday gesture so that the audience does not know whether I have stopped dancing or not and, carrying that irony further, I seek to disrupt their expectations by setting up an action to travel left and then cut right at the last moment unless I imagine they have caught on to me, in which case I might stand still. I make plays on movement, like rhyming or echoing an earlier gesture in another part of the body at a later time and perhaps out of kilter. I turn phrases upside down, reverse them or suggest an action and then not complete it, or else overstate it altogether. I make radical changes in a mundane way. I use weight, balance, momentum and physical actions like falling, pushing, etc. I say things to my company like, 'Toss your knees over there,' or, 'Start the phrase and then on the second count start it again,' or 'Do it and get off it.' I put all these movements together without transitions. I do not promote the next movement with a preceding transition and, therefore, I do not build up to something. If I do build up, I might end it with another build-up. I often return to a neutral standing position between moves; it is for me a way of measuring where I have been and where I am going. An even pulse (without musical accompaniment) does the same thing with time. A pulse brackets a unit of time that can be measured, divided, filled up completely or partially. If I am beginning to sound like a bricklayer with a sense of humour, you are beginning to understand my work.

I was thinking of *Locus* (1975) while talking about movement. *Locus* is organized around 27 points located on an imaginary cube of space slightly larger than the standing figure in a stride position. The points were correlated to the alphabet and a written statement, 1 being A, 2, B.

T	R	I	S	H	A		B	R	O	W	N	
20	18	9	19	8	1	27	2	18	15	23	14	27

W	A	S		B	O	R	N		I	N
23	1	19	27	2	15	18	14	27	9	14

I made four sections each three minutes long that move through, touch, look at, jump over, or do something about each point in the series, either one point at a time or clustered. There is spatial repetition, but not gestural. The dance does not observe front, it revolves. The cube base is multiplied to form a grid of five units wide and four deep. There are opportunities to move from one cube base to another without distorting the movement. By exercising these options, we travel. The choices of facing, placing and section are made in performance by the four performers. This describes the structure of the dance – you have to fill it in with the kinds of movement mentioned before.

The most recent accumulation entitled *Pyramid* (1975) also has a score. It is based on nine ascending and descending time units of nine counts in five measures. 1, 2, 3, 2, 1. The first fifteen measures are accumulated. When sixteen is added, one is dropped; add seventeen, drop two . . .; we continue this process up to 30 at which point we de-accumulate by dropping sixteen, return to 30, drop seventeen, return to 30, etc. until the piece erases itself. The four performers made their own movement. At this moment, I am working on a piece *Solo Olos* in which I am making a natural progression of non-functional movement. By natural progression I mean that movement B will be the simplest most obvious next move after A; C after B. When the sequence passes through a neutral position, there will be more than one obvious next move generating B1, B2 and more – an intersection of several directions. The progression and its alternatives will be executed forward and backward, and wherever possible to the left and right. The dancers will work side by side, back up, rejoin, wait, branch off, overlap, bunch, delay or pass in performance.

■ ■ ■

Source

Brown, T. and Livet, A. (1978) 'Trisha Brown: Edited Transcript of an Interview with Trisha Brown', *Contemporary Dance*, ed. A. Livet, New York: Abbeville: 44–54.

126

Trisha Brown (1936–)

American dancer and choreographer. She studied with Ann Halprin (1959), then with Robert Dunn at Merce Cunningham's New York Studio (1960). She was a founder member of Judson Dance Theatre (1962–66) and then of the Grand Union. She established the Trisha Brown Company in 1970.

Her choreography spans a huge range of improvisational and compositional means. In the early 1960s she explored various improvisational structures in *Trillium* (1962), *Rulegame 5* (1964) and *Yellowbelly* (1969). From 1968 she made a number of *Equipment Pieces* where her dancers were denied a 'natural' relationship with gravity by the intervention of various ropes, pullies and mechanical devices: *Rummage Sale* (1971), *Floor of the Forest* (1971) and, in particular, *Man Walking Down the Side of a Building* (1969). The last consisted precisely of what its title suggested. During the early 1970s she made a number of analytical dance pieces, notably the series based on accumulation as a process, including *Accumulation* (1971), *Group Accumulation* (1973), and culminating in *Accumulation with Talking plus Water Motor* (1978).

Brown has extended her investigations of choreographic method in collaboration with many visual artists and musicians, dating back to early explorations at Judson. Notable amongst these multifaceted theatre works have been *Glacial Decoy* (1979) with Robert Rauschenberg, *Son of Gone Fishing* (1981) with Donald Judd and Robert Ashley, and *Set and Reset* (1983) with Robert Rauschenberg and Laurie Anderson. Rauschenberg contributed visual presentations again for *Astral Convertible* (1989) and *Foray Forêt* (1990).

This edited transcript details key points in her career to 1978. It is especially valuable for its lucid description of her experiments into choreographic process. It details precisely what strategies she set up, and why she made the choices of process that she did. It shows her concern for herself as a performer, for performance and for her audience. Her description of the performance quality given by structured improvisation is exemplary, as is her description of her use of 'movement'.

Reader cross-references

Anderson – collaborated on the music for *Set and Reset*

Banes – a critical context to her work

Bausch – a contrasting European approach to dance making

Beck – a theatre contemporary with a different approach to the same times

Boal – comparison with a director working with non-theatrical processes and spaces

Cage and **Glass** – musicians working with concerns for structure and process

Hikikata – an antithetical approach to the body

Humphrey and **Wigman** – to compare with early modern dancers

Rainer – also at Judson, but whose strategies, although about process, were different.

Further reading

Banes, S. (1987) 'Gravity and Levity', *Terpsichore in Sneakers: Post-Modern Dance*, 2nd edition, Middletown: Conn.: Wesleyan University Press.

Brunel, C., Brown, T. and Delahaye, G. (1987) *Trisha Brown*, Paris: Editions Bougé.

Sayre, H.M. (1989) 'Tracing Dance: Collaboration and the New Gesamtkunstwerk', *The Object of Performance: The American Avant-Garde Since 1970*, Chicago: University of Chicago Press: 101–144.

Chapter 15

John Cage

FOUR STATEMENTS
ON THE DANCE

This article was part of a series, Percussion Music and Its Relation to the Modern Dance, *that appeared in* Dance Observer *in 1939. It was written in Seattle where I had organized a concert-giving percussion ensemble.*

Goal: New Music, New Dance

Percussion music is revolution. Sound and rhythm have too long been submissive to the restrictions of nineteenth-century music. Today we are fighting for their emancipation. Tomorrow, with electronic music in our ears, we will hear freedom.

Instead of giving us new sounds, the nineteenth-century composers have given us endless arrangements of the old sounds. We have turned on radios and always known when we were tuned to a symphony. The sound has always been the same, and there has not been even a hint of curiosity as to the possibilities of rhythm. For interesting rhythms we have listened to jazz.

At the present stage of revolution, a healthy lawlessness is warranted. Experiment must necessarily be carried on by hitting anything – tin pans, rice bowls, iron pipes – anything we can lay our hands on. Not only hitting, but rubbing,

smashing, making sound in every possible way. In short, we must explore the materials of music. What we can't do ourselves will be done by machines and electrical instruments which we will invent.

The conscientious objectors to modern music will, of course, attempt everything in the way of counterrevolution. Musicians will not admit that we are making music; they will say that we are interested in superficial effects, or, at most, are imitating Oriental or primitive music. New and original sounds will be labeled as 'noise.' But our common answer to every criticism must be to continue working and listening, making music with its materials, sound and rhythm, disregarding the cumbersome, top-heavy structure of musical prohibitions.

These prohibitions removed, the choreographer will be quick to realize a great advantage to the modern dance: the simultaneous composition of both dance and music. The materials of dance, already including rhythm, require only the addition of sound to become a rich, complete vocabulary. The dancer should be better equipped than the musician to use this vocabulary, for more of the materials are already at his command. Some dancers have made steps in this direction by making simple percussion accompaniments. Their use of percussion, unfortunately, has not been constructive. They have followed the rhythm of their own dance movement, accentuated it and punctuated it with percussion, but they have not given the sound its own and special part in the whole composition. They have made the music identical with the dance but not cooperative with it. Whatever method is used in composing the materials of the dance can be extended to the organization of the musical materials. The form of the music-dance composition should be a necessary working together of all materials used. The music will then be more than an accompaniment; it will be an integral part of the dance.

When I was growing up in California there were two things that everyone assumed were good for you. There were, of course, others – spinach and oatmeal, for instance – but right now I'm thinking of sunshine and orange juice. When we lived at Ocean Park, I was sent out every morning to the beach where I spent the day building rolly-coasters in the sand, complicated downhill tracks with tunnels and inclines upon which I rolled a small hard rubber ball. Every day toward noon I fainted because the sun was too much for me. When I fainted I didn't fall down, but I couldn't see; there were flocks of black spots wherever I looked. I soon learned to find my way in that blindness to a hamburger stand where I'd ask for something to eat. Sitting in the shade, I'd come to. It took me much longer, about thirty-five years in fact, to learn that orange juice was not good for me either.

Before studying Zen, men are men and mountains are mountains. While studying Zen, things become confused. After studying Zen, men are men and mountains are mountains. After telling this, Dr. Suzuki was asked, 'What is the difference between before and after?' He said, 'No difference, only the feet are a little bit off the ground.'

The following piece was printed in Dance Observer *in 1944.*

Grace and Clarity

The strength that comes from firmly established art practices is not present in the modern dance today. Insecure, not having any clear direction, the modern dancer is willing to compromise and to accept influences from other more rooted art manners, enabling one to remark that certain dancers are either borrowing from or selling themselves to Broadway, others are learning from folk and Oriental arts, and many are either introducing into their work elements of the ballet, or, in an all-out effort, devoting themselves to it. Confronted with its history, its former power, its present insecurity, the realization is unavoidable that the strength the modern dance once had was not impersonal but was intimately connected with and ultimately dependent on the personalities and even the actual physical bodies of the individuals who imparted it.

The techniques of the modern dance were once orthodox. It did not enter a dancer's mind that they might be altered. To add to them was the sole privilege of the originators.

Intensive summer courses were the scenes of the new dispensations, reverently transmitted by the master-students. When the fanatically followed leaders began, and when they continued, to desert their own teachings (adapting chiefly balletish movements to their own rapidly-growing-less-rigorous techniques), a general and profound insecurity fell over the modern dance.

Where any strength now exists in the modern dance, it is, as before, in isolated personalities and physiques. In the case of the young, this is unfortunate; for, no matter how impressive and revelatory their expressed outlooks on life are, they are overshadowed, in the minds of audiences, and often, understandably, in the dancers' own minds, by the more familiar, more respected, and more mature older personalities.

Personality is a flimsy thing on which to build an art. (This does not mean that it should not enter into an art, for, indeed, that is what is meant by the word *style*.) And the ballet is obviously not built on such an ephemeron, for, if it were, it would not at present thrive as it does, almost devoid of interesting personalities and certainly without the contribution of any individual's message or attitude toward life.

That the ballet *has* something seems reasonable to assume. That what it has is what the modern dance needs is here expressed as an opinion.

It is seriously to be doubted whether *tour jeté, entrechat six*, or *sur les pointes* (in general) are needed in the modern dance. Even the prettiness and fanciness of these movements would not seem to be requisite. Also, it is not true that the basis of the ballet lies in glittering costumes and sets, for many of the better ballets appear year after year in drab, weather-beaten accoutrements.

Ballets like *Les Sylphides, Swan Lake*, almost any *Pas de Deux* or *Quatre*, and currently, the exceptional *Danses Concertantes* have a strength and validity quite beyond and separate from the movements involved, whether or not they are done with style (expressed personality), the ornamented condition of the stage, quality of costumery, sound of the music, or any other particularities, including those of content. Nor does the secret lie in that mysterious quantity, form. (The forms of the ballet are mostly dull; symmetry is maintained practically without question.)

Good or bad, with or without meaning, well dressed or not, the ballet is always clear in its rhythmic structure. Phrases begin and end in such a way that *anyone* in the audience knows when they begin and end, and breathes accordingly. It may seem at first thought that rhythmic structure is not of primary importance. However, a dance, a poem, a piece of music (any of the time arts) occupies a length of time, and the manner in which this length of time is divided first into large parts and then into phrases (or built up from phrases to form eventual larger parts) is the work's very life structure. The ballet is in possession of a tradition of clarity of its rhythmic structure. Essential devices for bringing this about have been handed down generation after generation. These particular devices, again, are not to be borrowed from the ballet: they are private to it. But the function they fulfill is not private; it is, on the contrary, universal.

Oriental dancing, for instance, is clear in its phraseology. It has its own devices for obtaining it. Hot jazz is never unclear rhythmically. The poems of Gerard Manley Hopkins, with all their departure from tradition, enable the reader to breathe with them. The modern dance, on the other hand, is rarely clear.

When a modern dancer has followed music that was clear in its phrase structure, the dance has had a tendency to be clear. The widespread habit of choreographing the dance first, and obtaining music for it later, is not in itself here criticized. But the fact that modern choreographers have been concerned with things other than clarity of rhythmic structure has made the appearance of it, when the dance-first-music-later method was used, both accidental and isolated. This has led to a disregard of rhythmic structure even in the case of dancing to music already written, for, in a work like Martha Graham's *Deaths and Entrances*, an audience can know where it is in relation to the action only through repeated seeings and the belying action of memory. On the other hand, Martha Graham and Louis Horst together were able to make magnificently clear and moving works like their *Frontier*, which works, however, stand alarmingly alone in the history of the modern dance.

The will to compromise, mentioned above, and the admirable humility implied in the willingness to learn from other art manners is adolescent, but it is much closer to maturity than the childish blind following of leaders that was characteristic of the modern dance several years ago. If, in receiving influences from the outside, the modern dance is satisfied with copying, or adapting to itself, surface particularities (techniques, movements, devices of any kind), it will die before it reaches maturity; if, on the other hand, the common denominator of the completely developed time arts, the secret of art life, is discovered by the modern dance, Terpsichore will have a new and rich source of worshippers.

With clarity of rhythmic structure, *grace* forms a duality. Together they have a relation like that of body and soul. Clarity is cold, mathematical, inhuman, but basic and earthy. Grace is warm, incalculable, human, opposed to clarity, and like the air. Grace is not here used to mean prettiness; it is used to mean the play with and against the clarity of the rhythmic structure. The two are always present together in the best works of the time arts, endlessly, and life-givingly, opposed to each other.

'In the finest specimens of versification, there seems to be a perpetual conflict between the law of the verse and the freedom of the language, and each is incessantly, though insignificantly, violated for the purpose of giving effect to the other. The best poet is not he whose verses are the most easily scanned, and whose phraseology is the commonest in its materials, and the most direct in its arrangement; but rather he whose language combines the greatest imaginative accuracy with the most elaborate and sensible metrical organisation, and who, in his verse, preserves everywhere the living sense of the metre, not so much by unvarying obedience to, as by innumerable small departures from, its *modulus*.' (Coventry Patmore, *Prefatory Study on English Metrical Law*, 1879, pp. 12–13.)

The 'perpetual conflict' between clarity and grace is what makes hot jazz hot. The best performers continually anticipate or delay the phrase beginnings and endings. They also, in their performances, treat the beat or pulse, and indeed, the measure, with grace: putting more or fewer icti within the measure's limits than are expected (similar alterations of pitch and timbre are also customary), contracting or extending the duration of the unit. This, not syncopation, is what pleases the hep-cats.

Hindu music and dancing are replete with grace. This is possible because the rhythmic structure in Hindu time arts is highly systematized, has been so for many ages, and every Hindu who enjoys listening to music or looking at the dance is familiar with the laws of tala. Players, dancers, and audience enjoy hearing and seeing the laws of the rhythmic structure now observed and now ignored.

This is what occurs in a beautifully performed classic or neo-classic ballet. And it is what enables one to experience pleasure in such a performance, despite the fact that such works are relatively meaningless in our modern society. That one should, today, have to see *Swan Lake* or something equally empty of contemporary meaning in order to experience the pleasure of observing clarity and grace in the dance, is, on its face, lamentable. Modern society needs, as usual, and now desperately needs, a strong modern dance.

The opinion expressed here is that clarity of rhythmic structure with grace are essential to the time arts, that together they constitute an aesthetic (that is, they lie under and beneath, over and above, physical and personal particularities), and that they rarely occur in the modern dance; that the latter has no aesthetic (its strength having been and being the personal property of its originators and best exponents), that, in order for it to become strong and useful in society, mature in itself, the modern dance must clarify its rhythmic structure, then enliven it with grace, and so get itself a theory, the common, universal one about what is beautiful in a time art.

....

In Zen they say: If something is boring after two minutes, try it for four. If still boring, try it for eight, sixteen, thirty-two, and so on. Eventually one discovers that it's not boring at all but very interesting.

At the New School once I was substituting for Henry Cowell, teaching a class in Oriental music. I had told him I didn't know anything about the subject. He said, 'That's all right. Just go where the records are. Take one out. Play it and then discuss it with the class.' Well, I took out the first record. It was an LP of a Buddhist service. It began with a short microtonal chant with sliding tones, then soon settled into a single loud reiterated percussive beat. This noise continued relentlessly for about fifteen minutes with no perceptible variation. A lady got up and screamed, and then yelled, 'Take it off. I can't bear it any longer.' I took it off. A man in the class then said angrily, 'Why'd you take it off? I was just getting interested.'

During a counterpoint class at U.C.L.A., Schoenberg sent everybody to the blackboard. We were to solve a particular problem he had given and to turn around when finished so that he could check on the correctness of the solution. I did as directed. He said, 'That's good. Now find another solution.' I did. He said, 'Another.' Again I found one. Again he said, 'Another.' And so on. Finally, I said, 'There are no more solutions.' He said, 'What is the principle underlying all of the solutions?'

I went to a concert upstairs in Town Hall. The composer whose works were being performed had provided program notes. One of these notes was to the effect that there is too much pain in the world. After the concert I was walking along with the composer and he was telling me how the performances had not been quite up to snuff. So I said, 'Well, I enjoyed the music, but I didn't agree with that program note about there being too much pain in the world.' He said, 'What? Don't you think there's enough?' I said, 'I think there's just the right amount.'

Many of my performances with Merce Cunningham and Dance Company are given in academic situations. Now and then the director of the concert series asks for an introductory talk. The following remarks were written for audiences in St. Louis and at Principia College in the autumn of 1956. Then a few months later, in January 1957, they appeared in Dance Observer.

In This Day ...

In this day of TV-darkened homes, a live performance has become something of a rarity, so much so that Aaron Copland recently said a concert is a thing of the past. Nevertheless, I would like to say a few words regarding the new direction taken by our company of dancers and musicians.

Though some of the dances and music are easily enjoyed, others are perplexing to certain people, for they do not unfold along conventional lines. For one thing, there is an independence of the music and dance, which, if one closely observes, is present also in the seemingly usual works. This independence follows from Mr. Cunningham's faith, which I share, that the support of the dance is not to be found in the music but in the dancer himself, on his own two legs, that is, and occasionally on a single one.

Likewise the music sometimes consists of single sounds or groups of sounds which are not supported by harmonies but resound within a space of silence. From this independence of music and dance a rhythm results which is not that of horses' hoofs or other regular beats but which reminds us of a multiplicity of events in time and space – stars, for instance, in the sky, or activities on earth viewed from the air.

We are not, in these dances and music, saying something. We are simple-minded enough to think that if we were saying something we would use words. We are rather doing something. The meaning of what we do is determined by each one who sees and hears it. At a recent performance of ours at Cornell College in Iowa, a student turned to a teacher and said, 'What does it mean?' The teacher's reply was, 'Relax, there are no symbols here to confuse you. Enjoy yourself!' I may add there are no stories and no psychological problems. There is simply an activity of movement, sound, and light. The costumes are all simple in order that you may see the movement.

The movement is the movement of the body. It is here that Mr. Cunningham focuses his choreographic attention, not on the facial muscles. In daily life people customarily observe faces and hand gestures, translating what they see into psychological terms. Here, however, we are in the presence of a dance which utilizes the entire body, requiring for its enjoyment the use of your faculty of kinesthetic sympathy. It is this faculty we employ when, seeing the flight of birds, we ourselves, by identification, fly up, glide, and soar.

The activity of movement, sound, and light, we believe, is expressive, but what it expresses is determined by each one of you – who is right, as Pirandello's title has it, if he thinks he is.

The novelty of our work derives therefore from our having moved away from simply private human concerns towards the world of nature and society of which all of us are a part. Our intention is to affirm this life, not to bring order out of chaos nor to suggest improvements in creation, but simply to wake up to the very life we're living, which is so excellent once one gets one's mind and one's desires out of its way and lets it act of its own accord.

....

When Vera Williams first noticed that I was interested in wild mushrooms, she told her children not to touch any of them because they were all deadly poisonous. A few days later she bought a steak at Martino's and decided to serve it smothered with mushrooms. When she started to cook the mushrooms, the children all stopped whatever they were doing and watched her attentively. When she served dinner, they all burst into tears.

One day I went to the dentist. Over the radio they said it was the hottest day of the year. However, I was wearing a jacket, because going to a doctor has always struck me as a somewhat formal occasion. In the midst of his work, Dr. Heyman stopped and said, 'Why don't you take your jacket off?' I said, 'I have a hole in my shirt and that's why I have my jacket on.' He said, 'Well, I have a hole in my sock, and, if you like, I'll take my shoes off.'

This piece appeared in Dance Magazine, *November 1957. The two pages were given me in dummy form by the editors. The number of words was given by chance operations. Imperfections in the sheets of paper upon which I worked gave the position in space of the fragments of text. That position is different in this printing, for it is the result of working on two other sheets of paper, of another size and having their own differently placed imperfections.*

2 Pages, 122 Words on Music and Dance

To obtain the value
of a sound, a movement,
measure from zero. (Pay   A bird flies.
attention to what it is,
just as it is.)

Slavery is abolished.

the woods

A sound has no legs to stand on.

The world is teeming: anything
can happen.

movement

sound

Points in   Activities which are different

time, in   love   happen in a time which is a space:

space   mirth   are each central, original.

                   the heroic

                   wonder

The emotions   tranquillity   are in the audience.

                   fear

                   anger   The telephone rings.

                   sorrow   Each person is in the best seat.

                   disgust

Is there a glass of water?   War begins at any moment.

Each now is the time, the space.

lights

    inaction?

                  Are eyes open?

Where the bird flies, fly.   ears?

■   ■   ■

139

Source

Cage, J. (1961, 1973) 'Four Statements on the Dance', *Silence*, Middletown, Conn.: Wesleyan Univ. Press: 87–97.

'Goal: New Music, New Dance' first published in 1939 in *Dance Observer* as part of a series, 'Percussion Music and Its Relation to Modern Dance'.

'Grace and Clarity' first published in 1944 in *Dance Observer*.

'In This Day . . .' written in 1956 and published in 1957 in *Dance Observer*.

'2 Pages, 122 Words on Music and Dance' first published in *Dance Magazine*, November 1957.

John Cage (1912–93)

A composer and philosopher who used music as both a philosophic and an aesthetic medium, and who saw in performance a mode of enlarging our political as well as our aural horizons. His work spans the period from 1938 to 1993, during which time he worked extensively with the American dancer and choreographer Merce Cunningham. He was musical director of the Cunningham company from 1944, and their collaborations have provided some of the most stimulating formalist dance of the century.

Much of Cage's music investigates the medium, and questions assumptions about what is or what is not acceptable. His most famous composition, *4'33"* (1952), offers the listener a silent piano around which the ambient sounds provide the music, which is thus shaped by the individual listener. In 1946 he wrote *Theatre Piece*, which allows the performers to write their own scenario within prescribed time limits, using the notions of chance which Cage took from the Chinese. He was also much influenced by the Dada artists, and by his friendship with Marcel Duchamp.

The first of the four statements was written on the US West Coast in 1939, after he had studied with another American composer, Henry Cowell. The others, in 1944, 1956 and 1957 give a twenty-year span of his ideas on dance. It could be said that Cage's radical questioning of musical language parallels Beckett's reduction of the play text, and that his explorations into the process of music making may be usefully compared to Brecht's contemporaneous quest for a new acting technique. Cage wrote and delivered lectures for a large part of his life, and in many of them used similar rhythmical structures to those of his musical compositions. His unstated connections between seemingly disparate ideas reflect his lifelong interest in Zen Buddhism; an interest which led to connections between music and dance, and between the visual and performing arts, which influenced generations of performing artists. His writing is lucid, simple, and often startling. By making surprising connections he forces us to contemplate the obvious in a new light.

Reader cross-references

Barthes – the quality of music
Benjamin – for a different, contemporary, European perspective on art and its purpose
Brown – a dancer working with similar concerns for structure and processes
Cunningham – his major artistic collaborator
Eisler – a contemporary European theatre composer
Glass – another US view of contemporary music
Humphrey – a later statement on modern dance
Rainer – a later manifesto on dance
Schechner – interest in non-Western forms

Further reading

Cage, J. (1968) *A Year from Monday*, Middletown, Conn.: Weslyan University Press.
Kostelanetz, R. (ed.) (1970) *John Cage*, New York: Praeger.

141

Chapter 16

Edward Gordon Craig

THE ACTOR AND THE
ÜBER-MARIONETTE

NAPOLEON is reported to have said: 'In life there is much that is un-worthy which in art should be omitted; much of doubt and vacillation; and all should disappear in the representation of the hero. *We should see him as a statue in which the weakness and the tremors of the flesh are no longer percep-tible.*' And not only Napoleon, but Ben Jonson, Lessing, Edmund Scherer, Hans Christian Andersen, Lamb, Goethe, George Sand, Coleridge, Anatole France, Ruskin, Pater,[1] and I suppose all the intelligent men and women of Europe – one does not speak of Asia, for even the unintelligent in Asia fail to comprehend photographs while understanding art as a simple and clear manifestation – have protested against this *reproduction* of Nature, and with it photographic and weak actuality. They have protested against all this, and the theatrical managers have argued against them energetically, and so we look for the truth to emerge in due time. It is a reasonable conclusion. Do away with the real tree, do away with the reality of delivery, do away with the reality of action, and you tend towards the doing away with the actor. This is what must come to pass in time, and I like to see the managers supporting the idea already. Do away with the actor, and you do away with the means by which a debased stage-realism is produced and flourishes. No longer would there be a living figure to confuse us into connecting actuality and art; no longer a living figure in which the weakness and tremors of the flesh were perceptible.[2]

The actor must go, and in his place comes the inanimate figure – the Über-marionette we may call him, until he has won for himself a better name. Much has been written about the puppet, or marionette. There are some excellent volumes upon him, and he has also inspired several works of art. To-day in his least happy period many people come to regard him as rather a superior doll – and to think he has developed from the doll. This is incorrect. He is a descendant of the stone images of the old temples – he is to-day a rather degenerate form of a god. Always the close friend of children, he still knows how to select and attract his devotees.

When any one designs a puppet on paper, he draws a stiff and comic-looking thing. Such a one has not even perceived what is contained in the idea which we now call the marionette. He mistakes gravity of face and calmness of body for blank stupidity and angular deformity. Yet even modern puppets are extraordinary things. The applause may thunder or dribble, their hearts beat no faster, no slower, their signals do not grow hurried or confused; and, though drenched in a torrent of bouquets and love, the face of the leading lady remains as solemn, as beautiful and as remote as ever. There is something more than a flash of genius in the marionette, and there is something in him more than the flashiness of displayed personality. The marionette appears to me to be the last echo of some noble and beautiful art of a past civilization. But as with all art which has passed into fat or vulgar hands, the puppet has become a reproach. All puppets are now but low comedians.

They imitate the comedians of the larger and fuller blooded stage. They enter only to fall on their back. They drink only to reel, and make love only to raise a laugh. They have forgotten the counsel of their mother the Sphinx. Their bodies have lost their grave grace, they have become stiff. Their eyes have lost that infinite subtlety of seeming to see; now they only stare. They display and jingle their wires and are cocksure in their wooden wisdom. They have failed to remember that their art should carry on it the same stamp of reserve that we see at times on the work of other artists, and that the highest art is that which conceals the craft and forgets the craftsman. Am I mistaken, or is it not the old Greek Traveller of 800 B.C. who, describing a visit to the temple-theatre in Thebes, tells us that he was won to their beauty by their 'noble artificiality'? 'Coming into the House of Visions I saw afar off the fair brown Queen seated upon her throne – her tomb – for both it seemed to me. I sank back upon my couch and watched her symbolic movements. With so much ease did her rhythms alter as with her movements they passed from limb to limb; with such a show of calm did she unloose for us the thoughts of her breast; so gravely and so beautifully did she linger on the statement of her sorrow, that with us it seemed as if no sorrow could harm her; no distortion of body or feature allowed us to dream that she was conquered; the passion and the pain were continually being caught by her hands, held gently, and viewed calmly. Her arms and hands seemed at one moment like a thin warm fountain of water which rose, then broke and fell with all those sweet pale fingers like spray into her lap. It would have been as a revelation of art to us had I not already seen that the same spirit dwelt in the other examples of the art of these Egyptians. This 'Art of Showing and Veiling,' as they call it, is so great a spiritual force in the land that it plays the larger part in their religion. We may learn from it somewhat of the power and the grace of courage, for it is impossible to witness a perform-ance without a sense of physical and spiritual refreshment.' This in 800 B.C. And who knows whether the puppet shall not once again become the faithful medium for the beautiful thoughts of the artist. May we not look forward with hope to that day which shall bring back to us once more the figure, or symbolic creature, made also by the cunning of the artist, so that we can gain once more the 'noble artificiality' which the old writer speaks of? Then shall we no longer be under the cruel influence of the emotional confessions of weakness which are nightly witnessed by the people and which in their turn create in the beholders the very weaknesses which are exhibited. To that end we must study to remake these images – no longer content with a puppet, we must create an über-marionette. The über-marionette will not compete with life – rather will it go beyond it. Its ideal will not be the flesh and blood but rather the body in trance – it will aim to clothe itself with a death-like beauty while exhaling a living spirit. Several times in the course of this essay has a word or two about Death found its way on to the paper – called there by the incessant clamouring of 'Life! Life! Life!' which the realists keep up. And this might be easily mistaken for an affectation, espe-cially by those who have no sympathy or delight in the power and the mysterious joyousness which is in all passionless works of art. If the famous Rubens and the celebrated Raphael made none but passionate and exuberant statements, there were many artists before them and since to whom moder-ation in their art was the most precious of all their aims, and these more than all others exhibit the true masculine manner. The other flamboyant or drooping artists whose works and names catch the eye of to-day do not so much speak like men as bawl like animals, or lisp like women.

The wise, the moderate masters, strong because of the laws to which they swore to remain ever faithful – their names unknown for the most part

— a fine family — the creators of the great and tiny gods of the East and the West, the guardians of those larger times: these all bent their thoughts forward towards the unknown, searching for sights and sounds in that peaceful and joyous country, that they might raise a figure of stone or sing a verse, investing it with that same peace and joy seen from afar, so as to balance all the grief and turmoil here.

In America we can picture these brothers of that family of masters, living in their superb ancient cities, colossal cities, which I ever think of as able to be moved in a single day; cities of spacious tents of silk and canopies of gold under which dwelt their gods; dwellings which contained all the requirements of the most fastidious; those moving cities which, as they travelled from height to plain, over rivers and down valleys, seemed like some vast advancing army of peace. And in each city not one or two men called 'artists' whom the rest of the city looked upon as ne'er-do-well idlers, but many men chosen by the community because of their higher powers of perception — artists. For that is what the title of artist means: one who perceives more than his fellows, and who records more than he has seen. And not the least among those artists was the artist of the ceremonies, the creator of the visions, the minister whose duty it was to celebrate their guiding spirit — the spirit of Motion.

In Asia, too, the forgotten masters of the temples and all that those temples contained have permeated every thought, every mark, in their work with this sense of calm motion resembling death — glorifying and greeting it. In Africa (which some of us think we are but now to civilize) this spirit dwelt, the essence of the perfect civilization. There, too, dwelt the great masters, not individuals obsessed with the idea of each asserting his personality as if it were a valuable and mighty thing, but content because of a kind of holy patience to move their brains and their fingers only in that direction permitted by the law — in the service of the simple truths.

How stern the law was, and how little the artist of that day permitted himself to make an exhibition of his personal feelings, can be discovered by looking at any example of Egyptian art. Look at any limb ever carved by the Egyptians, search into all those carved eyes, they will deny you until the crack of doom. Their attitude is so silent that it is death-like. Yet tenderness is there, and charm is there; prettiness is even there side by side with the force; and love bathes each single work; but gush, emotion, swaggering personality of the artist? — not one single breath of it. Fierce doubts of hope? — not one hint of such a thing. Strenuous determination? — not a sign of it has escaped the artist; none of these confessions — stupidities. Nor pride, nor fear, nor the comic, nor any indication that the artist's mind or hand was for the thousandth part of a moment out of the command of the laws which ruled him. How superb ! This it is to be a great artist; and the amount of emotional outpourings of today and of yesterday are no signs of supreme intelligence, that is to say, are no signs of supreme art. To Europe came this spirit, hovered over Greece, could hardly be driven out of Italy, but finally fled, leaving a little stream of tears – pearls – before us. And we, having crushed most of them, munching them along with the acorns of our food, have gone farther and fared worse, and have prostrated ourselves before the so-called 'great masters,' and have worshipped these dangerous and flamboyant personalities. On an evil day we thought in our ignorance that it was us they were sent to draw; that it was our thoughts they were sent to express; that it was something to do with us that they were putting into their architecture, their music. And so it was we came to demand that we should be able to recognize ourselves in all that they put hand to; that is to say, in their architecture, in their sculpture, in their music, in their painting, and in their poetry we were to figure – and we also reminded them to invite us with the familiar words: 'Come as you are.'

The artists after many centuries have given in, that which we asked them for they have supplied. And so it came about that when this ignorance had driven off the fair spirit which once controlled the mind and hand of the artist, a dark spirit took its place; the happy-go-lucky hooligan in the seat of the law – that is to say, a stupid spirit reigning; and everybody began to shout about Renaissance! while all the time the painters, musicians, sculptors, architects, vied one with the other to supply the demand – that all these things should be so made that all people could recognize them as having something to do with themselves.

Up sprang portraits with flushed faces, eyes which bulged, mouths which leered, fingers itching to come out of their frames, wrists which exposed the pulse; all the colours higgledy-piggledy; all the lines in hubbub, like the ravings of lunacy. Form breaks into panic; the calm and cool whisper of life in trance which once had breathed out such an ineffable hope is heated, fired into a blaze and destroyed, and in its place – *realism*, the blunt statement of life, something everybody misunderstands while recognizing. And all far from the purpose of art: for its purpose is not to reflect the actual facts of this life, because it is not the custom of the artist to walk behind things, having won it as his privilege to walk in front of them – to lead. Rather should life reflect the likeness of the spirit, for it was the spirit which first chose the artist to chronicle its beauty.[3] And in that picture, if the form be that of the living, on account of its beauty and tenderness, the colour for it must be sought from that unknown land of the imagination, and what is that but the land where dwells that which we call Death? So it is not lightly and flippantly that I speak of puppets and their power to retain the beautiful and remote expressions in form and face even when subjected to a patter of praise, a torrent of applause. There are persons who have made a jest of these puppets. 'Puppet' is a term of contempt, though there still remain some who find beauty in these little figures, degenerate though they have become.

To speak of a puppet with most men and women is to cause them to giggle. They think at once of the wires; they think of the stiff hands and the jerky movements; they tell me it is 'a funny little doll.' But let me tell them a few things about these puppets. Let me again repeat that they are the descendants of a great and noble family of Images, images which were indeed made 'in the likeness of God'; and that many centuries ago these figures had a rhythmical movement and not a jerky one; had no need for wires to support them, nor did they speak through the nose of the hidden manipulator. [Poor Punch, I mean no slight to you! You stand alone, dignified in your despair, as you look back across the centuries with painted tears still wet upon your ancient cheeks, and you seem to cry out appealingly to your dog: 'Sister Anne, Sister Anne, is *nobody* coming?' And then with that superb bravado of yours, you turn the force of our laughter (and my tears) upon yourself with the heartrending shriek of 'Oh my nose! Oh my nose! Oh my nose!'] Did you think, ladies and gentlemen, that these puppets were always little things of but a foot high?

Indeed, no! The puppet had once a more generous form than yourselves.

Do you think that he kicked his feet about on a little platform six feet square, made to resemble a little old-fashioned theatre, so that his head almost touched the top of the proscenium? and do you think that he always lived in a little house where the door and windows were as small as a doll's house, with painted windowblinds parted in the centre, and where the flowers of his little garden had courageous petals as big as his head? Try and dispel this idea altogether from your minds, and let me tell you something of his habitation.

In Asia lay his first kingdom. On the banks of the Ganges they built him his home, a vast palace springing from column to column into the air and pouring from column to column down again into the water. Surrounded by gardens spread warm and rich with flowers and cooled by fountains; gardens into which no sounds entered, in which hardly anything stirred. Only in the cool and private chambers of this palace the swift minds of his attendants stirred incessantly. Something they were making which should become him, something to honour the spirit which had given him birth. And then, one day, the ceremony.

In this ceremony he took part; a celebration once more in praise of the Creation; the old thanksgiving, the hurrah for existence, and with it the sterner hurrah for the privilege of the existence to come, which is veiled by the word Death. And during this ceremony there appeared before the eyes of the brown worshippers the symbols of all things on earth and in Nirvana. The symbol of the beautiful tree, the symbol of the hills, the symbols of those rich ores which the hills contained; the symbol of the cloud, of the wind, and of all swift moving things; the symbol of the quickest of moving things, of thought, of remembrance; the symbol of the animal, the symbol of Buddha and of Man – and here he comes, the figure, the puppet at whom you all laugh so much. You laugh at him to-day because none but his weaknesses are left to him. He reflects these from you; but you would not have laughed had you seen him in his prime, in that age when he was called upon to be the symbol of man in the great ceremony, and, stepping forward, was the beautiful figure of our heart's delight. If we should laugh at and insult the memory of the puppet, we should be laughing at the fall that we have brought about in ourselves – laughing at the beliefs and images we have broken. A few centuries later, and we find his home a little the worse for wear. From a temple, it has become, I will not say a theatre, but something between a temple and a theatre, and he is losing his health in it. Something is in the air; his doctors tell him he must be careful. 'And what am I to fear most?' he asks them. They answer him: 'Fear most the vanity of men.' He thinks: 'But that is what I myself have always taught, that we who celebrated in joy this our existence, should have this one great fear. Is it possible that I, one who has ever revealed this truth, should be one to lose sight of it and should myself be one of the first to fall? Clearly some subtle attack is to be made on me. I will keep my eyes upon the heavens.' And he dismisses his doctors and ponders upon it.

And now let me tell you who it was that came to disturb the calm air which surrounded this curiously perfect thing. It is on record that somewhat later he took up his abode on the Far Eastern coast, and there came two women to look upon him. And at the ceremony to which they came he glowed with such earthly splendour and yet such unearthly simplicity, that though he proved an inspiration to the thousand nine hundred and ninety-eight souls who participated in the festival, an inspiration which cleared the mind even as it intoxicated, yet to these two women it proved an intoxication only. He did not see them, his eyes were fixed on the heavens; but he charged them full of a desire too great to be quenched; the desire to stand as the direct symbol of the divinity in man. No sooner thought than done; and arraying themselves as best they could in garments ('like his' they thought), moving with gestures ('like his' they said) and being able to cause wonderment in the minds of the beholders ('even as he does' they cried), they built themselves a temple ('like his,' 'like his'), and supplied the demand of the vulgar, the whole thing a poor parody.

This is on record. It is the first record in the East of the actor. The actor springs from the foolish vanity of two women who were not strong enough to look upon the symbol of godhead without desiring to tamper with it; and the parody proved profitable. In fifty or a hundred years places for such parodies were to be found in all parts of the land.

Weeds, they say, grow quickly, and that wilderness of weeds, the modern theatre, soon sprang up. The figure of the divine puppet attracted fewer and fewer lovers, and the women were quite the latest thing. With the fading of the puppet and the advance of these women who exhibited themselves on the stage in his place, came that darker spirit which is called Chaos, and in its wake the triumph of the riotous personality. Do you see, then, what has made me love and learn to value that which to-day we call the 'puppet' and to detest that which we call 'life' in art? I pray earnestly for the return of the image – the über-marionnette to the Theatre; and when he comes again and is but seen, he will be loved so well that once more will it be possible for the people to return to their ancient joy in ceremonies – once more will Creation be celebrated – homage rendered to existence – and divine and happy intercession made to Death.

Florence: March 1907

Notes

1   Of sculpture Pater writes: 'Its white light, purged from the angry, bloodlike stains of action and passion, reveals, not what is accidental in man, but the god in him, as opposed to man's restless movement.' Again: 'The base of all artistic genius is the power of conceiving humanity in a new, striking, rejoicing way, of putting a happy world of its own construction in place of the meaner world of common days, of generating around itself an atmosphere with a novel power of refraction, selecting, transforming, recombining the images it transmits, according to the choice of the imaginative intellect.' And again: 'All that is accidental, all that distracts the simple effect upon us of the supreme types of humanity, all traces in them of the commonnness of the world, it gradually purges away.'

2   From another point of view, and one not lightly to be either overlooked or discussed, Cardinal Manning, the Englishman, is particularly emphatic when he speaks of the actor's business as necessitating 'the prostitution of a body purified by baptism.'

3   'All forms are perfect in the poet's mind: but these are not abstracted or compounded from Nature; they are from Imagination.' – William Blake.

■   ■   ■

Source

Craig, E.G. (1911, 1956) 'The Actor and the Über-Marionette', *On the Art of the Theatre*, New York: Theatre Arts Books: 80–94.
Written in 1907, first published in 1911.

Edward Gordon Craig (1872–1966)

British theatre designer, actor, and visionary, who became the first British theatre artist to write a book of theatre theory. Craig's life was full of unresolved schemes for designs and performances, though he did manage to create a short-lived theatre school in Florence in 1913. However, his collaboration with Stanislavski on Hamlet (1912), which is well documented, has become a case study in the problems of international collaboration. On the whole Craig was rejected by the British theatre establishment, and was taken up in great measure by the French and the Russians. His ideas bear much resemblance to those of Adolph Appia, whom he met on one occasion. Together their thinking can be said to have influenced generations of European theatre directors. Craig died in France in 1966.

On the Art of the Theatre was published in 1911, and was described by its author as a 'dream put into words'. In it he discusses the nature of theatre as a collaborative art, but yet one where the visual must predominate, and where the performers need to be directed by a master figure who controls what the audience see. Like Meyerhold in Russia, he denied the psychology of traditional Western theatre, and in particular that of naturalism. For Craig a performance was a total kinaesthetic marriage of sound, shape, light, and movement. He saw the Western actor as a fallible, unreliable source, and in this extract he suggests that recourse to non-Western forms might produce the kind of precise visual and aural result that he sought.

His notorious theory of the Über-Marionette masks a passionate desire to question the role of the actor in the totality of the performance. If the theatre of the future is to move beyond the natural, then the actor needs to lose his personality, and as in certain forms of Asian theatre, take on the attributes of a puppet.

Reader cross-references

Appia and **Schlemmer** – parallel design aesthetics
Duncan – an extensive artistic and personal relationship
Meyerhold – a similar insistence on the performer's discipline
Schlemmer – a later, European, visual aesthetic

Stanislavski – the *Hamlet* collaboration
Wilson – later ideas on visual theatre

Further reading

Bablet, D. (1962, 1966) *The Theatre of Edward Gordon Craig*, trans. D. Woodward, London: Heinemann.
Innes, C. (1983) *Edward Gordon Craig*, Cambridge: Cambridge University Press.
Rood, A. (ed.) (1977, 1978) *Gordon Craig on Movement and Dance*, London: Dance Books.
Senelick, L. (1982) *Gordon Craig's Moscow Hamlet*, London: Greenwood Press.

Chapter 17

Merce Cunningham

YOU HAVE TO
LOVE DANCING
TO STICK TO IT

you have to love dancing to stick to it. it gives you nothing back, no manuscripts to store away, no paintings to show on walls and maybe hang in museums, no poems to be printed and sold, nothing but that single fleeting moment· when you feel alive. it is not for unsteady souls.

and though it appeals through the eye to the mind, the mind instantly reject its meaning unless the meaning is betrayed immediately by the action. the mind is not convinced by kinetics

alone, the meaning must be clear, or the language familiar and readily accessible.

the kinesthetic sense is a separate and fortunate behavior. it allows the experience of dancing to be part of all of us.

but clarity is the lowest form of poetry, and language, like all else in our lives, is always changing. our emotions are constantly being propelled by some new face in the sky, some new rocket to the moon, some new sound in the ear, but they are the same emotions.

you do not separate the human being from the actions he does, or the actions which surround him, but you can see what it is like to break these actions up in different ways, to allow the passion, and it is passion, to appear for each person in his own way.

it is hard for many people to accept that dancing has nothing in common with music other than the element of time and division of time. the mind can say how beautiful as the music hints at, or strikes out with color.

but the other extreme can be seen and heard in the music accompanying the movements of the wild animals in the Disney films. it robs them of their instinctual rhythms, and leaves them as caricatures. [s]ure, it is a man-made arrangement, but what isn't?

the sense of human emotion that a dance can give is governed by familiarity with the language, and the elements that act with the language; here those would be music, costume,

you have to love dancing to stick to it. it gives you
nothing back, no manuscripts to store away, no paintings
to show on walls and maybe hang in museums, no poems to
be printed and sold, nothing but that single fleeting
moment when you feel alive. it is not for unsteady souls.

and though it appeals through the eye
to the mind, the mind instantly reject
its meaning unless the meaning is
betrayed immediately by the action.
the mind is not convinced by kinetics

the kinesthetic sense is a separate and fortunate
behavior. it allows the experience of dancing to
be part of all of us.

alone, the meaning must be clear, or
the language familiar and readily
accessible.

but clarity is the lowest form of
poetry, and language, like all else
in our lives, is always changing.
our emotions are constantly being propelled by some new
face in the sky, some new rocket to the moon, some new
sound in the ear, but they are the same emotions.

you do not
separate
the human be-
from the
actions he
does, or
the actions
which sur-
round him,
but you can
see what it
is like to
break these
actions up
in differ-
ent ways, to
allow the
passion, and
it is pass-
sion, to ap-
pear for each
person in his
own way.

it is hard for many people to
accept that dancing has nothing
in common with music other than
the element of time and division
of time. the mind can say how
beautiful as the music hints at,
or strikes out with color.

but the other extreme can be seen
& heard in the musical accompany
ments to the movements of the
wild animals in the Disney films.
it robs them of their instinctual
rhythms, and leaves them as caricatures. ture, it is a man-made
arrangment, but what isn't?

the sense of human emotion that a
dance can give is governed by familiarity with the language, and the
elements that act with the language;
here those would be music, costume,

Original page from *Changes: Notes on Choreography*

154

Source

Cunningham, M. (1968) 'you have to love dancing to stick to it', *Changes: Notes on Choreography*, New York: Something Else.

Merce Cunningham (1919–)

American dancer and choreographer. He danced with Martha Graham (1939–45), and presented his first programme of solo works in 1944. He worked extensively with John Cage, especially in ventures at Black Mountain College. In 1952 he formed the Merce Cunningham Dance Company for whom he has choreographed ever since. He first began using chance operations in his choreography in 1951 for *16 Dances for Soloist and Company of Three*. Chance subsequently became a central part of his making processes. In 1964 he presented the first of his *Events* where dances and parts of dances from his repertoire were recombined into a choreographic collage. His stage work includes *Rainforest* (1968), *Walkaround Time* (1968) which pays homage to Duchamp, and *Duets* (1980). Cunningham has produced extensive repertory for television and video including *Westbeth* (1975), *Blue Studio: Five Segments* (1975), *Fractions I and II* (1978), and *Points in Space* (1989). He has collaborated with many musicians and artists, particularly John Cage, with whom he worked extensively to establish his particular relationship between dance and music; also David Tudor, Robert Rauschenberg, Frank Stella, Andy Warhol, Jasper Johns, Charles Atlas.

Cunningham's work is celebrated for the emphasis it places on dancing for its own sake. Critics and historians have variously spoken of the formalism of his work, its modernism and its invention. He has consistently made dance that stands on its own with the other arts and which speaks for itself: 'My work is without literary reference or without psychological determination in any way. The music does not support the dance in any conventional way. The music is made separately from the dance. What you have in my work is the dancing itself'.[1]

This extract is a series of observations on dancing. Although brief, they draw attention to many of Cunningham's main ideas. They emphasise that he is a dancer himself and that many of his concerns are to do with the transitory nature of dance.

Reader cross-references

Banes – contextual reference
Barthes – the grain in performance
Bausch – alternative, European, contemporary view of dance and theatre

Brown and **Rainer** – who later developed choreography in a more postmodern way, but who also stress the centrality of the dancer

Cage – his main musical collaborator, for relationship between music and dance

Meyerhold – an earlier precedent for alternative theatrical staging

Richter – Dada as historical antecedent for many of Cunningham's ideas

Schlemmer – Bauhaus antecedents

Wigman – contrasting idea of what it is to be a dancer

Wilson – later formal theatre explorations

Further reading

Cage, J., Cunningham, M., Johns, J. and Sontag, S. (1979, 1990) *Dancers on a Plane*, London: Thames & Hudson.

Cunningham, M. (1985) *The Dancer and the Dance: Conversations with Jacqueline Lesschaeve*, New York: Marion Boyars.

Klosty, J. (1975) *Merce Cunningham*, New York: Dutton.

Note

1   Cunningham, M. and Witts, D. (1980) Interview with Merce Cunningham, in *Merce Cunningham and Dance Company Programme*, Everyman Theatre, Liverpool, 25–28 June, p. 1.

Chapter 18

Isadora Duncan

THE DANCER
OF THE FUTURE

T HE MOVEMENT OF WAVES, of winds, of the earth is ever in the same lasting harmony. We do not stand on the beach and inquire of the ocean what was its movement in the past and what will be its movement in the future. We realize that the movement peculiar to its nature is eternal to its nature. The movement of the free animals and birds remains always in correspondence to their nature, the necessities and wants of that nature, and its correspondence to the earth nature. It is only when you put free animals under false restrictions that they lose the power of moving in harmony with nature, and adopt a movement expressive of the restrictions placed about them.

So it has been with civilized man. The movements of the savage, who lived in freedom in constant touch with Nature, were unrestricted, natural and beautiful. Only the movements of the naked body can be perfectly natural. Man, arrived at the end of civilization, will have to return to nakedness, not to the unconscious nakedness of the savage, but to the conscious and acknowledged nakedness of the mature Man, whose body will be the harmonious expression of his spiritual being.

And the movements of this Man will be natural and beautiful like those of the free animals.

The movement of the universe concentrating in an individual becomes what is termed the will; for example, the movement of the earth, being the concentration of surrounding forces, gives to the earth its individuality, its will of movement. So creatures of the earth, receiving in turn these concentrating forces in their different relations, as transmitted to them through their ancestors and to those by the earth, in themselves evolve the movement of individuals which is termed the will.

The dance should simply be, then, the natural gravitation of this will of the individual, which in the end is no more nor less than a human translation of the gravitation of the universe.

The school of the ballet of today, vainly striving against the natural laws of gravitation or the natural will of the individual, and working in discord in its form and movement with the form and movement of nature, produces a sterile movement which gives no birth to future movements, but dies as it is made.

The expression of the modern school of ballet, wherein each action is an end, and no movement, pose or rhythm is successive or can be made to evolve succeeding action, is an expression of degeneration, of living death. All the movements of our modern ballet school are sterile movements because they are unnatural: their purpose is to create the delusion that the law of gravitation does not exist for them.

The primary or fundamental movements of the new school of the dance must have within them the seeds from which will evolve all other movements, each in turn to give birth to others in unending sequence of still higher and greater expression, thoughts and ideas.

To those who nevertheless still enjoy the movements, for historical or choreographic or whatever other reasons, to those I answer: They see no farther than the skirts and tricots. But look – under the skirts, under the tricots are dancing deformed muscles. Look still farther – underneath the muscles are deformed bones. A deformed skeleton is dancing before you. This deformation through incorrect dress and incorrect movement is the result of the training necessary to the ballet.

The ballet condemns itself by enforcing the deformation of the beautiful woman's body! No historical, no choreographic reasons can prevail against that!

It is the mission of all art to express the highest and most beautiful ideals of man. What ideal does the ballet express?

No, the dance was once the most noble of all arts; and it shall be again. From the great depth to which it has fallen, it shall be raised. The dancer of the future shall attain so great a height that all other arts shall be helped thereby.

To express what is the most moral, healthful and beautiful in art – this is the mission of the dancer, and to this I dedicate my life.

These flowers before me contain the dream of a dance, it could be named 'The light falling on white flowers.' A dance that would be a subtle translation of the light and the whiteness. So pure, so strong, that people would say: it is a soul we see moving, a soul that has reached the light and found the whiteness. We are glad it should move so. Through its human medium we have a satisfying sense of movement, of light and glad things. Through this human medium, the movement of all nature runs also through us, is transmitted to us from the dancer. We feel the movement of light intermingled with the thought of whiteness. It is a prayer, this dance; each movement reaches in long undulations to the heavens and becomes a part of the eternal rhythm of the spheres.

To find those primary movements for the human body from which shall evolve the movements of the future dance in ever-varying, natural, unending sequences, that is the duty of the new dancer of today.

As an example of this, we might take the pose of the Hermes of the Greeks. He is represented as flying on the wind. If the artist had pleased to pose his foot in a vertical position, he might have done so, as the God, flying on the wind, is not touching the earth; but realizing that no movement is true unless suggesting sequence of movements, the sculptor placed the Hermes with the ball of his foot resting on the wind, giving the movement an eternal quality.

In the same way I might make an example of each pose and gesture in the thousands of figures we have left to us on the Greek vases and bas-reliefs; there is not one which in its movement does not presuppose another movement.

This is because the Greeks were the greatest students of the laws of nature, wherein all is the expression of unending, ever-increasing evolution, wherein are no ends and no stops.

Such movements will always have to depend on and correspond to the form that is moving. The movements of a beetle correspond to its form. So do those of the horse. Even so the movements of the human body must correspond to its form. The dances of no two persons should be alike.

People have thought that so long as one danced in rhythm, the form and design did not matter; but no, one must perfectly correspond to the other. The Greeks understood this very well. There is a statuette that shows a dancing cupid. It is a child's dance. The movements of the plump little feet and arms are perfectly suited to its form. The sole of the foot rests flat on the ground, a position which might be ugly in a more developed person, but is natural in a child trying to keep its balance. One of the legs is half raised; if it were outstretched it would irritate us, because the movement would be unnatural. There is also a statue of a satyr in a dance that is quite different from that of the cupid. His movements are those of a ripe and muscular man. They are in perfect harmony with the structure of his body.

The Greeks in all their painting, sculpture, architecture, literature, dance and tragedy evolved their movements from the movement of nature, as we plainly see expressed in all representations of the Greek gods, who, being no other than the representatives of natural forces, are always designed in a pose expressing the concentration and evolution of these forces. This is why the art of the Greeks is not a national or characteristic art but has been and will be the art of all humanity for all time.

Therefore dancing naked upon the earth I naturally fall into Greek positions, for Greek positions are only earth positions.

The noblest in art is the nude. This truth is recognized by all, and followed by painters, sculptors and poets; only the dancer has forgotten it, who should most remember it, as the instrument of her art is the human body itself.

Man's first conception of beauty is gained from the form and symmetry of the human body. The new school of the dance should begin with that movement which is in harmony with and will develop the highest form of the human body.

I intend to work for this dance of the future. I do not know whether I have the necessary qualities: I may have neither genius nor talent nor temperament. But I know that I have a Will; and will and energy sometimes prove greater than either genius or talent or temperament. . . .

My intention is, in due time, to found a school, to build a theatre where a hundred little girls shall be trained in my art, which they, in their turn, will better. In this school I shall not teach the children to imitate my movements, but to make their own. I shall not force them to study certain definite movements; I shall help them to develop those movements which are natural to them. Whosoever sees the movements of an untaught little child cannot deny that its movements are beautiful. They are beautiful because they are natural to the child. Even so the movements of the human body may be beautiful in every stage of development so long as they are in harmony with that stage and degree of maturity which the body has attained. There will always be movements which are the perfect expression of that individual body and that individual soul; so we must not force it to make movements which are not natural to it but which belong to a school. An intelligent child must be astonished to find that in the ballet school it is taught movements contrary to all those movements which it would make of its own accord.

This may seem a question of little importance, a question of differing opinions on the ballet and the new dance. But it is a great question. It is not only a question of true art, it is a question of race, of the development of the female sex to beauty and health, of the return to the original strength and to natural movements of woman's body. It is a question of the development of perfect mothers and the birth of healthy and beautiful children. The dancing school of the future is to develop and to show the ideal form of woman. It will be, as it were, a museum of the living beauty of the period.

Travellers coming into a country and seeing the dancers should find in them that country's ideal of the beauty of form and movement. But strangers who today come to any country, and there see the dancers of the ballet school, would get a strange notion indeed of the ideal of beauty in that country. More than this, dancing like any art of any time should reflect the highest point the spirit of mankind has reached in that special period. Does anybody think that the present day ballet school expresses this?

Why are its positions in such contrast to the beautiful positions of the antique sculptures which we preserve in our museums and which are constantly presented to us as perfect models of ideal beauty? Or have our museums been founded only out of historical and archaeological interest, and not for the sake of the beauty of the objects which they contain?

The ideal of beauty of the human body cannot change with fashion but only with evolution. Remember the story of the beautiful sculpture of a Roman girl which was discovered under the reign of Pope Innocent VIII, and which by its beauty created such a sensation that the men thronged to see it and made pilgrimages to it as to a holy shrine, so that the Pope, troubled by the movement which it originated, finally had it buried again.

And here I want to avoid a misunderstanding that might easily arise. From what I have said you might conclude that my intention is to return to the dances of the old Greeks, or that I think that the dance of the future will be a revival of the antique dances or even of those of the primitive tribes. No, the dance of the future will be a new movement, a consequence of the entire evolution which mankind has passed through. To return to the dances of the Greeks would be as impossible as it is unnecessary. We are not Greeks and therefore cannot dance Greek dances.

But the dance of the future will have to become again a high religious art as it was with the Greeks. For art which is not religious is not art, is mere merchandise.

The dancer of the future will be one whose body and soul have grown so harmoniously together that the natural language of that soul will have become the movement of the body. The dancer will not belong to a nation but to all humanity. She will dance not in the form of nymph, nor fairy, nor coquette, but in the form of woman in her greatest and purest expression. She will realize the mission of woman's body and the holiness of all its parts. She will dance the changing life of nature, showing how each part is transformed into the other. From all parts of her body shall shine radiant intelligence, bringing to the world the message of the thoughts and aspirations of thousands of women. She shall dance the freedom of woman. . . .

■   ■   ■

Source

Duncan, I. (1928) 'The Dancer of the Future', *The Art of the Dance*, New York: Theatre Arts Books.
  Written *c.* 1902 and first published 1928.

Isadora Duncan (1878–1927)

American dancer and choreographer. She was born in the USA but spent most of her professional life in Europe (1899–1927), where she gained a reputation as one of the foremost dancers of the age. She performed mainly as a solo dancer but also with children trained at the many schools that she set up from 1904 onwards. Her repertoire was extensive and she toured some of her works for two decades.[1] These included *Brahms Waltzes* (1905), *Fifth Symphony* (1915) to Beethoven, *Marseillaise* (1915), and *Marche Slave* (1917).

Duncan performed throughout Europe, visiting most major cities, especially Paris, London, St Petersburg (1905) and Berlin. She returned to the USA in 1909, 1911, 1917 and 1922 but was not always well received, firstly because of her private reputation, later, after 1917, because of her political affiliation. She was fêted by many major artists of the period, including Rodin and Edward Gordon Craig, with whom she had a personal and artistic relationship. In 1921 she was invited to establish a school in Moscow by Lenin's newly formed Soviet government. She became a Soviet citizen. She returned to Paris in 1927 where she gave her last concert at the age of 49; she died, prematurely, in a car accident in Nice in the same year.

It is evident from the extensive accounts of her dancing that Duncan was a remarkable performer who heralded the freedom and the political concern that later modern dancers would emulate. The evidence provided by contemporary critics makes it quite clear that it was her dancing that gained her a reputation as one of the most talked-about women in Europe. We are fortunate that Duncan committed her ideas to paper too.

In this early extract she surveys the dancer's position at the turn of the century and finds ballet wanting. Some of the writing now seems fanciful, but the rest contains the essentials of the ideas that became the foundations for the new modern dance. She looks to a new way of moving 'to find those primary movements for the human body from which shall evolve the movements of the future dance . . .' for the dancer of the future who 'shall dance the freedom of woman'.

Reader cross-references

Craig – artistic collaborator and father of her first child
Marinetti – another view of the promise of the new century
Martin – a critic who recognised her as a dancer and as a writer and theorist
Piscator – a contemporary theatre approach
Stanislavski – whom she met in St Petersburg, a great admirer of her work
Wigman and **Humphrey** – later women modern dancers

Further reading

Duncan, I. (1928) *The Art of the Dance*, New York: Theatre Arts Books.
Magriel, P. (ed.) (1948) *Isadora Duncan*, London: A & C Black.

Note

1   Layson, J. (1983) 'Isadora Duncan: A Preliminary Analysis of her Work' *Dance Research*, 1, 1: 39–49, lists at least 223 dances.

Chapter 19

Hanns Eisler

SOME REMARKS ON
THE SITUATION OF
THE MODERN COMPOSER

W HEN MEDICAL SCIENCE was not yet able to diagnose the cause of serious diseases, such as tuberculosis, beri-beri, or diseases of the blood, patients were in a sorry plight. These diseases were considered to be matters of chance, misfortunes for which there was little alleviation, or it was believed the sick were possessed and should be exorcised by prayer. When modern science and technology discovered new methods of diagnosis and new apparatus, it became known that these diseases were not personal disasters, but were caused by microbes and if recognized in time, were curable. Those were the great days of chemotherapy. The latest scientific research has produced a still more interesting result. It has been ascertained that a large number of these diseases, such as tuberculosis and beri-beri, are the result of social conditions, and many of them will disappear entirely when social conditions are changed. What a colossal development of human knowledge – disease, as fate, incurable; disease, caused by bacteria, curable. Disease, caused by social conditions, which are changeable, curable.

If we modern composers were able to apply some of this objectivity, common sense and knowledge to our own field, we would be more successful. But that requires a scientific approach instead of the noncommitted futile natterings about art. This is urgently necessary, since the crisis in modern music is sharpening, while barbarism in music is on the increase.

The people have become musical illiterates, despite technical progress in music. It is high time for contemporary composers to see reason and alter their attitude. In order to contend successfully with this state of anarchy and barbarism a new type of composer, teacher and musician is needed. I would appeal above all, to the modern composer, for as the producers of music, they are the most important. If we wish to create a new type of composer, then we must first challenge the old type wherever we find him. This can only be done with scientific methods, objectively and fairly; therefore it is necessary to raise the practice and theory of music to the level of contemporary thought. Unfortunately, it is true to say that at a time when new methods of working and reasoning have already been introduced in industry, medicine, chemistry, physics, sociology and political economy, wholly antiquated methods are still applied in the theory and practice of music. The so-called modern composer is mainly to blame for this state of affairs. We shall have to find a new definition for the word 'modern.' After all, it should be possible to determine what, for our time, is progressive or retrogressive in music.

The crisis in music has been caused by the general crisis in society. In music it appears concretely in the technique of composing. This, in turn, has contributed to the complete isolation of modern music from social life. The modern composer has meanwhile become a parasite, supported by wealthy patrons out of personal interests, and no longer carries out any rational work in society. Consequently, the composer's profession still has something of the subservient character of the seventeenth century. He can no longer maintain himself from his compositions, which is already suspect, but for example, has to hang around the salons in order to be seen. That is particularly detrimental to young composers for they are thus cut off from the realities of life. This seclusion leads to most modern works having nothing to say about the most urgent issues of the day. Some modern composers are only concerned with themselves. (So let them!) Others have form and technique problems. (It's a fine thing to contemplate technique, so why disturb them?) Lastly, there are the so-called lyrical temperaments, exquisitely sensitive and profound, who know definitely spring will come and the moon will shine when the nights are light. (That's a boost for Hollywood.) Now modern composers are of the opinion that 'absolute music,' more accurately music without words, cannot express anything definite at all, and certainly nothing about 'the urgent issues of our day.' Music without words, they say, cannot achieve this nor is it the purpose of music. (The purpose of music is only to be found in music itself. Music for music's sake.)

But we know from history that so-called absolute music reached the highest point of expression in one particular period. Beethoven's symphonies were the music of the struggle of the young bourgeoisie against decaying feudalism. We also know from history that instrumental music was not always predominant. In the fifteenth and sixteenth centuries instrumental music played a subordinate role to vocal music. Instrumental music and the concert (as the organized form of musical life) are not eternal, but historical forms. They arose and developed within capitalist society and they enter a crisis when capitalist society enters a crisis. In 1750 the Mannheim Symphonic School was new and revolutionary. In 1810 it embodied the highest musical expression of the period. By 1890 what was left was pedestrian naturalism à la Richard Strauss, or the artificial, sentimental *Weltanschauung* music of Gustav Mahler. By 1933 there were no longer any achievements of significance in this sphere and it is quite impossible to define the purpose of a symphony. So a really progressive composer will have to realize that this is a completely archaic art form, which should no longer be employed. Why continue the useless? We are witnessing a new blossoming and predominance of vocal music following the instrumental era of the nineteenth century. Instrumental music will play an increasingly subordinate and insignificant role in music. A solution to the music crisis emanating from purely instrumental music can't be found. The experiences of the last twenty years demonstrate this quite clearly. Modern composers have tried almost everything and the result is complete anarchy. The composer today depends only on his own personal recipe and his own taste. If this would guarantee a high musical culture, then there would be nothing against it. But since it inherently helps to produce barbarism and decay it is harmful. There were periods of great styles in the history of music, which were generally considered obligatory. As everybody knows it is often not easy to distinguish between an early Beethoven, Haydn or Mozart, without an exact analysis. Certain cadences were generally accepted as well as certain formal methods, such as the employment of additional musical elements in the transition, or as the development or the recapitulation. Despite all these generally accepted elements of form, the composers were not uniform; each possessed individuality.

Modern music will only exist when there is a new modern style which is obligatory for all and useful to society. At a time when modern music no longer has a public but is only promoted privately a composer can do as he likes. He can compose like Czerny and with a few false basses write a '*Book of Exercises for* non-*Dexterity*.' He can copy Brahms with the twelve tone technique or sit on top of the piano declaring he is expressing his innermost soul. Since these three methods are as useless as they are unsalable the difference is minute. We find the same sort of anarchy in aesthetics. Today there are no aesthetic standards in music, for the difference between beautiful and ugly has become a matter of personal taste and experience. A modern type of composer must take note of that. The terms 'beautiful' or 'not beautiful' which played such an important role fifty years ago are out of date. They no longer say anything about the value and therefore must be replaced by the new 'useful' and 'useless.' Many fellow musicians believe the only criterion is good or bad music. That sounds quite reasonable. Unfortunately, however, it is difficult today to agree on what is good and what is bad music. Some composers consider Stravinsky primitive, others consider Schönberg obsolete. There are a number of very talented modern composers, whose composing is technically bad from a certain point of view. Careless part writing, lack of artistry in the form, inability in the counterpoint. Yet there are others who will defend these composers, maintaining they intended to so write and it was not done out of ignorance, but to achieve certain 'effects.' Unfortunately, the terms 'good' and 'bad' alone are no longer adequate as criteria, nor yet the terms 'modern' and 'old-fashioned.' But when we combine these criteria with the new criteria of 'useful' and 'useless' we will make better headway, especially if we go one step further and ask 'useful for whom?' Technical standards among modern composers are bad, though generally not yet admitted. Among the best of them we often find only mannerisms instead of originality, style imitation instead of style, superficial tricks in place of fundamental technical workmanship. Anyone looking at what you might call a polyphonic work of a talented young composer would find little counterpoint, merely an imitation of it, or the use of certain counterpoint mannerisms. So today the terms 'good' and 'bad' must be applied with the greatest of care and in any case only in connection with 'useful' or 'useless.'

The new type of composer will also have to learn that the crisis in modern music has been brought about mainly by the growth in technical devices. The radio, gramophone records and sound film have created a completely new situation. The concert compared with sound film is just as old-fashioned as the mailcoach compared with the airplane. Sound film and radio are destroying the old forms of music listening for there is a big difference between listening to a symphony at a concert or on the radio. There is a glaring contradiction between classical music and the modern means of production. Take a simple experiment – if you turn on the radio in a car driving along the street of a big city then you will realize that classical music does not fit the modern way of life. It requires a passive listener who is easily affected and who can shut off his thinking. The technique of composing classical music is dependent on this and arose because of it. If listened to over the radio or in a film many of the formal devices seem antiquated. For instance, the principle of recapitulation, of the development, indeed the whole sonata form itself. Sound film is making the masses unaccustomed to listening to music in the abstract but accustomed to seeing pictures of real life while they hear music. So a more realistic type of listener is arising in contrast to the old idealist concert-goer. This is a very interesting process. It is not altered by the fact that the film industry is helping to produce a barbaric condition in culture and that it is a political and moral device for blunting the intellect of the masses. Whether film will become a wonderful art form for mankind or a sordid commodity is a question of power, that is to say, a political question and not an aesthetic-cultural one. The sound film will also decisively change the state of instrumental music. The first experiments have been made to produce music synthetically on the film sound track. The sound chart of the composer's score is copied onto the film track. It sounds adventurous, but it has already been done. It is known how the tone A looks graphically on the film track and this graphic sign can be changed back again into music. The manual labor of the musician is thus replaced by the machine; this will lead to a complete revolutionizing of techniques of composing. But this means the composer can make himself absolutely independent of the inadequacies of the instruments and musicians. The conductor, the virtuoso and the instrumentalist will become superfluous. The result will be a still greater mass poverty among musicians, if the present form of society is not changed by then. It will not take too long, if we think of the short time that it took for the sound film to develop. Music-making by man will then have a new function, it will be for the music-lover and the amateur. (Just as the train, the car and the plane have not made walking or rambling disappear.) Great music will be put directly by the composer onto the apparatus; with the help of technicians, but no longer of 'artists.' (There will no longer be problems about the tempi or the rendering.) These are the material fundamentals and prerequisites for a new style in music.

It is not possible in such a brief exposition to enlarge on such problems systematically. They can only be touched on, so to speak. Nevertheless, from what has already been stated it is clear along what lines the new type of modern composer should think in order to arrive at a new musical practice. What are our main difficulties? Certain social situations have produced certain musical forms, that is, they produce a certain musical diction. If the material productive forces of a society develop at a quicker speed than the music, then music will lag behind and a contradiction will arise between it and society. With modern composers it is as though they find themselves in an airtight room, where there is no possibility of solving even the smallest technical problem. (All these struggles for a new technique and new aesthetics expire without showing any result. There are no victors any more, only the vanquished.)

Even if modern composers were of one mind at least on some questions, another type of man with a rough voice and hard hands would appear, bang on the table and demand, 'For whose benefit?' And that is the main question.

In order to check the decay of music and to find a new technique, a new style and thus a new circle of listeners, the modern composer will have to leave his airtight room and find his place in society. It is not a question of sentimentality and kindheartedness but a question of music.

The modern composer must change *from a parasite into a fighter*. In the interests of music we must ask ourselves: What social attitude is the most useful? Once we have realized that the present form of society has produced musical barbarism, then we must try to change it. However, that is a very difficult matter, not easily achieved. We cannot conduct such struggles alone, but must form an alliance with those sections of the people who suffer under this order of society and who are combating it. That is an alliance of the progressive intellectuals, scholars, doctors, engineers, artists and the working class. The composer must understand once and for all that this alliance alone will provide the guarantee of bringing order into the chaos in music. This path is long and difficult, but in the interests of music it must be taken. It is also a question of character for there is a difference between a weakling, a futile dreamer (and whoever is futile is also harmful), or a modern man, a realist, who thinks and fights for his cause. In these times of mankind's great battles for a new world musicians should not desert the field. Let us join the struggle on the side of truth against falsehood. Then we will best serve our cause, the cause of modern music.

■　■　■

Source

Eisler, H. (1935, 1978) 'Some Remarks on the Situation of the Modern Composer', *Hanns Eisler: A Rebel in Music*, trans. M. Meyer, ed. M. Grabs, Berlin: Seven Seas Books: 106–113.[1]

Hanns Eisler (1892–1962)

Born in Leipzig and studied composition under Schoenberg and Webern, winning prizes for his early work. He became a committed Marxist, and was involved in some of the revolutionary activities of the German communist party in the 1920s. He wrote choral works and marching songs which became popular with left-wing groups throughout Europe, many of them in the minor key, which Eisler thought was more threatening or dangerously energetic.

In the 1930s he met Bertolt Brecht, with whom he formed a lifelong friendship, composing together at least two theatre works which have been seen as masterpieces – *Die Massnähme* (*The Measures Taken*) (1930), and *Die Mütter* (*The Mother*) (1932), from the novel by Maxim Gorky. Both works display a distinct theatrical relationship between words and music, and are pioneering in that these elements have an equal expressive weight, as well as being both memorable and powerfully uplifting. After Hitler came to power in Germany, Eisler's music was banned, and he moved to Hollywood, returning after the Second World War to the German Democratic Republic to work with Brecht once again within the new socialist state, with works including *The Mother* (1951) with Brecht's wife Helene Weigel in the title role. From 1948 to 1961 he wrote scores for seventeen plays, his view being that good theatre must also incorporate music that can both serve and elevate the performance as a major signifier of meaning, hence his inclusion in this book.

Eisler's essay on the modern composer demands new thinking and new compositional techniques to serve what he sees as the new anti-bourgeois era. Ironically it is only in the late twentieth century that Eisler's call for a new modern style has seen composers such as Adams, Glass, Bryars and Smith producing music that has bridged the gap between the classes, generations, and countries.

Reader cross-references

Benjamin – a fellow Marxist in Germany in the 1930s
Brecht – his main collaborator
Cage – on music and performance
Glass – another, later, theatre composer
Müller – a later German playwright
Wigman – a contemporary, dancer's, viewpoint

Further reading

Betz, A. (1976, 1982) *Hanns Eisler Political Musician*, trans. B. Hopkins, Cambridge: Cambridge University Press.
Willett, J. (1968) *The Theatre of Bertolt Brecht*, London: Methuen.

Note

1   *Einiges über die Lage des modernen Komponisten*, Typescript, Hanns Eisler
    Archives. Grabs notes (p. 113) that this was intended for publication in
    New Music and was published in a shortened version in the *Daily Worker*,
    New York, 5 December 1935 as 'The Composer in Society'.

Chapter 20

Philip Glass

NOTES ON

EINSTEIN

ON THE BEACH

Part 1

The music for *Einstein on the Beach* was written in the spring, summer and fall of 1975. Bob Wilson and I worked directly from a series of his drawings which eventually formed the designs for the sets. Prior to that period, we had reached agreement on the general thematic content, the overall length, its divisions into 4 acts, 9 scenes and 5 connecting 'knee plays.' We also determined the makeup of the company – 4 principal actors, 12 singers, doubling when possible as dancers and actors, a solo violinist, and the amplified ensemble of keyboards, winds and voices with which my music is usually associated.

The three main recurring visual themes of the opera (Train/Trial/Field with Spaceship) are linked to three main musical themes. The overall thematic divisions of the opera are as follows:

KNEE PLAY 1 (Chorus and electric organ)
    ·Act 1   Scene 1   TRAIN (ensemble with solo voice
                             and chorus joining at the end)
               Scene II   TRIAL (chorus, violin, electric organ
                             and flutes)

KNEE PLAY 2 (Violin solo)

Act II	Scene 1	DANCE 1 – Field with Spaceship (ensemble with solo voice/dancers)
	Scene 2	NIGHT TRAIN (2 voices, chorus and small ensemble)

KNEE PLAY 3 (Chorus *a capella*)

Act III	Scene 1	TRIAL/PRISON (chorus and electric organ, ensemble at the end)
	Scene 2	DANCE 2 – Field with Spaceship (6 voices, violin, electric organ)

KNEE PLAY 4 (Chorus and violin)

Act IV	Scene 1	BUILDING/TRAIN (chorus and ensemble)
	Scene 2	BED (solo electric organ and voice)
	Scene 3	SPACESHIP (chorus and ensemble)

KNEE PLAY 5 (Women's chorus, violin and electric organ)

The most important musical material appears in the knee plays and features the violin. Dramatically speaking, the violinist (dressed as Einstein, as are the performers on stage) appears as a soloist as well as a character in the opera. His playing position – midway between the orchestra and the stage performers – offers a clue to his role. He is seen then, perhaps as Einstein himself, or simply as a witness to the stage events; but, in any case, as a musical touchstone to the work as a whole.

It might be useful to delineate some of the visual/musical transformation of the material which makes up the opera:

The image of the train appears three times – first in Act I, Scene 1, then in Act II, Scene 2 (as the Night Train), and finally in Act IV, Scene 1, where it appears in the same perspective as the Night Train, but this time transformed into a building. The music for the first train is in three parts, or 'themes.' The first theme (based on the super-imposition of two shifting rhythmic patterns, one changing and one fixed) makes up most of the music of this scene.

The second appearance of the train image, the Night Train, is a reworking of the first theme, this time with a larger complement of voices. The music for the Building is a development of the second theme, recognizable by its highly accented rhythmic profile, in which the repeated figures form simple arithmetic progressions.

The third theme is a rhythmic expansion of a traditional cadential formula. This 'cadence' theme forms the principal material of the opera, being used for the 2nd, 3rd and 4th Knee Plays, as well as almost the entire music for Act IV, Scene 3, the Spaceship.

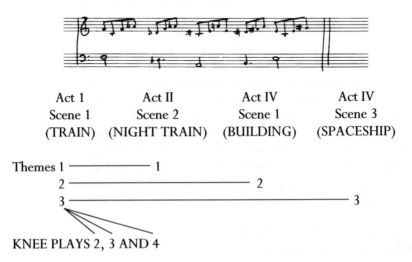

Act 1	Act II	Act IV	Act IV
Scene 1	Scene 2	Scene 1	Scene 3
(TRAIN)	(NIGHT TRAIN)	(BUILDING)	(SPACESHIP)

Themes 1 ——————— 1
     2 —————————————— 2
     3 ——————————————————————— 3

KNEE PLAYS 2, 3 AND 4

The second major visual image, the Trial, also appears three times in the opera – first in Act I, Scene 2, then in Act III, Scene 1 where, after the first few minutes, the stage divides, becoming half-trial/half-prison, and finally in Act IV, Scene 2, where the bed which has been in the center of the trial, and in half of the trial/prison, now occupies the entire stage. Here again the trial music is in three parts, or 'themes.' After the opening of the first trial we hear the violin, accompanied by men's voices, playing a simple, harmonically stable rhythmic pattern which, through an additive process, slowly expands and contracts.

Later, the women's voices join in, producing a somewhat thicker texture. Toward the end of this scene, during the judge's speech, the second theme is heard, more chordal in nature, for solo electric organ.

The Trial/Prison begins musically in the same way as the first Trial. After the stage divides, the third theme is heard – numbers sung by the men and women in the jury box and lightly accompanied by harmonically shifting arpeggios on electric organ. Toward the end of the scene, the witness remaining alone on the stage speaks and, as the scenery is removed, the second (chordal) theme appears – this time in soprano saxophone and bass clarinet.

The Bed scene begins with a cadenza for electric organ. As the bed lifts to a vertical position and flies upwards, we hear the first theme again. Then, for the last time, the second (chordal) theme is heard, now accompanied by a solo singing voice.

Act 1, Scene 2	Act III, Scene 1	Act IV, Scene 2
(TRIAL)	(TRIAL/PRISON)	(BED)
Theme 1	1	1
	Theme 3	
Theme 2	2	2

The first two appearances of the Field image are given over to dance and can be heard as similar reflections of the same musical material. For me they are two pillars equidistant from either end of the opera, sharing only superficial features with the musical content of the other scenes. During the first dance in Act II, Scene 1, a spaceship is seen in the distance. In the second dance, Act III, Scene 2, the spaceship appears closer. The third appearance of the Field, Act IV, Scene 3 takes place inside the spaceship and, as indicated earlier, the music comes from the third theme of the train music.

The Knee Plays are the short connecting pieces which appear throughout the work much as prelude, interludes and postlude. Taken together, they form a play in themselves. They can also be seen as the seeds which flower and take form in the larger scenes. In the first four Knee Plays, two characters are seen in a room, sitting at two tables, then sitting side-by-side in two chairs, next standing together in front of a large control board and then lying on top of two large glass tables. In the final knee play, the last moment of the opera, they are seen sitting on a bench waiting for a bus.

The musical structure of the Knee Plays can be seen in the following diagram:

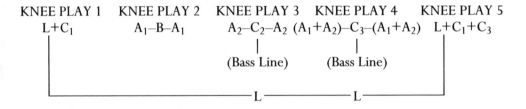

The 2nd, 3rd and 4th Knee Plays share the same form – first theme, second theme and return to first theme. The 'cadence' theme of the first train (Act I, Scene 1) makes up the first theme in all of these Knee Plays, either expressed as violin arpeggios (A_1), in a chorale setting for voices (A_2), or, in the 4th Knee Play, as a combination of the two ($A_1 + A_2$). The middle theme (B) of the 2nd Knee Play, based on simple scale passages, reappears during the second dance and in the middle section of the Spaceship music. The middle themes of the 3rd Knee Play (C_2) and the 4th Knee Play (C_3) are different arrangements of the same material, easily recognizable by its highly lyrical character.

The root movement (implied bass line) of this material is A-G-C. This becomes, in the pedal of an electric organ, the opening descending bass line (L) of the 1st Knee Play.

After a very extended beginning, during which the audience enters, the first vocal setting (C_1) of these harmonies appears. The descending bass line (L) reappears for the 5th Knee Play, joined shortly thereafter by women's voices singing the vocal music of the 1st Knee Play (C_1), and then by the violin, playing the middle theme of the 4th Knee Play (C_3).

The vocal texts used throughout the opera are based on numbers and solfege ('do, re, mi . . .') syllables. When numbers are used, they represent the rhythmic structure of the music. When solfege is used, the syllables represent the pitch structure of the music. In either case, the text is not secondary or supplementary, but is a description of the music itself.

To conclude this part of the notes, one might say that, in a general way, the opera begins with a 19th Century train and ends with a 20th Century spaceship. Events occur en route – trials, prison, dances – and throughout, the continuity of the Knee Plays. A number of principal characters appear and reappear in different combinations, often carrying with them an identifying gesture. The violinist, one of the Einsteins of the opera, remains (even during the final scene, the Spaceship, when the entire company is on stage) seated apart, a witness.

Part 2

'Einstein on the Beach' is part of an ongoing musical project begun with 'Another Look at Harmony' in the spring of 1975. This, in turn, is based on 'Music in 12 Parts' (completed 1974) which developed a vocabulary of techniques (additive processes, cyclic structure and combinations of the two) to apply to problems of rhythmic structure. 'Another Look at Harmony' turns to problems of harmonic structure or, more accurately, structural harmony – new solutions to problems of harmonic usage, where the evolution of material can become the basis of an overall formal structure intrinsic to the music itself (and without the harmonic language giving up its moment-to-moment content and 'flavor').

My main approach throughout has been to link harmonic structure directly to rhythmic structure, using the latter as a base. In doing so, easily perceptible 'root movement' (chords or 'changes') was chosen in order that the clarity of this relationship could be easily heard. Melodic material is for the most part a function, or result, of the harmony, as is true in earlier periods of Western music. However, it is clear that some of the priorities of Western music (harmony/melody first, then rhythm) have been reversed. Here we have rhythmic structure first, then harmony/melody. The result has been a reintegration of rhythm, harmony and melody into an idiom which is, hopefully, accessible to a general public, although, admittedly, somewhat unusual at first hearing.

Parts 1 and 2 of 'Another Look at Harmony' became the basis of Act I, Scene 1 (Train) and Act II, Scene 1 (Field) of the opera and were the starting points from which additional material and devices were developed.

The musical material of the opera is made up of series of 5 chords, 4 chords, 3 chords, 2 chords and 1 chord. Following is a brief description of each series and the techniques relevant to its use.

The most prominent 'theme' of the opera is made from the following progression of 5 chords:

$$\text{key of f}$$
$$f - D^b - B^{bb}$$
$$\text{(i) (VI) (IV}^b\text{)}$$

$$A - B - E$$
$$\text{(IV) (V) (I)}$$
$$\text{key of E}$$

This combines both a familiar cadence and a modulation in one formula. What makes the formula distinctive and even useful is, of course, the way in which the IV^b (B^{bb}) becomes IV (A) of the new key, thereby making the phrase resolve a half-step lower. This, in turn, provides the leading tone for the original i (f). As it is a formula which invites repetition, it is particularly suited to my kind of musical thinking. It can be heard in the opera as the third theme of the Train music (Act I, Scene 1,) with ensemble and chorus, then in arpeggio form as a violin solo in Knee Play 2, next in chorale form for chorus *a capella* in Knee Play 3, then in both arpeggio form and chorale form in Knee Play 4, and finally combining all the previous arrangements in the Spaceship (Act IV, Scene 3).

The progression of 4 chords appears at the end of the Trial (Act I; Scene 2), Trial/Prison (Act III, Scene 1) and Bed (Act IV, Scene 2). It is a rhythmic expansion of the 4 chords:

$$f - E^b - C - D$$

As indicated, the f and C harmonies are 'paired' rhythmically, as are the E^b and D harmonies. Beginning with a simple pattern of eighth notes,

$$(f)\,(E^b)(C)(D)$$
$$4-3-4-3,$$

the phrase gradually expands, each new phrase being played twice, until quite a long and elaborate final figure is produced. An example of the rhythmic/harmonic expansion in its early stage is as follows:

	(f)	(E^b)	(C)	(D)
(1)	4	3	4	3
(2)	(4+3)	4	(4+3)	(4)
(3)	(4+3)	(4+3)	(4+3)	(4+3)
(4)	(4+3+2)	(4+3)	(4+3+2)	(4+3)

etc.

The material involving the series of 3 chords makes up the music of the two dance sections (Act II, Scene 1 and Act III, Scene 2). The procedure here is quite different, setting three key centers (A, e^7 and B^b) 'around' a central key of d. At the beginning, each of the key centers is associated with its own meter and all are played over a common rhythmic pattern of 6/8. (This, incidentally, creates a secondary polymetric 'flavor' throughout the music.) The key of A appears in dotted quarters, e^7 in eighth notes (a substitute key of C^7 appears later) and B^b in half notes. After an excursion into one of these key centers the music returns, always, to the central key of d. As the music develops, the key centers begin to exchange metrical character. Later, these form complex accumulations of meters in the same key before returning to the central key, d. This accumulative process continues until the original key/meter associations are lost in an overall texture of harmonies and meters.

The sequence of two chords is found in the Trial/Prison music. The two harmonies, a^7 and g^7, are first heard as two alternating arpeggiated figures in 6/8 (played on electric organ with voices chanting numbers representing the rhythmic patterns). The music develops as each 'half' of the figure undergoes a process of rhythmic fragmentation (wherein small increments of the original figure are added to itself). At first the process occurs equally in both halves (represented by the two harmonies) of the figure, thereby maintaining an exact overall symmetry. Gradually, the two halves begin to differ rhythmically, reaching a point where they are completely different and the figure is asymmetrical. At this point two successive asymmetrical figures in the music begin to act as mirror images of each other, thereby seeming to form one doubly-long symmetrical pattern.

The music based on one chord is first heard in the Trial (Act I, Scene 2). The violin, playing a figure in 7/8, outlines an a^7 harmony. A simple additive process begins as each successive figure adds a single eighth note, thereby changing its overall rhythmic character and causing the figure to gradually expand. The figure later contracts when the process is reversed, returning finally to its original form. The same process is heard later at the beginning of the Trial/Prison (Act III, Scene 1) and finally in the Bed (Act IV, Scene 2).

■　■　■

Source

Glass, P. (1976) 'Notes on *Einstein on the Beach*', booklet accompanying *Einstein on the Beach*, New York: CBS: 9–11.

Philip Glass (1937–)

Composer; studied at the University of Chicago and at the Juilliard School, New York. He worked with Ravi Shankar (Paris 1965) and then travelled to India (1965–66), where he developed an interest in Indian music; at the same time, he began composing 'minimalist' works. He gave his first concert in 1967, which was followed by the formation of the Philip Glass Ensemble, in 1968. His work was first recorded in 1971, and his first opera performed in 1976.

Glass's work has been noted for its contribution to 'minimalism', especially his compositions of the period 1965–75, including *Music in 12 Parts* (1971–74). His subsequent work has included many collaborations with theatre devisers, choreographers and film makers. He worked with Robert Wilson and Lucinda Childs on *Einstein on the Beach* (1976) and with Wilson again on *Satyagraha* (1980), *Akhnaten* (1984) and *CIVIL warS* (1984). He collaborated again with Childs, *Dance nos. 1–5* (1979), and with Jerome Robbins, *Glass Pieces* (1983). His film music includes *North Star* (1977) for *Mark di Suvero, Sculptor* and the soundtrack for Godfrey Reggio's *Koyaanisquatsi* (1983).

The extract here includes Glass's notes for the New York production of *Einstein on the Beach*. The work was premièred at Avignon, France, on 25 July 1976. Its New York première (21 November 1976), at the Metropolitan Opera, helped make Glass famous. The opera also established many precedents for its staging, choreography and manner of collaboration. The notes are of particular interest in the way they detail how the composer has approached the music for a collaborative theatre piece. They are clearly written with the totality of the performance in mind.

Reader cross-references

Brown – a dancer working with concerns for structure and processes
Cage – a different approach to twentieth-century composition
Eisler – another theatre composer
Rainer – comparison with her ideas of minimalism
Wilson – a theatre collaborator

Further reading and listening

Glass, P. (1977) *North Star*, Virgin.
Glass, P. (1983) *Glassworks*, CBS.
Jones, R.T. (ed.) (1988) *Opera on the Beach: Philip Glass on His New World of Music Theatre*, London: Faber.

Chapter 21

Roselee Goldberg

PERFORMANCE ART
FROM FUTURISM
TO THE PRESENT

PERFORMANCE became accepted as a medium of artistic expression in its own right in the 1970s. At that time, conceptual art – which insisted on an art of ideas over product, and on an art that could not be bought and sold – was in its heyday and performance was often a demonstration, or an execution, of those ideas. Performance thus became the most tangible art form of the period. Art spaces devoted to performance sprang up in the major international art centres, museums sponsored festivals, art colleges introduced performance courses, and specialist magazines appeared.

It was during that period that this first history of performance was published (1979), demonstrating that there was a long tradition of artists turning to live performance as one means among many of expressing their ideas, and that such events had played an important part in the history of art. It is interesting that performance, until that time, had been consistently left out in the process of evaluating artistic development, especially in the modern period, more on account of the difficulty of placing it in the history of art than of any deliberate omission.

The extent and richness of this history made the question of omission an even more insistent one. For artists did not merely use performance as a means to attract publicity to themselves. Performance has been considered as a way of bringing to life the many formal and conceptual ideas on which the making of art is based. Live gestures have constantly been used as a weapon against the conventions of established art.

Such a radical stance has made performance a catalyst in the history of twentieth-century art; whenever a certain school, be it Cubism, Minimalism or conceptual art, seemed to have reached an impasse, artists have turned to performance as a way of breaking down categories and indicating new directions. Moreover, within the history of the avant garde — meaning those artists who led the field in breaking with each successive tradition — performance in the twentieth century has been at the forefront of such an activity: an avant avant garde. Despite the fact that most of what is written today about the work of the Futurists, Constructivists, Dadaists and Surrealists continues to concentrate on the art objects produced by each period, it was more often than not the case that these movements found their roots and attempted to resolve problematic issues in performance. When the members of such groups were still in their twenties or early thirties, it was in performance that they tested their ideas, only later expressing them in objects. Most of the original Zurich Dadaists, for example, were poets, cabaret artistes and performers who, before actually creating Dada objects themselves, exhibited works from immediately preceding movements, such as the Expressionists. Similarly, most of the Parisian Dadaists and Surrealists were poets, writers and agitators before they made Surrealist objects and paintings. Breton's text *Surrealism and Painting* (1928) was a belated attempt to find a painterly outlet for the Surrealist idea, and as such it continued to raise the question: 'What is Surrealist painting?' for some years after its publication. For was it not Breton who, four years earlier, had stated that the ultimate Surrealist *acte gratuit* would be to fire a revolver at random into a crowd on the street?

Performance manifestos, from the Futurists to the present, have been the expression of dissidents who have attempted to find other means to evaluate art experience in everyday life. Performance has been a way of appealing directly to a large public, as well as shocking audiences into reassessing their own notions of art and its relation to culture. Conversely, public interest in the medium, especially in the 1980s, stems from an apparent desire of that public to gain access to the art world, to be a spectator of its ritual and its distinct community, and to be surprised by the unexpected, always unorthodox presentations that the artists devise. The work may be presented solo or with a group, with lighting, music or visuals made by the performance artist him or herself, or in collaboration, and performed in places ranging from an art gallery or museum to an 'alternative space', a theatre, café, bar or street corner. Unlike theatre, the performer *is* the artist, seldom a character like an actor, and the content rarely follows a traditional plot or narrative. The performance might be a series of intimate gestures or large-scale visual theatre, lasting from a few minutes to many hours; it might be performed only once or repeated several times, with or without a prepared script, spontaneously improvised, or rehearsed over many months.

Whether tribal ritual, medieval passion play, Renaissance spectacle or the 'soirées' arranged by artists in the 1920s in their Paris studios, performance has provided a presence for the artist in society. This presence, depending on the nature of the performance, can be esoteric, shamanistic, instructive, provocative or entertaining. Renaissance examples even show the artist in the role of creator and director of public spectacles, fantastic triumphal parades that often required the construction of elaborate temporary architecture, or allegorical events that utilized the multi-media abilities attributed to Renaissance Man. A mock naval battle, designed by Polidoro da Caravaggio in 1589, took place in the specially flooded courtyard of the Pitti Palace in Florence; Leonardo da Vinci dressed his performers as planets and had them recite verses about the Golden Age in a pageant entitled *Paradiso* (1490); and the Baroque artist Gian Lorenzo Bernini staged spectacles for which he wrote scripts, designed scenes and costumes, built architectural elements and even constructed realistic flood scenes, as in *L'Inondazione* ('The Inundation of the Tiber', 1638).

The history of performance art in the twentieth century is the history of a permissive, open-ended medium with endless variables, executed by artists impatient with the limitations of more established art forms, and determined to take their art directly to the public. For this reason its base has always been anarchic. By its very nature, performance defies precise or easy definition beyond the simple declaration that it is live art by artists. Any stricter definition would immediately negate the possibility of performance itself. For it draws freely on any number of disciplines and media – literature, poetry, theatre, music, dance, architecture and painting, as well as video, film, slides and narrative – for material, deploying them in any combination. Indeed, no other artistic form of expression has such a boundless manifesto, since each performer makes his or her own definition in the very process and manner of execution.

This book is a record of those artists who use performance in trying to live, and who create work which takes life as its subject. It is also a record of the effort to assimilate more and more the realm of play and pleasure in an art which observes less and less the traditional limitations of making art objects, so that in the end the artist can take delight in almost any activity. It is, finally, about the desire of many artists to make art that functions outside the confines of museums and galleries.

In tracing an untold story, this first history inevitably works itself free of its material, because that material continues to raise questions about the very nature of art. It does not pretend to be a record of every performer in the twentieth century; rather, it pursues the development of a sensibility. The goal of this book is to raise questions and to gain new insights. It can only hint at life off the pages.

■   ■   ■

Source

Goldberg, R. (1979, 1988) 'Foreword', *Performance Art from Futurism to the Present*, London: Thames & Hudson: 7–9.
First published in 1979 as *Performance: Live Art 1909 to the Present*.

Roselee Goldberg

Performance historian and writer on art. She graduated from the Courtauld Institute, London, and became Director of the Royal College of Art Gallery, London and then Curator of the Kitchen Centre for Video, Music and Performance, New York. She has published in both the US and the UK.

Goldberg's first edition of *Performance* in 1979 was a ground-breaking history of twentieth-century 'live art' that established a precedent for later histories. In it she says that 'performance has only recently become accepted as a medium of artistic expression in its own right' (1979:6). By the time the second edition was published she could confidently say that it 'became accepted. . . . in the 1970s'. Among the reasons for this acceptance was precisely her popularisation of the idea.

Both editions of her history cover the twentieth century. Both editions, despite different titles, identify the first futurist manifesto of 20 February 1909 as a starting point. The first concludes with Robert Wilson and *Einstein on the Beach*. The second completely rewrites the recent period as 'the art of ideas and the media generation' and includes not only Wilson but also Anderson, Bausch and Butoh.

The foreword to the second edition is included here as it gives a concise, lucid summation of performance as seen from an artist's point of view. The crucial distinction that she makes is that 'unlike theatre, the performer *is* the artist'. It is therefore not surprising to find so many dancers included in her analysis. Her account remains the most comprehensive one to date.

Reader cross-references

Anderson, Barba, Brown, Duncan, Rainer and **Schlemmer** – the performer as
   artist
Marinetti – the historical futurist viewpoint on performance art
Richter – the founding of Dada
Schechner – a theatre/performance point of view

Chapter 22

Jerzy Grotowksi

STATEMENT OF PRINCIPLES

I

THE RHYTHM OF LIFE in modern civilization is char-acterized by pace, tension, a feeling of doom, the wish to hide our personal motives and the assumption of a variety of roles and masks in life (different ones with our family, at work, amongst friends or in community life, etc.). We like to be 'scientific', by which we mean discursive and cerebral, since this attitude is dictated by the course of civilisation. But we also want to pay tribute to our biological selves, to what we might call physiological pleasures. We do not want to be restricted in this sphere. Therefore we play a double game of intellect and instinct, thought and emotion; we try to divide ourselves artificially into body and soul. When we try to liberate ourselves from it all we start to shout and stamp, we convulse to the rhythm of music. In our search for liberation we reach biological chaos. We suffer most from a lack of totality, throwing ourselves away, squandering ourselves.

Theatre – through the actor's technique, his art in which the living organism strives for higher motives – provides an opportunity for what could be called integration, the discarding of masks, the revealing of the real substance: a totality of physical and mental reactions. This opportunity must be treated in a disciplined manner, with a full awareness of the responsibilities it involves. Here we can see the theatre's therapeutic function for people in our present day civilization. It is true that the actor accomplishes this act, but he can only do so through an encounter with the spectator – intimately, visibly, not hiding behind a cameraman, wardrobe mistress, stage designer or make-up girl – in direct confrontation with him, and somehow 'instead of' him. The actor's act – discarding half measures, revealing, opening up, emerging from himself as opposed to closing up – is an invitation to the spectator. This act could be compared to an act of the most deeply rooted, genuine love between two human beings – this is just a comparison since we can only refer to this 'emergence from oneself' through analogy. This act, paradoxical and borderline, we call a total act. In our opinion it epitomizes the actor's deepest calling.

II

Why do we sacrifice so much energy to our art? Not in order to teach others but to learn with them what our existence, our organism, our personal and unrepeatable experience have to give us; to learn to break down the barriers which surround us and to free ourselves from the breaks which hold us back, from the lies about ourselves which we manufacture daily for ourselves and for others; to destroy the limitations caused by our ignorance and lack of courage; in short, to fill the emptiness in us: to fulfil ourselves. Art is neither a state of the soul (in the sense of some extraordinary, unpredictable moment of inspiration) nor a state of man (in the sense of a profession or social function). Art is a ripening, an evolution, an uplifting which enables us to emerge from darkness into a blaze of light.

We fight then to discover, to experience the truth about ourselves; to tear away the masks behind which we hide daily. We see theatre – especially in its palpable, carnal aspect – as a place of provocation, a challenge the actor sets himself and also, indirectly, other people. Theatre only has a meaning if it allows us to transcend our stereotyped vision, our conventional feelings and customs, our standards of judgement – not just for the sake of doing so, but so that we may experience what is real and, having already given up all daily escapes and pretences, in a state of complete defenselessness unveil, give, discover ourselves. In this way – through shock, through the shudder which causes us to drop our daily masks and mannerisms – we are able, without hiding anything, to entrust ourselves to something we cannot name but in which live Eros and Charitas.

III

Art cannot be bound by the laws of common morality or any catechism. The actor, at least in part, is creator, model and creation rolled into one. He must not be shameless as that leads to exhibitionism. He must have courage, but not merely the courage to exhibit himself – a passive courage, we might say: the courage of the defenseless, the courage to reveal himself. Neither that which touches the interior sphere, nor the profound stripping bare of the self should be regarded as evil so long as in the process of preparation or in the completed work they produce an act of creation. If they do not come easily and if they are not signs of outburst but of mastership, then they are creative: they reveal and purify us **while we transcend ourselves**. Indeed, they improve us then.

For these reasons every aspect of an actor's work dealing with intimate matters should be protected from incidental remarks, indiscretions, nonchalance, idle comments and jokes. The personal realm – both spiritual and physical – must not be 'swamped' by triviality, the sordidness of life and lack of tact towards oneself and others; at least not in the place of work or anywhere connected with it. This postulate sounds like an abstract moral order. It is not. It involves the very essence of the actor's calling. This calling is realized through carnality. The actor must not **illustrate** but **accomplish** an 'act of the soul' by means of his own organism. Thus he is faced with two extreme alternatives: he can either sell, dishonour, his real 'incarnate' self, making himself an object of artistic prostitution; or he can give himself, sanctify his real 'incarnate' self.

IV

An actor can only be guided and inspired by someone who is whole-hearted in his creative activity. The producer, while guiding and inspiring the actor, must at the same time allow himself to be guided and inspired by him. It is a question of freedom, partnership, and this does not imply a lack of discipline but a respect for the autonomy of others. Respect for the actor's autonomy does not mean lawlessness, lack of demands, never ending discussions and the replacement of action by continuous streams of words. On the contrary, respect for autonomy means enormous demands, the expectation of a maximum creative effort and the most personal revelation. Understood thus, solicitude for the actor's freedom can only be born from the plenitude of the guide and not from his lack of plenitude. Such a lack implies imposition, dictatorship, superficial dressage.

V

An act of creation has nothing to do with either external comfort or conventional human civility; that is to say, working conditions in which everybody is happy. It demands a maximum of silence and a minimum of words. In this kind of creativity we discuss through proposals, actions and living organisms, not through explanations. When we finally find ourselves on the track of something difficult and often almost intangible, we have no right to lose it through frivolity and carelessness. Therefore, even during breaks after which we will be continuing with the creative process, we are obliged to observe certain natural reticences in our behaviour and even in our private affairs. This applies just as much to our own work as to the work of our partners. We must not interrupt and disorganize the work because we are hurrying to our own affairs; we must not peep, comment or make jokes about it privately. In any case, private ideas of fun have no place in the actor's calling. In our approach to creative tasks, even if the theme is a game, we must be in a state of readiness – one might even say 'solemnity'. Our working terminology which serves as a stimulus must not be dissociated from the work and used in a private context. Work terminology should be associated only with that which it serves.

A creative act of this quality is performed in a group, and therefore within certain limits we should restrain our creative egoism. An actor has no right to mould his partner so as to provide greater possibilities for his own performance. Nor has he the right to correct his partner unless authorized by the work leader. Intimate or drastic elements in the work of others are untouchable and should not be commented upon even in their absence. Private conflicts, quarrels, sentiments, animosities are unavoidable in any human group. It is our duty towards creation to keep them in check in so far as they might deform and wreck the work process. We are obliged to open ourselves up even towards an enemy.

VI

It has been mentioned several times already, but we can never stress and explain too often the fact that we must never exploit privately anything connected with the creative act: i.e. location, costume, props, an element from the acting score, a melodic theme or lines from the text. This rule applies to the smallest detail and there can be no exceptions. We did not make this rule simply to pay tribute to a special artistic devotion. We are not interested in grandeur and noble words, but our awareness and experience tell us that lack of strict adherence to such rules causes the actor's score to become deprived of its psychic motives and 'radiance'.

VII

Order and harmony in the work of each actor are essential conditions without which a creative act cannot take place. Here we demand consistency. We demand it from the actors who come to the theatre consciously to try themselves out in something extreme, a sort of challenge seeking a total response from every one of us. They come to test themselves in something very definite that reaches beyond the meaning of 'theatre' and is more like an act of living and way of existence. This outline probably sounds rather vague. If we try to explain it theoretically, we might say that the theatre and acting are for us a kind of vehicle allowing us to emerge from ourselves, to fulfil ourselves. We could go into this at great length. However, anyone who stays here longer than just the trial period is perfectly aware that what we are talking about can be grasped less through grandiose words than through details, demands and the rigours of work in all its elements. The individual who disturbs the basic elements, who does not for example respect his own and the others' acting score, destroying its structure by shamming or automatic reproduction, is the very one who shakes this undefinable higher motive of our common activity. Seemingly small details form the background against which fundamental questions are decided, as for example the duty to note down elements discovered in the course of the work. We must not rely on our memory unless we feel the spontaneity of our work is being threatened, and even then we must keep a partial record. This is just as basic a rule as is strict punctuality, the thorough memorizing of the text, etc. Any form of shamming in one's work is completely inadmissible. However it does sometimes happen that an actor has to go through a scene, just outline it, in order to check its organization and the elements of his partners' actions. But even then he must follow the actions carefully, measuring himself against them, in order to comprehend their motives. This is the difference between outlining and shamming.

An actor must always be ready to join the creative act at the exact moment determined by the group. In this respect his health, physical condition and all his private affairs cease to be just his own concern. A creative act of such quality flourishes only if nourished by the living organism. Therefore we are obliged to take daily care of our bodies so we are always ready for our tasks.

We must not go short of sleep for the sake of private enjoyment and then come to work tired or with a hangover. We must not come unable to concentrate. The rule here is not just one's compulsory presence in the place of work, but physical readiness to create.

VIII

Creativity, especially where acting is concerned, is boundless sincerity, yet disciplined: i.e. articulated through signs. The creator should not therefore find his material a barrier in this respect. And as the actor's material is his own body, it should be trained to obey, to be pliable, to respond passively to psychic impulses as if it did not exist during the moment of creation – by which we mean it does not offer any resistance. Spontaneity and discipline are the basic aspects of an actor's work and they require a methodical key.

Before a man decides to do something he must first work out a point of orientation and then act accordingly and in a coherent manner. This point of orientation should be quite evident to him, the result of natural convictions, prior observations and experiences in life. The basic foundations of this method constitute for our troupe this point of orientation. Our institute is geared to examining the consequences of this point of orientation. Therefore nobody who comes and stays here can claim a lack of knowledge of the troupe's methodical programme. Anyone who comes and works here and then wants to keep his distance (as regards creative consciousness) shows the wrong kind of care for his own individuality. The etymological meaning of 'individuality' is 'indivisibility' which means complete existence in something: individuality is the very opposite of half-heartedness. We maintain, therefore, that those who come and stay here discover in our method something deeply related to them, prepared by their lives and experiences. Since they accept this consciously, we presume that each of the participants feels obliged to train creatively and try to form his own variation inseparable from himself, his own reorientation open to risks and search. For what we here call 'the method' is the very opposite of any sort of prescription.

IX

The main point then is that an actor should not try to acquire any kind of recipe or build up a 'box of tricks'. This is no place for collecting all sorts of means of expression. The force of gravity in our work pushes the actor towards an interior ripening which expresses itself through a willingness to break through barriers, to search for a 'summit', for totality.

The actor's first duty is to grasp the fact that nobody here wants **to give** him anything; instead they plan **to take** a lot from him, to take away that to which he is usually very attached: his resistance, reticence, his inclination to hide behind masks, his half-heartedness, the obstacles his body places in the way of his creative act, his habits and even his usual 'good manners'.

X

Before an actor is able to achieve a total act he has to fulfil a number of requirements, some of which are so subtle, so intangible, as to be practically undefinable through words. They only become plain through practical application. It is easier, however, to define conditions under which a total act cannot be achieved and which of the actor's actions make it impossible.

This act cannot exist if the actor is more concerned with charm, personal success, applause and salary than with creation as understood in its highest form. It cannot exist if the actor conditions it according to the size of his part, his place in the performance, the day or kind of audience. There can be no total act if the actor, even away from the theatre, dissipates his creative impulse and, as we said before, sullies it, blocks it, particularly through incidental engagements of a doubtful nature or by the premeditated use of the creative act as a means to further his own career.

■ ■ ■

Source

Grotowski, J. (1968, 1969) 'Statement of Principles', *Towards a Poor Theatre*, trans. M. Buszewicz and J. Barba, ed. E. Barba, London: Methuen: 211–218.

Jerzy Grotowski (1933–)

Polish director. Along with Stanislavski and Brecht, he is credited with establishing a new form of actor training for the twentieth century. His purpose has always been, and remains, more philosophical – 'the quest for what is most essential in life ... something like a second birth'. Grotowski, with his Theatre of Thirteen Rows (Opole, 1959–62), then transformed into the Laboratory Theatre (1962–84), revolutionised the art of performance.

He insisted that the actor should be the prime energy and source of any theatre production and, moreover, that the space should be adapted to suit the dynamic of the individual theatre piece. From 1959 to 1970 he developed exercises and vocal techniques which produced some of Europe's most intense performances, such as *Kordian* (1962), *Akropolis* (1962), *Dr Faustus* (1963), and

The Constant Prince (1965), most of which were played in a small upper space in the centre of Wroclaw, from where the Laboratory Theatre toured extensively both within and outside Europe. *Apocalypsus Cum Figuris* (1969), which ran for over twelve years – a quasi-mystic collage of theatrical ideas – has been described by those few who saw it as one of the great theatrical productions of the twentieth century. Through the shock of exposure to Grotowski's theatre, audiences were expected to be transformed, and many throughout Europe have testified to its power. In 1984 the Laboratory Theatre was dissolved and its members went their individual ways, one of which led to the establishment of the Gardzienice Association under the leadership of Wlodzimierz Staniewski. Grotowski himself, after a period in the USA, now has a centre in Pontedera, Italy, where he concentrates on developing the para-theatrical work that formed the last stage of the Laboratory's work.

In this 'Statement' Grotowski outlines his belief that theatre can act as a catalyst for transcendence, and that the actor must, through his training, be a conduit for this change. The text was written for actors of the Laboratory Theatre undergoing a period of trial before being accepted as full members.

Reader cross-references

Artaud – for a similar messianic role for theatre
Barba – a student of Grotowski's, published his first book
Brook – acknowledged him as 'unique'
Brecht, Stanislavski and **Meyerhold** – comparison with other European systems of training
Hijikata – a contemporary, comparable Japanese account of the performer's role
Kantor – a contemporary Polish artist
Rainer – an approach to performance in many ways completely antithetical
Soyinka – a West African perspective on ritual

Further reading

Bradby, D. and Williams, D. (1988) *Directors' Theatre*, London: Macmillan.
Kumiega, J. (1985) *The Theatre of Grotowski*, London: Methuen.
Mitter, S. (1992) *Systems of Rehearsal*, London: Routledge.

Chapter 23

Tatsumi Hijikata

MAN, ONCE DEAD, CRAWL BACK!

A NXIETY has sown itself everywhere. It lies always ahead of the action, just like the school kid who pisses in his pants just as the whistle blows at the school races.

This form of anxiety is growing-anxiety over the present, anxiety over the future. However, there is not the slightest trace of fear in this condition. I wonder how it can be that this situation arose.

There is a lot of anxiety present at my dance lessons: one finds there many people festering due to their own turbid eroticism. All kinds gather at the studio, some forlorn, some just passing through. In teaching butoh my aim is to make them aware of a part of themselves that they have lost contact with, by making them study themselves body and soul. They are inhibited by their anxieties, but through the means of dance they can share their anxieties with each other.

Learning dance is not a matter of where to position an arm or a leg. Since I believe neither in a dance teaching method nor in controlling movement, I do not teach in this manner. I have never believed in these systems; I have been mistrustful of them since the day I was born.

Recently, it is possible to distinguish between the fighters and the pleasure seekers in this life. On the one hand, those who throw bombs, and on the other hand, those who are completely indifferent. Superficially they seem to be at extremes, but they share one thing in common: their homogeneity. They are mistaken in thinking that hurling bombs or turning away makes them diametrically opposed. One should do both!

As an example, the troops that fight continually in battle tire quickly. If they were immersed in the spirit of butoh, one man would be able to do the work of two and recovery would be quicker. This butoh spirit is what I try to impart during lessons in my studio. Younger people start with great enthusiasm in some endeavor, but their ardor quickly cools off. This is because they are acquainted only with the superficial and ostentatious aspects of life. Through immersing oneself wholly in dance one can encounter the butoh spirit. It is here, rather than in the stage performance, that one finds the real meaning of butoh.

When one considers the body in relation to dance, it is then that one truly realizes what suffering is: it is a part of our lives. No matter how much we search for it from the outside there is no way we can find it without delving into ourselves.

We are broken from birth. We are only corpses standing in the shadow of life. Therefore, what is the point of becoming a professional dancer? If a man becomes a laborer and a woman a servant, isn't that enough in itself!

That is the essence of butoh – and that is how I lead my communal life.

We should live in the present. We should do what we have to do now and not keep putting it on the long finger as the majority of adults do. This is why they exhaust themselves. For children, there is only the present. They are not afraid. Fear envelops us in a fine mesh. We must remove this mesh.

There is nothing to fear in the avant-garde; it's only a dry intellectual comprehension. We *should* be afraid! The reason that we suffer from anxiety is that we are unable to live with our fears. Anxiety is something created by adults. The dancer, through the butoh spirit, confronts the origins of his fears: a dance which crawls towards the bowel of the earth. I don't believe this is possible with European dance.

The body is fundamentally chaotic; the Japanese body particularly, which in comparison with the coherent body of the Occidental (both religiously and culturally), is unsure in its stance. Occidentals have their feet planted firmly on the ground, forming a pyramid, whereas the Japanese seem to be performing acrobatic feats on oil paper. Therefore, they have to find their balance on twisted legs.

For my next performance I plan to use *geta* (wooden sandals). There are now only seven artisans in Tokyo capable of inserting the 'teeth' for the foot strap. Eventually I will have to ask the craftsmen of the Osaka area. Gradually the environment in which we live is becoming a toothless one in every sense of the word.

Once fallen, man must rise again. It is not only a matter of straightening one's back and facing the sun. I am not interested in having an ordinary theater troupe, but rather a troupe which has experienced the vagaries of this world. Once, there was a very noticeable change in a member of the troupe who had returned after a period of absence. On being asked what had happened to him, he replied that he had been washing dishes! For these kind of people dance is a way of helping them from burning up; it acts as a lubricant. That is why I do not see any value in either literature or painting that does not contain the essence of butoh.

I abhor a world which is regulated from the cradle to the grave. I prefer the dark to the dazzling light. Darkness is the best symbol for light. There is no way that one can understand the nature of light if one never observes deeply the darkness. A proper understanding of both requires that both their inherent natures be truly understood.

One does not need to be dazzling like an alien from another star. I would like to construct a huge countryside in Tokyo.

The young should not become sensual addicts. They need a real desire and must act in accordance with it – dance with it, without imposing regulations on themselves.

Don't mince your steps, take a giant step!
One should believe in the energy born in oneself out of suffering.
One shouldn't become a *bonsai* (miniature tree).
Believe in your own energy and don't let yourself be affected by others.

■　　■　　■

Source

Hijikata, T. (1988) 'Man, once dead, crawl back!', *Butoh: Shades of Darkness*, ed. N. Masson-Sekine, Tokyo: Shufonotomo: 186–189.

Tatsumi Hijikata (1928–86)

Japanese dancer and choreographer. His early training in techniques derived from modern dance, notably with Kazuko Matsumura, whose work derived, via Takaya Eguchi, from Wigman. He began to present his own work in 1959, with *Kinjiki* (Forbidden Colours), based on a novel by Yukio Mishima (1915–70). In 1960 he termed his work Ankoku Buyo (Dance of Darkness), later Ankoku Butoh. He worked with Kazuo Ono, who became his pupil and collaborator. From the late 1960s he also worked with Yoko Ashikawa, Saga Kobayashi and Monoko Hinura among others.

Hijikata developed a form which was both uniquely Japanese and contemporary – Butoh. It could be seen as the antithesis of the liberation sought during the same period by contemporary Western dancers. In both its themes – cruelty, death, darkness, sexual perversion – and its concomitant attitude towards the body as 'fundamentally chaotic' it is a dance of denial. This is seen in *Saint Marquis – Dance of Darkness* (1960), *Secret Ceremony for an Hermaphrodite* (1961) and *Butoh Genet* (1967). His work with Kazuo Ono included the celebrated *Admiring La Argentina* (1977) and for Ashikawa *Nippon No Chibusa* (Breasts of Japan) (1983). Hijikata is ranked alongside Ono as the co-founder of Butoh. The many dance artists who followed him acknowledge his enormous influence. His work began to be seen more widely in the West in the early 1980s; as he said, 'we bring to the bright summer of Europe a little bit of violent darkness from Japan'.[1]

Hijikata comments here on his philosophy of dance. In this sense he outlines his attitude towards performance, rather than detailing process. Indeed, he speaks against a systematic approach to dance. His statements on the body will find resonance with those attracted by chaos as a defining feature of the postmodern condition, but not with those for whom reason is a virtue.

Reader cross-references

Artaud and **Marinetti** – early European celebrations of the irrational
Brown and **Rainer** – completely antithetical, contemporary views of dance
Grotowski and **Barba** – contemporary European parallels
Kantor – a contemporary view of a theatre of death
Richter – an earlier, Western view of chaos
Schechner – a Western view of the role of the avant-garde
Soyinka and **Bharucha** – different views on the place of traditional forms
Wigman – a Western, historical antecedent

Further reading

Blackwood, M. (1990) *Butoh: Body on the Edge of Crisis,* New York: Michael Blackwood.

Note

1   Hijikata, T. (1983) *Ankoku Buto,* Programme, Festival of Japanese Arts, Nottingham Playhouse, 24 June–1 July 1983.

Doris Humphrey

'CHECK LIST', FROM
THE ART OF
MAKING DANCES

HAVING HAD A CHANCE in five decades to make many choreographic mistakes, and having observed other people make them, too, I have compiled a short list of checks for the composer, something like a pocket set of rules for trueing up a work in progress. It is all too easy to become absorbed in one part of the complex act of composition, and, while the attention is fixed on that, allow fatal errors to creep in elsewhere. A final checking up on balances is a wise – indeed, an essential – procedure. These, then, are some reminders which have been learned by painful experience and which should help the choreographer to avoid some of the commonest mistakes:

> Symmetry is lifeless
> Two-dimensional design is lifeless
> The eye is faster than the ear
> Movement looks slower and weaker on the stage
> All dances are too long
> A good ending is forty per cent of the dance
> Monotony is fatal; look for contrasts
> Don't be a slave to, or a mutilator of, the music
> Listen to qualified advice; don't be arrogant

Don't intellectualize; motivate movement
Don't leave the ending to the end

There follows comment and explanation about each item on the list:

Symmetry is lifeless

In the chapters on design, it was pointed out that shape, per se, has significance and that symmetrical design always suggests stability, repose, a
passionless state, the condition before will and desire have begun to operate,
or after these have subsided. Therefore it is never exciting, and if it is misused
– that is, in the service of emotional sequences – it will weaken the dance
and result in tedium. Symmetry is good for calm states of being, ritual, or
beginnings; or endings, when a resolution is in order. Dancers, without
compositional training, almost invariably fall into symmetry, as children do
when they improvise. The child begins to dance with his feet, the arms held
out at the sides. This is in response to an instinctive reaction of the body
toward balancing; the imperfectly co-ordinated child is safer with the arms
out on either side of the straight trunk, to offset the changes of weight in
the feet. Moving in space, the child usually runs with tiny steps (this is safer
than jumping from one foot to the other), still with the arms extended
outward. Turns are often done with both arms over the head; this is also a
safety instinct – all the body weights are over the center of gravity, and the
difficulty of the turn is minimized. All these movements are symmetrical in
design. Children have to be taught to skip with arms in opposition to the
feet, where the weights, though balanced, are more precarious. Every teacher
knows the child who can only skip on one foot. My guess is that his instinct
is operating to bring him to earth safely, after that one adventurous hop.

Beginners in choreography behave exactly like children in their choice
of movement, and unfortunately some of them never learn otherwise, but
go on into elaborate group compositions in which each dancer uses the arms
symmetrically according to the safe-balance instinct, regardless of the subject
matter and the cluttered look of all-out arms.

The symmetrical design in form is by no means rare either – two to
one side, two to the other. Overuse of symmetry is not only naïve and
unimaginative, but also very dull. No painter would think of using unrelieved
symmetry; he knows this is for decorative art, such as wallpaper, fabrics,
rugs. The dancer, on the other hand, because his instrument is his own body,
is caught in physiological compulsions, and the snare of feeling good – that
is, moving without fear of imbalance – is most powerful. In children this is
charming, but in adults, deplorable.

Two-dimensional design is lifeless

The human body is three-dimensional. If composition is to speak of people, even abstractly, as in a pure-movement dance, the full dimensions must be used if the piece is to look warm and alive. Nothing dehumanizes movement so completely as the flat, linear design. This can be employed intermittently in a composition without too much damage, and sometimes very effectively, as it provides a welcome contrast. Nevertheless, the choreographer should always keep in mind its devitalizing tendency. Two-dimensional figures, as in Egyptian friezes and Greek vases, have been effectively stylized from the original models to make handsome decorative art. It is no longer human, but this is well within the province of the artist. Dance can also do this, to a limited extent, although the actual body can never be distorted and stylized as much as it can be with brush and chisel. Choreographers err most often in deciding when to use the flat design. In ritual, which has been traditionalized so that feeling is no longer dominant, and in other cold and impersonal subject matter, flat design is the very device to use; but too often, through habit or predilection, it is chosen to tell of warmth and feeling, and here it is a dismal failure.

The eye is faster than the ear

The eye is a far more educated instrument than the ear, which, along with the nose, has been retrogressing in sensitivity up the ladder of evolution. This is simply because the eye is a more valuable informer about our environment, is exercised more, and therefore is faster. That is, it grasps complex relationships more quickly, and also retains a more accurate memory of them. Not only is the eye faster, but, in a contest with the ear, will invariably take precedence. So movement must take the spotlight; it must not be repetitious or lazily lean on the music to carry it along.

Movement looks slower and weaker on the stage

One of the peaks of anxiety in choreography is that moment when the studio-born dance is transferred to the stage. Immediately space works magical and often appalling differences. Distance has weakened almost everything about the dance. Dynamics are not so strong, personalities are dimmer, timing looks slower; and so, with the essential vitality lessened, it now seems too long. In only one respect is it clearer – in its over-all design, because the eye can now see the whole in one glance without shifting from point to point, which is inevitable in the studio. Also, there is a seeming illogicality in the fact that detail is much more apparent at a distance. One would think that small movements and inaccuracies would be easier to see at close range. Not so, in practice. For instance, lack of precision in ensemble movements, overlooked in a studio, stands out on a stage embarrassingly. In fact, it screams for correction.

The obvious remedy for all this is to remember to compensate for the expected changes in the studio – what looks there a little too fast, too sharp, too big, too aggressive in general will probably be about right.

All dances are too long

In all my many years of looking at dances, I can remember only a scant handful that were too short. And this includes all kinds of dances: ballet, ethnic, modern and jazz. Almost all of them would have been improved by cutting and condensing. Everybody seems to recognize the overlong composition except the choreographer himself. In teaching young students, it has been proved over and over again that those who sit watching the efforts of one of the class need no prompting from me to judge accurately the length of what they are seeing. I am sure this is true of a lay audience in general; they know very well when a work is overextended, by means of that automatic timer of boredom they have in the nervous system. But the choreographer goes obliviously on and on, no doubt because he cannot be sufficiently objective. His self-fascination is working at a galloping pace. His own invention, child of his body and his brain, is truly wonderful to him, a proof to the ego that 'I am,' and no less dear than his very right hand. Anything so remarkable is surely worth repeating in all its movement, and drawing out to its full glorious length. Recurring shocks from those who feel it is a little too long never seem to deter him, except at the cost of much agony and resentment.

There is one other remedy besides cutting for the overlong dance, and that is more material, more intensity, more invention; in other words, a richer mixture might keep the whole thing alive in its original length.

A good ending is forty per cent of the dance

The ending is a highly important affair, which choreographers should worry about fully as much as playwrights with their third-act curtain. The theater is a place where the last impression is not only the strongest one, but tends to color the audience's opinion of the whole – which is perhaps not fair, but it is a fact. If the curtain – that abrupt effacing of the color, action, music – comes down on a weak, equivocal or illogical conclusion, the first reaction is one of disappointment, and there is an impression of total failure.

It takes an effort of goodwill to remember that, yes, the beginning was excellent, there was a high spot in the middle, the music was appropriate, etc. – still that fatal ending remains a psychological blight so strong as to mark the piece as unsuccessful. We are so constituted as individuals that we passionately long to be satisfied emotionally with our theatrical fare, and the supreme satisfaction is the final statement. When the last curtain comes down, we don't want to feel puzzled or at loose ends or cheated; we want to be refreshed and stimulated enough so that we, too, can break into the release of physical action – clap hands and rejoice. This does not mean that endings must necessarily be devised for theatrical dazzle, although this is a well-worn and reliable cliché. Rather, it means that they shall be true and, if possible, surprising. The inevitability of the ending must be apparent, and if to this is added an imaginative treatment, there is a double stimulation. Beware of originality without truth, however. This will not do.

Monotony is fatal; look for contrasts

The choreographer who can choose from a wide range of materials built right into his natural personality is rare. Most people live and die in narrow grooves. They meet all situations with fast nervous energy, or moderately and calmly; they plod or they fly, they are thinkers or doers, optimists or pessimists. The natural human being does not and cannot react in all these ways to his normal state. But to be successful, the choreographer, along with the playwright, the novelist and the composer, must enlarge his personal range, must seek to use and understand attitudes and timings quite foreign to his natural inclinations. Specifically, the dancer whose normal physical timing is moderate, and who is reluctant to leave the floor, will be badly handicapped as a composer if he stays in this range, not only because it will lead to monotony, but because moderation is the dullest area of all. Very fast or very slow tempi are much more exciting, because they are further away from the workaday pace. For the mover-in-moderation to lift himself out of his normal rhythm takes a very great effort indeed, plus enlightenment and conviction. I am afraid this happens all too rarely, and so there are too many dances of the deadly middle – medium pace, medium dynamics, medium everything, and extreme only in their dullness. Moderation in all things may be a good recipe for living, but in dancing it is fatal.

Don't be a slave to, or a mutilator of, the music

Procedures in regard to music alter radically almost from one decade to another. Not only do individuals change their minds about the selection and uses of music, but opposing ideas are now held, now abandoned in various centers of dance throughout the world. Perhaps the only thing everyone agrees on is that there should be music with dance. At this point, my own opinion is that the choreographer should not follow the music bar for bar, phrase for phrase, note for note. The dance should be related to, but not identical with, the music, because this is redundant – why say in dance exactly what the composer has already stated in music? – and because the dance is an entirely different art, subject to physical and psychological laws of its own. The ideal relationship is like a happy marriage in which two individuals go hand in hand, but are not identical twins. On the other hand, the choreographer should be a great respecter of music. Arbitrary cutting and juggling of parts to suit his own convenience should not be tolerated. For instance, snipping out the second movement of a well-known string quartet for a solo dance is a stupid affront to a great art. So is that other blunder that recurs so often, stopping short at an arbitrary point where there is no cadence, or ending with the remark, 'That's all I need.' These painful errors, and others like them, call for heavy doses of knowledge, taste and respect.

Listen to qualified advice; don't be arrogant

Independence and conviction are glorious qualities, and where would the human race be without them? Americans, especially, have the Declaration of Independence built right into their history and characters, and I have no doubt that our great contribution to the dance has resulted primarily from this outstanding trait. But this is also known by our derogators as brashness, arrogance and crudity. One must admit that there is something just about this criticism, and that such traits exist in the dance no less than elsewhere. It is impossible to mark exactly where independence changes into arrogance; but, tentatively, shall we say it is at the point where the very young, who seem to their elders to be promising and only partly educated, declare themselves to be artists with no further need for advice? Or perhaps they do feel a little shaky and uncertain, but the ego prompts them to stand alone, even at the peril of their artistic lives. Considering that it takes an average of ten years to make a dancer, and fifteen to make a choreographer, a declaration of independence much earlier than this seems premature. I think it would not hurt these young people to listen a little longer, and to exercise some humility. But one can easily make a mistake in judgments of this sort. History is full of examples where youth defied the elders and their traditions, and lived to be justified. Still, in general, there is not enough listening and too much egotism, and this applies not only to the very young, but also to older choreographers who cannot admit, at their stage of experience, that there might be something they don't know. These latter composers have had to grow up with whatever talent they possessed innately, but now there is a body of theory which it would be worth their while to investigate.

Don't intellectualize; motivate movement

There is a great difference of opinion about this point in the dance world, at least in the United States. In fact there is such a schism that the subject calls for a chapter of its own. At this point, it must be obvious that I belong to the faction that believes in motivation, feeling and emotion, as opposed to the widespread notion that these things are not only unnecessary but outmoded. It seems to me that an intellectual approach, which is central and not peripheral, is out of place in an art which has, as its medium, movement of the human body. Intellectual concepts are for the world of fact, for mental exercises such as philosophy and science, and for the word arts capable of making evaluations, which are, for the most part, foreign to the dance. One of the examples of intellectualism is the imitation of other arts, notably painting, which, with its quite different values of static relationships, can put a blight of immovability on the dance. I venture to say that dance cannot be completely intellectualized without forfeiting its audiences and endangering its very existence. Fortunately, such a ruinous procedure is not likely to take over completely, considering the vitality of the human being. Communication in terms of nonintellectualized movement seems to me the desirable goal.

Don't leave the ending to the end

I have already stressed the importance of endings, and because of this I strongly advise the choreographer to consider and shape the end long before it is upon him. This will mitigate some of the disasters caused by vagueness of conception — lack of time, the ending that seems perfect in the mind, but that is not right in practice. The workmanlike procedure, with all its logic, is not the best way to compose a dance. Things are usually made in a series of steps: the assembling of materials, the cutting or shaping, the fastening together and finally the polish or paint. Choreographers should not begin at the beginning and plod through like this. The dance is not an artifact, but is shot through with intangibles of feeling, intuition, inspiration, and a special psychological attitude to the ending. There is usually a high resistance to thinking about the ending at all. This is somehow supposed to come of itself, probably because the body of the dance is mostly concerned with movement, where dancers are happiest, and is the part that gets long and loving attention. But an end, a statement, a resolution, is a conception which must be considered and decided on. This takes thinking, always a painful process and one that dancers avoid if possible. So choreographers go skimming along, the time grows short, the deadline is upon them, and no ending yet. Something is put together in a hurry: Do this, do that, anything to get it done and over with; after all, it's a beautiful dance, and the last minute or two is such a small part of it. I would like to persuade choreographers not to work this way. My recommendation is to stop in the middle somewhere and spend many concentrated hours, if necessary, on the conceiving of, the shaping and redoing of the final statement.

It would be well to state again at this point that I am not a believer in the starting and shaping of a dance with the conscious use of all the technical information which a theory of choreography implies. Hence the placing of this chapter as a check list, and the craft section, which precedes it, as a preliminary study. The dance itself should be long dreamed over, the instinctive movement invited, glimpses and visions welcomed to entrap the imagination. The strict technical considerations, one may hope, are operating subconsciously to save the choreographer from the worst mistakes; but on the surface all is rapt excitement, the discovery of a new country. With this procedure, the wail of the young, 'Now I know so much about it I can't compose any more,' will not be heard in the land so frequently.

■   ■   ■

Source

Humphrey, D. (1959) 'Check List', from *The Art of Making Dances*, New York: Grove Press: 159–166.

Doris Humphrey (1895–1958)

American dancer and choreographer. She danced with St Denis and Shawn in their Denishawn Company 1917–28. She made her solo debut as a choreographer in 1920, and choreographed a number of solo and group works for groups of Denishawn dancers including *Air for the G String* to Bach (1928). She co-founded the Humphrey–Weidman Company in 1928, and premièred *Water Study* for 16 dancers. She made numerous solo and group works for this company until 1944 including the trilogy *New Dance, Theatre Piece* and *With My Red Fires* (1935–36). From 1933 she taught and danced at the Bennington College School of Dance. She stopped dancing in 1944, after which she choreographed for the José Limon Company, including *Day on Earth* (1947).

Humphrey is celebrated along with her partner Charles Weidman, Martha Graham and the German dancer Hanya Holm as one of the 'Four Pioneers', featured in the eponymous film. Her work typifies American early modern dance. It was characteristically angular, percussive, expressive, dealing with themes drawn from personal and socio-political life. The recognisable choreographic style results from both choreographic and technical developments by Humphrey. She developed a technique based on 'fall and recovery'. This technique was taught to her own dancers and passed on to later generations. At the same time, she systematised her approaches to choreography and these became widely known through her book, *The Art of Making Dances*, published the year after her death.

This extract is the penultimate chapter of the book. In the previous seventeen chapters she lays out her approach to the art and craft of choreography. She identifies choreographers as being 'special people' and lays great store on the appropriate choice of subject matter. The craft of choreography is described in terms of 'design, dynamics, rhythm, motivation and gesture, words, music, sets and props and, finally, form'. The 'check list' reminds the student of some of the basic principles. This approach, which sets out choreographic rules and verities, was challenged even in the year that it was published – by such as Halprin – and later by Judson Dance Theatre. Her book, and this extract, stand as a symbol of how early modern dance tried to impose order on a chaotic world. Whilst many of the assumptions behind her approach have been superseded, much of her advice remains relevant, notably her observation that 'all dances are too long'.

Reader cross-references

Bausch – a later idea of motivation
Brown and **Rainer** – a later, contrasting view of the choreographic process
Cage – an earlier statement on dance and music
Duncan and **Wigman** – early modern dance in Europe
Martin – a critical and theoretical context for early modern dance
Stanislavski – comparison with a sytematised approach to the actor's training

Further reading

Cohen, S.J. (ed.) (1972) *Doris Humphrey: An Artist First*, Middletown, Conn.: Wesleyan University Press.

Humphrey, D. (1937, 1980) 'What a Dancer Thinks About', *The Vision of Modern Dance*, ed. J. Morrison Brown, London: Dance Books: 55–64.

Chapter 25

Alfred Jarry

OF THE FUTILITY
OF THE 'THEATRICAL'
IN THEATER

I THINK THE QUESTION of whether the theater should
adapt itself to the public, or the public to the theater, has
been settled once and for all. The public only understood,
or looked as if they understood, the tragedies and comedies of
ancient Greece because they were based on universally known
fables which, anyway, were explained over and over again in
every play and, as often as not, hinted at by a character in the
prologue. Just as nowadays they go to hear the plays of Molière
and Racine at the Comédie Française because they are always
being played, even though they certainly don't really understand them. The theater has not yet won the freedom to eject
forcibly any member of the audience who doesn't understand,
or to comb out the potential hecklers and hooligans from the
auditorium during each interval. But we can content ourselves
with the established truth that if people do fight in the theater
it will be a work of popularization they are fighting over, one
that is not in the least original and is therefore more readily
accessible than the original. An original work will, at least on
the first night, be greeted by a public that remains bemused
and, consequently, dumb.

But first nights are attended by those capable of understanding!

If we want to lower ourselves to the level of the public there are two things we can do for them – and which *are* done for them. The first is to give them characters who think as they do (a Siamese or Chinese ambassador seeing *The Miser* would bet anything that the miser would be outwitted and his money box stolen), and whom they understand perfectly. When this is the case they receive two impressions;· firstly they think that they must themselves be very witty, as they laugh at what they take to be witty writing – and this never fails to happen to Monsieur Donnay's audiences. Secondly they get the impression that they are participating in the creation of the play, which relieves them of the effort of anticipating what is going to happen. The other thing we can do for them is give them a commonplace sort of plot – write about things that happen all the time to the common man, because the fact is that Shakespeare, Michelangelo, or Leonardo da Vinci are somewhat bulky; their diameter is a bit difficult to traverse because genius, intelligence, and even talent are larger than life and so inaccessible to most people.

If, in the whole universe, there are five hundred people who, compared with infinite mediocrity, have a touch of Shakespeare and Leonardo in them, is it not only fair to grant these five hundred healthy minds the same thing that is lavished on Monsieur Donnay's audiences – the relief of not seeing on the stage what they don't understand; the *active* pleasure of participating in the creation of the play and of anticipation?

What follows is a list of a few things which are particularly horrifying and incomprehensible to the five hundred, and which clutter up the stage to no purpose; first and foremost, the *decor* and the *actors*.

Decor is a hybrid, neither natural nor artificial. If it were exactly like nature it would be a superfluous duplication. . . . (We shall consider the use of nature as decor later.) It is not artificial, in the sense that it is not, for the five hundred, the embodiment of the outside world as the playwright has seen and re-created it.

And in any case it would be dangerous for the poet to impose on a public of artists the decor that he himself would conceive. In any written work there is a hidden meaning, and anyone who knows how to read sees that aspect of it that makes sense for him. He recognizes the eternal and invisible river and calls it *Anna Perenna*.[1] But there is hardly anyone for whom a painted backdrop has two meanings, as it is far more arduous to extract the quality from a quality than the quality from a quantity. Every spectator has a right to see a play in a decor which does not clash with his own view of it. For the general public, on the other hand, any 'artistic' decor will do, as the masses do not understand anything by themselves, but wait to be told how to see things.

There are two sorts of decor: indoor and outdoor. Both are supposed to represent either rooms or the countryside. We shall not revert to the question, which has been settled once and for all, of the stupidity of *trompe l'œil*. Let us state that the said *trompe l'œil* is aimed at people who only see things roughly, that is to say, who do not see at all: it scandalizes those who see nature in an intelligent and selective way, as it presents them with a caricature of it by someone who lacks all understanding. Zeuxis is supposed to have deceived some birds with his stone grapes, and Titian's virtuosity hoodwinked an innkeeper.

Decor by someone who cannot paint is nearer to abstract decor, as it gives only essentials. In the same way simplified decor picks out only relevant aspects.

We tried *heraldic* decors, where a single shade is used to represent a whole scene or act, with the characters poised harmonically *passant* against the heraldic field. This is a bit puerile, as the said color can only establish itself against a colorless background (but it is also more accurate, since we have to take into account the prevailing red-green color blindness, as well as other idiosyncrasies of perception). A colorless background can be achieved simply, and in a way which is symbolically accurate, by an unpainted backdrop or the reverse side of a set. Each spectator can then conjure up for himself the background he requires, or, better still, if the author knew what he was about, the spectator can imagine, by a process of exosmosis, that what he sees on the stage is the real decor. The placard brought in to mark each change in scene saves the onlooker from being regularly reminded of base 'reality' through a constant substitution of conventional sets which he really only sees properly at the moment the scene is being shifted.

In the conditions we are advocating, each piece of scenery needed for a special purpose – a window to be opened, for instance, or a door to be broken down – becomes a prop and can be brought in like a table or a torch.

The actor adapts his face to that of the character. He should adapt his whole body in the same way. The play of his features, his expressions, etc., are caused by various contractions and extensions of the muscles of his face. No one has realized that the muscles remain the same under the make-believe, made-up face, and that Mounet and Hamlet do not have the same zygomatics, even though in anatomical terms we think that they are the same man. Or else people say that the difference is negligible. The actor should use a mask to envelop his head, thus replacing it by the effigy of the CHARACTER. His mask should not follow the masks in the Greek theater to indicate simply tears or laughter, but should indicate the nature of the character: the Miser, the Waverer, the Covetous Man accumulating crimes. . . .

And if the eternal nature of the character is embodied in the mask, we can learn from the kaleidoscope, and particularly the gyroscope, a simple means of *illuminating*, one by one or several at a time, the critical moments.

With the old-style actor, masked only in a thinly applied make-up, each facial expression is raised to a power by color and particularly by relief, and then to cubes and higher powers by LIGHTING.

What we are about to describe was impossible in the Greek theater because the light was vertical, or at least never sufficiently horizontal, and therefore produced a shadow under every protuberance in the mask; it was a blurred shadow, though, because the light was diffused.

Contrary to the deductions of rudimentary and imperfect logic, there is no clear shadow in those sunny countries; and in Egypt, below the tropic of Cancer, there is hardly a trace of shadow left on the face. The light was reflected vertically as if by the face of the moon, and diffused by both the sand on the ground and the sand suspended in the air.

The *footlights* illumine the actor along the hypotenuse of a right-angled triangle, the actor's body forming one of the sides of the right angle. And as the footlights are a series of luminous points, that is to say a line which, in relation to the narrowness of the front view of the actor, extends indefinitely to right and left of its intersection with the actor's plane, these footlights should be considered as a single point of light situated at an indefinite distance, as if it were *behind* the audience.

It is true that the footlights are less than an infinite distance away, so that one cannot really regard all the rays reflected by the actor (or facial expressions) as traveling along parallel lines. But in practice each spectator sees the character's mask *equally*, with the differences which are certainly negligible compared to the idiosyncrasies and different perceptive attitudes of the individual spectator. These differences cannot be attenuated, though they cancel each other out in the audience *qua* herd, which is what an audience is.

By slow nodding and lateral movements of his head the actor can displace the shadows over the whole surface of his mask. And experience has shown that the six main positions (and the same number in profile, though these are less clear) suffice for every expression. We shall not cite any examples, as they vary according to the nature of the mask, and because everyone who knows how to watch a puppet show will have been able to observe this for himself.

They are simple expressions, and therefore universal. Present-day mime makes the great mistake of using conventional mime language, which is tiring and incomprehensible. An example of this convention is the hand describing a vertical ellipse around the face, and a kiss being implanted on this hand to suggest a beautiful woman – and love. An example of universal gesture is the marionette displaying its bewilderment by starting back violently and hitting its head against a flat.

Behind all these accidentals there remains the essential expression, and the finest thing in many scenes is the impassivity of the mask, which remains the same whether the words it emits are grave or gay. This can only be compared with the solid structure of the skeleton, deep down under its surrounding animal flesh; its tragicomic qualities have always been acknowledged.

It goes without saying that the actor must have a special *voice*, the voice that is appropriate to the part, as if the cavity forming the mouth of the mask were incapable of uttering anything other than what the mask would say, if the muscles of its lips could move. And it is better for them not to move, and that the whole play should be spoken in a monotone.

And we have also said that the actor must take on the body appropriate to the part.

Transvestism has been forbidden by the Church and by art. Witness Beaumarchais, who in one of his prefaces wrote: 'The young man does not exist who is sufficiently developed to . . .' And since women are beardless and their voices shrill all their lives, a boy of fourteen is traditionally played on the Paris stage by a twenty-year-old woman who, being six years older, has much more experience. This is small compensation for her ridiculous profile and unesthetic walk, or for the way the outline of all her muscles is vitiated by adipose tissue, which is odious because it has a function – it produces *milk*.

Given the difference in their brains, a boy of fifteen, if you pick an intelligent one, will play his part adequately (most women are vulgar and nearly all boys are stupid, with some outstanding exceptions). The young actor Baron, in Molière's company, is an example, and there is also the whole period in the English theater (and the whole history of the Greek theater) when no one would have dreamed of trusting a part to a woman.

A few words on natural decors, which exist without duplication if one tries to stage a play in the open air, on the slope of a hill, near a river, which is excellent for carrying the voice, especially when there is no awning, even though the sound may be weakened. Hills are all that is necessary, with a few trees for shade. At the moment *Le Diable Marchand de Goutte* is being played out of doors, as it was a year ago, and the production was discussed some time ago in the *Mercure* by Alfred Vallette. Three or four years ago Monsieur Lugné-Poe and some friends staged *La Gardienne* at Presles, on the edge of the Isle-Adam forest. In these days of universal cycling it would not be absurd to make use of summer Sundays in the countryside to stage a few very short performances (say from two to five o'clock in the afternoon) of literature which is not too abstract – *King Lear* would be a good example;

we do not understand the idea of a people's theater. The performances should be in places not too far distant, and arrangements should be made for people who come by train, without previous planning. The places in the sun should be free (Monsieur Barrucand was writing quite recently about the free theater), and as for the props, the bare necessities could be transported in one or several automobiles.

Note

1   Dido's sister, who came to Rome and drowned in a river, of which she became the nymph. *Amne perenne latens, Anna Perenna vocor.*

    (Ovid, *Fasti*, Book III, l. 654.) [Translator's note.]

■ ■ ■

Source

Jarry, A. (1896, 1985) 'Of the Futility of the "Theatrical" in the Theater', *Selected Works of Alfred Jarry*, trans. B. Wright, ed. R. Shattuck and S. Watson Taylor, London: Methuen: 69–75.

Alfred Jarry (1873–1907)

The first performance of Jarry's *Ubu Roi* on 10 December 1896 in many ways marks the beginning of the modernist play. A wild parody of Shakespeare, it was originally written for marionettes, and its performance by actors with masks and sets by Pierre Bonnard, Toulouse-Lautrec and others, directed by Lugné-Poe at the Théâtre de l'Œuvre, provoked scenes of violence and pandemonium in the audience. Jarry's work, in plays, essays, and fiction, was perceived as a direct attack on the fundamental concepts of Western civilisation. He promoted a bitingly satiric denigration of bourgeois values via parodies of existing nineteenth-century theatrical styles. *Ubu*, and the writings surrounding it – *Ubu Cocu, Ubu's Almanac* (1901), *Days and Nights* (1897), and *César Antéchrist* – are the key works in which Jarry questions all forms of rational thought and structure. Père Ubu was seen as a monstrous symbol of modern bourgeois society, which thus stands condemned by its own actions. Jarry eventually completely identified with Ubu, taking on the persona of Ubu himself, and invented the science of 'pataphysics,[1] which he defined as 'the science of imaginary solutions' and 'the science of the laws governing exceptions'.

Jarry's essay proposes to do away with realistic decor, to create a physical acting style that can utilise masks, and vocal skills that can produce emblematic performances that eschew all naturalistic devices. In other words the curse of theatre is its bogus theatricality, and the public needs more immediacy and less artifice, as society needs, in similar manner, to shed its bourgeois pretensions.

Reader cross-references

Artaud – who wished for a theatre which would stir audiences from their apathy
Beck – a later revolutionary view of change through theatre
Richter – for the origins of Dada, which owed much to Jarry's absurdist ideas

Further reading

Esslin, M. (1961) *The Theatre of the Absurd*, London: Anchor Books.
Shattuck, R. (1958) *The Banquet Years*, London: Harcourt Bràce.

Note

1   This introduction to Jarry has been approved by the Collège de 'Pataphysique.

Chapter 26

Tadeusz Kantor

THE THEATRE
OF DEATH:
A MANIFESTO

1 Craig's Postulate: to bring back the marionette.
Eliminate the live actor. Man — a creature of
nature — is a foreign intrusion into the abstract
structure of a work of art.

According to Gordon Craig, somewhere along the banks of the Ganges two women forced their way into the shrine of the Divine Marionette, which was jealously hiding the secrets of the true THEATRE. They envied the ROLE of this Perfect Being in illuminating human intellect with the sacred feeling of the existence of God, its GLORY; they spied on its Movements and Gestures, its sumptuous attire and, by cheap parody, began to satisfy the vulgar taste of the mob. At the moment when they finally ordered a similar monument built for themselves — the modern theatre, as we know it only too well and as it has lasted to this day, was born. A clamorous Public Service Institute. With it appeared the ACTOR. In defence of his theory Craig cites the opinion of Eleanor Duse: 'to save the theatre, it must be destroyed, it is necessary for all actors and actresses to die of plague . . . for it is they who render art impossible. . . .'

*2 Craig's Version: Man – the actor ousts the marionette,
takes its place, thereby causing the
demise of the theatre.*

There is something very impressive in the stand taken by the
great Utopian, when he says: 'In all seriousness I demand the
return to the theatre of the imagination of the super-marionette . . . and when it appears people will again, as before,
be able to worship the happiness of Existence, and render
divine and jubilant homage to DEATH . . .' Craig, inspired by
the aesthetics of SYMBOLISM, considered man to be subject to
unpredictable emotions, passions, and consequently to chance
as an element completely foreign to the homogenous nature
and structure of a work of art, which destroys its principal
trait; cohesion.

   Not only Craig's idea but also that whole elaborate
programme of symbolism – impressive in its own time – had
in the 19th century the support of isolated and unique
phenomena announcing a new era and new art: Heinrich von
Kleist, Ernst Theodor Amadeus Hoffman. Edgar Allan Poe.
. . . One hundred years earlier, Kleist for the same reasons as
Craig, demanded the substitution of the actor by the marionette: he regarded the human organism, which is subject to the
laws of NATURE, as a foreign intrusion into Artistic Fiction,
based on the principle of Construction and Intellect. This
accounts for his reproaches stressing the limited capabilities of
man and charges of an incessantly controlling consciousness,
which excludes the concepts of grace and beauty.

*3 From the romantic mysticism of mannequins and the
artificial creations of man in the XIX century – to
the rationalism of XX century abstract thought.*

On what seemed to be the safe road traversed by the man
of Enlightenment and Rationalism there appears out of the
darkness, suddenly and in increasingly greater numbers,
DOUBLES, MANNEQUINS, AUTOMATONS, HOMUNCULI. Artificial creations, a mockery of the creatures of NATURE, bearers
of absolute degradation, ALL human dreams, DEATH, Horror
and Terror. There is born a faith in the unknown powers of
MECHANICAL MOVEMENT, a maniacal passion for the invention

217

of a MECHANISM surpassing in perfection and severity the human organism and all its weaknesses.

And all this with an aura of demonism, on the brink of charlatanism, illegal practices, magic, transgression and nightmare. This was the SCIENCE FICTION of those days, in which the demonic human brain created ARTIFICIAL MAN.

At the same time all of this signified an abrupt loss of faith in NATURE and in that realm of man's activity which was closely tied with nature. Paradoxically, from these extremely romantic and diabolical efforts to take away nature's right of creation – there evolved a movement increasingly independent and more and more dangerously distant from NATURE – A RATIONALISTIC, even MATERIALISTIC MOVEMENT of a 'WORLD OF ABSTRACTION', CONSTRUCTIVISM, FUNCTIONALISM, MACHINISM, ABSTRACTION, finally PURIST VISUALISM, recognising only the 'physical presence' of a work of art. This risky hypothesis, whose origin is none too attractive for an age of technology and scientism. I take upon my conscience and for my personal satisfaction.

4 Dadaism, introducing 'ready-made' elements of life, destroys the concepts of homogeneity and cohesion in a work of art, as postulated by symbolism. Art Nouveau and Craig.

But let us return to Craig's marionette. Craig's idea of replacing the live actor with a mannequin – an artificial and mechanical creation – for the sake of preserving perfect cohesion in a work of art, is today invalid.

Later experience destroyed the unity of structure in a work of art by introducing FOREIGN elements in collages and assemblages; the acceptance of 'ready-made' reality, full recognition of the role of CHANCE, and the placing of a work of art on the sharp borderline between the REALITY OF LIFE AND ARTISTIC FICTION – made irrelevant those scruples from the beginning of this century, from the period of Symbolism and Art Nouveau. The two possible solutions – either autonomous art and intellectual structure, or naturalism – ceased to be the ONLY ones. When the theatre, in its moments of weakness, submitted to the live organism of man and his laws – it automatically and logically agreed to the form or imitation of life, its presentation and re-creation. In the opposite circumstances, when the theatre was strong and independent enough to free itself from the pressure of life and man, it created artificial equivalents to life which turned out to be more alive, because they submitted easily to the abstractions of space and time and were capable of achieving absolute unity.

Today these possibilities are neither appropriate nor valid alternatives. For a new situation and new conditions have arisen in art. The appearance of the concept of READY-MADE REALITY, extracted from life – and the possibilities of ANNEXING it, INTEGRATING it into a work of art through DECISION, GESTURE or RITUAL – has become a fascination much stronger than (artificially) CONSTRUED reality, than the creation of ABSTRACTION, or the surrealistic world, than Breton's MIRACULOUSNESS. Happenings, Events and Environments with their colossal momentum, have achieved the rehabilitation of whole regions of REALITY, disdained until this time, cleansing it of the ballast of life's intentions.

This 'DECALAGE' of life's reality, its derailment from life's practices, moved the human imagination more strongly than the surrealistic reality of dreams. As a result, fears of direct intervention by life and man in the scheme of art – became irrelevant.

5 From the 'Ready-Made Reality' of the happening – to the dematerialization of the elements of a work of art.

However, as with all fascination, so too this one, after a time, was transformed into a convention practised universally, senselessly and in a vulgar manner. These almost ritualistic manipulations of Reality, connected as they are with the contestation of ARTISTIC STATUS and the PLACE reserved for art, gradually started to acquire different sense and meaning. The material, physical PRESENCE of an object and PRESENT TIME, the only possible context for activity and action – turned out to be too burdensome, had reached their limits. The TRANSGRESSION signified: depriving these conditions of the material and functional IMPORTANCE, that is, of their COMMUNICATIVENESS. Because this is the latest period, still current and not yet closed, the observations which follow derive from and are tied with my own creativity.

The object (*The Chair*, Oslo, 1970) became *empty*, deprived of *expression*, *connections*, *references*, characteristics of programmed *communication*, its '*message*' directed 'nowhere', it changed into a *dummy*.

Situations and activities were locked into their own CIRCUMFERENCE: the ENIGMATIC (theatre of the impossible, 1973), in my manifesto entitled 'Cambriollage', followed the unlawful INTRUSION into that terrain where tangible reality was transformed into its INVISIBLE EXTENSIONS. The role of THOUGHT, memory and TIME becomes increasingly clear.

219

6 The rejection of the orthodoxy of conceptualism and the 'Official Avant-garde of the Masses'.

The certitude which impressed itself upon me more and more strongly that the concept of LIFE can be vindicated in art only through the ABSENCE OF LIFE in its conventional sense (again Craig and the Symbolists!), this process of DEMATERIALIZATION SETTLED on a path which circumvented in my creative work the whole orthodoxy of linguistics and conceptualism. This was probably caused in part by the colossal throng which arose on this already official course and which will unfortunately become the latest instalment of the DADAIST current with its slogans of TOTAL ART, EVERYTHING IS ART, ALL ARE ARTISTS, ART IS IN THE MIND, etc.

I hate crowds. In 1973 I wrote a draft of a new manifesto which takes into consideration this false situation. This is its beginning:

> From the time of Verdun, Voltaire's Cabaret and Marcel Duchamp's Water-Closet, when the 'status of art' was drowned out by the roar of Fat Bertha – DECISION became the only remaining human possibility, the reliance on something that was or is unthinkable, functioning as the first stimulant of creativity, conditioning and defining art. Lately thousands of mediocre individuals have been making decisions, without scruples or any hesitation whatever. We are witnesses of the banalization and conventionalization of decision. This once dangerous path has become a comfortable freeway with improved safety measures and information. Guides, maps, orientation tables, directional signs, signals, centres, Art Co-operatives guarantee the excellence of the functioning of creativity. We are witnesses of the GENERAL MOVEMENT of artist-commandos, street fighters, artist-mediators, artist-mailmen, epistologs, pedlars, street magicians, proprietors of Office and Agencies. Movements on this already official freeway, which threatens with a flood of graphomania and deeds of minimal significance, increases with each passing day. It is necessary to leave it as quickly as possible. This is not easily done. Particularly at the apogee of the UNIVERSAL AVANT-GARDE – blind and favoured with the highest prestige of the INTELLECT, which protects both the wise and the stupid.

7 On the side streets of the official avant-garde, Mannequins appear.

My deliberate rejection of the solutions of conceptualism, despite the fact that they seemed to be the only way out from the path upon which I had embarked, resulted in my placing the above-mentioned facts of the latest stage of my creativity and attempts to describe them, on side streets which left me more open to the UNKNOWN!!!

I have more confidence in such a situation. Any new era always begins with actions of little apparent significance and little note, incidents having little in common with the recognised trend, actions that are private, intimate, I would even say – shameful. Vague. And difficult! These are the most fascinating and essential moments of creativity.

> *All of a sudden I became interested in the nature of*
> MANNEQUINS
> *The mannequin in my production of* THE WATER HEN *1967 and the mannequins in* THE SHOEMAKERS *1970, had a very specific role: they were like a non-material extension, a kind of* ADDITIONAL ORGAN *for the actor, who was their 'master'. The mannequins already widely used in my production of Slowacki's* Balladyna *were* DOUBLES *of live characters, somehow endowed with a higher* CONSCIOUSNESS, *attained 'after the completion of their lives'.*

These mannequins were already clearly stamped with the sign of DEATH.

8 The mannequin as manifestation of 'REALITY OF THE LOWEST ORDER'.

The mannequin as dealings of TRANSGRESSION.

The mannequin as EMPTY object. The DUMMY. A message of DEATH. A model for the actor.

The mannequin I used in 1967 at the Cricot 2 Theatre (*The Water Hen*) was a successor to the 'Eternal Wanderer' and 'Human Ambellages', one which appeared naturally in my 'Collections' as yet another phenomenon consistent with my long-held conviction that only the reality of the lowest order, the poorest and least prestigious objects are capable of revealing their full objectivity in a work of art.

Mannequins and Wax Figures have always existed on the peripheries of sanctioned Culture. They were not admitted further; they occupied places in FAIR BOOTHS, suspicious MAGICIANS' CHAMBERS, far from the splendid shrines of art, treated condescendingly as CURIOSITIES intended for the tastes of the masses. For precisely this reason it was they, and not academic, museum creations, which caused the curtain to move at the blink of an eye.

MANNEQUINS also have their own version of TRANSGRESSION. The existence of these creatures, shaped in man's image, almost 'godlessly', in an illegal fashion, is the result of heretical dealings, a manifestation of the

Dark, Nocturnal, Rebellious side of human activity. Of Crimes and Traces of Death as sources of recognition. The vague and inexplicable feeling that through this entity so similar to a living human being but deprived of consciousness and purpose there is transmitted to us a terrifying message of Death and Nothingness – precisely this feeling becomes the cause – simultaneously – of that transgression, repudiation and attraction. Of accusation and fascination. All arguments have been exhausted in accusations. The very mechanism of action called their attention to itself, that mechanism which, if taken as the purpose, could easily be relegated to the lower forms of creativity! IMITATION AND DECEPTIVE SIMILARITY, which serve the conjurer in setting his TRAPS and fooling the viewer, the use of 'unsophisticated' means, evading the concepts of aesthetics, the abuse and fraudulent deception of APPEARANCES, practices from the realm of charlatans.

To make matters complete, the entire proceedings were accompanied by a philosophical world-view which, from the time of Plato to this day, often regards as the purpose of art the unmasking of Being and a Spiritual Sense of Existence and not involvement in the Material Shell of the world, in that faking of appearances which are the lowest stage of being.

I do not share the belief that the MANNEQUIN (or a WAX FIGURE) could replace the LIVE ACTOR, as Kleist and Craig wanted. This would be too simple and naive. I am trying to delineate the motives and intent of this unusual creature which has suddenly appeared in my thoughts and ideas. Its appearance complies with my ever-deepening conviction that it is possible to express *life* in art only through the *absence of life*, through an appeal to DEATH, through APPEARANCES, through EMPTINESS and the lack of a MESSAGE.

The MANNEQUIN in my theatre must become a MODEL, through which pass a strong sense of DEATH and the conditions of the DEAD. A model for the live ACTOR.

9 My elucidation of the situation described by Craig.
The appearance of the LIVE ACTOR as a revolutionary
moment. The discovery of the IMAGE OF MAN.

I derive my observations from the domain of the theatre, but they are relevant to all current art. We can suppose that Craig's suggestively-depicted and disastrously-incriminating picture of the circumstances surrounding the appearance of the Actor – was composed for his own use, as a point of departure for his idea of the 'SUPER-MARIONETTE'. Despite the fact that I remain an admirer of Craig's magnificent contempt and passionate accusations (especially since I see before me the absolute downfall of today's theatre) and then only after my full acceptance of the first part of his Credo, in which he denies the institutionalised theatre any reason for artistic existence – I dissociate myself from his renowned decisions on the fate of the ACTOR.

For the moment of the ACTOR'S first appearance before the HOUSE (to use current terminology) seems to me, on the contrary: *revolutionary* and *avant-garde*. I will even try to compile and 'ascribe to History' a completely different picture, in which the course of events will have a meaning quite the opposite. . . . ! From the common realm of customary and religious rituals, common ceremonies and common people's activities advanced SOMEONE, who made the risky decision to BREAK with the ritualistic Community. He was not driven by conceit (as in Craig) to become an object of universal attention. This would have been too simplistic. Rather it must have been a rebellious mind, sceptical, heretical, free and tragic, daring to remain alone with Fate and Destiny. If we also add 'with its ROLE', we will then have before us the ACTOR. This revolt took place in the realm of art. Said event, or rather manifestation, probably caused much confusion of thought and clashing of opinions. This ACT was undoubtedly seen as a disloyalty to the old ritualistic traditions and practices, as secular arrogance, as atheism, as dangerous subversive tendencies, as scandal, as amorality, as indecency; people must have seen in it elements of clownery, buffoonery, exhibitionism and deviation. The author himself, set apart from society, gained for himself not only implacable enemies, but also fanatical admirers. Condemnation and glory simultaneously. It would be guilty of a ludicrous and shallow formalism to interpret this act of SEVERANCE (RUPTURE) as egotism, as a lust for glory or latent inclinations toward acting. It must have implied something much greater, a MESSAGE of extraordinary import. We will try to illustrate this fascinating situation: OPPOSITE those who remained on this side there stood a MAN DECEPTIVELY SIMILAR to them, yet (by some secret and ingenious 'operation') infinitely DISTANT, shockingly FOREIGN, as if DEAD, cut off by an invisible BARRIER – no less horrible and inconceivable, whose real meaning and THREAT appears to us only in DREAMS. As though in a blinding flash of lightning, they suddenly perceived a glaring, tragically circus-like IMAGE OF MAN, as if they had seen him FOR THE FIRST TIME, as if they had seen THEIR VERY SELVES. This was certainly a shock – a meta-physical shock, we might even say. The live effigy of MAN emerging out of the shadows, as if constantly walking ahead of himself, was the dominant MESSAGE of its new HUMAN CONDITION, only HUMAN, with its RESPONSIBILITY, its tragic CONSCIOUSNESS, measuring its FATE on an inexorable and final scale, the *scale of DEATH*. This revelatory MESSAGE, which was transmitted from the realm of DEATH, evoked in the VIEWERS (let us now call them by our own term) a metaphysical shock. And the reference to DEATH, to its tragic and MENACING beauty, were the means and art of that ACTOR (also according to our own terminology).

It is necessary to re-establish the essential meaning of the relationship:
VIEWER and ACTOR.

IT IS NECESSARY TO RECOVER THE PRIMEVAL FORCE OF THE SHOCK
TAKING PLACE AT THE MOMENT WHEN OPPOSITE A MAN (THE VIEWER)
THERE STOOD FOR THE FIRST TIME A MAN (THE ACTOR) DECEPTIVELY
SIMILAR TO US YET AT THE SAME TIME INFINITELY FOREIGN, BEYOND AN
IMPASSABLE BARRIER.

10 Recapitulation.

Despite the fact that we may be suspected and even accused
of a certain scrupulousness, inappropriate under the circumstances,
in destroying inborn prejudices and fears,
for the sake of a more precise picture
and possible conclusions
let us establish the limits of that boundary, which has the name:
THE CONDITION OF DEATH
for it represents the most extreme point of reference,
no longer threatened by any conformity,
FOR THE CONDITION OF THE ARTIST AND ART

. . . this specific relationship
terrifying
but at the same time compelling
the relationship of *the living to the dead*
who not long ago, while still alive, gave not the slightest
reason for the unforseen spectacle
for creating unnecessary separation and confusion:
they did not distinguish themselves
did not place themselves above others
and as a result of this seemingly banal
but, as would later become evident, rather essential
and valuable attribute
they were simply, normally
in no way transgressing universal laws
unremarkable
and now suddenly
on the other side
opposite
they astound us
as though we

were seeing them for the first time
set on display
in an ambiguous ceremony:
pointless
and at the same time repudiated,
irrevocably different
and infinitely foreign
and more: somehow deprived of all meaning
of no account
without the meanest hope of occupying some position
in our 'full' life relationships
which to us alone are accessible, familiar
comprehensible
but for them meaningless.
If we agree that a trait
of living people
is the ease and ability
with which they enter into mutual and manifold
life relationships
only then
with regard to the dead
is there born in us a sudden and startling
realisation of the fact that
this basic trait of the living
is brought out and made possible by
their complete
lack of differentiation
by their
indistinguishability
by their universal *similarity*
mercilessly abolishing all other opposing delusions
common
consistent
all-binding.
Only then do the *dead*
become (for the living)
noteworthy
for that highest price
achieving
their individuality
distinction
their CHARACTER

glaring
and almost
circus-like.

■　■　■

Source

Kantor, T. (1984) 'The Theatre of Death: A Manifesto', *Twentieth Century Polish Theatre*, trans. V.T. and M. Stelmaszynski, ed. B. Drozdowski, English trans. and ed. C. Itzin, London: John Calder: 97–106.

Tadeusz Kantor (1915–90)

Polish designer, artist and director. He became one of the century's most extraordinary practitioners through the creation of relatively few, but highly travelled productions. Starting as a painter and stage designer, he soon moved towards theatrical form with a series of 'happenings' in Warsaw and on the Baltic coast in the early 1960s. He sought to redefine the language of theatre through a constant questioning of the relationship between the performance space and the performers. Like Wagner, Kantor created total theatre pieces, devised and controlled by himself. In 1955 he formed his performance company, Cricot[2], in Krakow, in conjunction with other visual artists. In 1975 he produced his most famous piece, *The Dead Class*, a surrealist evocation of a 'dead' Polish past, by a cast of artists of all ages, which toured Europe and the USA, receiving awards and prizes. This was followed by, *Wielopole, Wielopole* (1982), *Let the Artists Die* (1985), and *I Shall Never Return* (1989). Kantor continued to produce work with Cricot[2] until his death in 1990, rehearsing his last piece, *Today is My Birthday.*

Kantor's 'Manifesto' shows how he departs from all the main traditions of European theatre in advocating non-linear form. He encapsulates his concern with the theatrical object, and with the actor as object, emphasising his roots in the visual arts. He expresses his concept of theatre as vision; as a process of parallel actions and events folding back on themselves; continuously commenting on Polish life under the domination of communism, and on its collective memory and nationality.

Reader cross-references

Craig – to whom he refers at length
Grotowski – a contemporary Polish artist
Hijikata – a contemporary concern with death
Schlemmer – theatre as sculptural object
Wilson – another approach to non-linear theatre

Further reading

Drozdowski, B. (ed.) (1979) *Twentieth Century Polish Theatre*, London: John Calder.

Klossiwicz, J. (1986) 'Tadeusz Kantor's Journey' *Drama Review* 30, T111: 4.

Kobialka, M. (trans. and ed.) (1993) *A Journey Through Other Spaces: Essays and Manifestos by Tadeusz Kantor*, Berkeley, Calif.: University of California Press.

Chapter 27

Elizabeth LeCompte

INTERVIEW

In developing Brace Up! *(1990) did you work with the Japanese material before addressing* Three Sisters?

Yes.

Was this material linked to the notion of a Japanese theatre troupe?

I always use a framing device outside the material, so it's like an onion skin or a frame within a frame. In all the pieces there's some outside storyteller and there's a text within that story.

Do you see specific connections between the Japanese material and the Chekhov?

Well, I do after the fact, but it isn't something that informs the way we go about making the pieces. After the fact certain things become obvious, but they're never obvious to begin with. I didn't see any reason for them to be put together other than that I happen to be interested in the formal aspects of Japanese theatre and some of the Japanese pop culture stuff and that I happen to like Chekhov's writing. When I started working on *Route 1 & 9* (1981) I didn't have any idea that these routines from Pigmeat Markham would have anything to do with *Our Town*. I had no idea whatsoever that these two would go together. I was working on Pigmeat Markham material because I was interested in it formally, the way I'm interested in the Japanese material formally. Again, in a similar way, I was attracted to the writing, to Wilder's writing – specifically Wilder's writing as a sort of poetic text next to this popular material – 'poetic' in quotes – filled with sentimental meaning, but absolutely vacant of any *real* meaning taken apart from the characters. I then take these things as givens when we work. Of course, eventually – because I and the company are the catalysts for the two things coming together – I will see things.

You seem to be describing a process that allows very different kinds of material to inhabit the same space while, in some respects, remaining very much apart.

Yeah. Yeah, definitely. I think probably in *Brace Up!* they ended up coming too much together. I would really want something more disparate.

The emphasis you place on the formal qualities of the material seems to be in opposition to the kind of psychological basis of Wilder and Chekhov's texts.

I don't have a rejection of psychological motivation. I just have a rejection of psychological motivation existing in one form. I like to use the psychological motivation as a whole theatrical space. I can't imagine, in this day and age, not feeling the psychology in one way or another.

Were you interested in any way in the association between Chekhov's work and naturalism? Perhaps in opposition to the Japanese material?

You see, I don't know the history of the Chekhov. I hadn't, before I'd done this, seen a Chekhov play except in Dutch. I couldn't really tell what the psychology was. And the naturalism was – well, I don't speak the language. I don't have the history of that, I don't know what that is. I think I'm doing a naturalistic version of Chekhov.

One of the conventional things about naturalism is that it creates one unified world.

Yeah. That's what I think I'm doing. Perhaps Stanislavski was not – he was fragmenting it all into different characters – to me it's all one thing.

Did you see any Noh theatre live?

No. I did see some tapes in Japanese. I never saw it translated. I couldn't follow the content, but I could watch them come on and go off. That's very important. So, you know, I didn't read too much about what Noh was or what it's supposed to be. I just watched tapes in Japanese. So I think I was probably drawn to that structure, that physical architectonic structure. How they moved, how they dealt with entrances and exits.

Is it something you pursued in the piece particularly?

Entrances and exits are extremely important. That's the defining thing, isn't it? In theatre. That's essential. It's the deepest, deepest place for me. But, I've said this before.

One of the things that interests me about the use of Noh is its emphasis upon conti-nuity – and so its reflection upon its own history. This seems to be reflected in the Wooster Group's work. Performances seem to comment on previous productions, images are re-used, rehearsal procedures are remembered or re-presented. Were you interested in Noh's concern with its own history?

I don't know. I mean, I'm not a Japanese theatre artist. I don't study Japanese theatre. I don't have any academic interest in Japanese theatre.

I'm just interested in what these appropriations might have to offer. Or what the juxta-position of the Japanese material against the Chekhov might be doing.

I think we were getting to that when I said 'entrances and exits'.

MW [Marianne Weems, a Wooster Group associate, who was also present]: The way that I look at it is that it's more like a contrapuntal reading. The two things go, and sometimes connect in the audience member's mind and sometimes don't. But there's no didactic, polemical –

Attempt.

MW: connection being made. There's no attempt to connect them, really. I think there's a rhythmic attempt to make them relate, or perhaps to let them relate in the space.

Yes. To allow them to be in the space together, without this *demand* for meaning. 'Meaning' in quotes – that you're dealing with, very strongly.

Do you mean that I'm demanding meaning of you?

Yes, absolutely. That's not what I'm about. My meaning is in the piece itself. I'm not going to now make meaning separately from that piece for you. Again, it's not a thing where I'm withholding that – I don't have it. It only happens for me in the space. In the moment of the theatrical act. Here I can just tell you the way I came up with those images, the way they are brought to the stage. Then, I could, if I wanted to, spin off and say, Oh, yes, isn't it funny how this image looks good, or it's good with that sound. I could even, after the fact, probably – if I were a writer – write a whole thing on the meaning of Japanese culture and Western language. About meaning and lack of meaning, about Western poetry and Eastern poetry. But I don't have much interest in it.

It may be that we don't have a language to talk with.

It's possible.

Which is, on the one hand, a shame, on the other hand, it may be instructive.

I think it is. I think it's probably very instructive looking at the work next to other people's work, too, to be honest, just by my inability to grapple with whatever it is you're telling me. It has something to do with why the work is like it is.

It's important, from my point of view, because I don't intend to demand a meaning for the piece.

No, no. I know. Believe me, I'm not trying to be obfuscating. Maybe the language that you're using I don't use. Maybe you've talked to people who aren't as theatre-oriented as I am. That's why Joan Jonas came to work with us, because she wanted to make entrances and exits. She doesn't make them in her own work. I didn't come from theatre but from painting and film – which is, the cut, you know, entrances and exits again – when do you come into a scene and when do you leave it. It may be that.

And this is also connected with framing.

Well, of course. Again, I think what I'm saying to you is that form is extra-ordinarily important to me – certain kinds of theatrical form. And I'm always trying to see it in different ways. And of course I work to different theatre traditions – not only Japanese. I worked for a long time with vaudeville, American vaudeville. So –

And the focus upon form is a key to these very disparate elements coinciding in the same space.

Yes, absolutely. And anything can co-exist together – without, you know, losing its own uniqueness – without being absorbed and regurgitated. They are separate, and they can stay separate and at the same time inform each other – within the same work. At best, when the form is strong enough, that's what happens. If the form isn't strong enough, it's just chaos. That's the danger.

That kind of focus doesn't offer itself to any kind of question I might ask about meaning or theme, does it?

No. Again, you can talk to me about what's going on on the stage.

I'm interested in the emphasis you place on 'presence'. You've said that you use whatever methods you can to try and make – or allow – the actor to become as present as possible.

Yes.

Is this a formal quality in the work?

It can be. Usually that presence is something that I think is – kind of – always in conversation with the formal pattern. The formal pattern will tend to allow the performer to get lulled into feeling safe. Within this structure that I've made, there are always holes that pop up – that's part of the form. So you have to be vigilant, all the time. Vigilant. Tremendously vigilant. And be aware of everything behind you and in front of you, of the entire structure. Or you might drown. Drowning, I mean – you know, stop you from breathing – to fill you up with water so you can't breathe. I think the constant battle for me as a director is to find ways that an actor can be always present, always alive, always thinking this is the first and last moment that she's there – doing this thing – within a structure that is so strong and so sure.

Do you think about the audience in the making of work?

Yeah. I mean – it's like the audience is *there*. They're the air that you breathe. The audience is the other part of the exploration process for theatre. There is no theatre without audience, so there is no life without breath. It's that essential. But it's an involuntary thing, breathing. And my awareness of the audience is almost involuntary. Sometimes I'm conscious of it. Usually when they come in for the first time – it's like a pain in your chest. I become aware of them when things aren't working on the stage. When something's wrong, I become aware in a very conscious way. So then I work to become unaware of them in a way that I'm unaware of my breathing. It doesn't mean that I'm cutting them out. It's just that they should be part of the flow of the whole.

It strikes me that if you concentrate on these formal elements in a way that keeps the possibilities of the piece open, that keeps these things colliding or existing at the same moment, then – because there are many languages being held up at the same time – the work resists being read through a single language. I wonder if, as a consequence of this, the viewer might become more open to this 'presence'?

I know what you're saying – but I don't know. Again, I'm not always sure. It's no science. I was talking to a writer a while ago, who's a little older than me. He was saying how, you know, he now had become technically better. He could write more quickly. He knew when things weren't working. He'd acquired technique. And I had to realise when I was talking to him that I still don't know how to get that presence on the stage, that every time I go down for a new piece it's the same battle as it was for *Sakonnet Point* in 1975. That I had not gotten any clearer about how to get that presence, how to keep it, how to make the form balance with the –

Do you think it can succumb to technique?

Well, I don't know. I don't know. I wish I had the technique, because it's harder to do it.

Joe Chaikin tried to gear technique toward producing presence, didn't he?

Yes, he did. That's a good point. I hadn't thought about Chaikin in a long time. But it's also – I'll tell you what else. And this is where I'm different from the other people you've talked to, with the exception of John Cage. I think what keeps me unable to get that technique down so that I can, you know, produce more quickly, more easily and more fluidly what I need – again, I use *need* in a spiritual way – on the stage is that I'm always working with other people and other texts, not my own texts. You know, Ping Chong writes his own texts. He's controlling them all the time. Joan Jonas makes up her own actions. She doesn't go to a script. She's writing her own material. I'm not. I'm having to come up against a new person and new people down-stairs every single piece. So I have to rediscover, in every piece, what makes the balance. Because people are so different. Actors are so different. I think that that's part of it. And it's that unique place – that I'm making a new thing out of old material. I'm not just redecorating an old script. I'm not just going to do Chekhov. I'm trying to – I'm trying to make it present for me. Which means literally reinventing. I mean – 'reinventing' it – it's an over-used word. I mean reinventing it from the ground up. From the way that the language resonates in the body on the stage – every way – to the way the psychology has to be – (Claps once) – has to be crashed up against and fragmented and then reformed. So it's got a double problem. I'm reinventing something and I'm having to come up against material that I don't necessarily understand – my actors, a text – and that I don't know how to manipulate. And because I think on stage – I don't think separately, I don't sit down with the text and say, 'Ah, this means this – if I get Joan Jonas to do this on stage, then I'll get what I want from this text.' What I want from the text is what Joan Jonas and Chekhov give to me on the stage! Only on the stage. Not inside my head. So it makes it particularly difficult. I've got the worst of both worlds.

Does it not also mean that the work is difficult to talk about, in certain respects?

Well. It depends on what you mean by 'talk about'. I don't think it does. I just can't talk about it in literary terms, in the same way that most people talk about it. I've discovered more recently that theatre people – especially directors – don't talk in the same way that I do. They talk as if I'm writing. Yet I'm not a writer. I'm using other people's writing. The process is akin to that – the process of reinventing – it's akin to writing. I just have my characters, my words, my colleagues, all materialised on the stage. Writers can do it in their head. I can't. I have to take my head – I'm very literal, as you can see – I have to take my head and put it on the stage and move the little elements of ideas around the stage to see what it means. Maybe it's a little unusual.

So I'm really a classical director in the sense that – I do plays. You know. (Laughs.) The most important thing in all of this is that – when I go downstairs I don't have any thematic ideas – I don't even have a theme. I don't have anything except the literal objects – some flowers, some images, some television sets, a chair, some costumes I like. In the last piece, something someone brought in by mistake. That's it. And then ideas come after the fact. It's a total reversal of most of the processes. And probably if I reversed it I'd do a lot more work and be a lot happier. (Laughs.) On that note –

Thanks.

(The interviewer was Nick Kaye)

■　　■　　■

Source

LeCompte, E. and Kaye, N. (1993, 1995) 'Interview with Elizabeth LeCompte', *Art into Theatre*, London: Macmillan.

Elizabeth LeCompte (1944–)

Founder and director of the Wooster Group (1976–), the New York based performance company which grew out of Richard Schechner's Performance Group (1967–80). It developed out of a long tradition of rejection of American commercial theatre, redefining the position of the 'performer' and 'role', and the function of previously written playscripts, in particular plays by the established American and European writers, whose work often constitutes a base for the group's performance explorations. Creations such as *Sakonnet Point* (1975) and *Route 1 & 9 (The Last Act)* (1981) deliberately challenge the audience's expectations, through an essentially fragmentary and deconstructive approach. *Route 1 & 9* for example, juxtaposed extracts from Thornton Wilder's *Our Town* with the comedy routines of the black company of Pigmeat Markham, the Wooster Group performers being in blackface. *LSD . . . Just the High Points* (1984), attempted to confront Arthur Miller's *The Crucible* with a debate incorporating Timothy Leary, the drug guru of the 1960s. (Miller eventually forbade the use of his text.) In 1991 *Brace Up!* subverted the narrative and psychological slant of Chekhov's *Three Sisters* to produce a set of technologically brilliant comments on the play and its reception, at the same time taking its visual stimulus from Japanese theatre.

This interview with Nick Kaye, the postmodernist historian, attempts to elucidate LeCompte's 'meaning' in her work. It is illuminating for her refusal to adopt any explanations which avoid the fact that she creates 'theatrical', not literary or philosophical, meaning, instead maintaining that the meanings of the Wooster Group's creations lie in the pieces themselves and nowhere else.

Reader cross-references

Bausch – a confrontational theatre approach
Brecht – the roots of an anti-psychological stance
Lepage – a similar eclectic approach to material
Rainer – a contemporary woman postmodernist with a similar concern for process
Schechner – North American antecedents
Wilson – another deconstructive approach to narrative

Further reading

Gray, S. and LeCompte, E. (1980) 'Rumstick Road', *Performing Arts Journal* 111(2).

Savran, D. (1988) *Breaking the Rules*, New York: Theatre Communications Group.

Shank, T. (1982) *American Alternative Theatre*, New York: Grove Press.

Chapter 28

Robert Lepage

ROBERT LEPAGE
IN DISCUSSION WITH
RICHARD EYRE

RE   This is the end of a long but quite ordinary day for Robert: he's been rehearsing *A Midsummer Night's Dream* since 10.30 this morning, re-rehearsing his show *Needles and Opium*, which he has just performed, and is now rounding off the day with a light ten-mile jog through this Platform. I've been seeing Robert's work for maybe six years, since he brought a show to the ICA. Last year I was in a position to exercise my patronage – put the taxpayers' money where my heart is – and invite *Tectonic Plates* to the National. In addition, I've been able to pursue the real passion of a fan and ask Robert to direct a show for the National. This all begs the question of why I think Robert's work is so singular and so attractive. I think it's because the more I work in the theatre and the more theatre I see, the more I treasure and admire the characteristics about the theatre that can't be translated into any other medium. Robert Frost said that poetry is the bit that can't be translated, and that's what I think about theatre. I don't like theatre when it's a surrogate for TV or for debate or anything else. I like it when it's the thing itself and it happens to a live audience and employs a vocabulary of speech, gesture, music, space and light as the servants of expression and content. They are all things that you see in spades in the work of Robert Lepage. His work has a characteristic of the best art: it converts the commonplace into the magical and makes the magical real and accessible. He is a purveyor of dreams, and what's encouraging and exciting for me is that it's not that he works in a language or syntax that belongs to the world of performance art. It's absolutely, irreducibly, theatre. It uses sometimes very simple, very primitive theatrical methods and translates into a language that is entirely original. His work also places a very strong emphasis on the work of actors and on the human being. It's very humane, funny, touching, and I think entirely wonderful.

A bit of biography: Robert has worked since the beginning of the eighties with a company called Théâtre Repère. He's an actor – you may have seen him in *Jesus of Montreal* – director, writer, musician. He's also the artistic director of the French Theatre of the Canadian National Arts Centre, which effectively means he's responsible for the National Theatre. And what he does in his spare time, I can't imagine.

Robert, how did you get interested in theatre?

RL I've never really been interested in theatre as such. In my adolescence I was more interested in theatricality. The reason, in my opinion, there's such a big difference between theatre and theatricality is that where I come from theatrical history is extremely young – about 50 years old or so – so we don't have any classics, our classics are borrowed. Also the fact that Canada's a bi-cultural country – two cultures that are *starting* to talk to each other. We did have a pool of good authors 20 years ago when I started to be interested in theatre. When I say that I'm more interested in theatricality, it's because I think the taste for young creators, actors or directors in Quebec, at least in the seventies, came much more from seeing rock shows, dance shows, performance art, than from seeing theatre, because theatre is not as accessible as it is here in Britain. And the theatre that was there was a theatre that was already dead: not reflecting anybody's identity, not actually staging the preoccupations of the people. I always come back to political things because it's important to understand what Canada's about culturally. For a long time anybody in English Canada who was an artistic director of a big theatre company had a British accent, and in Quebec those people had a French accent from France. I don't want to sound racist or xenophobic but it took some time before young theatre people became artistic directors or even directors. There's not a theatrical tradition but there's a lot of theatricality. A lot of my taste for theatre came from seeing concerts of Genesis and Jethro Tull. It sounds pretty superficial now, but theatre for a long time, at least in North America, has been dispossessed from its theatricality. It started to imitate film more and more and got stuck with cinematic realism. The theatrical fun was when Pina Bausch started to do tours and festivals in

Toronto. In the late seventies or early eighties there was this movement of all these new directors who were theatrical, and it became a more exciting place to be.

RE I think a lot of your generation here felt that theatre was in some way an inadequate substitute for film. They thought film is where the action is, film is the language of the 20th century, theatre is the language of the 19th century. Certainly in the States that was a strong feeling, and you didn't feel that?

RL I think that film is an extraordinarily exciting place to be, to work in or to see. I think it's as exciting as theatre. But I think that it's more interesting to work in theatre and to borrow from film artistic ways of showing things or telling stories. For a long time theatre had been only using the naturalism from film – saying we need real food on stage, we need to pretend that there's a fourth wall. That's wrong. Theatre's theatre. There's no fourth wall; it's live, it changes every night. What I'm trying to say is that theatre borrowed all the wrong things from film. We're facing an audience now that knows what a flash-back or a flash-forward is, that has a very strong culture and education in how to tell stories in many different ways because of film and TV. Theatre has to go along with that and use that in a theatrical way. I'm afraid I see a lot of theatre that only borrows the realism, and only the people in the front rows get to appreciate it.

RE I don't know the origin of Théâtre Repère, but is that why you started to write your own work, because you felt existing texts were somehow too linear?

RL Not necessarily. I thought a lot of texts were inadequate because they didn't correspond to the time and place I was evolving in. That was a phenomenon that was happening in Montreal and Quebec City, where language was such a political debate. Words were so coloured with politics, at least in the seventies, that people turned to non-verbal theatre to try and get other messages across. Politics was so present in Canadian life in the seventies that a lot of the creative work in Canada was based only on politics of the mind, not politics of the body, of emotion, of relationships. I think an artist sometimes has to put words aside, to explore these types of politics. Also I got interested because I was very good at mime. I never thought I'd be working as an actor and as a director.

RE You went to the Jacques Lecoq School in Paris?

RL No, not to that school, I went to Alain Knapp who had something called the Institut de la Personalité Créatrice – translated as a place for good manners. I wasn't there a full year, only a part. He had a way of approaching theatre in a very creative way. He never distinguished what a director and an actor do. He worked mainly on improvisations – things would happen spontaneously and had to be written as they were going. So you learned to be an actor and at the same time be a director because you had to see what you were composing, and you had to be a writer so that the structure was also working. His goal was to try to make total theatrical creators. Later on I started to move on to improv games and things like that. I went to school at Quebec City Conservatory, almost a monastery, for three years. Most of the teachers there had done Lecoq and worked in Lecoq's way and philosophy. The school was based a lot on physical work. When I came out of school, I was very good physically, but at that point the bourgeoisie had incorporated clowns and Commedia and all of that. There's a company in Canada called Direct Film, that processes Kodak stuff. They have these clowns – so the only job you could get as a clown was with them.

So anyway, all the things I'd learned in school had been incorporated by the *théâtre bourgeois*. I had to find a way of using what I knew. I think my main talent was the ability to gather people around an idea and devise pieces, and slowly we developed this group called Théâtre Repère. It's rather strange because now I have this burden on my shoulder of having all of the success, the merit of this thing, but also all the criticism; in fact it's a collective venture. I'm not trying to be falsely humble or coy or whatever (and that wouldn't be very convincing in the mouth of someone who just did a solo piece) but I truly believe that theatre is a meeting place. I don't think film is, necessarily. Film is a much more individualistic type of event. I believe that we can go through another renaissance in theatre. I'm not saying I'm trying to create a renaissance in what I'm doing, but I believe in the spirit of Renaissance, I think it's still alive and still possible. A lot of structures in the way our society permits or organises culture do not allow that, but as artists we can allow that to ourselves.

RE In each of Robert's shows, there is at least one, but generally about thirty images which really burn themselves on the memory. One of the things about your work, for a fellow director, is that one just feels very jealous. You sit there thinking 'I wish I'd thought of that'. But it's partly because these moments are all very simple. Anyone can think of a Lycra screen doing all those things (in *Needles and Opium*) – it's in a sense a traditional device – but anyone didn't think of it. Let me take a moment in *Dragons' Trilogy* which was recently at Riverside Studios. There's an extraordinarily moving moment (I can't tell you the whole story, it would take four and a half hours) but there's a Chinese man, married to a French Canadian woman who has been won in a bet. They have a retarded daughter, and a French-speaking Chinese nun comes to this rather unhappy couple to take away the daughter to a special home. This nun chatters away in a mixture of Chinese, English and French for a long time; it's a funny and touching scene. The child's suitcase is brought out, and gradually, as the nun speaks, the mother starts to put the child's clothes into the suitcase. She takes off the nun's habit, puts it in the suitcase, and the nun becomes this retarded child. It's the most extraordinary metamorphosis, terribly moving, and the most brilliant piece of bravura acting and direction. I was asking Robert how it came about and he said 'I think it was because we didn't have enough actors to go round'. I'm also fascinated by a moment in *Tectonic Plates* which, as an idea and as a realisation of that idea, made me cry because it was so perfect. There was a pit of water in the Cottesloe theatre. The story was a complicated interweaving, including Chopin, George Sand, Jim Morrison and the Doors and many other things, some of it set in Venice. There was an image in the second half when you were in Père Lachaise cemetery and a statue came to life. The shroud was taken off this statue and laid into the pool, and as it was laid there, a huge image of George Sand appeared on it. Of course it was just a simple carousel projector from above with a small slide. It was exquisitely beautiful because it was there on the water but only realised because the sheet was there. Now, I want to know how do you arrive at that? I don't think you sit at home thinking 'That's a good idea, how can I work it into the show' . . .

RL I think there's an important word that has lost its sense in the theatre, and that's the word 'playing'. It's become a profession, a very serious word, but the concept of playing has disappeared from the staging of shows. The only way you can attain these ideas is if you play. I think we're trying to be grown-ups and taken seriously and all of that, and everything that's childish or inventive about us we put aside. I always give this example, and you probably all went through similar things . . . My father was a cab driver so he didn't have any money, but at Christmas they would buy some sophisticated toy I'd wanted badly, and I'd start playing around with it and after three days I'd be completely bored and have more fun with the box it came in. If you play around you get these ideas. Text and story-writing is very sacred, but, the thing with the nun really came about because she was playing both parts and didn't have time to go out and come in again, so we used that to become a moment of poetry. For it to work it meant that every element of clothing that we took off her had a line that went with it – we wrote to justify the costume change, which is a sacrilege in the world of writing for the theatre. You never start from form. You always work by the sacred word and of course you have problems if you don't reinvent it. I'm not saying it works every time, but I think theatre is a place of form. You explore mediums until one day you express something very profound that has some echo in the audience. Sometimes it doesn't work but at least if you put that word 'play' back, the audience is much more moved and feels much more stimulated and excited by something that allows them to be inventive with the actor. There are two ways of being attentive to a show, either you can watch in a very passive way or in a very active way. We have learnt, probably for budget reasons, that we want to give the audience their money's worth. We say 'They come here to relax, they don't want to think.' But it's not true. I believe in the intelligence of the audience, I believe that the audience wants to create. You have to give the audience food, not things that are already masticated and organised and painted. Sometimes I think I can do beautiful, magical images that are very stunning but they're too high-tec, they don't give the audience the opportunity to invent them. I think I've achieved something when it's extremely simple but triggers in 300 people in the house 300 different versions, like a word does.

RE The pool in *Tectonic Plates*, you said that Michael Levine, the designer said you must have this pool . . .

RL Of course if, after a while the pool gets in the way, we put it aside, we don't suffer. I believe a lot in intuition and in spontaneous propositions, mainly from actors because actors are extremely intuitive people. They often stutter and can't clearly explain theatrical ideas as well as writers or directors, but they can actually express intuitions, and that's what we have to look for in theatre. Sometimes it's completely clumsy, you come in with this image and you work on it and consider it and at some point it always comes out, that there's this inner connection between us, all these layers underneath our feet, secret connections that we have to discover. Then we work on the coincidences. When you work alone it's more difficult because it's much more egocentric, almost therapeutic. But these ideas come from coincidence and intuition. For *Needles and Opium*, I was interested in Jean Cocteau and fascinated by the fact that he wrote a book on a plane. In those days it took 15 hours to fly from New York City to Paris, so he had time to write a book. I was amazed because I only deliver one tenth of the contents of the book, but it's very fascinating. I read it on a plane to Barcelona and had the physical sensation of flying while this guy was on this old 1949 plane. So you start to investigate the effects it has on you, the coincidences. You say, how come I feel moved and inspired by this piece of work, which I might just have read, found interesting and put aside? It's the fact that you're in mid-air, in a privileged place, these events indicate to you what you should be using. I've done it so much, and worked with so many people that I don't have as much fear or apprehension about going into it. Of course, a lot of actors or writers who participate in my works are often destabilised when we start.

Talking about *Tectonic Plates*, I can't explain it, it made an impression on me intellectually, this thing of continents that are moving. It's just an intuition. Then everyone in the company gives their impression and at one point we see all these story lines. I didn't know anything about Romanticism before we did this show, or about Jim Morrison or Chopin. I mean, I knew *something* – I'm not totally uncultivated – but then you get so obsessed and so creative when you delve into a world you don't know. The thing that's interesting is to discover a text, an author. That's something I do when I direct actors. The main indication I give when I work on a text is: Discover what you're saying. The audience wants to discover things and it's in a state of discovery that the actor is on the wing.

RE You've had prolonged experience of directing conventional existing texts, some classics, in large theatres not dissimilar from the National, and at the moment you're working on an existing text (*A Midsummer Night's Dream*), which you have directed before, in Victor Hugo's French translation. If you've got a given text, is that an inhibition or is it simply like the pool?

RL It depends on the text of course. Dealing with Shakespeare we're dealing with an avalanche of resources, a box of toys to be taken out. There are some authors that are so infinitely rich and give so much permission, because theatre is the platform of allowing things to be expressed, emotions to meet. What's so extraordinary about Shakespeare is that this man was so intuitive, he gives us the story of mankind. I think he offers a lot of permission to the actor, the translator, the director. You don't feel in a literal environment when working with Shakespeare, Dante or authors like that. Probably that's also one of the responses to the theatrical crisis in the past decade. In France for example, Mnouchkine is re-staging all the Greeks – people are going back to these fundamental texts.

RE Is that because they're poetic texts and the verbal imagery in the text resonates sufficiently . . .

RL Yes but also there's something about these texts that are doubtful. I did the Scottish play two months ago in Toronto, the first time I directed Shakespeare in English. There are all of these theories about how maybe Shakespeare did not exist and these fifteen women wrote the plays . . . there's something doubtful about the property and the invention. The essence of

Romanticism and the Renaissance is that you're building a new world on the ruins of the old one, and that's creative, that's rich. All these people. Shakespeare and the Greeks, built a new world on an old one.

RE That's a wonderful metaphor for the whole continuing process of theatre, isn't it, particularly in this country where you're very conscious of the mountainous tradition, and every time you do a Shakespeare play you've got this huge baggage piled up behind you and you are building on the old world.

RL I think also it's something about the global theatrical community. Theatre's a world that is built on ripping other people off. It's a normal tradition. Mummenschanz, an extraordinary mask and mime company from Switzerland, have this recipe for this kind of plasticine they use for their masks. Everyone wants to know the recipe. You have to show the strings. If you don't see the strings, at some point you have to understand that there *are* strings, there are people taking make-up off. You have to share that.

RE One of the things I like about working in the theatre is that it's completely pragmatic, it's empirical, and you always say 'Does it work?' That's why I like British actors a lot, because they come from a completely empirical tradition. Some people, certainly from the perspective of German theatre, they're pragmatic to a fault. Is that your experience of working with British actors (and you're indemnified against slander)?

RL I think the first thing you identify when you start working with British actors is that they're so professional, the system is centuries old, and you're shocked by how available actors are to the director. You want them to be crazy, to say shut up, listen to me. That's what they do where I come from – there's all these crazy people running round the room and you say 'Hey, focus.' British actors are extremely focused. It's an interesting phenomenon, not just in the theatre but British society in general has the reputation of this cliche of phlegmatism. Is that an English word?

RE Yeah.

RL Most certainly is. There's this theory that England's history, not in its theatre, but its history is so bloody – Jack the Ripper, Richard III – the culture is so bloody that it kind of assassinated death. It took the sexy thing of violence out of it. I'm amazed when I see British productions of a Shakespearean tragedy, to see this extraordinary balance between seeming cold but actually boiling inside, as if the British theatre is also referring to this extremely boiling and violent past but is actually living in a very organised and cold society. I think that the British actors I love have that quality – it's very close to Japanese theatre where everything is happening inside and it takes half an hour for an actor to cross the stage. You can feel the intensity and it's something that is lacking in North America because we're used to doing theatre or film that is crazy. An actor has to be crazy, to be generous, and there's a modesty that has been lost in theatre in North America.

RE I think it's something to do with our greatest export being class and our obsession with class. As an English person you grow up being taught that you have to take on class roles that are allocated. There's a sense in which every English person is educated as an actor.

RL It's very present in the theatre, that hierarchy. In the rehearsal room there's a hierarchy which you don't necessarily feel in other countries. Here, using words betrays where you're from, what part of the country you're from, it's very distinct. People don't talk a lot here. They don't say things before they can formulate them into very organised and pristine sentences.

RE That's not entirely my experience. You must have some very articulate actors in your company.

RL It all depends with whom you hang out.

RE I don't know if you've worked in Germany, but if you think the British theatre is hierarchical, the German one is virtually feudal. The autocracy of the director is extreme.

RL Yes, in France and Germany right now the new auteur is the director. People don't talk about the piece, they say the new Chéreau or the new Stein. It's interesting, for example the Latin countries like metaphors. They like this show, *Needles and Opium*, because it's a metaphoric kind of storytelling, but they're not as excited by something like the *Dragons' Trilogy* which is more a traditional way of telling a story, where you follow characters in chronology. That seems to appeal more to the anglophone countries. I wonder if it's to do with the language or culture. In the past six years maybe half and half of the shows I've produced have been either like this or like the *Dragons' Trilogy*, and it's difficult because even if you are fascinated by multicultural casting as I am, it's difficult to have a show to tour all the countries. Even if you think of Europe getting together and merging, in fact there are very strong cultural ways of telling stories and approaching theatre and it will take centuries before they change.

Audience question

What do you want to do in three years' time?

RL I don't really know – I guess I'll always work in a very spontaneous way and I'm booked for the next three years on a lot of things, but I can never envision the future. I don't have any future projects. I have commitments but I don't have any things I want to explore. I always bump into other people's good ideas.

■ ■ ■

Source

Lepage, R. (1992) 'Robert Lepage in Discussion with Richard Eyre', *Platform Papers* 3: London, Royal National Theatre: 23–32.

Robert Lepage (1957–)

Artistic Director of the French Theatre of the Canadian National Arts Centre. Born in Quebec, he graduated from the Quebec Conservatoire in 1978, and in 1982 joined Théâtre Repère, where he has pioneered his major work, which has been seen in Europe: *Polygraph* (1981), *Tectonic Plates* (1988), and *Needles and Opium* (1991), his one-man show. In 1992 he directed Shakespeare's *A Midsummer Night's Dream* for London's Royal National Theatre, which caused a certain outrage among the conservative UK critics for setting the play in a mudbath. For Lepage theatre has the logic of a dream, and he uses the technology of the stage, and film and video to achieve his ends, which are often concerned with intuition rather than literal ideas and themes. He often writes his own material and constructs visually powerful images against which to perform. He is interested in the colliding, clashing, meeting and overlapping of ideas, hence his major work *Tectonic Plates* utilises the ideas of continents, cultures and personalities colliding in the act of transformation. He works often from improvisation, and is a representative of a Canadian generation that is post-nationalist and open to the world. His work has an originality that uses traditional theatre means to produce performances of strong visual and conceptual complexity. Even when he works with established texts such as Shakespeare, Lepage creates a performance where he has become the author of the total artefact, often illuminating where others merely interpret.

In this interview with Richard Eyre, then director of the Royal National Theatre, Lepage talks about his disillusion with modern theatre writing, leading to the devising of his own work. He also stresses the element of 'play' in theatre, which creates the eclecticism of his performances.

Reader cross-references

Appia – an earlier visual approach to theatre
Bausch – a comparable approach to staging dance theatre
Beck – an oppositional view of the function of performance
LeCompte – a similarly eclectic approach to material
Wilson and **Anderson** – similar concerns with visual theatre

Chapter 29

F.T. Marinetti

THE FOUNDING
AND MANIFESTO
OF FUTURISM

W E HAD STAYED UP ALL NIGHT, my friends and I, under hanging mosque lamps with domes of filigreed brass, domes starred like our spirits, shining like them with the prisoned radiance of electric hearts. For hours we had trampled our atavistic ennui into rich oriental rugs, arguing up to the last confines of logic and blackening many reams of paper with our frenzied scribbling.

An immense pride was buoying us up, because we felt ourselves alone at that hour, alone, awake, and on our feet, like proud beacons or forward sentries against an army of hostile stars glaring down at us from their celestial encampments. Alone with stokers feeding the hellish fires of great ships, alone with the black spectres who grope in the red-hot bellies of locomotives launched down their crazy courses, alone with drunkards reeling like wounded birds along the city walls.

Suddenly we jumped, hearing the mighty noise of the huge double-decker trams that rumbled by outside, ablaze with coloured lights, like villages on holiday suddenly struck and uprooted by the flooding Po and dragged over falls and through gorges to the sea.

Then the silence deepened. But, as we listened to the old canal muttering its feeble prayers and the creaking bones of sickly palaces above their damp green beards, under the windows we suddenly heard the famished roar of automobiles.

'Let's go!' I said. 'Friends, away! Let's go! Mythology and the Mystic Ideal are defeated at last. We're about to see the Centaur's birth and, soon after, the first flight of Angels! . . . We must shake the gates of life, test the bolts and hinges. Let's go! Look there, on the earth, the very first dawn! There's nothing to match the splendour of the sun's red sword, slashing for the first time through our millennial gloom!'

We went up to the three snorting beasts, to lay amorous hands on their torrid breasts. I stretched out on my car like a corpse on its bier, but revived at once under the steering wheel, a guillotine blade that threatened my stomach.

The raging broom of madness swept us out of ourselves and drove us through streets as rough and deep as the beds of torrents. Here and there, sick lamplight through window glass taught us to distrust the deceitful mathematics of our perishing eyes.

I cried, 'The scent, the scent alone is enough for our beasts.'

And like young lions we ran after Death, its dark pelt blotched with pale crosses as it escaped down the vast violet living and throbbing sky.

But we had no ideal Mistress raising her divine form to the clouds, nor any cruel Queen to whom to offer our bodies, twisted like Byzantine rings! There was nothing to make us wish for death, unless the wish to be free at last from the weight of our courage!

And on we raced, hurling watchdogs against doorsteps, curling them under our burning tyres like collars under a flat-iron. Death, domesticated, met me at every turn, gracefully holding out a paw, or once in a while hunkering down, making velvety caressing eyes at me from every puddle.

'Let's break out of the horrible shell of wisdom and throw ourselves like pride-ripened fruit into the wide, contorted mouth of the wind! Let's give ourselves utterly to the Unknown, not in desperation but only to replenish the deep wells of the Absurd!'

The words were scarcely out of my mouth when I spun my car around with the frenzy of a dog trying to bite its tail, and there, suddenly, were two cyclists coming towards me, shaking their fists, wobbling like two equally convincing but nevertheless contradictory arguments. Their stupid dilemma was blocking my way – Damn! Ouch! . . . I stopped short and to my disgust rolled over into a ditch with my wheels in the air. . . .

O maternal ditch, almost full of muddy water! Fair factory drain! I gulped down your nourishing sludge; and I remembered the blessed black breast of my Sudanese nurse. . . . When I came up – torn, filthy, and stinking – from under the capsized car, I felt the white-hot iron of joy deliciously pass through my heart!

A crowd of fishermen with handlines and gouty naturalists were already swarming around the prodigy. With patient, loving care those people rigged a tall derrick and iron grapnels to fish out my car, like a big beached shark. Up it came from the ditch, slowly, leaving in the bottom, like scales, its heavy framework of good sense and its soft upholstery of comfort.

They thought it was dead, my beautiful shark, but a caress from me was enough to revive it; and there it was, alive again, running on its powerful fins!

And so, faces smeared with good factory muck – plastered with metallic waste, with senseless sweat, with celestial soot – we, bruised, our arms in slings, but unafraid, declared our high intentions to all the *living* of the earth:

Manifesto of Futurism

1   We intend to sing the love of danger, the habit of energy and fearlessness.
2   Courage, audacity, and revolt will be essential elements of our poetry.
3   Up to now literature has exalted a pensive immobility, ecstasy, and sleep. We intend to exalt aggressive action, a feverish insomnia, the racer's stride, the mortal leap, the punch and the slap.
4   We affirm that the world's magnificence has been enriched by a new beauty: the beauty of speed. A racing car whose hood is adorned with great pipes, like serpents of explosive breath – a roaring car that seems to ride on grapeshot is more beautiful than the *Victory of Samothrace*.
5   We want to hymn the man at the wheel, who hurls the lance of his spirit across the Earth, along the circle of its orbit.
6   The poet must spend himself with ardour, splendour, and generosity, to swell the enthusiastic fervour of the primordial elements.
7   Except in struggle, there is no more beauty. No work without an aggressive character can be a masterpiece. Poetry must be conceived as a violent attack on unknown forces, to reduce and prostrate them before man.
8   We stand on the last promontory of the centuries! . . . Why should we look back, when what we want is to break down the mysterious doors of the Impossible? Time and Space died yesterday. We already live in the absolute, because we have created eternal, omnipresent speed.

9   We will glorify war – the world's only hygiene – militarism, patrio-
     tism, the destructive gesture of freedom-bringers, beautiful ideas worth
     dying for, and scorn for woman.

10   We will destroy the museums, libraries, academies of every kind, will
     fight moralism, feminism, every opportunistic or utilitarian cowardice.

11   We will sing of great crowds excited by work, by pleasure, and by riot;
     we will sing of the multicoloured, polyphonic tides of revolution in the
     modern capitals; we will sing of the vibrant nightly fervour of arsenals
     and shipyards blazing with violent electric moons; greedy railway
     stations that devour smoke-plumed serpents; factories hung on clouds
     by the crooked lines of their smoke; bridges that stride the rivers like
     giant gymnasts, flashing in the sun with a glitter of knives; adventurous
     steamers that sniff the horizon; deep-chested locomotives whose wheels
     paw the tracks like the hooves of enormous steel horses bridled by
     tubing; and the sleek flight of planes whose propellers chatter in the
     wind like banners and seem to cheer like an enthusiastic crowd.

It is from Italy that we launch through the world this violently upsetting incen-
diary manifesto of ours. With it, today, we establish *Futurism*, because we want
to free this land from its smelly gangrene of professors, archaeologists, *ciceroni*
and antiquarians. For too long has Italy been a dealer in second-hand clothes.
We mean to free her from the numberless museums that cover her like so
many graveyards.

Museums: cemeteries! . . . Identical, surely, in the sinister promiscuity
of so many bodies unknown to one another. Museums: public dormitories
where one lies forever beside hated or unknown beings. Museums: absurd
abattoirs of painters and sculptors ferociously slaughtering each other with
colour-blows and line-blows, the length of the fought-over walls!

That one should make an annual pilgrimage, just as one goes to the
graveyard on All Souls' Day – that I grant. That once a year one should leave
a floral tribute beneath the *Gioconda*, I grant you that. . . . But I don't admit
that our sorrows, our fragile courage, our morbid restlessness should be
given a daily conducted tour through the museums. Why poison ourselves?
Why rot?

And what is there to see in an old picture except the laborious contor-
tions of an artist throwing himself against the barriers that thwart his desire
to express his dream completely? . . . Admiring an old picture is the same
as pouring our sensibility into a funerary urn instead of hurling it far off, in
violent spasms of action and creation.

Do you, then, wish to waste all your best powers in this eternal
and futile worship of the past, from which you emerge fatally exhausted,
shrunken, beaten down?

In truth I tell you that daily visits to museums, libraries, and academies (cemeteries of empty exertion, Calvaries of crucified dreams, registries of aborted beginnings!) are, for artists, as damaging as the prolonged supervision by parents of certain young people drunk with their talent and their ambitious wills. When the future is barred to them, the admirable past may be a solace for the ills of the moribund, the sickly, the prisoner. . . . But we want no part of it, the past, we the young and strong *Futurists*!

So let them come, the gay incendiaries with charred fingers! Here they are! Here they are! . . . Come on! set fire to the library shelves! Turn aside the canals to flood the museums! . . . Oh, the joy of seeing the glorious old canvases bobbing adrift on those waters, discoloured and shredded! . . . Take up your pickaxes, your axes and hammers and wreck, wreck the venerable cities, pitilessly!

The oldest of us is thirty: so we have at least a decade for finishing our work. When we are forty, other younger and stronger men will probably throw us in the wastebasket like useless manuscripts – we want it to happen!

They will come against us, our successors, will come from far away, from every quarter, dancing to the winged cadence of their first songs, flexing the hooked claws of predators, sniffing doglike at the academy doors the strong odour of our decaying minds, which will already have been promised to the literary catacombs.

But we won't be there. . . . At last they'll find us – one winter's night – in open country, beneath a sad roof drummed by a monotonous rain. They'll see us crouched beside our trembling aeroplanes in the act of warming our hands at the poor little blaze that our books of today will give out when they take fire from the flight of our images.

They'll storm around us, panting with scorn and anguish, and all of them, exasperated by our proud daring, will hurtle to kill us, driven by a hatred the more implacable the more their hearts will be drunk with love and admiration for us.

Injustice, strong and sane, will break out radiantly in their eyes.

Art, in fact, can be nothing but violence, cruelty, and injustice.

The oldest of us is thirty: even so we have already scattered treasures, a thousand treasures of force, love, courage, astuteness, and raw will-power; have thrown them impatiently away, with fury, carelessly, unhesitatingly, breathless, and unresting. . . . Look at us! We are still untired! Our hearts know no weariness because they are fed with fire, hatred, and speed! . . . Does that amaze you? It should, because you can never remember having lived! Erect on the summit of the world, once again we hurl our defiance at the stars!

You have objections? – Enough! Enough! We know them. . . . We've understood! . . . Our fine deceitful intelligence tells us that we are the revival and extension of our ancestors – Perhaps! . . . If only it were so! – But who cares? We don't want to understand! . . . Woe to anyone who says those infamous words to us again!

Lift up your heads!

Erect on the summit of the world, once again we hurl defiance to the stars!

■ ■ ■

Source

Marinetti, F.T. (1909, 1973) 'The Founding and Manifesto of Futurism', *Marinetti's Selected Writings*, trans. R.W. Flint, New York: Farrar, Straus and Giroux: 19–24.

First published in *Le Figaro* (Paris), 20 February 1909, translated into English 1973.

F.T. Marinetti (1876–1944)

Performance as an act of engagement with its time found its most intense expression in the Italian futurist movement, a collection of artists, writers, composers, theatre-makers, whose first manifesto, written by Marinetti, was printed in *Le Figaro* on 20 February 1909. This proclaimed a new and sensational world of speed, dynamism, and aggression. Futurism was the first cultural movement of the twentieth century, and Marinetti was a new kind of arts entrepreneur – artist, writer, publicist, promoter – without whose skills the movement would have foundered. Futurism, although it produced art, was more of an ideology, whose essential element was rebellion against the past, especially the stultifying past of Italian art, and against Italian cultural stagnation. The movement embraced industrialisation, technical invention, and ultimately Mussolini's fascism, hence its low profile in cultural historical terms until recent years. Futurism was organised like a political campaign; it embraced painting, music, plays, film, scenic design, dance, and, for one of its members, Valentine de Saint Point, lust – 'the quest of the flesh for the unknown'. Theatre, as a major performance form, was of interest because of its immediacy, and the potential physical involvement of the spectators; it was able to maximise the sensory and minimalise the intellectual. Many of the performance scenarios – by Cangiullo, Boccioni, Balla, Settimelli, and others – were far in advance of their time in their use of simultaneity and compression, synthesising actions and events into the fewest numbers of dynamic words and sound.

In this first manifesto of futurism, Marinetti describes the excitement and potential of a new artistic dynamism, in words which are clearly intended to provoke readers to action which will sweep away the cobwebs of the past, and points to the necessity for the twentieth century to embrace radical forms of art.

Reader cross-references

Artaud – who also wished to sweep away logic and embrace physicality and sensuality
Beck – a similar messianic view of art's importance
Duncan – another voice heralding the new century
Goldberg – the historical importance of futurism
Hijikata – Butoh also rejects the rational
Rainer – another, later, 'manifesto'
Richter – the founding of Dada, a contemporary movement of disgust

Further reading

Kirby, M. (1971) *Futurist Performance*, New York: Dutton.
Tisdall, C. and Bozzolla, A. (1977) *Futurism*, London: Thames & Hudson.

Chapter 30

John Martin

CHARACTERISTICS
OF THE MODERN
DANCE

1 Introduction

The dance has only recently begun to be recognized as a major
art and there is still considerable confusion about it, not only in
the public mind, but in the minds of the dancers themselves as
a class. There is no literature, to speak of, in English on the subject except that which deals with the older forms no longer in
general use by the progressive artists, and the only source of
enlightenment has been the actual performances of the dancers
themselves. In the last analysis, this is the only reliable source,
to be sure, for all theory which is more than hypothetical must
be by deduction from the practice of the best artists. It has not
been an easy matter, however, for even the most sympathetic
spectator to determine what the basis of the modern dance is
when he sees no two dancers' performances apparently in any
way similar to each other. He has been further confused by the
neglect, the ignorance and even the hostility of the majority of
music critics on the newspapers who undertake without any
preparation and with even less sympathy to write critically of
dance performances.

In the past – the comparatively recent past – the dance
meant the ballet, and the ballet meant the ballet d'action. This
consisted of a plot of sorts interspersed with choreographic

numbers much as a musical comedy is interspersed with songs. This class of performance fell naturally into the category of theatrical productions and was judged by the dramatic critics. When Isadora Duncan and the romantic movement appeared, with the emphasis heavy on music instead of drama, but still with choreographic accompaniment, dancing became a subject for the music critics to deal with. Now, with the development of the modern dance in which dancing is the main issue and music and plot are secondary where they are not actually inessential, confusion reigns. To dispel as effectually as may be this confusion is the objective of these pages.

In spite of the fact that there are as many methods and systems of modern dancing as there are dancers, certain common principles and purposes underlie them all. We shall here attempt to isolate these purposes and principles so that they may be examined with care. Let it be said once more that these theoretical deductions are based not on any preconceived point to be proved, but upon the practice of the leading dancers of the day, both American and European. First, let us consider the distinguishing characteristics of the modern dance – what it is made up of and how it differs from other types of dance; then from this subject we must inevitably be led to a consideration of dance form, and the relation which exists between the dance and other arts.

2 'Modern' vs. classic and romantic

The term 'modern' dance is obviously an inadequate one. It is not synonymous with contemporary dance, for it is by no means that inclusive. It is only of temporary accuracy insofar as it is accurate at all, for to-morrow when a more advanced type of dance shall have arisen it will be impossible to refer to the dancing of to-day as modern. It is, nevertheless, a blanket word which has succeeded in making itself equally offensive in all the arts. It covers a multitude of minor isms – cubism, futurism, dadaism, and in the dance particularly, expressionism, absolutism, creativism, and scores of others.

By the modern dance we shall here intend to imply by a method of negation those types of dancing which are neither classic nor romantic. It is perhaps unnecessary to say that folk dancing and those popular theatrical forms known as 'tap and acrobatic' are excluded from consideration, not because they are felt to be inferior or without value, but because they do not come under the definition of dancing as a fine art. The classic dance was built on set forms, arbitrary and traditional. The romantic dance rebelled against the cold estheticism of this system and discarded all formalism in favor of a free, personal expression of emotional experience. Since both these schools are still largely in practice, and since it is in a sense in opposition to them that the modern dance has arisen, it is necessary to pause for a few moments to see in a very general way what they consist of.

The classic dance has a set vocabulary of movement which for perfection of execution must be performed in a prescribed manner. The predominant characteristic of its movements – or rather of its attitudes – is artificiality. They are required to measure up to standards of design in space irrespective of the natural tendencies of the body and of any relation to human experience. They are, in the fullest sense of the word, abstract. From time to time the vocabulary has been enlarged by additions devised by eminent dancers, just as the literary vocabulary is enlarged from time to time by new words, but it remains essentially a limited medium – limited, indeed, from choice. That it is a medium of great beauty when it is employed by a genuine artist is not important here, if for no other reason than that there are not a half dozen artists of any rank who employ it.

The romantic dance threw off this restrictive vocabulary. It was not interested in what it considered to be a collection of meaningless words, so to speak; it wanted to get at meaning irrespective of words. For Isadora Duncan this meaning was to be found in herself under the inspirational influence of romantic music. But obviously in order to be objectified, it must have a visible form. As a matter of fact, this form proved to be scarcely less limited than that of the classic ballet. It contained a quantity of pantomimic gesture, many actual ballet attitudes and steps, and bits of posture from Greek ceramics and Oriental art. Ruth St Denis added enormously to its vocabulary from Oriental sources, and realizing perhaps the necessity of something concrete in the matter of form, was largely responsible for the introduction of musical form into the dance. In her musical interpretations, the pattern of the dance was practically that of the music insofar as the two could be made identical.

The classic dance itself was fundamentally affected by this romantic revolution through the radical innovations of Fokine in the Russian Imperial Ballet. Here there occurred a great liberalising of the rigid forms of the classic prescription, animated by the desire to give to the dance the warmth and vitality of human emotion. But the ballet forms remained as a basis for the new method. Thus in the entire romantic movement, which if we interpret it in its strict sense has been of surprisingly brief duration, there was no essential form discovered in which to express the new spirit. The new wine, poured into the old or inadequate bottles, burst the bottles and was lost.

3 Movement as substance

The modern dance has actually arisen in fulfilment of the ideals of the romantic movement. It has set itself positively against the artifice of the classic ballet, making its chief aim the expression of an inner compulsion; but it has also seen the necessity for vital forms for this expression, and indeed has realised the aesthetic value of form in and of itself as an adjunct to this expression. In carrying out this purpose it has thrown aside everything that has gone before and started all over again from the beginning.

This beginning was the discovery of the actual substance of the dance, which it found to be movement. This is one of the four great basic points of the modern dance. With this discovery the dance became for the first time an independent art, – an absolute art, as they like to say in Germany – completely self-contained, related directly to life, subject to infinite variety.

Previously movement was only incidental. In the classic dance what counted primarily was poses, attitudes and prescribed combinations of them. The movement that united them was unimportant. Every attempt was made, indeed, to hide muscular action, to make the body appear to be acted upon as by some external force which eliminated effort. In the romantic developments it was the emotional idea that was the centre of interest. This was conveyed largely by means of the music and in part even by a sort of intense mental concentration. Movement resulted, of course, but it was not seen as the material out of which the dance was to be made. It seems difficult to dispute, however, that the germ of the new idea lay in this development, and if it had not been for the overpowering domination of the music it might have made itself felt.

In the classic dance a certain meaning came out of the combination of movements, as a meaning comes out of a combination of words; but the words are essentially separate entities. In music, on the other hand, the result is obtained not by putting together a succession of notes, but by creating in the medium of sound which in spite of variations in pitch and intensity remains a unified entity, a substance. Similarly, movement is seen by the modern dancer as a unified entity, a substance. It may be varied in range of space, duration of time, quality and intensity, and still remain a constant thing. . . .

7 Metakinesis

Movement, then, in and of itself is a medium for the transference of an aesthetic and emotional concept from the consciousness of one individual to that of another. This should not be as strange an idea as it seems to be. Back as far as Plato, and perhaps farther, it has been toyed with by the metaphysical philosophers. Kinesis is the name they gave to physical movement; and in an obscure footnote in Webster's Dictionary – so common a source of reference as that! – we find that there is correlated with kinesis a supposed psychic accompaniment called metakinesis, this correlation growing from the theory that the physical and the psychical are merely two aspects of a single underlying reality.

We are not here concerned with theories of metaphysics, and it makes very little difference what we may choose to believe about the relation in general between the physical and the psychical. It is extremely important, however, that we see in the dance the relation that exists between physical movement and mental – or psychical, if you will – intention. Metakinesis is perhaps a formidable word, but it is the only one the dictionary yields for the expression of one of the vital points of the modern dance.

A few minutes ago, it was said that the discovery of movement as the substance of the dance in the same sense that sound is the substance of music, was one of the four important discoveries of the modern dance. The second of these discoveries is that of metakinesis. Nobody invented it, it has always been true. It was true when the early man of savagery conveyed his sense of the mystery of death, and when he stirred a whole tribe into warlike frenzy by leading them into a particular kind of dance. It was true, and recognized in a degree, in the great days of the Greek theatre, where movement was an important feature of drama. Indeed, the Greek tragic chorus, which at moments of highest tragedy sought refuge in chanting songs of deep fervor and dancing to them, was used, as Gilbert Murray has said somewhere, to express the 'inexpressible residue of emotion' which mere rationality – words and pantomime – could not convey. It was also true during the many years of the classic ballet. Without it audiences would have had no more delight in watching a ballerina balance herself on one toe in defiance of gravity than they would have had in watching feathers float on the air. It was their own consciousness of gravity which held them to the earth that made them applaud the feat of some one else in defying it. But no conscious artistic use was made of metakinesis until the modern dance arose. You will still find many dancers who will laugh at it – while their audiences slip rapidly away into the performances of their colleagues who have not such keen senses of humor.

The Germans have realized the value of it to such an extent that they have named their type of dancing in general 'expressionistic,' or the kind of dancing which expresses through movement the dancer's feeling.

Because of this close relationship between movement and personal experience, temperament, mental and emotional equipment, it is manifestly impossible for every one to be taught to do the same type of movement.

The ideal dance education, therefore, is that which trains the student to find his own type of movement. Rudolf von Laban, the German theorist, has divided all people into three general types, according to their style of movement, much as singers are divided into such general types as soprano, tenor, bass, etc. He has arrived at certain interesting conclusions, based on physiological and psychological research, and colored always with a sense of metakinesis. Certain individuals, he has found, are tall and thin and move in a certain manner, always more or less alike. These he calls 'high dancers.' Others are short and squat and move in another manner. These he calls 'low dancers.' Between them are the 'middle dancers.' Now the reason they move in certain fashions is not that they are of a certain stature, and their stature is not what it is because of their type of movement. Both are the result of some personal, mental, psychological characteristics. This is a complete veri- fication, as far as it goes, of the metaphysicians' theory that kinesis and metakinesis are two aspects of a single underlying reality. . . .

9 The modern dance a point of view

From this desire to externalize personal, authentic experience, it is evident that the scheme of modern dancing is all in the direction of individualism and away from standardization. That is why it is likely to be so confusing for the man in the street to go to dance recitals. He goes to one, and though he is bewildered, he thinks it over at home – for the purpose of illustration it is perhaps permissible to idealize the man in the street to this extent – and decides that he sees the point. The next Sunday he goes to the recital of another dancer just to see if he is right about the theory he has worked out. But this second dancer does not do a single thing in the way the first one did. The poor fellow is hopelessly confused. If he is still courageous enough to try a third dancer on the chance of some possible reconciliation of theory, he does so only to find confusion worse confounded.

Nevertheless, there is a great similarity throughout the dance field – that is, of course, the modern dance field. The mistake that is made is in looking for a standard system, a code such as characterized the classic dance. The modern dance is not a system; it is a point of view. This point of view has been developing through the years, and it is by no means an isolated development. It has gone hand in hand with the development of points of view on other subjects.

We have all, I am sure, become weary of hearing about the machine age and how it is killing all that is fine in life and how art cannot hope to survive. It is people who stopped thinking when dear Queen Victoria mounted the throne who lament thus, and it is they who find dancing gone to the dogs. It is an outlook that is posited upon either the inability or the unwillingness to undergo a change of mind. A number of such people somehow find their way into dance recitals, and if a collection of their remarks by way of criticism were to be published, it would become over night a standard textbook of misinformation. The first appearance of Mary Wigman in any community gives rise to priceless gems in this category, and Martha Graham's performances are also a prolific source. It is not only radical artists of this calibre, however, who draw out ex cathedra opinions from the disgruntled, but even so comparatively conservative a dancer as La Argentina. She has been accused of everything from being a man in disguise to having no rhythm! . . .

14 Dynamism

So far we have considered two of the four distinctive points of the modern dance – movement as substance, and metakinesis. The third of these points is dynamism.

When we see that the dance is not a series of connected postures but is rather the stuff that connects the postures, so to speak, we arrive at the conclusion that the dance consists of continuous or sustained movement. This movement contains no static elements, no attitudes however decorative which might be considered as points of rest.

Now, as a matter of fact, we know that there are actually pauses in dances, and that if there were not we would have a hard time clarifying phrases. But there is never a moment when the dancer lapses into natural physical rest until the dance, or the particular section of the dance if it is a work in several parts, is finished. Perhaps it may illustrate this point to think of a ball bouncing. There may be moments when the ball is comparatively at rest, as for example when it is in the hand between bounces, but it is never actually so until the game ends. Similarly there are moments when the body of the dancer is comparatively at rest, when the muscular effort is less than at other times. Obviously it would be almost impossible and quite undesirable to keep sustained movement always at the same degree of intensity.

The new German dance lays great emphasis upon this element of dynamism. Throughout the studios of Germany you will hear the phrase 'Anspannung und Abspannung' over and over again – the ebb and flow of muscular impulses. It was perhaps Rudolf von Laban who was primarily responsible for this emphasis. In his early considerations of the dance it became clear that since the dance was composed of movement and movement resulted from muscular action, the whole range of the dance, as of movement, lay between the extremes of complete relaxation and complete tension.

All movement inherently possesses force and intensity. The quality of the movement, therefore, is to a great extent regulated by its quantity – by the degree or amount of force or intensity it contains. This gives to the dance its only purely muscular rhythm. It is in a sense akin to the musical variation from loud to soft, though it is much wider in its application and more vital to the actual substance of the dance. It is of value according to its degree, the speed and range of its variation, its distribution among the parts of the body, and its representational implications.

The fourth distinctive point of the modern dance is the discarding of all traditional requirements of form and the establishment of a new principle upon which each dance makes its own form. This is a subject that demands consideration on its own account at some length.

■ ■ ■

Source

Martin, J. (1933, 1965) 'Characteristics of the Modern Dance', *The Modern Dance*, New York: Dance Horizons: 1–7, 13–16, 19–21, 31–33.

John Martin (1893–1985)

American dance critic and historian. He graduated from the University of Louisville, studied violin at Chicago Conservatory, and became involved in community theatre. He was editor of the *Dramatic Mirror* (1919–22) and director of Boleslavsky's Laboratory Theatre (1924–26).

Martin was dance critic of the *New York Times* from 1927 until his retirement in 1962. He later taught at the University of California at Los Angeles. During the thirty-five years that he was with the paper he profoundly influenced the development of dance in America. He was not the first American critic to write about dance, but he could rightly be called the first to concentrate on and champion modern dance as a serious art form.

Martin began his *NYT* writing about dance the year after Martha Graham had made her New York debut, the year before the Humphrey-Weidman Company was formed, and three years before Mary Wigman's first American tour. He championed the emergent modern dance from the very start: 'The amazing growth of the art consciousness of the American people during the last twenty years is nowhere more clearly manifested than in the field of dance.'[1] He wrote supportively and brilliantly about American modern dance. He set down his views on the aesthetics of modern dance in *The Modern Dance* (1933). This was followed by the all-embracing *Introduction to the Dance* (1939). These books greatly contributed to the status accorded dance as a serious art in the USA. His views, although now superseded by later historians, encapsulate the period and remain relevant in placing the concerns of that time.

In this extract Martin identifies what he sees as modern dance's formal characteristics. His thesis is that there is a new form of dance which differs from ballet's traditions of romanticism and classicism. He identifies this new modern dance as being a phenomenon that arose in Europe and America,[2] and writes about Duncan, Humphrey and Wigman in particular. It remains, sixty years on, a definitive American period statement.

Reader cross-references

Banes– a later critical perspective on dance
Benjamin – a contemporary, different, critical view of performance
Humphrey – a dancer on the choreography of modern dance
Stanislavski – whom he refers to in locating dance among the other arts
Wigman – a contemporary dancer's philosophy of modern dance

Further reading

Martin, J. (1933, 1965) *The Modern Dance*, New York: Dance Horizons.
Martin, J. (1989) *The Dance in Theory*, Princeton, N.J.: Dance Horizons, republication of the first third of *Introduction to the Dance* (1939).

Notes

1   Martin, J. (1927) *New York Times*, 27 November.
2   A perspective forgotten by some later historians who claimed it as uniquely American.

Chapter 31

Vsevolod Meyerhold

FIRST ATTEMPTS
AT A
STYLIZED THEATRE

T HE FIRST ATTEMPTS to realize a Stylized Theatre as conceived by Maeterlinck and Bryusov were made at the Theatre-Studio. In my opinion, this first experimental theatre came very near to achieving ideal stylized drama with its first production, *The Death of Tintagiles*; so I think it is appropriate to describe the work of the directors, actors and designers on this play, and to consider the lessons learnt during its production.

The theatre is constantly revealing a lack of harmony amongst those engaged in presenting their collective creative work to the public. One never sees an ideal blend of author, director, actor, designer, composer and prop-erty-master. For this reason, Wagner's notion of a synthesis of the arts seems to me impossible. Both the artist and the composer should remain in their own fields: the artist in a special *decorative* theatre where he could exhibit canvases which require a stage rather than an art gallery, artificial rather than natural light, several planes instead of just two dimensions, and so on; the composer should concentrate on symphonies like Beethoven's Ninth, for the dramatic theatre, where music has merely an auxiliary role, has nothing to offer him.

These thoughts came to me after our early experiments (*The Death of Tintagiles*) had been superseded by the second phase (*Pelléas and Mélisande*). But even when we started work on *The Death of Tintagiles* I was plagued already by the question of disharmony between the various creative elements; even if it was impossible to reach agreement with the composer and the artist, each of whom was trying instinctively to delineate his own function, at least I hoped to unify the efforts of the author, the director and the actor.

It became clear that these three, the basis of the theatre, could work as one, but only if given the approach which we adopted in the rehearsals of *The Death of Tintagiles* at the Theatre-Studio.

In the course of the usual discussions of the play (before which, of course, the director acquainted himself with it by reading everything written on the subject), the director and actors read through Maeterlinck's verses and extracts from those of his dramas containing scenes corresponding in mood to *The Death of Tintagiles* (the play, itself, was left until we understood how to treat it, lest it became transformed into a mere exercise). The verses and extracts were read by each actor in turn. For them, this work corresponded to the sketches of a painter or the exercises of a musician. The artist must perfect his technique before embarking on a picture. Whilst reading, the actor looked for new means of expression. The audience (everybody, not just the director) made comments and assisted the reader to develop these new means. The entire creative act was directed towards finding those inflections which contained the true ring of the author's own voice. When the author was 'revealed' through this collective work, when a single verse or extract 'rang true', the audience immediately analysed the means of expression which had conveyed the author's style and tone.

Before enumerating the various new aspects of technique developed through this intuitive method, and while I still retain a clear picture of these combined exercises of director and actors, I should like to mention two distinct methods of establishing contact between the director and his actors: one deprives not only the actor but also the spectator of creative freedom; the other leaves them both free, and forces the spectator to create instead of merely looking on (for a start, by stimulating his imagination).

The two methods may be explained by illustrating the four basic theatrical elements (author, director, actor and spectator) as follows:

1   A triangle, in which the apex is the director and the two remaining corners, the author and the actor. The spectator comprehends the creation of the latter two through

265

the creation of the director. This is method one, which we shall call the 'Theatre-Triangle'.

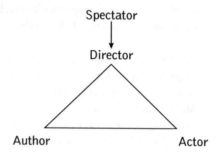

Spectator

Director

Author   Actor

2　A straight, horizontal line with the four theatrical elements (author, director, actor, spectator) marked from left to right represents the other method, which we shall call the 'Theatre of the Straight Line'. The actor reveals his soul freely to the spectator, having assimilated the creation of the director, who, in his turn, has assimilated the creation of the author.

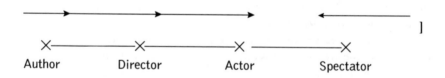

]

Author　　　　　Director　　　　Actor　　　　Spectator

1　In the 'Theatre-Triangle' the director explains his *mise en scène* in detail, describes the characters as he sees them, prescribes every pause, and then rehearses the play until his personal conception of it is exactly reproduced in performance. This 'Theatre-Triangle' may be likened to a symphony orchestra with the director acting as the conductor.

However, the very architecture of the theatre, lacking any provision for conductor's rostrum, points to the difference between the two.

People will say that there are occasions when a symphony orchestra plays without a conductor. Let us consider Nikisch[2] and the symphony orchestra which has been playing under him for years with scarcely a change in its personnel; take a composition which it has played several times a year over a period of ten years. If Nikisch were absent from the conductor's rostrum on one occasion, would the orchestra play the composition according to his interpretation? Yes, it is possible that the listener would recognize it as Nikisch's interpretation. But would the performance sound exactly as though Nikisch were conducting? Obviously, it would be worse, although we should still be hearing Nikisch's interpretation.

So I contend this: true, a symphony orchestra without a conductor is possible, but nevertheless it is impossible to draw a parallel between it and the theatre, where the actors invariably perform on the stage without a director. A symphony orchestra without a conductor is possible, but no matter how well rehearsed, it could never stir the public, only acquaint the listener with the interpretation of this or that conductor, and could blend into an ensemble only to the extent that an artist can re-create a conception which is not his own.

The actor's art consists in far more than merely acquainting the spectator with the director's conception. The actor will grip the spectator only if he assimilates both the director and the author and then gives of himself from the stage.

By contrast, an orchestral musician is distinguished by his ability to carry out the conductor's directions precisely, by dint of his virtuoso technique and *by depersonalizing himself*

In common with the symphony orchestra, the 'Theatre-Triangle' must employ actors with virtuoso technique, but at all costs lacking in indviduality, so that they are able to convey the director's exact concept.

2   In the 'Theatre of the Straight Line', the director, having absorbed the author's conception, conveys his own creation (now a blend of the author and the director) to the actor. The actor, having assimilated the author's conception via the director, stands face to face with the spectator (with director and author behind him), and *freely* reveals his soul to him, thus intensifying the fundamental theatrical relationship of performer and spectator.

In order for the straight line not to bend[2], the director must remain the sole arbiter of the mood and style of the production, but nevertheless, the actor's art remains free in the 'Theatre of the Straight Line'.

The director describes his plan during the discussion of the play. The entire production is coloured by his view of it. He inspires the actors with his devotion to the work, and imbues them with the spirit of the author and with his own interpretation. But after the discussion all the performers remain completely independent. Then the director calls a further general meeting to create harmony from all the separate pieces. How does he set about this? Simply by balancing all the parts which have been freely created by the various individuals involved in the collective enterprise. In establishing the harmony vital to the production, he does not insist on the exact representation of his own conception, which was intended only to ensure unanimity and to prevent the work created collectively from disintegrating. Instead he retires behind the scenes at the earliest possible moment and leaves the stage to the actors.

Then, either they are out of accord with the director or the author (if, say, they are not of the new school)[3] and 'set fire to the ship', or they reveal their souls through almost improvisatory additions, not to the text but to the mere suggestions of the director. In this way the spectator is made to comprehend the author and the director through the prism of the actor's art. *Above all, drama is the art of the actor.*

If you read any of the works of Maeterlinck, his poetry or his drama, his preface to the last collected edition,[4] his book *Le Trésor des Humbles*, where he speaks of the Static Theatre in a tone embodying all the colour and atmosphere of his works, you will see that he has no desire to evoke horror on the stage; nor does he seek to drive the spectator to such hysteria that he wants to flee in terror. On the contrary, he aims to provoke a fearful yet reasoning acceptance of the inevitability of life, to move the spectator to tears and suffering, and yet to soothe and console him. His first task is 'to alleviate our grief by implanting that hope which flags and then springs to life again'.[5] When the spectator leaves the theatre, life with all its pain resumes its course, but the pain no longer seems in vain; life flows on with its joys, its sorrows and its exigencies, but everything acquires meaning because we have seen that it is possible to emerge from the gloom, or at least to endure it without bitterness. Maeterlinck's art is healthy and life-giving. It summons people to a wise acceptance of the might of fate, and his theatre acquires all the significance of a temple. Pastore has good reason for extolling Maeterlinck's mysticism as the last refuge of apostates who refuse to recognize the temporal power of the Church yet cannot bring themselves to discard their free belief in another world. Such a theatre is fit for the presentation of religious subjects. No matter how sombre the colours of a work, so long as it is a *mystery*, it contains an indefatigable affirmation of life.

To us it seems that the whole mistake of our predecessors lay in their attempts at frightening the spectator instead of reconciling him with the inevitability of fate. 'At the foundation of my dramas' – writes Maeterlinck – 'lies the idea of a Christian God together with the ancient concept of Fate.' The author hears the words and lamentations of men as a muffled sound, as though they were falling into a deep abyss. He sees men from a vantage-point beyond the clouds as faintly glittering sparks. All he desires is to overhear in their souls a few words of humility, of hope, of compassion, of terror, and to show us the might of the fate which guides our destiny.

Our aim was to ensure that our production of Maeterlinck produced the same effect of reconciliation in the spectator's mind as the author himself intended. A performance of Maeterlinck is a *mystery*; either there is a barely audible harmony of voices, a chorus of soft weeping, of muted sobs and a stirring of hope (as in *The Death of Tintagiles*), or there is an ecstasy which is transformed into a universal religious festival with dancing to the music of organ and trumpets, or a bacchanalia to celebrate a great miracle (as in Act Two of *Sister Beatrice*). The dramas of Maeterlinck are 'above all else a manifestation and purification of the spirit'. They are '. . . a chorus of souls singing *sotto voce* of suffering, love, beauty and death'. They have a *simplicity* which transports one to the realms of fantasy, a harmony which brings calm, a joy bordering on the ecstatic. It was with this understanding of the spirit of Maeterlinck's theatre that we began work on the rehearsal exercises.

What Muther[6] said of Il Perugino, one of the most fascinating painters of the Quattrocento, seems to me true of Maeterlinck: 'The contemplative lyrical character of his subjects, the quiet grandeur and archaic splendour of his pictures could only be achieved by a composition whose harmony is unmarred by the slightest abrupt movement or the merest harsh contrast.'

Proceeding from this general evaluation of Maeterlinck's art, our directors and actors intuitively established the following principles during the course of preliminary rehearsals:

A   Diction

1   The words must be coldly 'coined', free from all tremolo and the familiar break in the voice. There must be a total absence of tension and lugubrious intonation.

2   The sound must always be 'reinforced'; the words must fall like drops into a deep well, the fall being clearly audible without any vibration in space. There must be no diffusion of sound, no drawing out of word-endings (as in the reading of the Decadents' verses).

3   The internal mystical vibration is more powerful than the histrionics of the old theatre, which were invariably uncontrolled and ugly to look at, with flailing of arms, beating of breasts and slapping of thighs. The internal mystical vibration is conveyed through the eyes, the lips, the sound and manner of delivery: the exterior calm which covers volcanic emotions, with everything light and unforced.

4   In the expression of the tragic sorrows of the soul the form is dictated by the content. Maeterlinck prescribes one form and no other in order to convey that which is so simple and so long-familiar.[7]

5   The dialogue should never be gabbled; this is permissible only in those *neurasthenic* dramas where much play is made with lines of dots. Epic calm does not exclude tragic emotions, which always possess a certain grandeur.

6   Tragedy with a smile on the lips. I did not grasp fully the need for this until I happened to read the following words of Savonarola:

269

Do not assume that Mary cried out at the death of her Son and roamed the streets, tearing her hair and acting like a madwoman. She followed Him with great humility. Certainly she shed tears, but her appearance revealed not so much sheer grief as a combination of *grief and joy*. Even at the foot of the Cross she stood in grief and joy, engrossed in the mystery of God's great mercy.

If an actor of the old school wished to move the audience deeply, he would cry out, weep, groan and beat his breast with his fists. Let the new actor express the highest point of tragedy just as the grief and joy of Mary were expressed: with an outward repose, almost *coldly*, without shouting or lamentation. He can achieve profundity without recourse to exaggerated tremolo.

B Plasticity

1   Richard Wagner reveals inner dialogue through the orchestra; the sung musical phrase lacks the power to express the inner passions of his heroes. Wagner summons the orchestra to his assistance, believing that only the orchestra is capable of conveying what is ineffable, of revealing the mystery to the spectator. Like the singer's phrase in the 'Musikdrama', the actor's word in the drama is an insufficiently powerful means of conveying inner dialogue. Surely if the *word* were the sole means of conveying the essence of tragedy, everybody would be capable of acting in the theatre. But merely by declaiming words, even by declaiming them well, one does not necessarily *say* anything. We need some new means of expressing the ineffable, of revealing that which is concealed.

Just as Wagner employs the orchestra to convey spiritual emotions, I employ *plastic movement*. But the old theatre, too, regarded plasticity as an essential means of expression; one has only to consider Salvini[1] in *Othello* or *Hamlet*. Plasticity itself is not new, but the form which I have in mind is new. Before, it corresponded closely to the spoken dialogue, but I am speaking of a *plasticity which does not correspond to the words*. What do I mean by this?

Two people are discussing the weather, art, apartments. A third – given, of course, that he is reasonably sensitive and observant – can tell exactly by listening to this conversation, which has no bearing on the relationship between the two, whether they are friends, enemies or lovers. He can tell this from the way they gesticulate, stand, move their eyes. This is because they move in a way unrelated to their words, a way which reveals their relationship.

The director erects a bridge between actor and spectator. He depicts friends, enemies or lovers in accordance with the author's instructions, yet by means of movement and poses he must present a picture which enables the spectator not only to hear the spoken dialogue but to penetrate through to the *inner* dialogue. If he has steeped himself in the author's theme and grasped the music of this inner dialogue, he will suggest plastic movements to the actor which will help the spectator to perceive the inner dialogue as the actors and he, himself, understand it.

The essence of human relationships is determined by gestures, poses, glances and silences. Words alone cannot say everything. Hence there must be a *pattern of movement* on the stage to transform the spectator into a vigilant observer, to furnish him with that material which the two people in conversation yielded to the third, the material which helps him grasp the true feelings of the characters. Words catch the ear, plasticity – the eye. Thus the spectator's imagination is exposed to two stimuli: the oral and the visual. The difference between the old theatre and the new is that in the new theatre speech and plasticity are each subordinated to their own separate rhythms and the two do not necessarily coincide. However, it does not follow that plasticity has always to contradict speech; a phrase may be supported by a wholly appropriate movement, but this is no more natural than the coincidence of the logical and the poetic stress in verse.

2   Maeterlinck's images are archaized; the names are like the names on icons; Arkel[9] is like a picture by Ambrogio Borgognoni; Gothic arches; wooden statues, carved and polished like palissander. One senses the need for symmetrical groupings in the manner of Peru-gino, for thus do they resemble most closely the divine nature of the universe.

'Women, effeminate boys and harmless, weary old men best express the gentle, dreamlike thoughts' which Perugino was striving to convey. Is not the same true of Maeterlinck? It is this which prompted an iconic style of portrayal.

The unsightly clutter of the naturalistic stage was replaced in the New Theatre by constructions rigidly subordinated to rhythmical movement and to the musical harmony of colour masses.

An iconic style was employed, too, in the construction of scenery – before scenery was abolished altogether. And since plastic movement acquired primary importance as a means of revealing inner dialogue, it was essential that scenery should do nothing to distract attention from this movement. It was necessary to focus the spectator's entire attention on the actors' movements. Therefore, we employed only one backdrop in *The Death of Tintagiles*. When rehearsed against a plain canvas drop, the tragedy produced a powerful impression because the play of gestures was seen in such sharp relief. But when the actors were transferred to a stage with scenery and space in which to move about, the play suffered. Hence we developed the decorative panel.

But when we tried it out in a number of plays (*Sister Beatrice, Hedda Gabler, The Eternal Story*[10]) it was a failure.[11] We found that it was no more effective than suspended scenery, against which the effect of plastic movement is dissipated because it is not seen in firm relief. In Giotto, nothing detracts from the fluidity of his lines, because all his work has a decorative rather than a naturalistic basis. But just as the theatre must not revert to naturalism, equally it must not become merely 'decorative' (unless the word be interpreted in the same sense as in the Japanese theatre).

Like symphonic music, the decorative panel serves its own specialized purpose, and if figures are necessary – as in a painting – they must be painted figures, or in the case of the theatre, cardboard marionettes – but not wax, wooden, or flesh-and-blood figures. A two-dimensional decorative panel demands two-dimensional figures.

The human body and the objects surrounding it – tables, chairs, beds, cupboards – are all three-dimensional; therefore the theatre, where the main element is the actor, must find inspiration in the plastic arts, not in painting. The actor must study *the plasticity of the statue*.

These were the conclusions reached at the close of the first cycle of experiments in the New Theatre. A historically vital circle was completed and yielded a fund of experience in stylized production, which gave rise to a new view of the role of decorative art in the theatre.

On learning that the theatre intends to reject the decorative principle, actors of the old school will be delighted, interpreting this as no less than a return to the old theatre. Surely, they will argue, the old theatre was the theatre of three dimensions. So this means – down with the stylized theatre!

My answer is that the placing of the decorative artist firmly in the decorative theatre and the musician in the concert hall signifies not the death of the stylized theatre but its adoption of an even bolder course.

In rejecting the decorative panel the New Theatre has not discarded the technique of stylized production; neither has it rejected the presentation of Maeterlinck in iconic terms. The means of expression must now be architectural, rather than pictorial as they were before. All our plans for stylized productions of *The Death of Tintagiles, Sister Beatrice, Hedda Gabler* and *The Eternal Story* have been preserved intact, but they have been translated into the terms of the liberated stylized theatre. Meanwhile, the painter has retired to a realm where actors and concrete objects are not admitted, because the aims of the actor and the non-theatrical painter are quite distinct.

Notes

1   Arthur Nikisch (1855–1922), celebrated conductor of the Leipzig Gewandhaus Orchestra.

2   Alexander Blok (*Pereval*, Moscow, 1906, no. 2) fears that the actors 'might set fire to the ship of the play', but to my mind, discord and disaster could occur only if the straight line were allowed to become crooked. This danger is eliminated if the director accurately interprets the author, accurately transmits him to the actors, and if they accurately understand him. [Meyerhold's note.]

3   The 'Theatre-Triangle' requires non-individualistic actors who none the less are outstanding virtuosi, regardless of their school. In the 'Theatre of the Straight Line' individual flair is most important, for without it free creativity is inconceivable. It needs a new school of acting, which must not be a school where new techniques are taught, but rather, one which will arise just once to give birth to a free theatre and then die.

    'The Theatre of the Straight Line' will grow from a single school as one plant grows from one seed. As each succeeding plant needs a new seed to be sown, so a new theatre must grow every time from a new school.

    'The Theatre-Triangle' tolerates schools attached to theatres which provide a regular stream of graduates, who imitate the great actors who founded the theatre, and fill vacancies in the company as they occur. I am convinced that it is these schools which are to blame for the absence of genuine, fresh talent in our theatres. [Meyerhold's note.]

4   Published in Russian in six volumes in Moscow, 1903–9.

5   Hannibale Pastore, 'Maurice Maeterlinck', in *Vestnik inostrannoy literatury*, September 1903.

6   Richard Muther, German art historian.

7   In practice, a question arose which I shall not attempt to answer, but content myself by merely stating: should the actor seek to discover the inner content of his part right from the start, give play to his emotions, and then shape it later into some form or other, or vice versa? At the time we adopted the procedure of restraining the emotions until the form was mastered, and that still seems to me the correct order. People will object that this only leads to the form fettering the emotions. This is not so. Our teachers, the actors of the old naturalistic school, used to say: if you do not want to ruin the part, start by reading it over to yourself, and do not read it aloud until it sounds right in your heart. One should approach a role in a realistic drama by first reading through the text to oneself; in a non-realistic drama one should master first the rhythm of the language and the movement – the same method is right for both. [Meyerhold's note.]

8   Tommaso Salvini: leading Italian Shakespearian actor. He toured in Russia on several occasions from 1880 to 1901.

9   In *Pelléas and Mélisande*.

10 By Przybyszewski.

11 All staged at Komissarzhevskaya's Theatre in 1906.

■   ■   ■

Source

Meyerhold, V. (1908, 1969) 'First Attempts at a Stylized Theatre', *Meyerhold on Theatre*, trans. and ed. E. Braun, New York: Hill & Wang: 49–58.

Written in 1907, first published in *Teatr, kniga o novom teatre*, Petersburg (1908), reprinted in Meyerhold's *O Teatre*, Petersburg (1913), English translation published (1969) by Hill & Wang.

Vsevolod Meyerhold (1874–1940)

Russian theatre director. A colleague of Stanislavski, he stands in relation to modern theatre much as Schoenberg does to music. Through his work with the Moscow Art Studio, set up for him by Stanislavski, and in a variety of other ensembles, he explored and redefined the possibilities of theatre language in the twentieth century. Meyerhold reacted against naturalistic theatre from inside the fount of naturalism, holding that performers were capable of more than imitation by the extended and trained use of the body, for which he designed a system of exercises known as Bio-Mechanics.

The productions with which he was involved, via a variety of different performing groups, numbered over five hundred, and included a famous version of Gogol's play *The Government Inspector* (1926). His innovative work on the revolutionary plays of Mayakovsky – *Mystery Bouffe* (1921), *The Bedbug* (1929), and *The Bathhouse* (1930) – promotes a view of theatre where the performer and scenery became interchangeable; where the actor, combined with the dynamic form of constructivist settings, produced a totally new and physical theatre. Meyerhold's experiments, which took Russian theatre away from the great naturalist tradition, were such that, although revolutionary, they did not suit the aesthetic of the communist government. To the country's shame Meyerhold was tried in prison in 1940 and shot, after making a speech to the All-Union Conference of Theatre Directors, where he was bitterly attacked. It is only since the 1960s that his work has become known in translation in the West, thanks to the efforts of dedicated scholars, and to those who preserved the memory of his work in Russia. Now that his experiments are being rediscovered it is clear that Meyerhold foreshadowed much of the exciting visual and physical theatre of recent years.

In this essay he explains the possible new forms of relationship between the creative forces of the theatre, together with his physical principles for performers, from which many of his detailed exercises followed.

Reader cross-references

Appia, Craig and **Schlemmer** – contemporary European visual perspectives
Brecht – a similar anti-naturalist approach
Cunningham – the dancer as the total element of production
Grotowski – the physical training of the performer
Stanislavski – the naturalism that Meyerhold rejected
Wigman – a European dance contemporary with a concern for modernism
Wilson – a later example of total theatre

Further reading

Braun, E. (1978) *The Theatre of Meyerhold*, London: Eyre Methuen.
—— (1978, 1995), *Meyerhold: A Revolution in Theatre*, 2nd edition, London: Methuen.
Leach, R. (1989) *Vsevolod Meyerhold*, Cambridge: Cambridge University Press.

Chapter 32

Heiner Müller

19 ANSWERS
BY HEINER MÜLLER

A couple of years ago you were invited to a conference on Postmodernism in New York. You couldn't attend the conference but submitted a paper defining your position versus some aspects of contemporary art. Could you explain what in your opinion would constitute a Postmodern drama, a Postmodern theatre?

The only Postmodernist I know of was August Stramm, a modernist who worked in a post office.

Language takes a central position in your work, much more than it usually does in contemporary American drama. Could you explain what you feel language's function is in the contemporary theatre?

I would take issue with the premise in the first part of your question. Language is also important in American drama and other media but it is a different language, I think, with perhaps a different function. A film critic once asked me why stage and film productions in the GDR tend to use a poeticizing rather than what he called a naturalistic language, why the tendency toward stylization rather than realism. The extent to which that is valid comes from the fact that the GDR is not photographable, the fact that here actors cannot even say 'Guten Tag' without it sounding like a lie. Realism doesn't work at all, only stylization works – a variation of Brecht's remark that a photograph of the Krupp Works says nothing really about the Krupp Works. The actors in the West are much better at Naturalism, at working with photographic texts or plays or films. Here they are better in productions of the classics, i.e., in anything that entails a stylized removal from immediate reality.

What is the role of language versus the rich visual imagery you employ to an ever increasing degree in your plays?

The worst experience I had during my stay in the United States was a film I saw called *Fantasia*, by Disney. I had never heard of it and actually ended up watching it by mistake. There were three films playing in the same movie house and I went into the wrong one. The most barbaric thing about this film, something I learned later, was that almost every American child between the ages of six and eight gets to view it. Which means that these people will never again be able to hear specific works by Beethoven, Bach, Handel, Tchaikovsky, etc., without seeing the Disney figures and images. The horrifying thing for me in this is the occupation of the imagination by clichés and images which will never go away; the use of images to prevent experiences, to prevent the having of experiences.

What has this got to do with your theatre?

Wolfgang Heise, a philosopher here in the GDR, once said that theatre is a laboratory for the social imagination. I find that relevant for what we are talking about. If one starts with the assumption that capitalist societies, indeed every industrial society, the GDR included, tends to repress and instrumentalize imagination – to throttle it – then for me the political task of art today is precisely the mobilization of imagination. To return to our example of *Fantasia*, the metaphorical function of the Disney film is to reduce the symbolic force of images to one meaning, to make them immediately allegorical. The imagery one finds in the early Russian cinema, on the other hand, is like the torrent of metaphors at the heart of Elizabethan literature. Here metaphors are constructed as a kind of visual protection against a much too rapidly changing reality, a reality that can only be dealt with and assimilated in this very special way. A world of images is created that does *not* lend itself to conceptual formulation and that cannot be reduced to a one-dimensional metaphor. This is what I try to do in my theatre.

You have written in other literary forms, poetry, short story, etc., but you always returned to the theatre, recently even as the director of your plays. Do you believe then that the theatre is a superior medium to investigate the complex problems of our time?

I have a real difficulty writing prose. I don't believe in literature as a work of art to be read. I don't believe in reading. I couldn't imagine writing a novel.

Where does your distrust of prose come from?

Writing prose you are all alone. You can't hide yourself. I also don't think I can write prose in the third person. I can't write: 'Washington got up and went to 42nd Street.' I can only imagine writing prose in the first person. Writing drama you always have masks and roles and you can talk through them. That's why I prefer drama – because of the masks. I can say one thing and say the contrary. I have a need to get rid of contradictions and that is easier to do with drama.

The theatre seems to have increasing difficulties in reaching wider audiences, larger sections of society, especially when it tries to interact with, or activate, its audiences. Where do you see reasons for this development and how should one cope with this danger of elitism?

This 'elitism,' as you call it, this not being immediately accessible, can also have its advantages. For accessibility is often connected with commercialization. Art becomes commercial at precisely the moment when its time is past. The tension between success and impact, which Brecht spoke of, is important in this respect: that one is always overtaken by success before a real impact can occur. As long as a thing works it is not successful, and when success is there then the impact is over. This is because there can only be an impact if, as for example in the theatre, the audience is split, brought home to its real situation. But that means there will be no agreement, no success. Success happens when everybody is cheering, in other words, when there is nothing more to say. For me the theatre is a medium which still permits one to avoid that kind of success. In film that is difficult because of the money involved.

But what about the GDR?

In our country, theatre allows you to have 500 or 800 people together in one room reacting at the same time, in the same space, to what is happening on stage. The impact of the theatre here is based on the absence of other ways of getting messages across to people. Films are not as important either because there is so much control. As a result, the theatre here has taken over the function of the other media in the West. I don't believe theatre has a great impact in West Germany, for instance. (We can forget about the United States.) You can do anything on the stage there but it doesn't mean anything to the society. Here the slogan of the Napoleonic era still applies: Theatre is the Revolution on the march.

In many of your texts you deal with topics which in this country would be defined as 'feminist'; and female characters often have a central place in your work. Could you explain how you think women should be presented on the contemporary stage?

As a playwright I don't deal with 'isms' but with reality. Can you tell me what a real female character is?

Your work is firmly rooted in history and/or mythology. American drama deals rarely with the past. What do you conceive as the function of mythology and history in the contemporary theatre?

The dead are in the overwhelming majority when compared to the living. And Europe has a wealth of dead stored up on that side of the ledger. The United States, not satisfied just with dead Indians, is fighting to close the gap. Literature, as an instrument of democracy, while not submitting to, should nevertheless be respectful of, majorities as well as of minorities.

Some of your critics maintain that at the center of your recent work is the conflict between the individual's desire 'to pursue happiness' and the individual's responsibility to history and mankind's progress. Do you agree with this view? If yes, could you speak to this contradiction and its present manifestations?

'We Germans were not put here on earth to enjoy ourselves but to do our duty.' (Bismarck)

If you disagree, what would you regard as a central issue in your recent texts?

How should I know, and if I knew why should I tell you?

If you reject this idea of a central issue, could you mention some of the interests you pursue in your writing?

See above.

Your plays have been performed in East and West Germany, in the United States, and in many other countries. You participated in many of these productions and recently have directed your plays in both Germanies. What difference could you observe in the theatrework of these different social and cultural systems, and what did they have in common?

To answer this question I am going to have to wait for more performances in East and West.

a) Where is the theatre, in your opinion, a more efficient instrument of social impact?
b) Where would you prefer to direct, and to watch, your plays on stage?

a) In the East. b) I would like to stage MACBETH on top of the World Trade Center for an audience in helicopters.

There has been a lot of attention given to the so-called 'New Subjectivity' in German letters, as exemplified by writers like Handke, Strauss, Laederach, etc. Do you see yourself in any relation to them and their work?

No. Nor do I see any relation of them to each other.

Terms like 'Despair,' 'Pessimism,' 'Guilt,' are often used by critics writing about your work. Do you think these are adequate definitions of your intentions and/or values?

Three times No.

People familiar with your recent texts often complain about a total lack of hope in your writing. What is your opinion?

I am neither a dope- nor a hope-dealer.

Would you care to comment on your views about the future of our world which you paint so darkly in your work?

The future of the world is not my future.
'Show me a mousehole and I'll fuck the world.' (Railworker at the soft-coal strip mine Klettwitz, GDR.)

■   ■   ■

Source

Müller, H. (1984) 'Interview: 19 Answers by Heiner Müller. "I am Neither A Dope- Nor a Hope-Dealer" ', *Hamlet Machine and Other Texts for the Stage*, ed. C. Weber, New York: Performing Arts Journal: 137–140.

Heiner Müller (1929–1995)

German playwright; one of Europe's most radical, in his most innovative work equal in stature to Samuel Beckett. For most of its existence Müller was a citizen of the German Democratic Republic, and worked with Brecht at the Berliner Ensemble, of which he was a director since the collapse of the Berlin Wall. As an admirer of Brecht his theatre texts – he deliberately did not call them plays – do not attempt to dictate fixed meanings, instead allowing the individual performer and director free play with the collage of materials that he presents. His major pieces often have elliptical titles – *Hamletmachine* (1977), *Despoiled Shore Medeamaterial Landscape with Argonauts* (1982), *Gunding's Life Frederick of PrussiaLessings Sleep Dream Scream* (1976), *Germania Death in Berlin* (1973). He was interested in a totally different theatre from the predominantly inter-pretative theatre that grew up in Germany post-war. 'I have no message,' he says, 'I just want conflicts, even between the audience and the text.' Müller's work presents formidable challenges for performers and directors, who must, by choices, 'make' the performance out of the texts which he presents. The pieces are often collages of different ideas, assemblages of literary fragments 'to escape the prison of meaning' – essential for a citizen of a country where all meanings were decided by decree, a tendency that caught up with Brecht in his later years. This social tension nevertheless produced some of the most challenging texts of the century, hence Müller's inclusion in this book. His collaborations with Robert Wilson – most notably on *CIVIL warS* (1984) have brought to the fore attitudes that both artists have in common with Beckett – that a work of art is not about some-thing – it is something. He was also an admirer of Pina Bausch, of whose work he said, 'the image is a thorn in our eye'. Similarly, this set of replies displays a typically Müllerian cast of thought.

Reader cross-references

Bausch – a dance theatre that Müller admires
Brecht – his philosophical antecedent
Eisler – an earlier German viewpoint

Richter – the conflicts of Dada
Wilson – one of his major collaborators

Further reading

Calandra, D. (1983) *New German Dramatists*, London: Macmillan.

Chapter 33

Erwin Piscator

EPIC SATIRE

The theatrical form

This was the first time we had been faced with a novel and not with a play which, whether it was good or bad, was at least conceived in terms of dialogue and scenery, and with some regard for theatrical form. A novel, furthermore, where despite the passivity of the hero there is constant movement; Schwejk is sent to prison, then discharged from prison, Schwejk follows the curate as he celebrates Mass, Schwejk is wheeled on to parade in a wheelchair, Schwejk is dispatched to the front in a train, marches for days in search of his regiment – in short, things around him are always moving, always in flux. It is fantastic how the constant shifting of the plot seems to express the restless instability of war.

Sample of stage movements as used in 'Schwejk'

II.2 (Anabasis):
Belt 1 from right to left:
    Schwejk is marching. From left to right. Singing.
On Belt 1 (from right to left):

Old lady is carried on standing.

Meeting.

Belt 1 stops:

    Dialogue to '. . . regiment hurries.'

Belt 1 from right to left:

    Schwejk marches on.

    Old lady travels out standing.

Belt 1 carries on milestones, trees, signposts: village of Malchin.

Belt 2 from right to left:

    A bar travels on.

Belts 1 and 2 stop:

    Scene to '. . . to the regiment as quickly as possible.'

Belts 1 and 2 from right to left:

    Bar travels off.

    Schwejk marches.

On Belt 2 traveling on stage:

    Haystack (snoring 8 sec.).

    Scene to '. . . if they hadn't deserted.'

Belt 1 runs (½ min.).

Belt 2 moves left to right.

Even when I first read the novel, long before we thought of dramatizing it, I had a mental picture of events following one another in a ceaseless, uninterrupted stream. Faced with the problem of putting this novel on the stage, this impression in my mind assumed the concrete form of a conveyor belt.

So here again the stage technique emerged ready-made from the subject of the play, or at least from what I like to call the artistic aggregate of the subject matter. The fact that this technique 'symbolized' a stage of society (the dissolution and decline of a social order) was secondary and fortuitous. And the stage technique in its turn predetermined the textual shape of the play.

P. has a technical imagination the like of which we have never seen before; he releases all the power of the stage, he wheedles out all its secrets, his conveyor belt is more than a gimmick, P. has dissolved the classical unities of time, place and space and given the dimension of the marvelous, the magical back to the theater, thanks to his inspired mastery of the most modern technical devices.

        Die Welt am Abend, January 24, 1928 (Kurt Kersten)

The dramatic principles of the conveyor belt

All previous attempts to put novels on the stage have essentially failed. In most cases they retained nothing but the figure of the hero whom they robbed of his characteristic atmosphere by placing him in a new plot and thus making him unconvincing as a character.

It was a doubly difficult task to dramatize Jaroslav Hašek's novel. For this was not a neatly constructed whole, but a huge agglomeration of anecdotes and adventures with no adequate conclusion. Schwejk's character was established at the beginning and did not develop at all in the course of the novel. He only ever appeared in a passive, never in an active role, and he could be imagined in any possible situation except the one in which he met his end. The action of the novel was determined solely by events from 1914 till the middle of the Great War. So even when one left aside the epic breadth of the book, all its other elements conspired to defy dramatization.

The first method we tried was dramatization in the traditional manner mentioned above. We extracted the figure of Schwejk from the novel and placed him in an action of our own invention. Predictably enough, this attempt produced nothing that could be used. We used all the best episodes in the original and still we deprived Schwejk of the atmosphere he needed. His stories and his gags were too abrupt. It was clear that they needed the build-up afforded by Hašek's involved style, and that dramatization could only shrink and diminish the events. The plot which we had superimposed on Schwejk (a love story, incidentally) also robbed Hašek's work of its political-theoretical dimension. His milieu and the people who make it work ceased to be decisive and were supplanted by the mechanical requirements of the comedy which produced its own inconsequential figures. Hašek's thrusts at the [Hapsburg] Monarchy, the Bureaucracy, the Military and the Church were thus robbed of their venom. We turned Schwejk, who takes everything so seriously that he makes it ludicrous, who obeys orders so literally that they turn into sabotage, who demolishes everything he supports, into an idiotic orderly whose witless efforts on behalf of his lieutenant eventually turn out for the best.

The failure of this attempt – and the adapters went as far as to produce an actable play – was further proof that this method of doctoring novels for the stage was wrong. So we abandoned the 'dramatization' of the hero and decided to stage sequences of the novel, instead of producing a play around the figure of Schwejk.

There was just one single objection to this plan: the form of the present-day stage. It seemed impossible to capture the epic movement of the novel with traditional theatrical techniques. With a fixed stage, the flow of Hašek's plot was bound to be chopped up into single scenes, and this would falsify the fluid character of the novel. Piscator overcame this problem by replacing the fixed stage floor with a moving floor, and with this one skillful touch he found the appropriate staging for the epic development of the novel: the conveyor belt.

And this solved our textual problems as well as our technical problems. The adapters no longer needed a framework other than the original story; they could limit themselves to choosing the most effective scenes in the novel and turning them into actable texts. The grouping of the action could follow Hašek's original closely, and the only problem left was how we could adequately stage Schwejk's environment, which had a decisive effect on him. And as usual, Piscator solved this question with film, but here with the difference that he had an animated cartoon made. At the beginning of each chapter where Hašek made direct general comments on his theme, Piscator projected cartoons, drawn by George Grosz. In this way he could effectively condense the forces which were opposed to Schwejk.

(It should be mentioned here that Piscator toyed for a while with the idea of making Schwejk the only figure to appear on the stage and representing all the other figures with cartoons.)

The figures alongside Schwejk, where they had no active part in the action, were represented by dolls or puppets. Originally these were to have been much more rigidly classified according to the various class ideologies of the figures.

Once the set and staging had been decided upon, the writers had only to compress the essentials of the novel – which at a conservative estimate takes twenty-four hours to read – into two and one-half hours without losing its particular style. (It is unfortunately impossible to spread Schwejk out over five evenings, as Piscator once suggested). The original novel had to be radically shortened and condensed and completely rearranged in places to make it playable at all. On the other hand, we strictly avoided using any material other than Hašek's original text.

The ending presented a special difficulty which was, in fact, never completely resolved. Hašek had died while writing the novel, without leaving any indication of a possible ending. Any ending we might contrive would seem to do violence to the original manuscript, and a natural ending was not effective theater. The controversial scene in Heaven, which in fact derived from one of Hašek's own passages, 'Cadet Biegler's Dream,' would have necessitated a disruptive reworking of the whole figure, since the novel did not afford all the material we would have needed. So for better or for worse, we had to adopt a compromise which was both effective theater and Schwejk-like.

The path followed here opens extraordinary prospects for the future. The intellectual revolution going on around us is not only radically transforming purely technical materials, but is also opening up new subjects and new forms. The theater can no longer restrict itself to a dramatic form which was once produced by a particular set of social and technical conditions, at a time when these very conditions are subject to far-reaching changes. A new form of play is evolving, one which is imperfect and transitional, but rich in new possibilities. Bourgeois art-historians may set out aesthetic principles which fortify the 'purity' of their art forms against the 'vandalism' of the rising classes. Piscator has captured the revolutionary novel for the stage, an achievement worth much more than all their wordy aestheticizing.

Gasbarra (*Welt am Abend*, January, 1928)

The conveyor belt

We were also faced with new problems in acting technique. It was the first time an actor had been required to perform his entire role while he was being carried along or was walking or running. This made it imperative that the belts should function silently. During the first discussions the manufacturer accepted this basic condition. But when we heard the belts in action for the first time – on January 28, 1928 – they sounded like a traction engine under full steam. The belts rattled and snorted and pounded so that the whole house quaked. Even at the top of your voice you could hardly make yourself heard. The idea of dialogue on these raging monsters was quite unthinkable. I seem to remember we just sank into the orchestra seats and laughed hysterically. There were twelve days to opening night. The technicians assured us that they could cut down the noise, but there was no longer any mention of the silent operation that we had been promised. The process threatened to be long and put the production in jeopardy. As usual, I was made to see that only a fraction of my idea could be put into practice. And in this case the problem was more difficult because in Pallenberg we had an actor of unheard-of good will who would make any sacrifice to cooperate, but he was at the same time a very temperamental artist, and naturally apprehensive about the unusual apparatus, especially if it was not even going to work. The long, hard task of modifying the belts began; it occupied every minute that I did not need the stage for rehearsals. With huge quantities of graphite, soap and lubricating oil, by strengthening the stage floor with heavy wooden props, fitting new bearings, lining the chains with felt, and putting a felt underlay beneath the whole machine, the noise was reduced to a level where it no longer drowned the text completely. Nonetheless, the actors still had to keep their voices up to make themselves heard.

The rest of the set was utterly simple. The only things on the whole stage apart from the conveyor belts were two flats joined by borders, one behind the other and a cloth screen at the back. Some of the props were carried onto the open stage by the conveyor belt, others hung in the flies, so that everything could be put in and taken out quickly. It was the cleanest, simplest and most versatile set I had ever devised. Everything went off quickly as if by clockwork.

It seemed to me that this apparatus had a quality of its own; it was inherently comic. Every application of the machinery somehow made you want to laugh. There seemed to be absolute harmony between subject and machinery. And for the whole thing I had in mind a sort of knockabout style, reminiscent of Chaplin or vaudeville.

■   ■   ■

Source

Piscator, E. (1929, 1980) 'Epic Satire: The Adventures of the Good Soldier Schwejk January 23, 1928 to April 12, 1928', *The Political Theatre*, trans. H. Rorrison, London: Eyre Methuen: 254–269.

First published in 1929 in *Das Politische Theater*, first published in Great Britain 1980.

Erwin Piscator (1893–1966)

The work of Piscator contains the most consistent set of experiments in staging, using all the possibilities that early twentieth-century stage technology allowed. Through his productions in Berlin throughout the 1920s and 1930s – *Sturmflut* (1926), *Hoppla, wir Leben!* (1927), *Der Kaisers Kulis* (1930) – in exile in America during the Second World War, and on his final return to Germany in the 1960s, Piscator showed a new awareness of the stage as a physical resource. He fought in the First World War, and became involved in many of the post-war Dada happenings in Berlin. The influence of Dada's harsh juxtapositions, grotesque masks, and attempts at immediacy gave Piscator's theatre a unique and exciting contemporaneity, in particular his production of Alfons Paquet's *Sturmflut* (Tidal Wave), where the permanent setting was backed by a transparent screen with a black frame and variable aperture, on to which was projected film from four backstage projectors. In 1928 the Piscator-Bühne's greatest success was a free dramatisation of Jaroslav Hašek's novel *The Good Soldier Schwejk*, where Piscator cast a famous Viennese comedian, Max Pallenberg, as Schwejk. For the production he designed two electrically powered conveyor-belts, parallel to the line of the sets and backed by white flats. The background to Schwejk's progress across Europe was conveyed by naturalistic film and by means of a series of savage animated cartoons drawn by the satirist Georg Grosz.

After the war Brecht, who had collaborated with Piscator earlier, invited him back to Berlin to join in reviving the Berlin theatre. By this time Piscator had moved away from a directly political theatre, having also worked at the Dramatic Workshop of the New School of Social Research in New York (which trained such actors as Marlon Brando). However, in the last years of his life in West Germany he re-established himself as a master of theatrical staging in his work on a series of documentary plays such as Rolf Hochuth's *The Representative* (1964), Weiss's *The Investigation* (1965), and Kippard's *In the Case of Robert Oppenheimer* (1967).

In 1929 Piscator published his only book, *The Political Theatre*, from which this extract is taken. In it we see the directorial mind at work on one staging problem of the Schwejk play, the detail of which demonstrates how he maintained that theatre was a constant search 'for the basic artistic, philosophical, social, and political principles of human thought and action in our age'. The extract contains Piscator's own notes as well as extensive quotes from a contemporary account.

Reader cross-references

Appia and **Craig** – similar concentration on the aesthetics of staging
Brecht – with whom Piscator sought for a new theatre
Duncan and **Wigman** – contemporaries working in Europe in dance
Richter – Dada, early influences on his conception of staging
Schlemmer – a contemporary consideration of the staging of dance
Wilson – visual theatre

Further reading

Innes, C. (1972) *Erwin Piscator's Political Theatre*, Cambridge: Cambridge University Press.
Piscator, M.L. (1967) *The Piscator Experiment*, New York: James Heinemann.

Chapter 34

Yvonne Rainer

A QUASI SURVEY OF SOME 'MINIMALIST' TENDENCIES IN THE QUANTITATIVELY MINIMAL DANCE ACTIVITY MIDST THE PLETHORA, OR AN ANALYSIS OF *TRIO A*

ALTHOUGH THE BENEFIT to be derived from making a one-to-one relationship between aspects of so-called minimal sculpture and recent dancing is questionable, I have drawn up a chart that does exactly that. Those who need alternatives to subtle distinction-making will be elated, but nevertheless such a device may serve as a shortcut to ploughing through some of the things that have been happening in a specialized area of dancing and once stated can be ignored or culled from at will.

It should not be thought that the two groups of elements are mutually exclusive ('eliminate' and 'substitute'). Much work being done today – both in theater and art – has concerns in both categories. Neither should it be thought that the type of dance I shall discuss has been influenced exclusively by art. The changes in theater and dance reflect changes in ideas about man and his environment that have affected all the arts. That dance should reflect these changes at all is of interest, since for obvious reasons it has always been the most isolated and inbred of the arts. What is perhaps unprecedented in the short history of the modern dance is the close correspondence between concurrent developments in dance and the plastic arts.

Isadora Duncan went back to the Greeks; Humphrey and Graham[1] used primitive ritual and/or music for structuring, and although the people who came out of the Humphrey-Graham companies and were active during the thirties and forties shared socio-political concerns and activity in common with artists of the period, their work did not reflect any direct influence from or dialogue with the art so much as a reaction to the time. (Those who took off in their own directions in the forties and fifties – Cunningham, Shearer, Litz, Marsicano, et al. – must be appraised individually. Such a task is beyond the scope of this article.) The one previous area of correspondence might be German Expressionism and Mary Wigman and her followers, but photographs and descriptions of the work show little connection.

Within the realm of movement invention – and I am talking for the time being about movement generated by means other than accomplishment of a task or dealing with an object – the most impressive change has been in the attitude to phrasing, which can be defined as the way in which energy is distributed in the execution of a movement or series of movements. What makes one kind of movement different from another is not so much variations in arrangements of parts of the body as differences in energy investment.

It is important to distinguish between real energy and what I shall call 'apparent' energy. The former refers to actual output in terms of physical expenditure on the part of the performer. It is common to hear a dance teacher tell a student that he is using 'too much energy' or that a particular movement does not require 'so much energy.' This view of energy is related to a notion of economy and ideal movement technique. Unless otherwise indicated, what I shall be talking about here is 'apparent' energy, or what is seen in terms of motion and stillness rather than of actual work, regardless of the physiological or kinesthetic experience of the dancer. The two observations – that of the performer and that of the spectator – do not always correspond. A vivid illustration of this is my *Trio A*: Upon completion two of us are always dripping with sweat while the third is dry. The correct conclusion to draw is not that the dry one is expending less energy, but that the dry one is a 'non-sweater.'

Objects	Dances

eliminate

or

minimize

Objects	Dances
1 role of artist's hand	1 phrasing
2 hierarchical relationships of parts	2 development and climax
3 texture	3 variation: rhythm, shape, dynamics
4 figure reference	4 character
5 illusionism	5 performance
6 complexity and detail	6 variety: phases and the spatial field
7 monumentality	7 the virtuosic feat and the fully extended body

substitute

Objects	Dances
1 factory fabrication	1 energy equality and 'found' movement
2 unitary forms, modules	2 equality of parts, repetition
3 uninterrupted surface	3 repetition or discrete events
4 nonreferential forms	4 neutral performance
5 literalness	5 task or tasklike activity
6 simplicity	6 singular action, event, or tone
7 human scale	7 human scale

Much of the western dancing we are familiar with can be character-ized by a particular distribution of energy: maximal output or 'attack' at the beginning of a phrase,[2] recovery at the end, with energy often arrested some-where in the middle. This means that one part of the phrase – usually the part that is the most still – becomes the focus of attention, registering like a photograph or suspended moment of climax. In the Graham-oriented modern dance these climaxes can come one on the heels of the other. In types of dancing that depend on less impulsive controls, the climaxes are farther apart and are not so dramatically 'framed.' Where extremes in tempi are imposed, this ebb-and-flow of effort is also pronounced: in the instance of speed the contrast between movement and rest is sharp, and in the adagio, or supposedly continuous kind of phrasing, the execution of transitions demonstrates more subtly the mechanics of getting from one point of still 'registration' to another.

The term 'phrase' can also serve as a metaphor for a longer or total duration containing beginning, middle, and end. Whatever the implications of a continuity that contains high points or focal climaxes, such an approach now seems to be excessively dramatic and more simply, unnecessary.

Energy has also been used to implement heroic more-than-human technical feats and to maintain a more-than-human look of physical exten-sion, which is familiar as the dancer's muscular 'set.' In the early days of the Judson Dance Theatre someone wrote an article and asked 'Why are they so intent on just being themselves?' It is not accurate to say that everyone at that time had this in mind. (I certainly didn't; I was more involved in experiencing a lion's share of ecstasy and madness than in 'being myself' or doing a job.) But where the question applies, it might be answered on two levels: 1) The artifice of performance has been reevaluated in that action, or what one does, is more interesting and important than the exhibition of char-acter and attitude, and that action can best be focused on through the submerging of the personality; so ideally one is not even oneself, one is a neutral 'doer.' 2) The display of technical virtuosity and the display of the dancer's specialized body no longer make any sense. Dancers have been driven to search for an alternative context that allows for a more matter-of-fact, more concrete, more banal quality of physical being in performance, a context wherein people are engaged in actions and movements making a less spec-tacular demand on the body and in which skill is hard to locate.

It is easy to see why the *grand jeté* (along with its ilk) had to be aban-doned. One cannot 'do' a *grand jeté*; one must 'dance' it to get it done at all, i.e., invest it with all the necessary nuances of energy distribution that will produce the look of climax together with a still, suspended extension in the middle of the movement. Like a romantic, overblown plot this partic-ular kind of display – with its emphasis on nuance and skilled accomplishment, its accessibility to comparison and interpretation, its involvement with connoisseurship, its introversion, narcissism, and self-congratulatoriness – has finally in this decade exhausted itself, closed back on itself, and perpetuates itself solely by consuming its own tail.

The alternatives that were explored now are obvious: stand, walk, run, eat, carry bricks, show movies, or move or be moved by some *thing* rather than oneself. Some of the early activity in the area of self-movement utilized games, 'found' movement (walking, running, etc.), and people with no previous training. (One of the most notable of these early efforts was Steve Paxton's solo, *Transit*, in which he performed movement by 'marking' it. 'Marking' is what dancers do in rehearsal when they do not want to expend the full amount of energy required for the execution of a given movement. It has a very special look, tending to blur boundaries between consecutive movements.) These descriptions are not complete. Different people have sought different solutions.

Since I am primarily a dancer, I am interested in finding solutions primarily in the area of moving oneself, however many excursions I have made into pure and not-so-pure thing-moving. In 1964 I began to play around with simple one- and two-motion phrases that required no skill and little energy and contained few accents. The way in which they were put together was indeterminate, or decided upon in the act of performing, because at that time the idea of a different kind of continuity as embodied in transitions or connections between phrases did not seem to be as important as the material itself. The result was that the movements or phrases appeared as isolated bits framed by stoppages. Underscored by their smallness and separateness, they projected as perverse *tours-de-force*. Everytime 'elbow-wiggle' came up one felt like applauding. It was obvious that the idea of an unmodulated energy output as demonstrated in the movement was not being applied to the continuity. A continuum of energy was required. Duration and transition had to be considered.

Which brings me to *The Mind is a Muscle, Trio A*. Without giving an account of the drawn-out process through which this four-and-a-half-minute movement series (performed simultaneously by three people) was made, let me talk about its implications in the direction of movement-as-task or movement-as-object.

One of the most singular elements in it is that there are no pauses between phrases. The phrases themselves often consist of separate parts, such as consecutive limb articulations – 'right leg, left leg, arms, jump,' etc. – but the end of each phrase merges immediately into the beginning of the next with no observable accent. The limbs are never in a fixed, still relationship and they are stretched to their fullest extension only in transit, creating the impression that the body is constantly engaged in transitions.

Another factor contributing to the smoothness of the continuity is that no one part of the series is made any more important than any other. For four and a half minutes a great variety of movement shapes occur, but they are of equal weight and are equally emphasized. This is probably attributable both to the sameness of physical 'tone' that colors all the movements and to the attention to the pacing. I can't talk about one without talking about the other.

The execution of each movement conveys a sense of unhurried control. The body is weighty without being completely relaxed. What is seen is a control that seems geared to the *actual* time it takes the *actual* weight of the body to go through the prescribed motions, rather than an adherence to an imposed ordering of time. In other words, the demands made on the body's (actual) energy resources appear to be commensurate with the task – be it getting up from the floor, raising an arm, tilting the pelvis, etc. – much as one would get out of a chair, reach for a high shelf, or walk down stairs when one is not in a hurry.[3] The movements are not mimetic, so they do not remind one of such actions, but I like to think that in their manner of execution they have the factual quality of such actions.

Of course, I have been talking about the 'look' of the movements. In order to achieve this look in a continuity of separate phrases that does not allow for pauses, accents, or stillness, one must bring to bear many different degrees of effort just in getting from one thing to another. Endurance comes into play very much with its necessity for conserving (actual) energy (like the long-distance runner). The irony here is in the reversal of a kind of illusionism: I have exposed a type of effort where it has been traditionally concealed and have concealed phrasing where it has been traditionally displayed.

So much for phrasing. My *Trio A* contained other elements mentioned in the chart that have been touched on in passing, not being central to my concerns of the moment. For example, the 'problem' of performance was dealt with by never permitting the performers to confront the audience. Either the gaze was averted or the head was engaged in movement. The desired effect was a worklike rather than exhibitionlike presentation.

I shall deal briefly with the remaining categories on the chart as they relate to *Trio A*. Variation was not a method of development. No one of the individual movements in the series was made by varying a quality of any other one. Each is intact and separate with respect to its nature. In a strict sense neither is there any repetition (with the exception of occasional consecutive traveling steps). The series progresses by the fact of one discrete thing following another. This procedure was consciously pursued as a change from my previous work, which often had one identical thing following another – either consecutively or recurrently. Naturally the question arises as to what constitutes repetition. In *Trio A*, where there is no consistent consecutive repetition, can the simultaneity of three identical sequences be called repetition? Or can the consistency of energy tone be called repetition? Or does repetition apply only to successive specific actions?

All of these considerations have supplanted the desire for dance structures wherein elements are connected thematically (through variation) and for a diversity in the use of phrases and space. I think two assumptions are implicit here: 1) A movement is a complete and self-contained event; elaboration in the sense of varying some aspect of it can only blur its distinctness; and 2) Dance is hard to see. It must either be made less fancy, or the fact of that intrinsic difficulty must be emphasized to the point that it becomes almost impossible to see.

Repetition can serve to enforce the discreteness of a movement, objectify it, make it more objectlike. It also offers an alternative way of ordering material, literally making the material easier to see. That most theatre audiences are irritated by it is not yet a disqualification.

My *Trio A* dealt with the 'seeing' difficulty by dint of its continual and unremitting revelation of gestural detail that did *not* repeat itself, thereby focusing on the fact that the material could not easily be encompassed.

There is at least one circumstance that the chart does not include (because it does not relate to 'minimization'), viz., the static singular object versus the object with interchangeable parts. The dance equivalent is the indeterminate performance that produces variations ranging from small details to a total image. Usually indeterminacy has been used to change the sequentialness – either phrases or larger sections – of a work, or to permute the details of a work. It has also been used with respect to timing. Where the duration of separate, simultaneous events is not prescribed exactly, variations in the relationship of these events occur. Such is the case with the trio I have been speaking about, in which small discrepancies in the tempo of individually executed phrases result in the three simultaneous performances constantly moving in and out of phase and in and out of synchronization. The overall look of it is constant from one performance to another, but the distribution of bodies in space at any given instant changes.

I am almost done. *Trio A* is the first section of *The Mind is a Muscle*. There are six people involved and four more sections. *Trio B* might be described as a VARIATION of *Trio A* in its use of unison with three people; they move in exact unison thruout. *Trio A* is about the EFFORTS of two men and a woman in getting each other aloft in VARIOUS ways while REPEATING the same diagonal SPACE pattern throughout. In *Horses* the group travels about as a unit, recurrently REPEATING six different ACTIONS. *Lecture* is a solo that REPEATS the MOVEMENT series of *Trio A*. There will be at least three more sections.

There are many concerns in this dance. The concerns may appear to fall on my tidy chart as randomly dropped toothpicks might. However, I think there is sufficient separating-out in my work as well as that of certain of my contemporaries to justify an attempt at organizing those points of departure from previous work. Comparing the dance to Minimal Art provided a convenient method of organization. Omissions and overstatements are a hazard of any systematizing in art. I hope that some degree of redress will be offered by whatever clarification results from this essay.

This article was written before the final version of *The Mind is a Muscle* had been made. (*Mat*, *Stairs*, and *Film* are not discussed.)

Notes

1   In the case of Graham, it is hardly possible to relate her work to anything outside of theatre, since it was usually dramatic and psychological necessity that determined it.
2   The term 'phrase' must be distinguished from 'phrasing.' A phrase is simply two or more consecutive movements, while phrasing, as noted previously, refers to the manner of execution.
3   I do not mean to imply that the demand of musical or metric phrasing makes dancing look effortless. What it produces is a different kind of effort, where the body looks more extended, 'pulled up,' highly energized, ready to go, etc. The dancer's 'set' again.

■   ■   ■

Source

Rainer, Y. (1968, 1974) 'A Quasi Survey of Some "Minimalist" Tendencies in the Quantitatively Minimal Dance Activity Midst the Plethora, or an Analysis of *Trio A*', *Work 1961–73*, Halifax, Nova Scotia: The Press of the Nova Scotia College of Art and Design: 63–69.
     Written in 1966, first published (1968) in G. Battcock (ed.) *Minimal Art*.

Yvonne Rainer (1934–)

American dancer and film maker, who began her dance training with Martha Graham in New York in 1957. In 1960 she did a summer workshop in San Francisco with Ann Halprin, where she met, amongst others, Trisha Brown and La Monte Young. She returned to New York, performed in work by Simone Forti and with James Waring and took Robert Dunn's workshop at the Cunningham

Studio. In 1962 she formed Judson Dance Theatre with Steve Paxton and Ruth Emerson. Rainer made a number of dances between 1960 and 1966 that used a variety of vocabularies, props, forms and tasks. She presented *Dance for 3 People and 6 Arms* and *Ordinary Dance* as part of *A Concert of Dance* (1962), the first Judson performance.

In 1966 Rainer presented a short trio for Steve Paxton, David Gordon and herself at Judson Church, *The Mind is a Muscle, Part 1*. This 4½-minute phrase became known as *Trio A* and is celebrated as a 'paradigmatic statement of the aesthetic goals of post-modern dance' (Banes 1987:44). Both the phrase itself and the context in which it was shown radically questioned ideas of theatricality that were current in modern dance. Its vocabulary, structure and function were democratic. It was recyclable and became part of seven of Rainer's other works in the late 1960s and in her last dance performance, *This is the story of a woman who . . .* (1973). Between 1970 and 1973 Rainer was part of the improvisational collective, Grand Union, whose performances included her *Continuous Project Altered Daily*.

In the early 1970s she began to concentrate on film making, beginning with *Lives of Performers* (1972), *Film About a Woman Who . . .* (1974) and *Kristina Talking Pictures* (1976). She developed many of the concerns that had been first stated in her dance work, especially those concerned with formalism, narrative and gender.

Her 'analysis' was written shortly after the first performance of *Trio A*. She gives a detailed consideration of why she made the choices she did, comparing it to notions of minimalism then current in sculpture. She has frequently been misinterpreted and therefore regarded as a modernist. In fact, *Trio A* can be seen as an early postmodernist statement (see Burt 1995), and it is the original context for this article that might have led to the confusion.

Reader cross-references

Bausch – a different, European, perspective on dance

Beck – a contemporary, but contrasting, response to the times

Boal – whose work in a South American context stressed democracy as a political goal

Brown – a postmodern concern for process

Cage – an earlier North American statement on dance

Glass – musical idea of minimalism in theatre

Grotowski and **Hijikata** – antithetical approaches to the body

LeCompte – a contemporary woman postmodernist with a concern for process

Marinetti – an earlier manifesto that sought to sweep away the past

Wigman – an early modern dancer's viewpoint

Further reading

Banes, S. (1981) *Democracy's Body: Judson Dance Theatre 1962–1964*, Ann Arbor, Mich.: UMI Research Press.

Banes, S. (1987) 'The Aesthetics of Denial', *Terpsichore in Sneakers: Post-Modern Dance*, Middletown: Conn.: 41–54.

Burt, R. (1995) ' "Purity" vs "Theatricality": A Re-reading of the Position of Minimalist Theatre Dance in Relation to Modernism/Postmodernism', *Border Tensions: Dance and Discourse*, University of Surrey, 22 April 1995.

Lippard, L.R. (1977) 'Talking Pictures, Silent Words: Yvonne Rainer's Recent Movies', *Art in America* 65, May–June: 86.

Chapter 35

Hans Richter

HOW DID
DADA BEGIN?

I N 1915, SOON AFTER the outbreak of the First World War, a rather undernourished, slightly pock-marked, very tall and thin writer and producer came to Switzerland. It was Hugo Ball, with his mistress Emmy Hennings who was a singer and poetry reader. He belonged to the 'nation of thinkers and poets', which was engaged, at that time, in quite different activities. Ball, however, had remained both a thinker and a poet: he was philosopher, novelist, cabaret performer, journalist and mystic.

> I had no love for the death's-head hussars,
> Nor for the mortars with the girls' names on them,
> And when at last the glorious days arrived,
> I unobtrusively went on my way.
>
> (Hugo Ball)

It is impossible to understand Dada without understanding the state of mental tension in which it grew up, and without following in the mental and physical footsteps of this remarkable sceptic. (The diaries of this extraordinary man were published after his death in 1927, under the title *Flucht aus der Zeit* ['Flight from Time'].) Guided and perhaps plagued by his conscience, Ball became the human catalyst who united around himself all the elements which finally produced Dada.

It was not until many years later, when he already lay in his grave at San Abbondio, in Ticino, the little village where he had lived with his wife

Emmy, that I learned about the latter part of his life. He had renounced all the excesses of his youth, had become very devout, and had lived among poor peasants, poorer than they, giving them help whenever he could. Fourteen years after his death, people in Ticino still spoke with love and admiration of his nobility and goodness.

There can be no doubt of Ball's unswerving search for a *meaning* which he could set up against the absurd meaninglessness of the age in which he lived. He was an idealist and a sceptic, whose belief in life had not been destroyed by the deep scepticism with which he regarded the world around him.

On 1st February 1916, Ball founded the Cabaret Voltaire. He had come to an arrangement with Herr Ephraim, the owner of the Meierei, a bar in Niederdorf, a slightly disreputable quarter of the highly reputable town of Zurich. He promised Herr Ephraim that he would increase his sales of beer, sausage and rolls by means of a literary cabaret. Emmy Hennings sang *chansons*, accompanied by Ball at the piano. Ball's personality soon attracted a group of artists and kindred spirits who fulfilled all the expectations of the owner of the Meierei.

In the first Dada publication Ball writes:

When I founded the Cabaret Voltaire, I was sure that there must be a few young people in Switzerland who like me were interested not only in enjoying their independence but also in giving proof of it. I went to Herr Ephraim, the owner of the Meierei, and said, 'Herr Ephraim, please let me have your room. I want to start a night-club.' Herr Ephraim agreed and gave me the room. And I went to some people I knew and said, 'Please give me a picture, or a drawing, or an engraving. I should like to put on an exhibition in my night-club.' I went to the friendly Zurich press and said, 'Put in some announcements. There is going to be an international cabaret. We shall do great things.' And they gave me pictures and they put in my announcements. So on 5th February we had a cabaret. Mademoiselle Hennings and Mademoiselle Leconte sang French and Danish *chansons*. Herr Tristan Tzara recited Rumanian poetry. A balalaika orchestra played delightful folk-songs and dances.

I received much support and encouragement from Herr M. Slodki, who designed the poster, and from Herr

Hans Arp, who supplied some Picassos, as well as works of his own, and obtained for me pictures by his friends O. van Rees and Artur Segall. Much support also from Messrs. Tristan Tzara, Marcel Janco and Max Oppenheimer, who readily agreed to take part in the cabaret. We organized a *Russian* evening and, a little later, a *French* one (works by Apollinaire, Max Jacob, André Salmon, A. Jarry, Laforgue and Rimbaud). On 26th February Richard Huelsenbeck arrived from Berlin, and on 30th March we performed some stupendous Negro music (toujours avec la grosse caisse: boum boum boum boum − drabatja mo gere drabatja mo bonoooooooooo −). Monsieur Laban was present at the performance and was very enthusiastic. Herr Tristan Tzara was the initiator of a performance by Messrs. Tzara, Huelsenbeck and Janco (the first in Zurich and in the world) of simultaneist verse by Messrs. Henri Barzun and Fernand Divoire, as well as a *poème simultané* of his own composition, which is reproduced on pages six and seven. The present booklet is published by us with the support of our friends in France, *Italy* and Russia. It is intended to present to the Public the activities and interests of the Cabaret Voltaire, which has as its sole purpose to draw attention, across the barriers of war and nationalism, to the few independent spirits who live for other ideals. The next objective of the artists who are assembled here is the publication of a *revue internationale*. La revue paraîtra à Zurich et portera le nom 'Dada' ('Dada'). Dada Dada Dada Dada.

Zurich, 15th May 1916

I shall often quote from Ball's diaries, because I know of no better source of evidence on the moral and philosophical origins of the Dada revolt which started in the Cabaret Voltaire. It is entirely possible that any or all of the other Dadaists − Arp, Duchamp, Huelsenbeck, Janco, Schwitters, Ernst, Serner, or another − went through the same inner development, fought similar battles and were plagued by the same doubts, but no one but Ball left a record of these inner conflicts. And no one achieved, even in fragmentary form, such precise formulations as Ball, the poet and thinker.

To understand the climate in which Dada began, it is necessary to recall how much freedom there was in Zurich, even during a world war. The Cabaret Voltaire played and raised hell at No. 1, Spiegelgasse. Diagonally opposite, at No. 12, Spiegelgasse, the same narrow thoroughfare in which the Cabaret Voltaire mounted its nightly orgies of singing, poetry and dancing, lived Lenin. Radek, Lenin and Zinoviev were allowed complete liberty. I saw Lenin in the library several times and once heard him speak at a meeting in Berne. He spoke good German. It seemed to me that the Swiss authorities were much more suspicious of the Dadaists, who were after all capable of perpetrating some new enormity at any moment, than of these quiet, studious Russians . . . even though the latter were planning a world revolution and later astonished the authorities by carrying it out.

Press announcement, 2nd February 1916:

Cabaret Voltaire. Under this name a group of young artists and writers has formed with the object of becoming a centre for artistic enter-tainment. The Cabaret Voltaire will be run on the principle of daily meetings where visiting artists will perform their music and poetry. The young artists of Zurich are invited to bring along their ideas and contributions.

They brought them along.

On 5th February 1916, Ball writes: 'The place was full to bursting; many could not get in. About six in the evening, when we were still busy hammering and putting up Futurist posters, there appeared an oriental-looking deputation of four little men with portfolios and pictures under their arms, bowing politely many times.

'They introduced themselves: Marcel Janco the painter, Tristan Tzara, Georges Janco and a fourth, whose name I did not catch. Arp was also there, and we came to an understanding without many words. Soon Janco's opulent *Archangels* hung alongside the other objects of beauty, and, that same evening Tzara gave a reading of poems, conservative in style, which he rather endear-ingly fished out of the various pockets of his coat.'

Ball's night-club was an overnight sensation in Zurich.

Cabaret

The exhibitionist assumes his stance before the curtain
and Pimpronella tempts him with her petticoats of scarlet.
Koko the green god claps loudly in the audience –
and the hoariest of old goats are roused again to lust.
Tsingtara! There is a long brass instrument.
From it dangles a pennant of spittle. On it is written: Snake.
All their ladies stow this in their fiddle-cases now
and withdraw, overcome with fear.

At the door sits the oily Camoedine.
She hammers gold coins into her thighs for sequins.
An arc-lamp puts out both her eyes;
And her grandson is crushed by the burning roof as it falls.

From the pointed ear of the donkey a clown catches
flies. His home is in another land.
Through little verdant tubes which bend
he has his links with barons in the city.

In lofty aerial tracks, where inharmonious
ropes intersect on which we whir away,
a small-bore camel makes platonic
attempts to climb; the fun becomes confused.

The exhibitionist, who in the past has tended
the curtain with a patient eye for tips,
quite suddenly forgets the sequence of events
and drives new-sprouted hordes of girls before him.

(Hugo Ball)

Readings of modern French poetry alternated with recitals by German, Russian and Swiss poets. Old music was played as well as new. This produced some unlikely combinations: Cendrars and van Hoddis, Hardekopf and Aristide Bruant, a balalaika orchestra and Werfel. Delaunay's pictures were exhibited and Erich Mühsam's poems performed. Rubinstein played Saint-Saëns. There were readings of Kandinsky and Lasker-Schüler, as well as Max Jacob and André Salmon.

He is a humble patron of a tenth-rate music-hall,
where, florally tattooed, the devil-women stamp.
Their pitchforks lure him on to sweet perditions,
blinded and fooled, but always in their thrall.

(Hugo Ball)

The poster for the Cabaret Voltaire was by the Ukrainian painter Marcel Slodki. He was later to participate from time to time, both through personal appearances and by submitting his works, but he never really belonged to Dada. He was a quiet, withdrawn individual whose voice could hardly be heard above the general uproar of the Cabaret Voltaire – or, later, that of the Dada movement.

Thus the Cabaret Voltaire was first of all a literary phenomenon. The creative energies of the group were devoted to the composition, performance and publication of poems, stories and songs. For each of these poems, songs and stories there was an appropriate style of delivery.

Cabaret Voltaire: its members and collaborators

Ball's qualities of thoughtfulness, profundity and restraint were complemented by the fiery vivacity, the pugnacity and the incredible intellectual mobility of the Rumanian poet Tristan Tzara. He was a small man, but this made him all the more uninhibited. He was a David who knew how to hit every Goliath in exactly the right spot with a bit of stone, earth or manure, with or without the accompaniment of witty *bons-mots*, back-answers and sharp splinters of linguistic granite. Life and language were his chosen arts, and the wilder the surrounding fracas, the livelier he became. The total antithesis between him and Ball brought out more clearly the qualities of each. In the movement's early, 'idealistic' period, these anti-*Dioscuri* formed a dynamic, even if serio-comic, unity.

What Tzara did not know, could not do, would not dare to do, had not yet been thought of. His crafty grin was full of humour but also full of tricks; there was never a dull moment with him. Always on the move, chattering away in German, French or Rumanian, he was the natural antithesis of the quiet, thoughtful Ball – and, like Ball, indispensable. In fact, each of these fighters for the spirit and anti-spirit of Dada was indispensable in his own way. What would Dada have been without Tzara's poems, his insatiable ambition, his manifestos, not to speak of the riots he produced in such a masterly fashion? He declaimed, sang and spoke in French, although he could do so just as well in German, and punctuated his performances with screams, sobs and whistles.

Bells, drums, cow-bells, blows on the table or on empty boxes, all enlivened the already wild accents of the new poetic language, and excited, by purely physical means, an audience which had begun by sitting impassively behind its beer-mugs. From this state of immobility it was roused into frenzied involvement with what was going on. This was Art, this was Life, and this was what they wanted! The Futurists had already introduced the idea of provocation into art and practised it in their own performances. As an art it was called Bruitism, and was later given musical status by Edgar Varèse, who followed up Russolo's discoveries in the field of noise-music, which was one of the basic contributions made by Futurism to modern music. In 1911 Russolo had built a noise-organ on which he could conjure up all the distracting sounds of everyday existence – the same sounds that Varèse later used as a musical elements. This unique instrument was destroyed at the première of the Buñuel-Dali film *L'Age d'Or* at the *Cinéma 28* in Paris in 1930, when the *camelots du roi* and other reactionary groups threw stink-bombs at the screen on which this 'anti-' [Catholic] film was being shown, and then broke up the whole place: chairs, tables, pictures by Picasso, Picabia and Man Ray, and Russolo's 'bruitistic' organ, which was on show in the foyer along with the pictures. Bruitism was taken up again by the Cabaret Voltaire and gained a good deal from the furious momentum of the new movement: upwards and downwards, left and right, inwards (the groan) and outwards (the roar).

■　■　■

Source

Richter, H. (1964, 1965) 'How Did Dada Begin?', *Dada: Art and Anti-Art*, trans. D. Britt, London: Thames & Hudson: 12–19.
    First published in 1964 by DuMont Schauberg, Köln, English edition 1965.

Hans Richter (1888–1976)

Artist, film maker and writer. Together with fellow artists Hugo Ball, Hans Arp, Tristan Tzara, Marcel Janco and Richard Huelsenbeck, he launched the Dada movement in Switzerland in 1916, with the founding of the Cabaret Voltaire, in a run-down bar in Zurich. He became a film maker, and is noted especially for *Rhythmus 21* (1921), an early abstract film, and for *8X8* (1957). He was Director of New York City College Institute of Film Techniques (1942–52), and historian of the Dada movement.

    Dada was essentially a reaction against what its participants saw as the meaninglessness of the war in Europe. Similarly its artistic manifestations – sound poems, collages, chance procedures, masks, dances – were anarchic reactions against established forms. The formation of the Cabaret gave a means of creating performance forms which could unite the arts, and from its beginnings in poetry and the visual arts, Dada was carried into film, music, typography, and articles of everyday use. The principle was for poetry to discard language as painting had already discarded the object, and in so doing to create provocative responses from the public: a logical destruction of logic in a futile world. Often chance became a major determinant in producing literature and performance poetry, the techniques of free association producing unexpected juxtapositions of words and sounds, seen as a creative basis on which to build a 'new and universal consciousness of art' (Huelsenbeck 1969). Dada ideas soon spread to Berlin, Cologne, Hanover, Paris, and New York, where the influential presence of Marcel Duchamp became crucial in the development of American performance in dance and music.

    There has always been confusion over the origins of Dada – its name, the individuals involved, its purpose and implications – and in 1964 Richter published his book to try and record what up to then had been subject to distorted accounts. In this essay he gives an apparently authoritative account of the founding of Dada, drawing largely on the diaries of Hugo Ball, the *éminence grise* behind the Dada idea.

Reader cross-references

Artaud – whose theatre attempted to stir audiences from their apathy
Cunningham – an American approach which acknowledges Dada as an antecedent
Goldberg – locates the historical importance of Dada
Hijikata – a later exponent of chaos
Jarry – antecedent of Dada
Marinetti – the contemporary, futurist, viewpoint
Müller – later theatrical development of collage and conflict
Piscator – early staging was influenced by Dada
Schlemmer – another, contemporary, art perspective from the Bauhaus

Further reading

Ball, H. (1974) *Flight Out of Time*, New York: Viking Press.
Huelsenbeck, R. (1969) *Memories of a Dada Drummer*, New York: Viking Press.
Motherwell, R. (ed.) (1951) *The Dada Painters and Poets*, New York: Wittenborn, Schultz.
Richter, H. (1971) *Hans Richter*, ed. C. Gray, New York: Holt, Rinehart & Winston.

Chapter 36

Richard Schechner

THE FIVE
AVANT GARDES OR . . .
OR NONE?

The five avant-gardes or . . .

What the avant-garde has become during the past 100 years or so is much too complicated to be organized under one heading. There is an historical avant-garde, a current avant-garde (always changing), a forward-looking avant-garde, a tradition-seeking avant-garde, and an intercultural avant-garde. A single work can belong to more than one of these categories. The five avant-gardes have emerged as separable tendencies because 'avant-garde' meaning 'what's in advance of' – a harbinger, an experimental prototype, the cutting edge – no longer describes the multifid activities undertaken by performance artists, auteurs, directors, designers, actors, and scholars operating in one or more of the various 'worlds' the planet has been partitioned into. At this point, even as I use them, I voice my objection to these outdated categories. The end of the cold war dissolved the opposition between the first world and the second. The collapse of Soviet hegemony over Eastern Europe and even the territories of the USSR itself was not a spasm temporally limited to 1989–91 or spatially localized in Europe. A steady and long-term infiltration of possibilities and alternatives accompanied, forced, and highlighted the failure of Soviet communism to deliver the goods or permit an open play of ideas. Similar historical processes are at work eliding and topsy-turvying other apparently stable systems, including Europe, China, and that most stable of them all, the USA. If by 'new world order' George

Bush means American hegemony (as he surely does), he is mistaken. The third and fourth worlds are everywhere. The pressures on America from the south are steadily increasing. There is a large and growing south in the USA, the UK, France, and other northern European countries. Change is coming both to China and the USA, forced on them by circumstances working themselves through in historical rather than journalistic time. As for the third world, it is characterized by tumult and often uncontrollable transformations. The task for cultural workers is to express as clearly as we can both the emotional and the logical sense of the changes taking place. We need to find ways to celebrate individual and cultural differences, even as people work towards economic and political parity. Is such a differential egalitarianism possible?

The historical avant-garde took shape in Europe during the last decades of the nineteenth century. It soon spread to many places around the world. The plays of Ibsen, and the naturalistic style of presenting them, for example, affected the modernization of Japan and the liberation of China from the Qing Dynasty. But the first great modern avant-garde, naturalism, soon evoked its opposites in an explosion of heterodoxies: symbolism, futurism, cubism, expressionism, dada, surrealism, constructivism . . . and many more with names, manifestos, and actions that came and went with such speed as to suggest their true aim: the propagation of artistic difference. Along with this was a political agenda, one of sharp opposition. Poggioli is near right when he detects in the historical avant-garde a 'prevalence of the anarchistic mentality . . . an eschatological state of mind, simultaneously messianic and apocalyptic' (1968: 99–100). Avant-gardists were on the left because the right was in power. When the left came to power, in the USSR for example, experimentalists were treated like kulaks, ripe for repression and extermination. Look what happened to Mayakovsky and Meyerhold, who, among a host of others, were reclassified from 'revolutionary comrades' to 'enemies of the people.' Stalin protected remnants of bourgeois culture, Stanislavski among them, and fostered the dullest kind of 'socialist realism.' Decades later, marching under the authority of Mao Zedong's 'little red book,' China's cultural revolution, orchestrated by Jiang Qing, actress and Mao's second wife, razed Chinese culture, both traditional and avant-garde. What Jiang produced were 'model operas,' brilliant but wooden performances expressing her own political and aesthetic values. At present, categories like 'left' and 'right' have lost much of their meaning; they are useful only in very particular historical circumstances, not as general principles.

Regarding the historical avant-garde, Michael Kirby is on the mark when he says that

> 'avant-garde' refers specifically to a concern with the historical *direc-tionality* of art. An advanced guard implies a rear guard or at least the main body of troops following behind. . . . Some artists may accept the limits of art as defined, as known, as given; others may attempt to alter, expand, or escape from the stylistic aesthetic rules passed on to them by the culture.
>
> (1969: 18–19)

What Kirby identifies as the avant-garde's 'impulse to redefine, to contradict, to continue the sensed directionality of art' (1969: 18–19) is the energy source and connecting link holding together the disparate movements of the historical avant-garde.

The historical avant-garde was characterized by the twin tendency to make something new that was also in opposition to prevailing values. Since Romanticism, these values have been seen as social and political as well as aesthetic. The Romantics introduced the idea that artists lived their lives in terms of their art – that experience, display, and expression were inextricably linked, each one functioning in terms of the others. 'Action,' whether poetic, personal, or political (trying to affect the way society was organized) became key. Wordsworth's description of poetry (in the 1800 'Preface' to his *Lyrical Ballads*) as the spontaneous overflow of powerful feelings . . . 'emotion recollected in tranquillity' was soon replaced by Shelley's call for direct radical action. This affection for radical thought, rhetoric, and action in opposition to accepted values was at the heart not only of the historical avant-garde's politics, but also of its bohemian lifestyle.

Even the *ancien régime* was not hated as much as the new dominant class, the bourgeoisie. Not only was the middle class in power, and to avant-gardists therefore the cause of what was wrong with society, it was also uncultured, grossly materialistic and greedy. Ironically, some of Shelley's heirs, in their hatred of bourgeois values and manners, adopted aristocratic airs. Paris's Left Bank and New York's Greenwich Village were famous as places where artists, dandies, and radicals (not mutually exclusive categories) lived their eccentric and libidinous lives, making art, mocking the bourgeoisie, and plotting revolution. Middle-class people considered the artists to be neurotic, childlike, and savage – a trinity formulated by Freud (in many ways an apologist for the Victorianism to whose practices his 'talking cure' adjusted errants). From the bourgeois perspective, artists were thought 'naturally' to be impetuous and irresponsible when it came to money, sex, and politics.

After the Russian Revolution of 1917, the conjunction of revolutionary thought and art grew stronger. Meyerhold was the most visible of a large cohort who wanted to find a place for experimental performance in what he believed was a new and progressive social order. For a time, until the paranoid 'man of steel' Josef Stalin turned it off, light came from the East in the form of biomechanics, constructivism, Russian futurism, montage, multimedia, and vibrant performance styles combining the most recent technological innovations with traditional popular entertainments, such as *commedia dell'arte*, circus, and the cabaret. And just as Germans fleeing Hitler in the 1930s and 1940s fertilized the artistic and intellectual life of Great Britain and the Americas, so Russians (Czarists as well as progressives) vitalized Western European and American theatre, film, and visual arts.

The 'current avant-garde' (second of the five types of avant-garde) is by definition what's happening *now*. Of course, 'now' is always changing – it will be different when this writing is published from what it is as I write in New York in November 1991. Today's current theatre avant-garde includes reruns of the historical avant-garde as well as the practices of formerly experimental artists whose work is by now 'classical' in terms of its predictability, solidity, and acceptance. You know what to expect from Robert Wilson, Laurie Anderson, Elizabeth LeCompte, Meredith Monk, Lee Breuer, Richard Foreman, Merce Cunningham, Pina Bausch, Rachel Rosenthal – and a bunch of younger people working in roughly the same ways as their predecessors and mentors; people like Anne Bogart, Julie Taymor, Bill T. Jones, and Martha Clarke.

The work of the current avant-garde is often excellent, virtuosic in its mastery of formerly experimental and risky materials and techniques. This mastery, coupled with a second and third generation of artists working in the same way, is what makes the current avant-garde classical. Over time, the historical avant-garde modulated into the current avant-garde: what were once radical activities in terms of artistic experimentation, politics, and lifestyles have become a cluster of alternatives open to people who wish to practice or see various kinds of theatrical art. The current avant-garde offers no surprises in terms of theatrical techniques, themes, audience interactions, or anything else. Like naturalism before it, 'avant-garde' has become a style, a way of working, rather than a bellwether. But unlike naturalism, the current avant-garde is not 'mainstream,' not what most theatres do. It is simply a menu of options drained of the fervor of their original impulses.

The current avant-garde certainly may be considered a 'new establish-ment.' As Graham Ley wrote, 'The continuing admiration for a select group of experimental practitioners prompts the question of whether we can have a theatrical avant-garde that would seem to be so well-established' (1991: 348). Ley identifies certain qualities of the current avant-garde that are anti-thetical to what drove the historical avant-garde. Chief among these are the heavy doses of money – most of it from government, big business, and foundations (where the robber barons and their descendants buried their pots of gold) – underwriting almost all of the established current avant-garde biggies from Robert Wilson and Peter Brook through to Grotowski and the Wooster Group. (Ley does not exclude me from the list of the subsidized, due to my long employment by first Tulane and then New York University.) Not only do well-known avant-gardists feed from various patrons (as did artists in the days before the marketplace), subsidy is what further genera-tions of theatre, dance, and other artists expect as their birthright. One has to go to popular entertainments – pop music, sports, movies, and TV – to find arts conditioned by the rough-and-ready economics of the market. However 'vulgar' these entertainments, they are also often both lively and innovative, especially in the development of physical techniques (lighting, sound, ways of including the audience, 'special effects'). The current avant-garde is not only dominated by a group of oldsters (of which I am, for better or worse, one), but it is also quite clearly an established style of perfor-mance, one that in many ways is not distinguishable from orthodox theatre and dance. What innovation comes from the current avant-garde, is mostly emanating from performance art, where people are exploring such things as explicit sexual art and the combining of the extremely personal with the political.

Another wing of the current avant-garde is the activist political theatre – heir to the guerrilla and street theatre movements of the 1960s. This work is avant-garde because there has been free trade of techniques, persons, and ideas between the avant-garde and political theatre from the days of Meyerhold, Brecht, and dada. People and groups like the gay activists of ACT UP (AIDS Coalition to Unleash Power) who use guerrilla theatre to demand more AIDS research and treatment, the radical environmentalists of Greenpeace, and the 'theatre of the oppressed' of Augusto Boal are in the forefront of this kind of theatre. There are very active political theatres in Latin America, Africa, and Asia. ACT UP and Greenpeace work along two lines simultaneously: to get their message across graphically to the general public by using sudden, often disruptive, and dramatic means: and to instill solidarity among their members – nothing brings a group together faster or with more enthusiasm than collectively taking action in an atmosphere of risk. When ACT UP members lie down in the streets simulating the dead and dying of AIDS, or when a Greenpeace ship intercepts a polluting or nuclear arms-bearing vessel, not only does the media catch the event and broadcast it, but group members are also invigorated, reaffirming in public their belief in their cause and each other. In this way, the activist political theatre is a religious and ritual theatre, a theatre of 'witnesses' in the Buddhist, Christian, and Hindu sense. Indeed, the strategies of Gandhi live in the work of political theatres everywhere.

Boal's techniques, originating as opposition to Latin American fascists – Boal himself fled Brazil in the late 1960s and was later forced from Argentina; he is now based in Paris and back in Rio – are somewhat different from those of ACT UP, Greenpeace, and other guerrilla theatre operations. More than wanting to unmask, attack, and ridicule systems and people he feels are oppressive, Boal wants to empower the oppressed. To do this, he has developed, over nearly twenty-five years of work, a non-Aristotelian form of improvisational participatory performance. Boal has written extensively about his work. And his Center for the Theatre of the Oppressed in Paris regularly issues publications.

Political performance, formalist theatre, personal expression, meditative performances . . . and on through a long list of styles, objectives, social and political contexts, and venues: for a long time, since the late 1970s at least, the trend has been away from hegemony toward a situation where there are a number of styles, each of which is an alternative to all the others. Instead of fiercely contentious 'isms' struggling against the mainstream and each other (a characteristic of the historical avant-garde), the current avant-garde is one where producing organizations and particular venues celebrate their receptivity to various styles. So, for example, in New York, the Brooklyn Academy of Music's (BAM) 'Next Wave' festival is actually a compilation of many different kinds of nonnaturalistic theatre and dance, none of it really new, none of it about to replace everything that came before. BAM has no ideological or artistic program beyond presenting what Harvey Lichtenstein and his cohorts think is 'hot.' BAM titles its annual avant-garde festival the 'Next Wave,' an absurd appellation for artists most of whom have been on the scene for decades. Or take the 1991–2 season at the Public Theatre arranged by the organization's new artistic director, JoAnne Akalaitis, a Mabou Mines founder. Works range from solo pieces by people of color ('curated by George C. Wolf'), to performance art, to productions of Shakespeare, Ford, and Lorca, to Anne Bogart directing the Mabou Mines company in Brecht's *In the Jungle of Cities*. The former dominant mainstream – Broadway, the West End, regional theatres – for their part freely borrow techniques and people from the current avant-garde. Such willy-nilly eclecticism, a monoculturalist's nightmare, is the way things are going to be for a long time.

But it's not enough to divide the avant-garde in two, the historical and the current. Since at least the last great burst of new activity in performance, the late 1950s through the mid-1970s – the time of happenings (later to become performance art), environmental theatre, guerrilla theatre, ritual arts – there have been two strong themes within the avant-garde: the forward-looking and the tradition-seeking. Those who are forward-looking advocate and celebrate artistic innovation and originality. This branch of the avant-garde is heir to the historical avant-garde, on the lookout for new ideas and techniques – multimedia, video hookups and interactive telecommunications, megasound, laser light shows, cybernetics, and hyper or virtual time/space. The works of Robert LePage, Laurie Anderson, John Jesurun, and the Wooster Group come to mind. Naim June Paik and many performance artists are forward-looking in the way I am specifying; or those who showed their works at one of the PULSE shows (People Using Light, Sound, and Energy) in Santa Barbara, California. Often this kind of work fuses the avant-garde with popular entertainments because so much of pop culture is not only technologically driven but also where the money is.

The forward-looking avant-garde enacts a future that is both amazing and apocalyptic. The very technology that is celebrated is also feared; it obliterates even as it liberates. The film *Total Recall* very clearly shows this. In the movie the boundary between inner fantasy life and outer 'real' life is blurred. As in Indian tales where the dreamer wakes up into his own dream, the Schwarzenegger character in *Total Recall* doesn't know if his vacation to Mars – a violent, grotesque, and erotic place – is happening inside his mind or in ordinary time/space. The movie ends with the hero and heroine barely escaping death as they witness the violently explosive terraforming of Mars. The old, desiccated planet is transformed into a new, fertile Edenic world. Unfortunately, this exciting denouement becomes pure Hollywood when it's stripped of its ambiguity and it's made clear that it's no dream; it's really happening.

The tradition-seeking avant-garde, so strongly present in Grotowski and Barba but visible as well in 'roots' movements and 'shamanic' performances, rejects fancy technology and cybernetics, preferring the 'wisdom of the ages,' most often found in nonWestern cultures. Jerzy Grotowski's journeys, both actual and conceptual, are paradigmatic of this tendency in the avant-garde. Grotowski's theatre education in Poland and the USSR was nothing unusual. He got his certificate in acting from the Krakow theatre school in 1955; from August 1955 until 1956 he studied directing in Moscow at the State Institute of Theatre Arts, where he became a 'fanatic disciple of Stanislavsky' and 'discovered Meyerhold' (Osinski 1986: 17–18). Then in the summer of 1956, he traveled through central Asia where, it seems, he experienced an epiphany. In Grotowski's own (translated) words:

314

During my expeditions in Central Asia in 1956, between an old Turkmenian town, Ashkhabad, and the western range of the Hindu Kush Mountains, I met an old Afghan named Abdullah who performed for me a pantomime 'of the whole world,' which had been a tradition in his family. Encouraged by my enthusiasm, he told me a myth about the pantomime as a metaphor for 'the whole world.' It occurred to me then that I'm listening to my own thoughts. Nature – changeable, moveable, but permanently unique at the same time – has always been embodied in my imagination as the dancing mime, unique and universal, hiding under the glittering of multiple gestures, colors, and the grimace of life.

(In Osinski 1986: 18)

Grotowski returned to Poland where he studied directing and became involved in the anti-Stalinist movements then gaining strength.

But his interest in things Asian and traditional continued. In 1957 he gave public lectures on 'The philosophical thought of the Orient,' including discussions of yoga, the Upanishads, Buddhism, Zen-Buddhism, Advaita-Vedanta, Taoism, and Confucius. In 1957 and again in 1959, Grotowski traveled to France where he saw works of Jean Vilar and Marcel Marceau, whom he greatly admired. All the while, Grotowski was directing Western works ranging from Ionesco's *The Chairs* and Chekhov's *Uncle Vanya* to an adaptation for radio of Mark Twain's *The White Elephant*. In 1959, Grotowski and critic-dramaturg Ludwik Flaszen took over Opole's Theatre of 13 Rows where they and their colleagues developed what was to be known as 'poor theatre' (see Grotowski 1968, Kumiega 1985, Osinski 1986). This style of performing – emphasizing the actors' psycho-physical abilities, refusing theatrical sets, redefining audience-performer interactions according to the needs of each production, constructing a textual montage from many sources (rather than interpreting a drama written by a single author) – was based on rigorous training founded at least initially on yoga and other principles Grotowski derived from his studies of Asian theatre and philosophies, combined with a deeply Polish Catholic and Hassidic mystic practice. In fact, Grotowski felt the similarity between these traditions, a similarity that Eugenio Barba some years later dubbed 'Eurasian theatre' (Barba: 1988). The stripped-down stage, the ritualized nature of the encounter between performers and spectators, the startling confrontation of extremely personal expression and totally composed face and body 'masks,' all were modeled to a degree after what Grotowski knew of Asian theatre, ritual, and thought. Grotowski's most audacious and experimental inventions are founded on tradition. What Artaud intuited and theorized, Grotowski researched and practiced.

In the late 1960s, Grotowski 'left the theatre.' He stopped directing plays. He began a series of research projects taking him to and putting him in touch with many artists and ritual specialists from different cultures in an attempt to find and express in specific theatrical ways – dances, songs, gestures, utterances, words – universals of performance. These research projects have had several names: theatre of sources, objective drama, ritual arts. The work is not yet complete and is probably uncompletable. It has taken Grotowski to Asia, the Americas, the Caribbean (and possibly other places too: Grotowski often travels incognito). Grotowski has not been silent regarding his work after poor theatre; and often enough he sounds classically avant-gardist:

Art is profoundly rebellious. Bad artists *speak* of rebelling; real artists *actually* rebel. They respond to the powers that be with a concrete act: this is both the most important and the most dangerous point. Real rebellion in art is something which persists and is competent and never dilettante. When I began working with the Theatre of Sources (it was still the period of participatory theatre) it was quite clear that in certain traditional human activities – which may be called religious – from different cultures where tradition still existed, it was possible to see, in some cases, participatory theatre without banality. It soon became clear that not all the differences can be reduced, that we can't alter our own conditioning, that I shall never be a Hindu even if I am conse-crated by the Hindus. One can, however, move toward what precedes the differences. Why do the African hunter from the Kalahari, the French hunter from the outskirts of Saintes, the Bengali hunter, and the Huichol hunter from Mexico all adopt the same body position when they go hunting, with the spinal backbone leaning slightly forward, and the knees slightly bent in a position that is sustained at the base by the sacrum-pelvis complex? And why can only one kind of rhythmic move-ment derive from this position? And what use can be made of this way of walking? There is a very simple, very easy level of analysis: if the weight of the body is on one foot and you move the other foot, you don't make any noise and you can also move very slowly without stop-ping. In this way certain animals remain unaware of your presence. But this isn't the important thing. What is important is that there exists a certain primary position of the human body. It's a position which goes back so far that it was probably the position not only of homo sapiens, but also of homo erectus, and connected in some way with the appear-ance of man. An extremely ancient position connected with what some Tibetans call the 'reptile' aspect. In the Afro-Caribbean culture this position is linked more precisely with the grass snake, and in the Hindu culture linked with the Tantra, you have this snake asleep at the base of the backbone. We are now touching on something which concerns my present work [1985]. I began asking myself, at the end of the period of the Theatre of Sources, how people used this primary energy, how, through differing techniques elaborated in the traditions, people found access to this ancient body of man. I have traveled a lot, I've read numerous books, I have found numerous traces.

(Grotowski 1987: 30–5)

It is not necessary to summarize Grotowski's work over the past twenty-five years to note two things. It remains in the vanguard of experimental work concerning performance (if not strictly theatre in the Western sense); and it is deeply traditional in a way that Grotowski himself, among others, is defining.

Eugenio Barba, Grotowski's longtime colleague and the founder-director of Odin Teatret, one of Europe's leading experimental theatres, challenges Western orthodoxy with Asian practice.

Why in the Western tradition, as opposed to what happens in the Orient, has the actor become specialised [. . . instead of being able to act, dance, mime, and sing?]. Why in the West does the actor tend to confine herself within the skin of only one character in each production? Why does she not explore the possibility of creating the context of an entire story, with many characters, with leaps from the general to the particular, from the first to the third person, from the past to the present, from the whole to the part, from persons to things?

(1988: 126)

Barba proposes an experimental theatre of roots.

Here the term 'roots' becomes paradoxical: it does not imply a bond with ties to a place, but an ethos which permits us to change places. Or better: it represents the force which causes us to change our horizons precisely because it roots us to a center.

(1988: 128)

The roots movement is not only of the West. Re-examining and redefining tradition is a characteristic of the avant-garde in India, Japan, and elsewhere. Suresh Awasthi writes:

I am taking the risk of giving a label – 'theatre of roots' – to the unconventional theatre which has been evolving for some two decades in India as a result of modern theatre's encounter with tradition. . . . Directors like B. V. Karanth, K. N. Panikkar, and Ratan Thiyam have had meaning-ful encounters with tradition, and, with their work, reversed the colonial course of contemporary theatre. . . . It sounds paradoxical, but their theatre is both avant-garde in the context of conventional realistic theatre, and part of the 2,000-year-old *Natyasastra* tradition.

(1989: 48)

Awasthi points out that the 'theatre of roots' must be seen against the back-drop of more than a century of Western naturalistic theatre which is the mainstream in India. Some qualities of the 'theatre of roots' – rejection of the proscenium stage, closer contact between spectators and performers, integration of music, mime, gesture, and literary text – are identical to the experimental theatre program practiced by environmental theatre workers in the West. Of course, this would be so: many of the Western experiments were modeled on the kinds of performances directors like me studied and/or saw in India or elsewhere. That this same avant-garde impulse should now be affecting modern (that is, orthodox or mainstream) Indian theatre is only to be expected.

In Japan, butoh, a word which used to mean 'ancient dance,' now refers to an intense, physically extreme, and rebellious avant-garde performance art developed by Kazuo Ohno and the late Tatsumi Hijikata. Butoh is practiced by Kazuko Shiraishi, Min Tanaka, Natsuo Nakajima, and several groups (Dai Rakuda-kan, Muteki-sha, and Sankai Juku are the best known). Described by Bonnie Sue Stein as 'shocking, provocative, physical, spiritual, erotic, grotesque, violent, cosmic, nihilistic, cathartic, [and] mysterious' (1986: 111), butoh is closely linked to noh and kabuki as well as other traditional Japanese arts.

> Butoh is an anti-traditional tradition seeking to erase the heavy imprint of Japan's strict society and offering unprecedented freedom of artistic expression. . . . Nakajima said, 'We found that we were making the same discoveries·as noh actors made, using some of the same termi-nology, but we had never learned these forms.'
>
> (Stein 1986: 111)

The images and actions butoh performers create are striking. Ohno in his eighties still performs the movements of a young coquette, her face painted white, her lips scarlet. 'He drapes himself across the edge of the stage in the serpentine curves of traditional femininity, then kicks his foot high like a carefree young lover. To the slow koto music, he skips, flutters, and poses' (Stein 1986: 107). Or Sankai Juku's nearly naked performers, their bodies powdered white, who dangle upside down far above the street, held aloft by ropes tied around their ankles. In Seattle in 1985, a rope broke and a Sankai Juku dancer plunged to his death. But risk is what butoh is about. Often performing outdoors in extremely harsh weather, forcing their bodies against rocks or into icy seawater, their teeth blacked out or painted, butoh performers awaken Japan's shamanic heritage, demonic mythology, and folk theatre. Butoh performers are also disruptive bohemians, canny city-based artists consciously playing out their subversive countertext mocking Japan's hyperorganized social life.

Examples like 'roots' from India and butoh from Japan could be multiplied from all around the world. There is no area, be it Micronesia, the Pacific Rim, West Africa, the Circumpolar Region, or wherever, which does not have artists actively trying to use, appropriate, reconcile, come to terms with, exploit, understand – the words and political tone vary, but the substance doesn't – the relationships between local cultures in their extreme particular historical development and the increasingly complex and multiple contacts and interactions not only among various cultures locally and regionally but on a global and interspecific scale. Fitfully, unevenly, and with plenty of cruelty, a planetary human culture is emerging which is aware of, if not yet acting responsibly toward, the whole geobiocultural system. Founded on certain accepted values which express themselves abstractly as mathematics and materially as technology, this planetary culture is engaging more and more scientists, social activists, and artists concerned with mapping, understanding, representing, and preserving the earth as an integrated geobiocultural system.

When I say 'accepted values' I don't mean these are God-given or inherent in nature or experience. They are constructed and imposed. These imposed values – mathematics and its expression in technology – can be used for good or bad. What constitutes good and bad is, of course, what philosophers, religious and spiritual people, and artists want to find out – and impose. No matter what is written or spoken at any given time – the Bible, the Koran, the Upanishads – history teaches that the question of good and bad is always open. Inquisitors used the Bible, bloody Muslim zealots the Koran, and the architects of the Indian caste system the Upanishads. Which leads me to the fifth kind of avant-garde, the intercultural. For whatever reasons – leftover colonialism, American imperialism, the hunger of people everywhere for material goods, the planetary spread of modernism, the ubiquity of a 'cosmopolitan style' in everything from airports to clothes – artists of the avant-garde are producing works on or across various borders: political, geographical, personal, generic, and conceptual. In a world where so-called universal values each day run up against deeply held local values and experiences, the result is clash, disturbance, turbulence, unease about the future, and hot argument about what the past was.

As intercultural performance artist Guillermo Gomez-Pena says:

> I physically live between two cultures and two epochs. . . . When I am on the US side, I have access to high-technology and specialized information. When I cross back to Mexico, I get immersed in a rich political culture. . . . When I return to California, I am part of the multicultural thinking emerging from the interstices of the US's ethnic milieus. . . . I walk the fibres of this transition in my everyday life, and I make art about it.
>
> (1991: 22–3)

This kind of uneasiness marks many in the intercultural avant-garde. It is not mostly a question of the artist not knowing where she lives. It is about belonging to more than one culture, subscribing to contradictory values, conflicting aesthetic canons. Salman Rushdie well knows the contradictions between Western liberal and Muslim fundamentalist values as they apply to literature and life. Rushdie has said he'd like to belong both to the Western and Islamic worlds. And within every nation many people are living difficult, sometimes exciting, multiple lives. The 'nation' no longer describes how or even where hundreds of millions of people live. As Sun Huizhu, aka William Sun, a leading young Chinese playwright who since the crushing of the democracy movement in Tiananmen Square in June 1989 has been unable to return to his native Shanghai, says:

> I would like to call on artists to pay more attention to an increasingly important reality. More and more people of different cultures are interacting and having problems in their interactions. As intercultural artists – often as ambassadors to other cultures – can we artists do something to address this issue and help solve some of those problems?[1]

Engaging intercultural fractures, philosophical difficulties, ideological contradictions, and crumbling national myths does not necessarily lead to avant-garde performances. Intercultural performances occur across an enormous range of venues, styles, and purposes. What is avant-garde is when the performance does not try to heal over rifts or fractures but further opens these for exploration. For example, I would say that Peter Brook's *The Mahabharata* was intercultural but not avant-garde, while Gomez-Pena's solo performances as *Border Brujo* or the *Warrior for Gringostroika* definitely are. The difference is that Brook wants to elide difference; he is looking for what unites, universalizes, makes the same. The conflicts in his Euro-Indic epic are philosophical, personal, familial, and religious – not intercultural. Brook assumes – as the English who own Shakespeare do – that certain works operate at the 'human' rather than cultural level. His *Mahabharata* does not interrogate the epic or subvert it; nor are spectators to regard with anything but liberal approval the 'international cast' Brook assembled to enact not only the epic story but also the universalist doctrine that under the skin all humans are the same. Don't get me wrong. I support nontraditional, color-blind, culture-blind casting (see Schechner 1989a). But in the case of Brook's *Mahabharata* such casting could have been the occasion for an exploration of the tensions between nonracialist universalism and the ethnic, nationalist, religious, and racial jungle of current world politics and personal relations.

... Or none?

Of what use is dividing the avant-garde into five? These categories clearly overlap. The current avant-garde includes work that is forward-looking, tradition-seeking, and intercultural. But despite the rudeness of the division, the operation reminds us of how complex, how multiple, the avant-garde has become. We can also see how very far the current avant-garde is from the historical avant-garde. The current avant-garde is neither innovative nor in advance of. Like a mountain, it just is. Although the term 'avant-garde' persists in scholarship as well as journalism, it no longer serves a useful purpose. It really doesn't mean anything today. It should be used only to describe the historical avant-garde, a period of innovation extending roughly from the end of the nineteenth century to the mid-1970s (at most). Saying something is avant-garde may carry a cache of shock, of newness, but in the West, at least, there is little artists can do, or even ought to do, to shock audiences (though quite a bit can offend them). And why try to shock? There are no surprises in terms of technique, theme, or approach. Everything from explicit sex shows, site-specific work, participatory performance, political theatre and guerrilla theatre (of the kind Greenpeace or ACT UP now do), to postmodern dance, the mixing of personal narratives with received texts, the deconstruction of texts, the blurring of boundaries between genres and so on, has been done and done again many times, over the past forty years. And if the scope is opened to 100 years, what in today's performance world can be said to be new? But the question is not, 'Can anything new happen?', but 'Who cares? Does it matter?' Who today could write manifestos comparable to the febrile outpourings of Artaud, palpitating with hatred, rage, and hope? Who would want to? Is anyone waiting for an Artaud to come around again?

I doubt it. A Rubicon has been crossed. Events today are recorded, replayed, ritualized, and recycled. And if Artaud were to show up, he would be accepted, put in his proper place. The limitless horizons of expectations that marked the modern epoch and called into existence endless newness have been transformed into a global hothouse, a closed environment. I do not agree with Baudrillard that everything is a simulation. But neither do we live in a world of infinite possibilities or originalities. A long neomedieval period has begun. Or, if one is looking for historical analogies, perhaps neo-Hellenistic is more precise. A certain kind of Euro-American cultural style is being extended, imposed, willingly received (the reactions differ) by many peoples in all parts of the world. Exactly what shape this style will take, what its dominant modes of thought will be, are not yet clear. But it will be a conservative age intellectually and artistically. That does not mean reactionary or without compassion. Nor is the kind of conservatism I am talking about incompatible with democratic socialism. It is a conservatism based on the need to save, recycle, use resources parsimoniously. It is founded on the availability of various in-depth 'archives' of many different prior experiences, artworks, ideas, feelings, and texts. This stored and recallable prior knowledge is being used to avoid repeating certain kinds of events as well as to promote certain new kinds of events. Local violence increases, no one seems to care how many die if the bloodshed, starvation, or plague is 'limited' (not in danger of becoming pandemic). What those in control fear is global violence, a threat to the established order not simply emergent but already firmly in place. The world's peoples are reminded daily of what will happen if global violence – to the environment, to populations, to species – is not brought under control. At the same time, entertainment expands its scope to include almost anything that happens that is technically witnessed and can be edited and played back. Art comes in several mutually reinforcing varieties: that which passes the time of those with enough money to buy tickets; that which excites without satisfying the appetites of its consumers; that which shows off the wealth, power, and taste of its patrons; that which is acquired as an investment. Popular entertainment follows roughly the same path.

To recycle, reuse, archive and recall, to perform in order to be included in an archive (as a lot of performance artists do), to seek roots, explore and maybe even plunder religious experiences, expressions, practices, and liturgies to make art (as Grotowski and others are doing) is to ritualize; not just in terms of subject matter and theme, but also structurally, as form. Ethologists and psychologists have shown that the 'oceanic feeling' of belonging, ecstasy, and total participation that many experience when ritualizing works by means of repetitive rhythms, sounds, and tones which effectively 'tune' to each other the left and right hemispheres of the cerebral cortex (see d'Aquili et al. 1979; Eibl-Eibesfeldt 1979; Fischer 1971; and Turner 1983). This understanding of ritual, as a process applying to a great range of human activities rather than as something tethered to religion, is a very important development. The relatively tight boundaries that locked the various spheres of performance off from each other have been punctured. It is doubtful if these boundaries ever really functioned, in fact. Certainly they didn't in popular entertainments and religious rituals. The boundaries, in fact, are the ghosts of neoclassical and Renaissance readings of the Aristotelian 'unities.' Keeping each genre in its place is a last ditch regressive action mounted by some critics and academics.

The four great spheres of performance – entertainment, healing, education, and ritualizing – are in play with each other. This playing (and it can be a very serious matter) is the subject of this book. What used to be a tightly boundaried, limited field has expanded exponentially. Each of the performance spheres can be called by other names. Entertainment includes aesthetics, the arrangement and display of actions in ways that are 'satisfying' or 'beautiful' (according to particular and local cultural canons). Education includes all kinds of political performances designed to exhort, convince, and move to action. Healing performances include shamanism, the ostensive display of hi-tech medical equipment, the bedside manner, and all kinds of interactive psychotherapies.

As the writings in this book show, I am of at least two minds regarding all this. I am enthusiastic about the expanding field of performance and its scholarly adjunct, performance studies. Performative analysis is not the only interpretation possible, but it is a very effective method for a time of charged rhetorics, simulations and scenarios, and games played on a global scale. It has always been a good method for looking at small-scale, face-to-face interactions. The public display of these 'for fun' may be taken as an operative definition of drama. But only a small number of artworks relate creatively and critically to the worlds around them. These are what used to be the avant-garde, but which today, as I've been saying, barely owns its name. A century from now the world may be running on new fuels, the automobile may have passed away, human settlements may exist on the moon and elsewhere – and on through a list of as yet barely imaginable changes and technological improvements. The basic tendency of all these changes has already been set. That tendency is to use without using up; to reserve the ability to repeat; to test through modeling, virtual experience, and other kinds of mathematical and analogical rehearsing.

Where does that leave Jayaganesh?

The writings in this book all relate to aspects of what I have called the 'broad spectrum' of performance (see Schechner 1988, 1989b, 1990). The broad spectrum includes performative behavior, not just the performing arts, as a subject for serious scholarly study. This book is one contribution to this big project. How is performance used in politics, medicine, religion, popular entertainments, and ordinary face-to-face interactions? What are the similarities and differences between live and mediated performances? The various and complex relationships among players – spectators, performers, authors, and directors – can be pictured as a rectangle, a performance 'quadrilogue.' Studying the interactions, sometimes easy, sometimes tense, among the speakers in the quadrilogue is what performance studies people do. These studies are intensely interdisciplinary, intercultural, and intergenric. Performance studies builds on the emergence of a postcolonial world where cultures are colliding, interfering with, and fertilizing each other. Arts and academic disciplines alike are most alive at their ever-changing borders. The once distinct (in the West at least) genres of music, theatre, and dance are interacting with each other in ways undreamt-of just thirty-five years ago. These interactions are both expressive of and part of a larger movement culturally.

Note

1   Sun made this statement during a five-day conference on intercultural performance held in Bellagio, Italy in February 1991. . . . Papers and proceedings from the conference will be published in 1994.

References

Awasthi, S. (1989), ' "Theatre of roots": encounter with tradition' *TDR, The Drama Review* 33 (4): 48–69.
Barba, E. (1986), *Beyond the Floating Islands*, New York: PAJ Publications.
d'Aquili, E.G., Laughlin, C.D. Jr., and McManus, J. (1979), *The Spectrum of the Ritual*, New York: Columbia University Press.
Eibl-Eibesfeldt, I. (1979), 'Ritual and ritualization from a biological perspective,' in M. von Cranach, K. Foppa, W. Lepenies and D. Ploog (eds) *Human Ethology*, Cambridge: Cambridge University Press.
Fischer, R. (1971), 'A cartography of the ecstatic and meditative states,' *Science* 174 (26 November): 897–904.
Gomez-Pena, G. (1991), 'A binational performance pilgrimage,' *TDR, The Drama Review* 35 (3): 22–45.
Grotowski, J. (1968), *Towards a Poor Theatre*, Holstebro: Odin Teatret Verlag.
—— (1987), 'Tu es le fils de quelqu'un [You are someone's son],' *TDR, The Drama Review* 31 (3): 30–41.
Kirby, M. (1969), *The Art of Time*, New York: E.P. Dutton.
Kumiega, J. (1985), *The Theatre of Grotowski*, London and New York: Methuen.
Ley, G. (1991), 'Sacred idiocy: the avant-garde as alternative establishment,' *New Theatre Quarterly* VII (28) (November): 348–52.
Osinski, Z. (1986), *Grotowski and His Laboratory*, New York: PAJ Publications.

Poggioloi, R. (1968), *The Theory of the Avantgarde*, Cambridge, Mass.: Harvard University Press.

Schechner, R. (1988), 'Performance Studies: the broad spectrum approach,' *TDR, The Drama Review* 32 (3): 4–6.

—— (1989a), 'Race free, gender free, body-type free, age free casting,' *TDR, The Drama Review* 33 (1): 4–12.

—— (1989b), '*PAJ* distorts the broad spectrum,' *TDR, The Drama Review* 33 (2): 4–9.

—— (1990), 'Performance Studies: the broad spectrum approach,' *National Forum* 70 (3): 15–16.

Stein, B.S. (1986), "Butoh: 'Twenty Years Ago We Were Crazy, Dirty, and Mad,' " *TDR, The Drama Review* 30 (2): 107–26.

Turner, V. (1983), 'Body, brain and culture,' *Zygon* 18 (3): 221–45.

■ ■ ■

Source

Schechner, R. (1993) 'Introduction: The five avant gardes or . . . [and] . . . Or none?', *The Future of Ritual: Writings on Culture and Performance* London: Routledge: 5–21.

Richard Schechner (1934–)

Director, writer, theorist; founder of the Performance Group, New York (1967–80). His 1968 theatre piece, *Dionysus in 69*, introduced major elements of ritual into performance, one of his recurrent interests as both director and writer. In 1962 he became editor of the influential *Tulane Drama Review* at Tulane University,[1] specifically to explore modes of non-verbal performance communication, and continues to edit *The Drama Review*. In *Commune* (1971) he selected at random fifteen members of the audience to act as villagers in a reconstruction of the Vietnam My Lai massacre, emphasising the Performance Group's interest in creating direct participation on the part of the spectators. Schechner coined the term 'Environmental Theatre' to describe performances which took inspiration from the specific reception conditions, and the work often blurred reality and performance as in his version of *The Balcony* (1979), the last of the Performance Group's creations, after which it was dissolved. He is University Professor at New York University, Tisch School of the Arts.

Schechner's theoretical and critical writings are also of profound importance in the approach he adopts as a result of his practice as director. His distinctions between drama, theatre, script and performance relate the field to that of historians, archaeologists and anthropologists, and have influenced generations of Western practitioners and thinkers. For Schechner, therefore, the drama is 'what the writer writes'; the script is the code of a particular production; the theatre is 'the specific set of gestures performed by the performer in any given performance'; the performance is the totality of the event for both performers and audience. As both director and writer Schechner is concerned to make performers and audience aware of the interlinking of all these ideas and definitions, often taking examples from non-Western cultures, and drawing on his travels in Asia and the Far East.

Schechner's essay attempts a historical and philosophical definition of the notion of the avant-garde. In doing so he refers to most of the figures included in this book. It is an excellent example of both the clarity and the importance of his theoretical writing, marking him out as one of the few director-theorists whose work is constantly breaking new boundaries in the analysis of performance.

Reader cross-references

Banes – a contemporary, contrasting, view of postmodernism
Beck – an American theatre contemporary
Bharucha – a contrasting, Indian, viewpoint on tradition
Brook – a European view of intercultural experiment
Cage – who also used non-Western thought and forms
Goldberg – an art historical view
Hijikata – a Japanese view of the avant garde
LeCompte – who worked with Schechner before founding the Wooster Group
Williams – an earlier discussion on the idea of text

Further reading

Schechner, R. (1978) *Environmental Theatre*, New York: Hawthorn.
Schechner, R. (1988) *Performance Theory*, London: Routledge.
Turner, V. (1969) *The Ritual Process*, Chicago: Aldine.

Note

1   Then known as *The Tulane Drama Review*, later as *The Drama Review*, published from New York University, and now, usually, simply *TDR*.

Chapter 37

Oskar Schlemmer

MAN AND ART
FIGURE

T HE HISTORY of the theater is the history of the transfiguration of the human form. It is the history of *man* as
the actor of physical and spiritual events, ranging from naïveté
to reflection, from naturalness to artifice.

The materials involved in this transfiguration are form
and color, the materials of the painter and sculptor. The arena
for this transfiguration is found in the con-structive fusion of
space and building, the realm of the architect. Through the
manipulation of these materials the role of the artist, the
synthesizer of these elements, is determined.

One of the emblems of our time is *abstraction*. It functions, on
the one hand, to disconnect components from an existing and
persisting whole, either to lead them individually *ad absurdum*
or to elevate them to their greatest potential. On the other
hand, abstraction can result in generalization and summation,
in the construction in bold outline of a new totality.

A further emblem of our time is *mechanization*, the inexorable process which now lays claim to every sphere of life
and art. Everything which can be mechanized *is* mechanized.
The result: our recognition of that which can *not* be mechanized.

And last, but not the least, among the emblems of our time are the new potentials of technology and invention which we can use to create altogether new hypotheses and which can thus engender, or at least give promise of, the boldest fantasies.

The theater, which should be the image of our time and perhaps the one art form most peculiarly conditioned by it, must not ignore these signs.

Stage (*Bühne*), taken in its general sense, is what we may call the entire realm lying between religious cult and naïve popular entertainment. Neither of these things, however, is really the same thing as stage. Stage is *representation* abstracted from the natural and directing its effect at the human being.

This confrontation of passive spectator and animate actor preconditions also the form of the stage, at its most monumental as the antique arena and at its most primitive as the scaffold in the market place. The need for concentration resulted in the peep show or 'picture frame,' today the 'universal' form of the stage. The term *theater* designates the most basic nature of the stage: make-believe, mummery, metamorphosis. Between cult and theater lies 'the stage seen as a moral institution'; between theater and popular entertainment lie variety (vaudeville) and circus: the stage as an institution for the artiste. [See diagram opposite.]

The question as to the origin of life and the cosmos, that is, whether in the beginning there was Word, Deed, or Form – Spirit, Act, or Shape – Mind, Happening, or Manifestation – pertains also to the world of the stage, and leads us to a differentiation of:

the *oral or sound stage* (*Sprech-oder Tonbühne*) of a literary or musical event;
the *play stage* (*Spielbühne*) of a physical-mimetic event;
the *visual stage* (*Schaubühne*) of an optical event.

Each of these stage forms has its corresponding representative, thus:

the *author* (as writer or composer) who is the creator of the word or musical
    sound;
the *actor* whose body and its movements make him the player;
the *designer* who is the builder of form and color.

Each of these stage forms can exist for itself and be complete within itself.

The combination of two or all three stage forms – with one of them always predominating – is a question of weight distribution, and is something that can be perfected with mathematical precision. The executor of this process is the universal *regisseur* or *director*. E.g.:

SCHEME FOR STAGE, CULT, AND POPULAR ENTERTAINMENT ACCORDING TO:

Central diagram — GENRE: a large circle labelled **STAGE** / **PEEP SHOW** ("picture frame"), containing three overlapping circles: **CONSECRATED STAGE / FESTIVAL STAGE** (ARENA) — BORDERLINE — **THEATER** — BORDERLINE — **CABARET / VARIETÉ (Vaudeville) / CIRCUS** (ARENA). Top band: **RELIGIOUS CULT ACTIVITY**. Bottom band: **FOLK ENTERTAINMENT**.

PLACE	PERSON	GENRE	SPEECH	MUSIC	DANCE
TEMPLE	PRIEST	RELIGIOUS CULT ACTIVITY	SERMON	ORATORIO	DERVISH
ARCHITECTURAL STAGE	PROPHET		ANCIENT TRAGEDY	EARLY OPERA (e.g. Handel)	MASS GYMNASTICS
STYLIZED OR SPACE STAGE	SPEAKER		SCHILLER ("BRIDE OF MESSINA")	WAGNER	CHORIC DANCE
THEATER OF ILLUSION	ACTOR	STAGE / PEEP SHOW ("picture frame")	SHAKESPEARE	MOZART	BALLET
WINGS AND BORDERS	PERFORMER (COMMEDIAN)		IMPROVISATION—COMMEDIA DELL'ARTE	OPERA BUFFA OPERETTA	MIME & MUMMERY
SIMPLEST STAGE OR APPARATUS & MACHINERY	ARTISTE		CONFERENCIER (M.C.)	MUSIC HALL SONG JAZZ BAND	CARICATURE & PARODY
PODIUM SCAFFOLD	ARTISTE		CLOWNERY	CIRCUS BAND	ACROBATICS
FAIRGROUND SIDESHOW	FOOL JESTER	FOLK ENTERTAINMENT	DOGGEREL BALLAD	FOLK SONG	FOLK DANCE

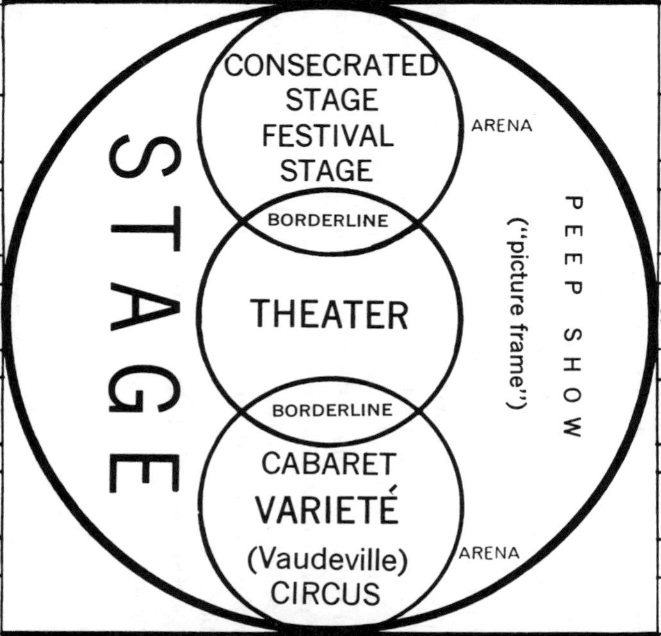

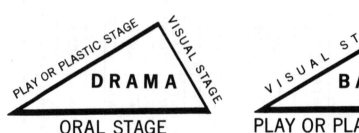

From the standpoint of *material* the actor has the advantages of immediacy and independence. He constitutes his own material with his body, his voice, his gestures, and his movements. Today, however, the once noble type who was both the poet and the projector of his own word has become an ideal. At one time Shakespeare, who was an actor before he was a poet, filled this role – so, too, did the improvising actors of the *commedia dell' arte*. Today's actor bases his existence as player on the writer's word. Yet when the word is silent, when the body alone is articulate and its play is on exhibition – as a dancer's is – then it is free and is its own lawgiver.

The material of the author is *word or sound*.

Except for the unusual circumstance in which he is his own actor, singer, or musician, he creates the representational material for transmission and reproduction on the stage, whether it is meant for the organic human voice or for artificial, abstract instruments. The higher the state of perfection of the latter, the broader their formative potential, while the human voice is and remains a limited, if unique, phenomenon. Mechanical reproduction by means of various kinds of technological equipment is now capable of replacing the sound of the musical instrument and the human voice or of detaching it from its source, and can enlarge it beyond its dimensional and temporal limitations.

The material of the formative artist – painter, sculptor, architect – is *form and color*.

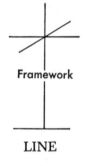

LINE   PLANE   SOLID (Volume)

These formative means, invented by the human mind, can be called *abstract* by virtue of their artificiality and insofar as they represent an undertaking whose purpose, contrary to nature, is order. Form is manifest in extensions of height, breadth, and depth; as line, as plane, and as solid or volume. Depending on these extensions, form becomes then linear framework, wall, or space, and, as such, rigid – i.e., tangible – form.

Non-rigid, intangible form occurs as light, whose linear effect appears in the geometry of the light beam and of pyrotechnical display, and whose solid- and space-creating effect comes through illumination. To each of these manifestations of light (which in themselves are already colored – only nothingness is without color) can be added *coloring* (*intensifying*) *color*.

Color and form reveal their elementary values within the constructive manipulation of architectonic space. Here they constitute both object and receptacle, that which is to be filled and fulfilled by Man, the living organism.

In painting and sculpture, form and color are the means of establishing these connections with organic nature through the representation of its phenomena. Man, its chief phenomenon, is both an organism of flesh and blood and at the same time the exponent of number and 'Measure of All Things' (the Golden Section).

These arts – architecture, sculpture, painting – are fixed. They are momentary, frozen motion. Their nature is the immutability of not an accidental but a typified condition, the stability of forces in equilibrium. And thus what may appear at first as a deficiency, particularly in our age of motion, is actually their greatest merit.

The stage as the arena for successive and transient action, however, offers *form and color in motion*, in the first instance in their primary aspect as separate and individual mobile, colored or uncolored, linear, flat, or plastic forms, but furthermore as fluctuating, mobile space and as transformable architectonic structures. Such kaleidoscopic play, at once infinitely variable and strictly organized, would constitute – theoretically – the *absolute* visual stage (*Schaubühne*). Man, the animated being, would be banned from view in this mechanistic organism. He would stand as 'the perfect engineer' at the central switchboard, from where he would direct this feast for the eyes.

Yet all the while Man seeks *meaning*. Whether it is the Faustian problem whose goal is the creation of Homunculus or the anthropomorphic impulse in Man which created his gods and idols, he is incessantly seeking his likeness, his image, or the sublime. He seeks his equal, the superman, or the figures of his fancy.

Man, the human organism, stands in the cubical, abstract space of the stage. Man and Space. Each has different laws of order. Whose shall prevail?

331

Either abstract space is adapted in deference to natural man and transformed back into nature or the imitation of nature. This happens in the theater of illusionistic realism.

Or natural man, in deference to abstract space, is recast to fit its mold. This happens on the abstract stage.

The laws of cubical space are the invisible linear network of planimetric and stereometric relationships. (See above sketch.) This mathematic corresponds to the inherent mathematic of the human body and creates its balance by means of movements, which by their very nature are determined *mechanically and rationally*. It is the geometry of calisthenics, eurhythmics, and gymnastics. These involve the *physical attributes* (together with facial stereotypy) which find expression in acrobatic precision and in the mass calisthenics of the stadium, although there is no conscious awareness of spatial relationships here. (See sketch, p. 333, top.)

The laws of organic man, on the other hand, reside in the invisible functions of his inner self: heartbeat, circulation, respiration, the activities of the brain and nervous system. If these are to be the determining factors, then their center is the human being, whose movements and emanations create an imaginary space. (See sketch, p. 333, bottom.) Cubical-abstract space is then only the horizontal and vertical framework for this flow. These movements are *determined organically and emotionally*. They constitute the

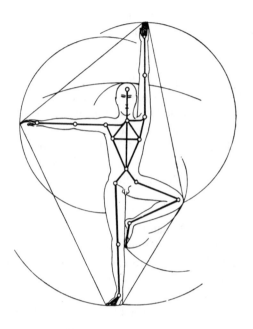

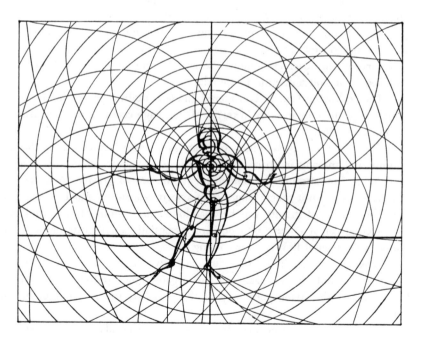

psychical impulses (together with the mimetics of the face), which find expression in the great actor and in the mass scenes of great tragedy.

Invisibly involved with all these laws is Man as Dancer (Tänzermensch). *He obeys the law of the body as well as the law of space; he follows his sense of himself as well as his sense of embracing space.* As the one who gives birth to an almost endless range of expression, whether in free abstract movement or in symbolic pantomime, whether he is on the bare stage or in a scenic environment constructed for him, whether he speaks or sings, whether he is naked or costumed, the *Tänzermensch* is the medium of transition into the great world of the theater (*das grosse theatralische Geschehen*). Only one branch of this world, the metamorphosis of the human figure and its abstraction, is to be outlined here.

The transformation of the human body, its metamorphosis, is made possible by the *costume*, the disguise. Costume and mask emphasize the body's identity or they change it; they express its nature or they are purposely misleading about it; they stress its conformity to organic or mechanical laws or they invalidate this conformity.

The native costume, as produced by the conventions of religion, state, and society, is different from the theatrical stage costume. Yet the two are generally confused. Great as has been the variety of native costumes developed during the course of human history, the number of genuine stage costumes has stayed very small. They are the few standardized costumes of the *commedia dell' arte*: Harlequin, Pierrot, Columbine, etc.; and they have remained basic and authentic to this day.

The following can be considered fundamentally decisive in the transformation of the human body in terms of this stage costume (see illustrations pp. 335 and 336).

These are the possibilities of Man as Dancer, transformed through costume and moving in space. Yet there is no costume which can suspend the primary limitation of the human form: the law of gravity, to which it is subject. A step is not much longer than a yard, a leap not much higher than two. The center of gravity can be abandoned only momentarily. And only for a second can it endure in a position essentially alien to its natural one, such as a horizontal hovering or soaring.

Acrobatics make it possible to partially overcome physical limitations, though only in the realm of the organic: the contortionist with his double joints, the living geometry of the aerialist, the pyramid of human bodies.

The endeavor to free man from his physical bondage and to heighten his freedom of movement beyond his native potential resulted in substituting for the organism the mechanical human figure (*Kunstfigur*): *the automaton and*

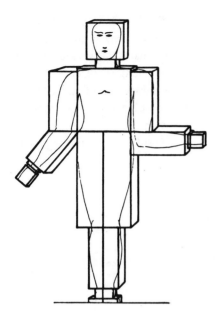

The laws of the surrounding cubical space. Here the cubical forms are transferred to the human shape: head, torso, arms, legs are transformed into spatial-cubical constructions.
Result: *ambulant architecture.*

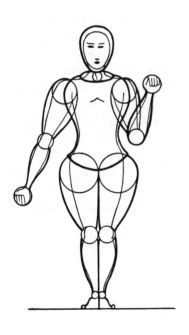

The functional laws of the human body in their relationship to space. These laws bring about a typification of the bodily forms: the egg shape of the head, the vase shape of the torso, the club shape of the arms and legs, the ball shape of the joints.
Result: *the marionette.*

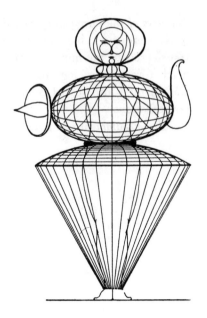

The laws of motion of the human body in space. Here we have the various aspects of rotation, direction, and intersection of space: the spinning top, snail, spiral, disk.
Result: *a technical organism.*

The metaphysical forms of expression symbolizing various members of the human body: the star shape of the spread hand, the ∞ sign of the folded arms, the cross shape of the backbone and shoulders; the double head, multiple limbs, division and suppression of forms.
Result: *dematerialization.*

the marionette. E.T.A. Hoffmann extolled the first of these, Heinrich von Kleist the second.

The English stage reformer Gordon Craig demands: 'The actor must go, and in his place comes the inanimate figure – the Übermarionette we may call him.' And the Russian Brjusov demands that we 'replace actors with mechanized dolls, into each of which a phonograph shall be built.'

Such, indeed, are two actual conclusions arrived at by the stage designer whose mind is constantly concerned with form and transformation, with figure and configuration. As far as the stage is concerned, such paradoxical exclusiveness is less significant than the enrichment of modes of expression which is brought about by it.

Possibilities are extraordinary in light of today's technological advancements: precision machinery, scientific apparatus of glass and metal, the artificial limbs developed by surgery, the fantastic costumes of the deep-sea diver and the modern soldier, and so forth. . . .

Consequently, potentialities of constructive configuration are extraordinary on the metaphysical side as well.

The artificial human figure (*Kunstfigur*) permits any kind of movement and any kind of position for as long a time as desired. It also permits – an artistic device from the periods of greatest art – a variable relative scale for figures: important ones can be large, unimportant ones small.

An equally significant aspect of this is the possibility of relating the figure of natural 'naked' Man to the abstract figure, both of which experience, through this confrontation, an intensification of their peculiar natures.

Endless perspectives are opened up: from the supernatural to the nonsensical, from the sublime to the comic. Precursors in the use of pathos, of the sublime, are the actors of ancient tragedy, monumentalized by means of masks, cothurni, and stilts. Precursors in the comic style are the gigantic and the grotesque figures of carnival and fair.

Wondrous figures of this new sort, personifications of the loftiest concepts and ideas, made of the most exquisite material, will be capable also of embodying symbolically a new faith.

Seen from this perspective, it might even be predicted that the situation will completely reverse itself: the stage designer will develop optical phenomena and will then seek out a poet who will give them their appropriate language through words and musical sounds.

And so, in accordance with idea, style, and technology, the following still await their creation (see p. 338):

the Abstract-Formal and Color
the Static, Dynamic, and Tectonic
the Mechanical, Automatic, and Electric
the Gymnastic, Acrobatic, and Equilibristic   } Theater
the Comic, Grotesque, and Burlesque
the Serious, Sublime, and Monumental
the Political, Philosophical, and Metaphysical

Utopia? It is indeed astonishing how little has been accomplished so far in this direction. This materialistic and practical age has in fact lost the genuine feeling for play and for the miraculous. Utilitarianism has gone a long way in killing it. Amazed at the flood of technological advance, we accept these wonders of utility as being already perfected art form, while actually they are only prerequisites for its creation. 'Art is without purpose' insofar as the imaginary needs of the soul can be said to be without purpose. In this time of crumbling religion, which kills the sublime, and of a decaying society, which is able to enjoy only play that is drastically erotic or artistically outré, all profound artistic tendencies take on the character of exclusiveness or of sectarianism.

And so there remain only three possibilities for the artist in the theater today!

He may seek realization within the confines of the given situation. This means cooperation with the stage in its present form – productions in which he places himself at the service of writers and actors in order to give to their work the appropriate optical form. It is a rare case when his intentions coincide with those of the author.

Or he may seek realization under conditions of the greatest possible freedom. This exists for him in those areas of staging which are primarily visual display, where author and actor step back in favor of the optical or else achieve their effect only by virtue of it: ballet, pantomime, musical theater, and the like. It also exists in those areas – independent of writer and actor – of the anonymous or mechanically controlled play of forms, colors, and figures.

Or he may isolate himself altogether from the existing theater and cast his anchor far out into the sea of fantasy and distant possibilities. In this case his projects remain paper and model, materials for demonstration lectures and exhibitions of theater art. His plans founder on the impossibility of materialization. In the final analysis this is unimportant to him. His idea has been demonstrated, and its realization is a question of time, material, and technology.

This realization will come with the construction of the new theater of glass, metal, and the inventions of tomorrow.

It depends as well upon the inner transformation of the spectator — Man as alpha and omega of every artistic creation which, even in its realization, is doomed to remain Utopia so long as it does not find intellectual and spiritual receptivity and response.

■ ■ ■

Source

Schlemmer, O. (1924, 1961) 'Man and Art Figure', in W. Gropius and A. Wensinger (eds) *The Theater of the Bauhaus*, Middletown, Conn.: Wesleyan: 17–32.

Oskar Schlemmer (1888–1943)

German painter, choreographer, dancer, theorist, teacher. Schlemmer trained as a painter in Stuttgart, and became increasingly interested in the other arts and attracted to dance. He described ideas for a new type of dance as early as 1912.[1] In 1920 he became Master of the Stone Masonry Workshop at the newly created Bauhaus (1919) in Weimar, under Walter Gropius. He designed productions at Stuttgart Landestheater, including Kokoschka's *Murderer, Hope of Women*. His most famous choreography, *The Triadic Ballet*, was completed and premièred in Stuttgart on 30 September 1922. He was Head of the Bauhaus Stage Workshop 1923–29 in Dessau, working with Kurt Schmidt, Xanti Schawinsky and Wassily Kandinsky. He made a number of works, *Dances for the Experimental Stage*, including *Gesture Dance* (1926) and *Stick Dance* (1927). When Meyer took over the Bauhaus (1929), Schlemmer left, rather than sacrifice his ideals. *The Triadic Ballet* was restaged for Rolf de Maré's International Choreographic Competition, Paris (1932). Schlemmer became a professor at art schools in Breslau, then in Berlin. In 1933, following the ascendancy of Nazism (and attendant disapproval of modernism), he was dismissed as 'degenerate' by the authorities. The Bauhaus was dissolved in the same year. During the Second World War he was a worker in an enamel factory, before taking his life in 1943.

The Bauhaus was perhaps the most important art school of the twentieth century, certainly one of the most influential. Its example of democratising the distinctions between artists and craftsmen, theory and practice, and between the arts is unparalleled. Significantly, it had an experimental stage workshop; dance was central to this experiment, and there was a lively interface between choreography and art.[2]

In this article Schlemmer describes the theoretical foundations of theatre in terms of relationships between the stage, the performer, and its visual constituents. It ranges widely and is one of the most comprehensive such statements. It was written a year after *The Triadic Ballet* and reflects this as a definitive theatre experiment of its time.

Reader cross-references

Appia – a contemporary on visual theatre
Craig – a contemporary, and to whom Schlemmer refers
Cunningham and **Cage** – the Black Mountain Connection
Kantor – a later concern with sculptural qualities of performance
Meyerhold and **Piscator** – concern with staging
Richter – a contemporary, but different, art perspective – Dada
Wigman – contemporary, European modern dance – the individual and expression
Anderson and **Wilson** – later views of visual theatre

Further reading

bitterberg, k.-g. (1968, 1975) *bauhaus*, stuttgart: institut für auslandsbeziehungen.
Scheyer, E. (1970) 'The Shapes of Space: The Art of Mary Wigman and Oskar Schlemmer', *Dance Perspectives* 41, Spring.
Schlemmer, O. (1969, 1971) *Man: Teaching Notes from the Bauhaus*, trans. J. Seligman, London: Lund Humphries.

Notes

1   Described in his diaries but not realised until 1916. Contemporaneous with Kandinsky's similar *Der Gelbe Klange* (1912) and with the first seasons of the Ballet Russe from 1909.
2   This valuable connection continued at Black Mountain College, USA in the 1950s (see Cage and Cunningham) and, more informally, at Judson in the 1960s.

Chapter 38

Wole Soyinka

THEATRE IN AFRICAN TRADITIONAL CULTURES: SURVIVAL PATTERNS

E VEN WHERE other resources of pre-colonial society are
unevenly shared, culture tends to suggest a comparatively
even-handed distribution or – perhaps more simply – mass
appropriation. This may help to explain why it is always a
primary target of assault by an invading force. As an instrument of self-definition, its destruction or successful attrition
reaches into the reserves of racial/national will on a comprehensive scale. Conversely, the commencement of resistance and
self-liberation by the suppressed people is not infrequently
linked with the survival strategies of key cultural patterns,
manifested through various art forms. The experience of
West Africa has been no different. The history of West African
theatre in the colonial period reveals itself therefore as largely
a history of cultural resistance and survival. Confronted by the
hostility of both Islamic and Christian values, in addition to the
destructive imperatives of colonialism, it has continued until
today to vitalize contemporary theatrical forms both in the
tradition of 'folk opera' and in the works of those playwrights
and directors commonly regarded as 'Westernized'.

We must not lose sight of the fact that drama, like any
other art form, is created and executed within a specific physical environment. It naturally interacts with that environment,

is influenced by it, influences that environment in turn and acts together with the environment in the larger and far more complex history of society. The history of a dramatic pattern or its evolution is therefore very much the history of other art forms of society. And when we consider art forms from the point of view of survival strategies, the dynamics of cultural interaction with society become even more aesthetically challenging and fulfilling. We discover, for instance, that under certain conditions some art forms are transformed into others – simply to ensure the survival of the threatened forms. Drama may give way to poetry and song in order to disseminate dangerous sentiments under the watchful eye of the oppressor, the latter forms being more easily communicable. On the other hand, drama may become more manifestly invigorated in order to counteract the effect of an alienating environment.

Nigeria offers a valuable example of the dual process of cultural attenuation and resurgence. For example, theatrical professionalism was synonymous, by the middle nineteenth century, with the artistic proficiency and organisation of a particular theatrical form which had emerged from the burial rituals associated with the Oyo monarchy, the *egungun*. The question of when a performed event became theatre as opposed to ritualism is of course a vexed one that we need not bother about in this context. It is, however, commonly agreed that what started out – probably – as a ritualistic ruse to effect the funeral obsequies of an Oyo king had, by the mid-century, evolved into a theatrical form in substance and practice. From an annual celebration rite of the smuggling-in of the corpse of that king and its burial, the *egungun* ancestral play became, firstly, a court re-enactment, then a secular form of performance which was next appropriated by the artists themselves. Its techniques were perfected by family guilds and township cults. About this time, however, Islam had begun its push southwards. The Oyo empire, already in disintegration from internal rivalries and other stresses, found itself under increasing military pressure from the Hausa-Fulani in the north, a situation which came on the heels of a rebellion of tributary states to the south. The fall of Oyo took down with it the security which the theatrical art had enjoyed under its patronage. The Muslims, victorious in northern Yorubaland, banned most forms of theatrical performance as contrary to the spirit of Islam. The *Agbegijo, Alarinjo* and allied genres, with their dramatic use of the paraphernalia of carved masks and other representations of ancestral spirits, came most readily under religious disapproval. It did not matter that, by now, they had lost most of their pretence to the mysterious or numinous.

Southern Nigeria and its neighbouring territories were, however, only temporary beneficiaries from this disruption of political life in the old Oyo empire. The Christian missionaries had also begun their northward drive, usually only a few steps ahead of the colonial forces. The philistinic task begun by the Moslems was rounded out by the Christians' ban on the activities of suspect cults. The Christians went further. They did not content themselves with banning just the dramatic performance; they placed their veto also on indigenous musical instruments – *bata, gangan, dundun* and so on – the very backbone of traditional theatre. It was into this vacuum that the returned slaves stepped with their Western (and therefore Christian) instruments, their definitely Christian dramatic themes and their Western forms.

Another historical factor aided the temporary eclipse of indigenous theatre forms: the slave trade and its supply which involved inter-state wars, raids and casual kidnappings. The missionary compounds often offered the securest havens from these perennial hazards, just as did (in West Africa) submission to the protective spheres of the Muslim overlords. It is difficult to imagine a group of refugees from the old Oyo empire encouraged by their Muslim or Christian protectors to revert to the ways of their 'pagan art'. The records do not reveal any such acts of disinterested artistic patronage. Artistic forms might be appropriated, but only in the cause of religious promotion; thus, for example, the appropriation of musical forms by the nineteenth-century Christian missionaries in Buganda for hymns. This, however, was only a later refinement, a sensible strategy for rendering the patently alien words and sentiments less abrasive to the indigenes by coating them in traditional harmonies.

It is difficult to trace, at present, the effect of the Oyo *egungun* dispersal on the development of theatrical forms in neighbouring areas. This is always the case with any situation of artistic hiatus – a period, that is, when a particular form of art goes underground or disappears temporarily, especially under the pressures of a dominant political and artistic ethos. The records simply ignore them, or treat them merely as isolated nuisances. The substitution of new forms belonging to the dominant culture takes pride of place in records, and this is the situation we encounter in the development of Western 'concerts' and variety shows in the colonized territories of West Africa. At this point, therefore, let us clarify in our minds what theatre is. That this is more than a merely academic exercise is easily grasped if we refer to a sister art, sculpture, an achievement which the missionary-colonizer pioneers found convenient to deny to the African. The redressing assessment was made by other Europeans – the artists themselves, notably the Expressionists; they had no overriding reasons to deny the obvious, to ignore what was even a potential source of inspiration to their own creative endeavours. The vexed question of what constitutes drama and what is merely ritual, ceremony, festival and so on, while it continues to be legitimately argued, must always be posed against an awareness of early prejudiced reading of the manifestations encountered by culture denigrators, definitions which today still form the language of orthodox theatre criticism. To assist our own definition we need look only at any one cultural event within which diversified forms are found, forms which – through their visual impact – tend towards the creation of differing categories for a comparative description. In other words if, within one performance or cluster of performances (say, a festival or a celebration) in any given community, we discover consciously differing qualitative enactments, we are obliged to rummage around in our artistic vocabulary for categories that reflect such differences. Thus we find that, sooner or later, we arrive at the moment when only the expression 'drama' or 'theatre' seems apposite, and then the search is over. We will take an example from the Afikpo masquerades of south-east Nigeria.

A contrast between the *okumkpa* event and the *oje ogwu*, both being components of this Afikpo festival, actually furnishes us with the basic definition we need. This masquerade, which is the professional handiwork of a male initiation society, varies, we discover, from basically balletic sequences as contained in the *oje ogwu* to the *mimetic* as contained in the *okumkpa*. The latter is indeed performed as a climax to what appears to be the prominent *oje ogwu* turn by the masqueraders. Both are basically audience-oriented – in other words, we are not really concerned here with the complication of a *ritual* definition but one of performance and reception. The audience plays a prominent appreciative role in this outdoor performance, judging, booing or approving on purely aesthetic grounds. Whatever symbolism may be contained in the actual movements of the *oje ogwu* is of no significance in the actual judgement. What the audience looks for and judges are the finer points of leaps, turns, control and general spatial domination. The poorer performers are soon banished to the group sessions – which demonstrates the importance given to individual technical mastery.

The *okumkpa* event, by contrast, consists of satirical mimesis. Masks are also used but the *action* forms the basis of performance. This action consists of a satirical rendition of actual events both in neighbouring settlements and in the village itself. Personalities are ridiculed, the events in which they were involved are re-enacted. In short, events are transformed artistically both for audience delectation and for the imparting of moral principles. Additionally, however, one standard repertoire consists of the taking of female roles by the young male initiates, this role being of a rather derogatory character. The satirized female is invariably what we might call 'the reluctant bride'. As the young actor minces and prances around, sung dialogues accompany him, built around the same theme: 'How much longer are you going to reject all suitors on the grounds that they are not sufficiently handsome/strong/industrious etc., etc.?' Competition is keen among the initiates for the honour of playing this central female impersonator. The various sketches in this vein are rounded off in the end by a massed parade of the various actors in the *njenji* where the less accomplished actors have their own hour of glory and the entire female world is satirically lectured on the unkindness of keeping the male rooster waiting too long.

We will not examine the sociological motivation of this kind of drama except to point out that this example is actually more rewarding, in our search for an explanation of man's motives in *dramatizing*, than, for instance, the theory of the origin in the Oyo masquerade. Clearly, in the Afikpo masquerade we encounter a male-prejudiced device. It ensures man's claim to social superiority and creates guilt in the woman for not fulfilling on demand man's need for female companionship. It is of no more mystifying an order of things than, for instance, the disparagement by male undergraduates in their press of female undergraduates who have not submitted to their own desires – except, of course, that traditional society imposed heavy penalties on libellous fabrication (which is, by the way, a reliable indication of artistic barrenness). What we obtain from one, therefore, is genuine art; from their modern progeny, alas, only dirty pictures and fevered fantasies. The *okumkpa* provides us with drama – variety, satire. We are left with no other definition when we contrast it with its consciously differentiated companion piece – the *oje ogwu*.

Similarly, festivals such as the Ogun or Osun (River) festivals in Yorubaland provide us with multi-media and multi-formal experiences within which it is not at all difficult to find unambiguous examples of dramatic enactments. The high point of the festival of the Yoruba hero-deity Obatala is, for instance, undoubted drama, consisting of all the elements that act on the emotions, the excitations of conflict and resolution and the human appreciation of spectacle. We begin to understand now why dating the origin of African drama, locating it in a specific event, time and place is an impossible task – indeed, a meaningless one. In the study of art forms, it is clearly more appealing to look into extant material for what may be deduced as primitive or early forms of the particular art, noting along the way what factors have contributed to their survival in the specific forms. Festivals, comprising as they do such a variety of forms, from the most spectacular to the most secretive and emotionally charged, offer the most familiar hunting-ground. What is more, they constitute in themselves *pure theatre* at its most prodigal and resourceful. In short, the persistent habit of dismissing festivals as belonging to a 'spontaneous' inartistic expression of communities demands re-examination. The level of organization involved, the integration of the sublime with the mundane, the endowment of the familiar with properties of the unique (and this, spread over days) all indicate that it is into the heart of many African festivals that we should look for the most stirring expressions of man's instinct and need for drama at its most comprehensive and community-involving. Herbert M. Cole renders this point of view in penetrating terms:

> A festival is a relatively rare climatic event in the life of any community. It is bounded by a definite beginning and end, and is unified thereby, as well as being set apart from the above daily life. Its structure is built on a core or armature of ritual. The festival brings about a suspension of ordinary time, a transformation of ordinary space, a formaliser of ordinary behaviour. It is as if a community becomes a stage set and its people actors with a battery of seldom-seen props and cos-tumes. Meals become feasts, and greetings, normally simple, become ceremonies. Although dependent upon life-sustaining rituals, the festival is an elaborated and stylised phenomenon which far surpasses ritual necessity. It often becomes the social, ritual and political apotheosis of community life in a year. At festival time one level of reality – the common and everyday – gives way to another, a more intense, symbolic and expressive level of reality.[1]

What this implies is that instead of considering festivals from one point of view only – that of providing, in a primitive form, the ingredients of drama – we may even begin examining the opposite point of view: that contemporary drama, as we experience it today, is a contraction of drama, necessitated by the productive order of society in other directions. That is, drama undergoes parallel changes with other structuring mechanisms of society. As communities outgrow certain patterns of producing what they require to sustain themselves or of transforming what exists around them, the structures which sustain the arts are affected in parallel ways, affecting in turn the very forms of the arts. That the earlier forms are not necessarily more 'primitive' or 'crude' is borne out by the fact that more and more of the highly developed societies are turning to the so-called 'primitive' forms of drama as representing the significant dramatic forms for contemporary society. These societies, which vary from such ideologically disparate countries as the United States and East European countries, are re-introducing on stage, in both formal theatre structures and improvised spaces, dramatic forms such as we have described, from the macro-conceptual (as represented in festivals) to the micro-conceptual, as ritual may be held to epitomize.

In this vein, what are we to make of the famous Return-to-the-Village Festival of the Koumina canton in Bobo-Dioulasso, Upper Volta?[2] Here we encounter a people who, like many others in West Africa, have experienced the culturally disrupting influences of Muslim and Christian cultures. The traders came first, the Mande traders, in the early sixteenth century. In their next significant migration, the mid-eighteenth century, they were accompanied by Muslim clerics, with the cultural results with which we are by now familiar. By 1775 proselytization had become so successful that an Imamate had been established by the famous Saghnughu family of scholars. The late nineteenth century saw the take-over by colonial administrators and Christian missionaries. Yet under this double assault, Bobo traditional arts have survived until today, and nowhere are they given more vital expression than in the 'Tagaho' season festival which marks the return of the Bobo to their village after their seasonal migrations to their farmsteads. The festival, which has for its core the funeral ceremonies for those who died during the period of farmland migration, has a far more important function for the living: the re-installation of the cohering, communal spirit and existential reality. Costumes are elaborately prepared, formal patterns both of 'ritual' and 'pageant' worked out and rehearsed, individual events enacted by masked figures for a delayed participation by the community as one entity. It is all of course a conscious performance, informed and controlled by aesthetic ideas, by the competitive desire also of 'showing off' dramatic skills. Simultaneously it is an affirmation of social solidarity. Can this form of theatre, considered in its most fundamental purpose and orientation, be viewed much differently from the theatre of 'happenings' which began in America and Europe in the sixties and is still encountered in parts of those societies today? To be sure, the former is more disciplined, formal and community-inspired, which are all attributes that we experience from unalienating forms of theatre.

At this point, it may be useful to consider instances where an art form evolves into another art form in one geographical/cultural area but fails to do so in another. The heroic tradition is one that is common to most parts of Africa (and, indeed, to most societies). Within this tradition may be grouped, at any level of its development, the epic, saga, praise-chants, ballads and so on, but here we are concerned with the performance aspect from which dramatization most naturally evolves. East, Central and South Africa are particularly rich in the tradition of the heroic recitative. Among the Luo of Kenya and Uganda, for instance, we may note the form known as the *pakrouk*, a kind of virtue-boasting which takes place at ceremonial gatherings, usually to the accompaniment of a harp. The individual performer emerges from the group, utters praises of his own person and his achievements, and is replaced or contended with by another. Similar manifestations are found among the Ankole tribes, while further south, among the Sotho and the Zulu, sustained lyrical recitations on important historical events have become highly developed.

Among the Ijaw people of south-eastern Nigeria, however, the same tradition has actually developed dramatic variants, has moved beyond the merely recited to the enacted, a *tour de force* sustained by a principal actor for over three days. The saga of *Ozidi*, the principal source for J.P. Clark's play of the same name, is an example. By contrast, the history of the performance arts in Central and Southern Africa reveals a tendency towards virtual stasis of the putative dramatic elements. Even the dramatic potential of such rituals as the *Nyasi-iye*, the boat-building and launching ceremonies of the Luo, with its symbolic cutting of the 'umbilical cord' as the boat is freed from its moorings, even the abundant parallelisms with nuptial rites, have somehow failed to move towards a truly dramatic render-ing of the significance and life-intertwining role of the boats in the daily pre-occupations of the Luo. One need only contrast this with the various rites and festivals of the coastal and riverine peoples of West Africa, where both religious observances and economic practicalities of the same activity have taken on, over the centuries, a distinctly dramatic ordering. One may speculate at length on the reasons for this contrast; the reality remains, however, that drama as an integral phenomenon in the lives of the peoples of Central and Southern Africa has followed a comparatively meagre devel-opment.

Well then, let us, using one of our early examples, follow how tradi-tional theatre forms adjusted or re-surfaced from the preliminary repressions of alien cultures. We find that the 'pagan' theatre ultimately withstood the onslaught, not only preserving its forms but turning itself consciously into a base of resistance against both dominating systems. We are able to witness the closing of a cycle of cultural substitution in a curious irony of this slavery-colonial experience. Having first broken up the cultural life of the people, the slave era, now in its dying phase in the first half of the nineteenth century, brought back the sons of the land with a new culture in place of the old. The returnees constituted a new elite: they possessed after all the cultural tools of the colonial masters. But – and now we emphasize the place of theatre among these cultural tools – even where they were fully assimilated into the cultural values of their erstwhile masters (or saviours), they found on their return company servants, civil servants, missionary converts who belonged in the same social class as themselves, but were culturally unalien-ated. These stay-at-homes had had what was more or less an equivalent colonial education, yet had also acquired a nationalist awareness which mani-fested itself in cultural attitudes. As the nineteenth century entered its last quarter, the stay-at-homes were able to provide a balancing development pattern to cultural life on the West coast which came predominantly under the creative influence of the returnee Christians, despite the latter's confi-dence in the superiority of their acquired arts and their eagerness to prove to the white population that the black man was capable not only of receiving but also of practising the refined arts of the European.

The cultural difference between the settlers of Liberia and Sierra Leone on the one hand, and the coastal societies of Ghana and Nigeria on the other can be translated in terms of the degree of cultural identification with, and adaptation of the authentic resources of the hinterland. To the former – mostly returnee slaves – the indigenous people remained savage, crude and barbaric, to be regarded only as material for missionary conversion and possible education. The converts who had remained at home, however, set off a process of schisms within social and religious institutions whose value-system was Eurocentric, delving again and again into the living resources of indigenous society. Naturally there were exceptions on both sides, but this dichotomy did hold in general. The direction of *new* forms of theatrical entertainment therefore followed an eastward pattern from the new returnee settlements; inevitably it received increasing native blood-transfusion as it moved further east away from the bastardized vaudeville of the 'Nova Scotians', so that by the time it arrived in Ghana, Dahomey (now Benin) and Nigeria, both in form and content, a distinct West African theatrical idiom had evolved.

'Academies', to begin with, were formed for the performance of concerts which were modelled on the Victorian music hall or the American vaudeville. The Christian churches organized their own concerts, schools were drawn into the concert rage – prize-giving days, visits of the District Officer, Queen Victoria's birthday and so on. The black missionaries refused to be outdone; Rev. Ajayi Crowther was a famous example, a black prelate who patronized and encouraged this form of the arts, while the Rev. James Johnson turned the famous Breadfruit church in Lagos into a springboard for theatrical performances. The Brazilian returnees added an exotic yet familiar flavour, their music finding a ready echo in the traditional melodies of the West Coast and the Congo whose urban suppression had not occurred long enough for such melodies to be totally forgotten. At the turn of the century and in the first decades of the twentieth century, Christmas and New Year saw the streets of the capital cities of Freetown and Lagos transformed by mini-pageants reminiscent of Latin fiestas, of which the 'caretta', a kind of satyr masquerade, appears to have been the most durable.

Cultural nationalism was, however, constantly at work against a total usurpation by imported forms. Once again religion and its institutions provided the base. Unable to accept the excesses of the Christian cultural imperialism, such as the embargo on African instruments and tunes in a 'universal' church, and the prohibition of drumming on tranquil Anglican Sundays, the breakaway movements began. The period 1888 to the early 1930s witnessed a proliferation of secessionist movements, mostly inspired by a need to worship God in the cultural mode of the forefathers. And now began also a unique 'operatic' tradition in West Africa, but especially Lagos, beginning with church cantatas which developed into dramatizations of biblical stories until it asserted its independence in secular stories and the development of professional touring troupes. The process, reminiscent of the evolution of the 'miracle' or 'mystery' plays of medieval Europe, is identical with the evolution of the Agbegijo theatre (then temporarily effaced) from the sacred funeral rites of the Alafin of Oyo to court entertainment and, thereafter, independent existence and geographical dispersion. From the genteel concerts of classical music and English folk songs by the 'Academy' of the 1880s to the historical play *King Elejigbo* of the Egbe Ife Church Dramatic Society in 1902, a transformation of thought and sensibility had recognizably taken place even among the Westernized elite of southern Nigeria. The Churches did not take kindly to it. They closed their church-yards and schools to the evolving art. Alas, they only succeeded in accelerating the defiant erection of theatre halls, specifically designed for the performing arts. It was in reality a tussle between groups of colonial elites, fairly balanced in the matter of resources. By 1912 the secularization of theatrical enter-tainment in southern Nigeria was sufficiently advanced for the colonial government to gazette a 'Theatre and Public Performance Regulations Ordinance', which required that performing groups obtain a licence before going before the public. In the climate of cultural nationalism which obtained in Lagos at that time, it is doubtful whether this disguised attempt at polit-ical censorship would have worked; it is significant that the ordinance was never made into law.

Ironically, yet another breakaway church, the Cherubim and Seraphim movement, swung the pendulum back towards a rejection of traditional forms and was followed shortly by other emulators in the Christian re-consecration of theatrical forms. The furthest these churches would go in the use of musical instruments was the tambourine; local instruments which had created a new tonality in the operettas now touring the West Coast – sekere, dundun, gangan, and so on – were damned as instruments of the Devil. Secular stories, even of historic personages and events, were banned and the new theatre halls, church halls and schoolrooms echoed once more to the Passion of Christ, the anguish of Nebuchadnezzar, the trials of Job, and other dramatic passages from the Bible. The Aladura, Cherubim and Seraphim, and their adherents did not however stop there. These 'prophetist' cults spread rapidly along the West Coast waging a crusade against all 'pagan' worship and their sacred objects. Descending on the provinces of the established churches, they ignited bonfires with their hot-gospelling in which perished thousands of works of art, especially in Nigeria, Cameroons, Ghana and the Ivory Coast. The vision of a fifteen-year-old girl, Abiodun Akinsowon, about 1921, was to prove a costly dream for the cultural heritage of West Africa, the heaviest brunt of which was borne by Yoruba sculpture. This period may also be justly said to constitute the lowest ebb in the fortunes of traditional theatre, participation in the cultural life even of the villages being subjected to lightning descents from the fanatical hordes of the prophetic sects. In the physical confrontations that often took place, the position of authority was predictable. Embarrassed as they sometimes were by the excesses of the sectarians, the European missionaries and their black priests had no hesitation about their alliances – and their voice was weighty in the processes of imposing the colonial peace.

But the 'vaudeville' troupes prospered. Names of groups such as we encounter in 'Two Bobs and their Carolina Girl' tell us something of the inspiration of much of these. Master Yalley, a schoolteacher, is credited with having begun the tradition of the vaudeville variety act in Ghana. His pupil Bob Johnson and his 'Axim Trio' soon surpassed the master and became a familiar figure on Ghana's cultural landscape, also later in Nigeria. More important still, Bob Johnson's innovations must be credited with having given birth to the tradition of the 'concert party' of Ghana, groups which specialize in variety routine: songs, jokes, dances, impersonations, comic scenes. However, the most notable achievement in the sense of cultural continuity was their thrusting on to the fore-state of contemporary repertoire a stock character from traditional lore, the wily trickster Anansi. This quickly developed into a vehicle for social and political commentary, apart from its popularity in comic situations.

The Jaguar Jokers, for example, transformed Anansi into the more urban character of Opia, while Efua Sutherland's more recent *The Marriage of Anansewa* takes this tradition into an even more tightly-knit and disciplined play format – the term 'disciplined' being employed here merely in the sense of reducing the areas of spontaneous improvization, without however eliminating them. Those who saw this piece during Festac 77 will have observed how attractively the element of formal discipline and free improvization blended together to encourage a controlled audience interaction. By the middle 1930s, Bob Johnson had become sufficiently established to take his brand of vaudeville to other West African cities. West Africa in this decade could boast of a repertoire of shows displaying the most bizarre products of eclectic art in the history of theatre. Even cinema, an infant art, had by then left its mark on West African theatre: some of Bob Johnson's acts were adaptations of Charlie Chaplin's escapades, not omitting his costume and celebrated shuffle. And the thought of Empire Day celebration concerts at which songs like 'Mini the Moocher' formed part of the evening musical recitals, side by side with 'God's Gospel is our Heritage' and vignettes from the life of a Liberian stevedore, stretches the contemporary imagination, distanced from the historical realities of colonial West Africa.

Again, another irony of colonial intentions: while Bob Johnson was preparing his first West African tour and Hubert Ogunde, later to become Nigeria's foremost 'concert party' leader, was undergoing his aesthetic formation from the vying forces of a clergyman father and a grandmother who was a priestess of the *Osugbo* cult, a European educationist, Charles Beart in Senegal, was beginning to reverse the policy of European acculturation in a leading secondary school in Senegal. The extent of this development – including also an appreciation of the slow pace of such an evolution – will be better grasped by recalling the educational charter of assimilationism, spelt in diverse ways by the publications of such dedicated African Francophiles as the Abbe Boillat, Paul Holle and so on. Boillat, in spite of extensive sociological research (*Esquisses senegalaises*),[3] the result of his examination of the culture and philosophy of the Bambara, Sarakole, Wolof, Serer, the Tukulor and Moorish groups in Senegal, found no lessons to be drawn from African society for modern cultural development, no future but to witness the fall of all those 'gross, if not dishonourable, ways known as the *custom of the country*'. If his addresses to the metropolitan centre of the French world did not become the cornerstone of French assimilationist policies, they undoubtedly played a key role in their formulation. Against this background, and ensuring decades of such conservatism, the Ecole William Ponty was founded. A famous teachers' college, it served Francophone Africa in the same way as did Achimota College in the Anglophone West and Makerere College in East Africa. They were all designed to provide a basic European education for would-be teachers and low-echelon civil servants. Such humanistic education as came into the curriculum of the Ecole William Ponty was of necessity French – French plays, poetry, music, art, history. Charles Beart, during his principalship, embarked however on a new orientation of the students' cultural instructions. From 1930 onwards the students were encouraged to return to their own societies for cultural directions. Assignments were given which resulted in the students' exploration of both the form and the substance of indigenous art. Groups from every colonial territory represented at William Ponty were then expected to return from vacation armed with a theatrical presentation based on their researches, the entire direction being left in the hands of the students themselves. Since the new theatrical sociology did not confine itself to the usual audiences of European officials and 'educated' Africans, nor to Senegal alone, its influence spread widely through different social strata of French-speaking Africa. Was it, however, a satisfying development of the culture from which it derived?

The answer must be in the negative, though the experiment was not without its instructive values. It would be too much to expect that, at that period, the classic model of French theatre could yield completely to the expression of traditional forms. The community represented by William

Ponty was an artificial one. It was distanced from the society whose cultural hoard it rifled both in qualitative thought and material product. The situation was of course not peculiar to William Ponty since it also obtained in the other schools and institutions set up by the colonizer for the fulfilment of his own mission in Africa. Thus the theatre of William Ponty served the needs of exotic satisfaction for the community of French colonials. Even when it 'went to the people', and with their own material, it remained a curiosity that left the social life and authentic cultural awareness of the people untouched.

We will conclude with the 'new' theatre form which has proved the most durable; hybrid in its beginnings, the 'folk opera' has become the most expressive language of theatre in West Africa. What were the themes that mostly engaged the various groups spread along the Coast? The Nigerian Hubert Ogunde provides a convenient compendium, since he does appear to be more consistently varied in his dramatic fare than any comparable group to date in West Africa. His repertoire ranges from outright fantasy through biblical dramatizations to social commentary and political protest, both in the colonial and post-colonial era. A comparative study of the repertoire of the Jaguar Jokers, the Axim Trio, or the current Anansekrom groups of Ghana for example would reveal that these concentrate almost exclusively on social commentary, mostly with a moralistic touch – the evils of witchcraft, maladjustment in the social status of the cash-crop nouveaux riches, generational problems, changing status of women in society, sexual mores and so on, all of which also preoccupy the pamphlet drama of the Onitsha market literateurs. Hubert Ogunde explored these themes in his plays and more. His biblical adaptations became in effect a vehicle for direct commentaries on contemporary society. Reference is hardly necessary to those plays which have earned him the ire of colonial and post-colonial governments: Bread and Bullets, a play not merely on the famous Iva Valley strike by miners in eastern Nigeria but on the general inequity of labour exploitation; and Yoruba Ronu, an indictment of the corruption and repression of the government of the then Western Region. Both plays were proscribed by the affected governments. They have entered the lore of theatrical commitment in Nigeria.

And additionally, Hubert Ogunde exemplifies what we have referred to up until now as the survival patterns of traditional theatrical art. From the outset of his theatrical career, Ogunde's theatre belonged only partially to what we have described as the 'Nova Scotian' tradition. His musical instrumentation was all borrowed from the West, movement on stage was pure Western chorus-line night-club variety. Nevertheless, the attachment to traditional musical forms (albeit with Western impurities) gradually became more assertive. Encouraged no doubt by the appearance of more tradition-grounded

353

groups such as Kola Ogunmola and Duro Ladipo, Hubert Ogunde in the early sixties began to employ traditional instruments in his performance, his music delved deeper into home melodies, and even his costumes began to eschew the purely fabricated, theatrically glossy, for recognizable local gear. Rituals appeared with greater frequency and masquerades became a frequent feature – often, it must be added, as gratuitous insertions. Ogunde's greatest contribution to West African drama – quite apart from his innovative energy and his commitment to a particular political line – lies in his as yet little appreciated musical 'recitative' style, one which he has made unique to himself. It has few imitators, but the success of his records in this genre of 'dramatic monologue' testifies to the responsive chord it elicits from his audience. Based in principle on the Yoruba *rara* style of chanting, but in stricter rhythm, it is melodically a modernistic departure, flexibly manipulated to suit a variety of themes. Once again, we find that drama draws on other art forms for its own survival and extension. It is no exaggeration to claim that Hubert Ogunde's highest development of the chanted dramatic monologue can be fixed at the period of the political ban on his *Yoruba Ronu*. Evidently all art forms flow into one another, confirming, as earlier claimed, that the temporary historic obstacles to the flowering of a particular form sometimes lead to its transformation into other media of expression, or even the birth of totally different groups.

This survey stops at the emergence of the latest forms of traditional drama. The finest representatives of this to date have been the late Kola Ogunmola (comedy and satire) and Duro Ladipo (history and tragedy). Their contribution to contemporary drama and their innovations from indigenous forms require a far more detailed study, just as Moses Olaiya (Baba Sala) demands a chapter of his own iconoclastic brand of theatrical wit. The foregoing attempts to highlight ways in which artistic forms return to life again and again after their seeming demise, ways by which this process emphasizes the fundamental unity of various art forms and the social environment that gives expression to them; how certain creative ideas are the very offspring of historic convulsions. Finally, while for purposes of demarcation we may speak of Nigerian, Ghanaian or perhaps Togolese drama, it must constantly be borne in mind that, like the economic intercourse of the people themselves, the various developments we have touched upon here in drama and the arts do not obey the laws of political boundaries though they might respond to the events within them. The various artistes we have mentioned had, and still enjoy, instant *rapport* with audiences far from their national and linguistic boundaries. Their art finds a ready response in most audiences since their themes are rooted in everyday experience, fleshed out in shared idioms of cultural adjustment.

Notes

1   Herbert M. Cole in *African arts*, VIII (3).
2   Now renamed Burkina Faso.
3   Abbe Boillat, *Esquisses Sénégalaises*, 1858; new edition, Paris, 1984, Editions Karthala.

∎   ∎   ∎

Source

Soyinka, W. (1982, 1988, 1993) 'Theatre in African Traditional Cultures: Survival Patterns', *Art, Dialogue and Outrage*, ed. B. Jeyifo, London: Methuen: 134–146.

Originally published in 1982 in *African History and Culture* and first republished in 1988 by New Horn Press.

Wole Soyinka (1934–)

Nigerian playwright, novelist, critic, poet, essayist. He was born and educated in Nigeria, then in England where he lived (1954–70). He worked for the Royal Court, London (1957–59) where excerpts from his early plays were produced. *The Swamp Dwellers* was produced in London in 1957, then in Ibadan, Nigeria with *The Lion and the Jewel* (1959). Soyinka produced plays in both Nigeria and England, notably *A Dance of the Forests* (1963). He worked at the University of Ife, then the University of Lagos, and in 1969 was appointed Head of Theatre at the University of Ibadan. He continued to write extensively there, then later at the University of Ife.

Soyinka's writing became recognised world-wide and in 1986 he was awarded the Nobel prize for literature. At the same time, in his own country, he was arrested and detained for his intellectual and political views on a number of occasions, especially for the two years 1967–69 (described in *The Man Died*, 1979). He has continued to speak out against injustice, however unpopular this has made him. He left Nigeria in 1994.[1]

Soyinka's work is remarkable for the way it combines a profound understanding of the history and myths of the Yoruba and other African peoples and his ability to draw on a wide range of sources from both the European and Asian traditions. He is truly a pan-cultural writer and has been at the forefront of such a worldview for some thirty years.

This essay is about the resilience of West African theatre forms within the wider contexts of both Christian and Muslim colonisers. It shows a deep understanding of all three cultures and the interplay between them at the level of performance.

Reader cross-references

Artaud, Grotowski and **Barba** – European notions of ritual
Barthes – with whom Soyinka takes issue
Benjamin – comparative, European intellectual stance
Bharucha and **Hijikata** – different notions of the traditional

Further reading

Jones, E.D. (1973) *The Writings of Wole Soyinka*, London: Heinemann.
Soyinka, W. (1974) *Collected Plays 1 and 2*, Oxford: Oxford University Press.

Note

1   The way in which he was treated as an intellectual in Nigeria was reported, after his departure, in S. Hughes (1994) 'Long road to freedom', *Times Higher Education Supplement* No. 1151, 25 November: 1.

Chapter 39

Konstantin Stanislavski

INTONATIONS
AND PAUSES

1

IN THE AUDITORIUM of the school theatre we found, when we came in to-day, a large placard with the words 'Speech on the Stage'. As is his custom Tortsov congratulated us on reaching a new phase in our work:

'At our last lesson I explained to you that actors must acquire the feel of vowels and consonants of syllables, get inside them.

'To-day we go on, in the same way, to consider whole words and phrases. Do not expect me to read you a lecture on the subject, that is the job of a specialist. All I shall tell you concerns several aspects of the art of speaking on the stage that I have learned about in my own practical experience. It will help you in your approach to your new studies in the 'laws of speech!'

'Many fine books have been written about these laws and about words. Study them carefully. The most appropriate to the needs of Russian actors is the well worked out book of S.M. Volkonski on *The Expressive Word*. I shall be constantly having recourse to it, I shall quote it and draw examples from it in these introductory lessons on stage speech. An actor should know his own tongue in every particular. Of what use will all the subtleties of emotion be if they are expressed in poor speech? A first-class musician should never play on an instrument out of tune. In this field of speech we need science but we must be intelligent and forehanded about acquiring it. There is no point in filling our heads with a lot of new ideas and rushing on the stage to exploit them before we have learned the elementary rules. That kind of a student will lose his head, he will either forget his science or think about it to the exclusion of everything else. Science can help art only when they support and complement each other.'

Tortsov reflected for a moment and then went on:

'You have often heard me say that each person who goes on to the stage has to re-train himself from the beginning: to see, walk, move about, hold intercourse with people and, finally, to speak. The vast majority of people make use of poor, vulgar ways of speaking in ordinary life, but they are not aware of this because they are accustomed to these defects in themselves and in others. I do not say that you are an exception to this rule. Therefore, before you begin your regular speech work it is absolutely necessary to be made aware of the deficiencies in your speech so that you can break yourselves permanently of the habit, widespread among actors, of giving their own incorrect everyday speech as an excuse for the slovenly ways of speaking on the stage.

'Words and the way they are spoken show up much more on the stage than in ordinary life. In most theatres actors are required to repeat the text half-way decently. Even this is done in a slipshod, routine way.

'There are many reasons for this and the first of them is that in ordinary life one says what one is obliged to, or what one desires to, for a purpose, to accomplish an end, because of necessity or, actually, for the sake of some real, fruitful, pointed verbal action. It even happens rather frequently that even when one chatters along without paying much attention to the words, one is still using them for a reason: to pass the time quickly, to distract the attention and so on.

'On the stage it is different. There we speak the text of another, the author's, and often it is at variance with our needs and desires.

'Moreover in ordinary life we talk about things we actually see or have in our minds, things that actually exist. On the stage we have to talk about things we do not see, feel, think about for ourselves but in the imaginary persons of our parts.

'In ordinary life we know how to listen, because we are interested in or need to hear something. On the stage, in most cases, all we do is make a pretence of attentive listening. We do not feel any practical necessity to penetrate the thoughts and words of our stage partner. We have to oblige ourselves to do it. And that forcing ends in over-acting, routine, clichés.

'There are other distressing circumstances too, which tend to kill lively human reactions. The lines, repeated so often in rehearsals and numerous performances, are parroted. The inner content of the text evaporates, all that is left is mechanical sound. In order to earn the right to be on the stage the actors have to be doing something. One of the things they do to fill up the blank spaces inside their parts is to engage in automatic repetition of their lines.

'The consequence of this is that actors acquire a habit of mechanical speech on the stage, the thoughtless parrot-like pronunciation of lines learned by heart without any regard for their inner essence. The more rein they give to this habit, the keener their mechanical memory, the more stubborn the habit of such prattle becomes. And gradually we see the development of a specifically stereotyped kind of stage speech.

'In ordinary life we also meet with mechanical expressions such as: "How do you do?" "Pretty well, thank you." Or "Good-bye. Best of luck!"

'What is a person thinking of while he is saying those automatic words? He is subject neither to the thought nor the feeling essentially contained in them. They just pop out of us while we are absorbed by entirely different interests. We see the same thing in school. While a pupil is reciting something he has learned by rote he is often thinking about his own affairs and the mark the teacher will give him. Actors are prone to the same habits.

'To such actors the feelings and ideas of a part are step-children. In the beginning, when they first read the play the words, both their own lines and those of the others who play opposite them, seem interesting, new; they have some point. But after they have heard them kicked around at rehearsal, the words lose all essential meaning. They do not exist in the hearts or even in the consciousness of the actors, but only in the muscles of their tongues. By then it makes little difference to him what his or anyone else's lines are. The only important thing is to keep going, never to stop in his tracks.

'How senseless it is when an actor on the stage, without even hearing out what is being said to or asked of him, without allowing a thought, even an important one, to be fully expressed to him, hurries to break in on his partner's lines. It also happens that the key word in a cue is so skimped that it does not reach the public, so that the sense of the reply to it is entirely lost, the partner has nothing to reply to. There is no use in his asking to have the question repeated because the first actor has no real comprehension of what he was asking in the first place. All these falsifications add up to conventional, cliché acting which kills all belief in the lines spoken and in their living content.

'The situation is worsened of course when actors consciously give an incorrect turn to their lines. We all know that many of them use their lines as a vehicle to exhibit some vocal attributes, diction, manner of recitation, the technique of their voice production. Such actors have no more relation to art than the salesman of musical instruments who brashly demonstrates his wares by pyrotechnical execution, not for the purpose of conveying the intent of the composer, but merely to sell the instrument.

'Actors do the same when they indulge in calculated cadences and technical effects by emphasizing individual letters of syllables, crooning over or bellowing them without any purpose other than to show off their voices, and to make the eardrums of their hearers tingle with pleasant admiration.'

2

Tortsov began with a question to-day: What do we mean by subtext? What is it that lies behind and beneath the actual words of a part?

He expressed his answer this way:

'It is the manifest, the inwardly felt expression of a human being in a part, which flows uninterruptedly beneath the words of the text, giving them life and a basis for existing. The subtext is a web of innumerable, varied inner patterns inside a play and a part, woven from "magic ifs", given circumstances, all sorts of figments of the imagination, inner movements, objects of attention, smaller and greater truths and a belief in them, adaptations, adjustments and other similar elements. It is the subtext that makes us say the words we do in a play.

'All these intentionally intertwined elements are like the individual threads in a cable, they run all through the play and lead to the ultimate super-objective.

'It is only when our feelings reach down into the subtextual stream that the "through line of action" of a play or a part comes into being. It is made manifest not only by physical movements but also by speech: it is possible to act not only with the body but also with sound, with words.

'What we call the through line as related to action has its equivalent in the subtext, as related to speech.

'It is superfluous to state that a word taken separately and devoid of inner content is nothing but an external name. The text of a part if it is made up of no more than that will be a series of empty sounds.

'Take as an example the word "love". For a foreigner it is only a strange combination of letters. It is an empty sound because it is devoid of all the inner connotations which quicken the heart. But let feelings, thoughts, imagination give life to the empty sound and an entirely different attitude is produced, the word becomes significant. Then the sounds 'I love' acquire the power to fire a man with passion and change the course of his whole life.

'The word "onward" when inwardly coloured by patriotic emotion is capable of leading regiments to sure death. The simplest words, that convey complex thoughts affect our whole outlook on the world. It is not for nothing that the word has become the most concrete expression of man's thought.

'A word can arouse in him all five senses. One needs to do no more than recall the title of a piece of music, the name of a painter, of a dish, of favourite perfumes and so on and one immediately resurrects the auditory and visual images, tastes, smells or tactile sensations suggested by the word.

'It can bring back painful sensations. In *My Life in Art* a story about a toothache caused a toothache in the person who heard it.

'There should never be any soulless or feelingless words used on the stage. Words should no more be divorced from ideas there than from action. On the stage it is the part of the word to arouse all sorts of feelings, desires, thoughts, inner images, visual, auditory and other sensations in the actor, in those playing opposite him and through them together in the audience.

'This suggests that the spoken word, the text of a play is not valuable in and of itself, but is made so by the inner content of the subtext and what is contained in it. This is something we are prone to forget when we step on to the stage.

'We are also inclined to forget that the printed play is not a finished piece of work until it is played on the stage by actors and brought to life by genuine human emotions; the same can be said of a musical score, it is not really a symphony until it is executed by an orchestra of musicians in a concert. As soon as people, either actors or musicians, breathe the life of their own sentiment into the subtext of a piece of writing to be conveyed to an audience, the spiritual well springs, the inner essence is released – the real things which inspired the writing of the play, the poem, the score of music. The whole point of any such creation is in the underlying subtext. Without it the words have no excuse for being presented on the stage. When they are spoken the words come from the author, the subtext from the actor. If this were not so the public would not make the effort of coming to the theatre, they would sit at home and read the printed play.

'Yet it is only on the stage that a drama can be revealed in all its full-ness and significance. Only in a performance can we feel the true spirit which animates a play and its subtext – this is recreated, and conveyed by the actors every time the play is given.

'It is up to the actor to compose the music of his feelings to the text of his part and learn how to sing those feelings in words. When we hear the melody of a living soul we then, and only then, can come to a full appreci-ation of the worth and beauty of the lines and of all that they hold concealed.

'From your earlier work in this school you are familiar with the inner line of a part with its progressive action leading to the super-objective. You know too how these lines are formed to create an inner state in which you live your part, and how you have recourse to the aids of psycho-technique when this does not occur spontaneously.

'This whole process is equally valid and necessary in the relation to the spoken word.'

■   ■   ■

Source

Stanislavski, K. (1950), Intonations and Pauses, (parts 1 and 2), *Building a Character*, trans. E.R. Hapgood, London: Max Reinhardt: 109–115.
Completed in 1930 and first published in English in 1950.

Konstantin Stanislavski (1863–1938)

Russian actor and director. The work and teaching of Stanislavski have been the major influence on actor training in Europe in the twentieth century. It is still the only substantial and completely worked-out method of acting available. Brecht's and Meyerhold's attempts at recording their training methods are, by comparison, crude and partial. Stanislavski's System, as it has come to be known, is available in two major books, *An Actor Prepares*, and *Building a Character*, first published in English in 1936 and 1950 respectively. They are the result of a life of directing and training actors, mostly those of the Moscow Art Theatre, which Stanislavski founded with Vladimir Nemirovitch-Danchenko in 1898. The company became associated in particular with the plays of Anton Chekov, and it is mainly to the problems of producing Chekov's plays that much of the advice of the System refers. As such it is taught all over Europe and the USA, China, and parts of the rest of the world. In a modified form, known as the Method, it has trained many of the best North American performers, and has been a profound influence on Hollywood. In the UK most professional drama schools are still dedicated to exploring the implications of the System. It is thus the most pervasive performer training conducted in the Western world, and has held its own against the tide of anti-naturalist approaches unleashed in modern and postmodern contexts.

In this extract from *Building a Character* Stanislavski deliberately uses a fictional situation – the actors and teachers in a studio – in order to give the sense of a practical acting method. The book is essentially a guide to the attainment of a certain style, but it is interesting to note the emphasis that Stanislavski puts on observation and analysis of everyday human behaviour as a basis for discovering a way of internalising knowledge of which the results will be shown on stage. In this emphasis he agrees with Brecht, for whom observation was the paramount performer's skill.

Reader cross-references

Artaud – a contemporary, but different, approach
Beck – similar intensity of purpose in training
Boal and **Barba** – alternative training methods
Brecht – similar insights to opposing ends
Craig – the *Hamlet* collaboration
Duncan – a contemporary whom Stanislavski admired for her performance
Humphrey – a systematised approach to dance
Martin – who considers Stanislavski in defining modernism in dance
Meyerhold – an opposing Russian method
Wigman – a contemporary, dance viewpoint

Further reading

Benedetti, J. (1988) *Stanislavski: A Biography*, London: Methuen.
Nemirovitch-Danchenko, V. (1936) *My Life in the Russian Theatre*, trans. J. Conrad, New York: Theatre Arts Books.
Stanislavski, K. (1924) *My Life in Art*, trans. J.J. Robbins, London: Geoffrey Bles.

Chapter 40

Mary Wigman

THE PHILOSOPHY
OF MODERN DANCE

T HE DANCE is one of many human experiences which cannot be
suppressed. Dancing has existed at all times, and among all people and
races. The dance is a form of expression given to man just as speech, philosophy, painting or music. Like music, the dance is a language which all human
beings understand without the use of speech. Granted, the dance is as little
an everyday expression as music: the man who begins to dance because of
an inner urge does so perhaps from a feeling of joyousness, or a spiritual
ecstasy which transforms his normal steps into dance steps, although he
himself may not be conscious of this change.

In short, the dance, like every other artistic expression, presupposes a
heightened, increased life response. Moreover, the heightened response does
not always have to have a happy background. Sorrow, pain, even horror and
fear may also tend to release a welling-up of feeling, and therefore of the
dancer's whole being.

There is something alive in every individual which makes him capable
of giving outward manifestation, (through the medium of bodily movement)
to his feelings, or rather, to that which inwardly stirs him. . . .

I feel that the dance is a language which is inherent, but slumbering in
every one of us. It is possible for every human to experience the dance as
an expression in his own body, and in his own way.

What we expect from the professional dancer is the creative dance in
its most intense representation. We never insist upon such an intense representation from the lay-dancer. The professional dancer is distinguished for his

particular qualifications, and for his artistic contribution to the dance. He must have the divine capacity to portray the difficult language of the dance: to recreate and objectify what he feels inside of himself.

The same desire for artistic liberation, for exaltation, for personal ecstasy, for bodily movement, in short, for activating his own imagination is also present in the non-professional dancer, and therefore gives him the right to seek for himself the intense expression of the dance.

We all know that the body is an end in itself. The dancer must learn, however, when and how to control his body. He ought not to regard his body simply for itself. He must transform and cultivate it as an instrument of the dance. The dance begins where gymnastics leave off. There are subtle differences between these two forms, and it is somewhat difficult to demarcate between them. Suffice it to say, the differences are neither in the kind [n]or in the style of bearing, but rather in those unexplainable disparities which cannot be easily put into words. The single gestures, isolated in themselves, do not make the dance, but rather the manner in which the gestures are connected in and by movement: the way in which one form of movement is organically developed from its preceding movement, and the manner in which it leads as organically into the next movement. That which is no longer apparent or obvious, which may be said to 'lie between the lines' of dancing, is what transforms the gymnastic movement into that of the dance.

To recapitulate: dancing is a simple rhythmic swinging, or ebb and flow, in which even the minutest gesture is part of this flow, and which is carried along the unending tide of movement.

The dance always remains bound by the human body, which is, after all, the dancer's instrument. However, with the emotion which stirs him, and the spirituality which uplifts him, the dance becomes more than mere physical movement in space, and the dancer more than its mobile agent. From then on, it represents the internal experiences of the dancer. To put it another way: we dance the mutation or change of our spiritual and emotional conditions as they are alive in our own body, in a rhythmic to and fro.

The idealistic substance of the dance, and of the dance creation, are the same as that of other creative and inter-pretative arts. In any event, it treats of man and his fate, — not necessarily the fate of men of today, nor of yesterday, nor even of tomorrow. But the fate of man caught in his eternal and perpetual web forms the old and yet ever new theme of the dance-creation. From the crudest reality to the sublimest abstraction, man is personified in the dance. All his struggles, griefs, joys are thus represented. Man himself forms the general theme for a limitless and ever significant congeries of variations.

'What idea do you think of when you dance?' A question which is often asked me, and which is difficult to answer. For the process which we call thinking has really nothing to do with the dance. The idea for a dance may come to a creative artist in his sleep, or at any moment of the day; that is to say, it is suddenly there. The idea finds root in one's consciousness without the conjuration of thought. Just as a melodic theme comes to a composer without his knowing why or where, so an idea of movement, a dance-theme, occurs just as spontaneously to the dancer. It often happens that the dancer carries the germ of the dance-theme inside of himself for a long time before it is released. It gives him no peace until it begins to take shape and form as movement. Once this theme, which is the eventual starting point of the entire dance, is at hand, the real work on the dance-creation begins; its composition and its interpretation. This formative period keeps the dancer in a constant state of excitement until the idea of the dance has reached its final point, until it has matured into a work of art. When this moment has arrived, the dance-creator becomes the dance-interpreter. It is absolutely necessary then that the dancer portray the dance in a way that will convey the meaning and force of the inner experiences which have inspired him to conceive this dance.

The primary concern of the creative dancer should be that his audience not think of the dance objectively, or look at it from an aloof and intellectual point of view, — in other words, separate itself from the very life of the dancer's experiences; — the audience should allow the dance to affect it emotionally and without reserve. It should allow the rhythm, the music, the very movement of the dancer's body to stimulate the same feeling and emotional mood within itself, as this mood and emotional condition has stimulated the dancer. It is only then that the audience will feel a strong emotional kinship with the dancer: and will live through the vital experiences behind the dance-creation. Shock, ecstasy, joy, melancholy, grief, gaiety, the dance can express all of these emotions through movement. But the expression without the inner experience in the dance is valueless.

A definite change in dancing, particularly in Germany, has been taking place these past twenty years. The revised mode of terpsichorean expression we designate as the 'modern dance' in contrast to the 'classic dance' or the ballet.

The ballet had reached such a state of perfection that it could be developed no further. Its forms had become so refined, so sublimated to the ideal of purity, that the artistic content was too often lost or obscured. The great 'ballet dancer' was no longer a representative of a great inner emotion, (like the musician or poet) but had become defined as a great virtuoso. The ballet-dancer developed an ideal of agility and lightness. He sought to conquer and annihilate gravitation. He banned the dark, the heavy, the earthbound, not only because it conflicted with his ideal of supple, airy, graceful technique, but because it also conflicted with his pretty aesthetic principles.

Times, however, became bad. War had changed life. Revolution and suffering tended to destroy and shatter all the ideals of prettiness. Traditions, aged and cherished, were left behind. How could these old and broken-down traditions remain firm throughout this awful period of destruction? Youth seeking for some spiritual relief could no longer turn to these anile panaceas. And so youth destroyed whatever appeared static, superfluous and moribund; and in its stead set up its own spiritual demands, its own material challenges.

What this new youth demanded of life and mankind, it also demanded from the artistic expression of its time, namely, the honest reflection of its own emotional experiences in symbols of artistic creation and interpretation. It demanded this positive reflection from its literature, drama, poetry, painting, architecture, music and the dance. All of these new things were direct outgrowths from its spiritual restiveness, its material challenges.

It is therefore easy to understand why this new youth should be attracted to the modern dance, the latter being one of the things which grew out of the youth's new world. The modern dance is the expression of youth and of today, and it is as positive in its expression as all the other modern arts. . . .

■ ■ ■

Source

Wigman, M. (1933) 'The Philosophy of Modern Dance', *Europa* 1 (1), (May–July).

Mary Wigman (1886–1973)

German dancer and choreographer whose career as a performer began in 1914 at the outbreak of the First World War with her solo *Witch Dance* and ended in 1942, during the Second World War, with another solo *Farewell and Thanksgiving*.

During these twenty-eight years she ran and choreographed her own company (1920–35) and she continued to choreograph for the theatre until 1961. Among her better known works are her second version of *Witch Dance* (1926), *Shifting Landscape* (1929) and *Totenmal* (1930).

Wigman was an early pupil of, and collaborator with, Rudolf Laban with whom she worked for some years. She established her own school in Dresden in 1920 and her pupils included Harald Kreutzberg, Gret Palucca and Hanya Holm. The last opened her New York branch of the Wigman school in 1931.

She wrote extensively, and her writings on dance are collected in Wigman 1966 and 1975 in excellent translations. This article, first published in July 1933, is a statement of her commitment to a particular approach to making dance which is typical of its time and definitive of European early modern dance. The concern with expression is consistent with the form that she worked within – Ausdruckstanz. It was published at the height of her career, when she had achieved success and recognition in Europe and in North America. In the same year Hitler became Chancellor of the new German Reich and it is unsurprising to find that Wigman's modernist ideas (as expressed here) fell increasingly into disfavour with the new regime.

Reader cross-references

Bausch – a later exponent of dance theatre, who owes much to her precedent
Brown, Cunningham and **Rainer** – later dancers who largely reject the idea of dance as expression
Duncan – her contemporary
Hijikata – a later Japanese exponent of Butoh, in direct lineage
Humphrey – another early modern dancer
Martin – a contemporary definition of early modern dance
Schlemmer – a contemporary, European modern choreographer who placed emphasis on the visual
Stanislavski, Artaud, **Brecht, Eisler, Meyerhold** and **Piscator** – useful comparisons within the period.

Further reading

Manning, S. (1993) *Ecstasy and the Demon: Feminism and Nationalism in the Dance of Mary Wigman*, Los Angeles: University of California Press.
Wigman, M. (1966) *The Language of Dance*, trans. W. Sorrell, London: Macdonald & Evans.
Wigman, M. (1975) *The Mary Wigman Book*, trans. and ed. W. Sorell, Middletown, Conn.: Wesleyan University Press.

Chapter 41

Raymond Williams

ARGUMENT:
TEXT AND
PERFORMANCE

T HE WORD *drama* is used in two main ways: first, to describe a literary work, the text of a play; and, second, to describe the performance of this work, its production. Thus, the text of *King Lear* is drama, and Shakespeare, as a writer, a dramatist; while a performance of *King Lear* is also drama, its players engaged in a dramatic activity. The acts of writing a play and of performing it are clearly distinct, as are the experiences of reading a play and of watching its performance, yet the word *drama* is equally meaningful when applied to either. Nor is the coincidence of the word accidental: for drama, as a literary form, is a work intended for performance, and, similarly, the great majority of performances are of literary works. It is true that we find, at one extreme, works which are cast in a dramatic form, but which are now very difficult or impossible to perform, and are therefore mainly known to us through reading; and again, at the other extreme, we find some performances which are not based on any written work, or on any complete written work, or which, if so based, are not accompanied by publication, so that we can know the work only in performance. These extremes are both drama; but the normal situation is that there is a work of literature, the play, which is intended to be performed, but can also be read, and which, in either case, we shall properly recognize as drama.

When a dramatist writes a play, he is not writing a story which others can adapt for performance: he is writing a literary work in such a manner that it can be directly performed.

Dramatic action

Drama can be further defined as *action*, which is the meaning of the original Greek word δρᾶμα. *Action*, as a definition, can usefully indicate the method of the literary form, or the process of the theatrical performance. It must not be used, however, as if it were equivalent to a certain kind of performance, or a certain kind of dramatic substance. *Action* refers to the nature of the literary conception; to the method of the literary work; and to the manner of its communication. Further, because of the great variety of the dramatic tradition, it refers, at different times and in different places, to methods which differ, and which have to be distinguished. On the basis of the performances that have been considered, we can distinguish four kinds of dramatic action:

(a) *Acted Speech:* the kind of action found in the *Antigone*, in the medieval plays, and in parts of the Elizabethan drama. Here, the drama is conceived, and the literary work is written, in such a way that when, in the known conditions of performance, the words are enacted, the whole of the drama is thereby communicated. Further, the literary form – the detailed arrangement of the words – prescribes, in the known conditions, the exact action. There is no important action that is separate from the words – 'the poetry is the action'. The action is a necessary unity of speech and movement – 'acted speech'; and where there are minor actions that are separate, these again are prescribed by the form as a whole, which is fully realized in the words, written for known performance conditions.

(b) *Visual Enactment:* the kind of action developed from the separate minor actions of the previous form. Here, an action exactly prescribed by the literary form, but not directly accompanied by speech, is separately performed. When a performer enacts an emotion, in response to the speech of *another*, the beginnings of this method are evident. It is taken further, as in the final ascent of Everyman, when an action is made *necessary* by the speech of another. Finally, a situation that has already been defined in speech may be separately enacted, without speech, as in the duel of Hamlet and Laertes; or may be separately enacted, to the accompaniment of the speech of a *narrator*; or, in the simplest example, may (as in the early Elizabethan dumb-show) precede the full performance. This kind of action has been separately developed, as in various forms of dance-drama, and of ballet: in Yeats's *At the Hawk's Well*, the form of the hawk's dance is prescribed by the literary work, but the detail is determined by the actual dancer; in ballet, the separate enactment has become a whole art, and does not directly depend on a literary work.

(c) *Activity*: the kind of action, as in *The Feast at Solhoug*, which, in our time, is often thought to be the *only* kind of dramatic action. Here, there is no direct unity of speech and movement; but the movement, usually arranged in a pattern of exciting events, is primary, and the dramatic speech exists mainly to give the cue for these events, to explain them, and to punctuate them by simple cries of alarm, warning, shock and so on. It is not a verbal design being communicated in a whole action, but a series of events being intermittently accompanied by words.

(d) *Behaviour*: the kind of action, as in *The Seagull*, where the words and movement have no direct and necessary relation, but derive, as it were separately, from a conception of 'probable behaviour' in the circumstances presented. Words and movements often equally communicate the dramatic experience, but not in a design of 'acted speech'; the speech, as we have seen in the performance of *The Seagull*, is often separate from the 'acting'. The speech is prescribed, but the 'acting', and 'setting', and therefore the action as a whole must often be separately inferred, even where the conditions of performance are known.

The distinction of these four kinds of *action* is, it will be noted, based largely on matters of emphasis. We often find a single play containing action of more than one type, but the range nevertheless remains clear. It is in these terms that we can understand the essential difference between, say, the *Antigone* and *The Seagull*, although both are works of dramatic literature. It is in these terms, also, that the varying relation between text and performance in drama must be understood.

The relation of text and performance

Drama is commonly made of four elements: *speech* (in its most general sense, including, at times, singing and recitative, as well as dialogue and conversation); *movement* (including gesture, dance, physical enactment, and acted

371

event); *design* (including scene, scenery, costume and effects of lighting); and *sound* (as distinct from the use of the human voice – e.g. music, 'sound effects'). All these elements can appear in performance; what is variable is their relation to the literary work, the text. For example, in the categories of action already distinguished:

(a) Acted Speech: when a text of this kind – e.g. the *Antigone* – is set in the known conditions of performance for which the dramatist was writing, the full detail of the performance is seen to be prescribed. Speech and movement are determined by the arrangement of the words, according to the known conventions; design and sound are again conventional, known to the dramatist from the conditions of performance, and controlled by him in these terms. In such a case, the dramatist is not only writing a literary work; he is also, by the use of exact conventions, *writing the performance.* Performance, here, is a physical communication of a work that is, in its text, dramatically complete.

(b) *Visual Enactment:* here the relation of text and performance will vary according to the degree of convention of what is to be visually enacted. Where this is fully conventional (a precisely known action or pattern of movements) the text exactly prescribes the performance, by stage direction, or by necessary inference from the verbal design. In other cases, the text does no more than prescribe an *effect*, of which the *means* must be worked out in performance.

(c) *Activity:* here, although the text may in a general way prescribe the action, the effect of the performance will usually be very different from the effect of the text alone. The physical action will take charge, and the words will be subordinate to it. It is unusual for a dramatist writing a play of this type to realize, in his own work, the full dramatic movement; and there will usually be scope for considerable variation in performance; especially since the movements will normally be a representation of events, detailed means of which will be usually left to performance.

(d) *Behaviour:* here we find the widest separation between text and performance. The prescribed dramatic speech is 'probable conversation', and because in this there can be no exact relation between the arrangement of words and the method of speaking them, the performance will inevitably be an 'interpretation' of the text, and hence subject to wide variation. Movement and scene will be described in general terms, of which the detail is left to performance; but because they are under-

stood as 'probable behaviour' and 'probable setting', they will be subject to further variations of interpretation. Indeed, the performance of a text of this kind is based less on the text than on a *response to the text*. This type, in fact, is often nearer to 'a story which others adapt for performance' than to the text which has only to be communicated to be fully performed.

On the basis of these distinctions, it is evident that there is no constant relation between text and performance in drama. Moreover, the variations have always to be understood in terms of changing methods of dramatic writing and playing. As a matter of theory, the variations have to be recognized; we must always clarify the alternative areas of fact. Because, in our own time, the normal types of dramatic action are 'activity' and 'behaviour', the necessary separation of text and performance has often been taken for granted, and, as a consequence, a separation has been assumed between literature and theatre. The separation is real, in much of our own drama; but we must not allow ourselves to be persuaded that it is inherent in all drama. At first, we can say that 'here it is so, and there not so', and this is important, as a counter to dogma. But then, inevitably, we must go on to express preferences between the alternatives. We must make, not only the theoretical recognition, but also a practical criticism; and, in this, the emphasis will tend to fall on the dramatic problems of our own day.

Action and reality

We have been looking at methods of writing and methods of performance. These methods acquire, at a certain point, a material reality: most notably in the structures of theatres, but also in forms of texts. Any reality inherited in this way sets certain limits, indicates certain bearings, for the making of drama. Without this inheritance, the drama could not work at all, but in periods of change the restrictions can be very obvious. In fact, during the last hundred years, most serious dramatists have complained of these restrictions, and many of them have been in active revolt against what seemed a settled and frustrating establishment. Out of the energy of this revolt, most of the important new work has come.

Yet we must not put our whole emphasis on this revolt against established structures and conventions. For if we do, we are describing it in too negative a way. The only positive description we shall be left with is an unfocused, an imprecise, creative energy. What has always to be emphasized is the profound relation between methods of writing and performance and particular views of reality. In each generation, the old methods are called conventional, but in an art like the drama the successful new method is in itself a convention. The writing and performance of drama depends on that kind of agreement – it need not altogether be prior agreement; it can be reached in the act itself – on the nature of the action being presented. What is called conventional, in the sense of an old routine, is a method or set of methods which presents a different kind of action, and through it a different kind of reality.

An audience is always the most decisive inheritance, in any art. It is the way in which people have learned to see and respond that creates the first essential condition for drama. Thus we often take for granted that any audience will understand the highly conventional nature of any dramatic performance: that the action inhabits its own dimension, and is in that sense different from other kinds of action. Yet it is not only that in some other societies, where there is no effective dramatic tradition, we find that this very particular response – depending on very intricate assumptions, adjustments and restraints, as is obvious when it has to be stated theoretically – can fail to be made. It is also that even in societies with an effective and widespread dramatic tradition, there is great practical variation in the response itself. It is obvious, for example, in our own society, that there is great uncertainty about the reality, and the implications for reality, of certain kinds of dramatic action, and about the criteria, the references, by which the reality of any particular play should be judged. This uncertainty has been much more evident since drama became a true majority form, especially on television. It is easy to respond to this, and to the kinds of complaint it continually generates, with an apparent sophistication, derived from a particular and learned distinction between art and reality: 'it is only, after all, a play', or 'we are not so naïve as to expect a play to reproduce reality exactly'. But this is not much more than a class habit. The responses being argued, the references being made, often in very confused local ways, seem to any historian of the drama the permanent and essential and very difficult questions, with which the long history of the art has always been directly concerned.

The relation between a dramatic action and reality, that is to say, is not to be settled by a formula: by the effective dramatic methods, the conventions, of a particular period. Dramatic actions at once express and test the many versions of reality which are possible, and it is in the end a more serious response to a play to complain that a character 'should not have behaved like that' – since the relation between the action and the reality is then being actively weighed – than to retreat from such questions into some notion of aesthetic propriety, which in ruling out such a question would rule out also the major dramatic interests of the whole European tradition.

When the argument can be seen as an argument about convention, there is a possibility of moving on from what is often an angry and very local confusion. But then to see the problem as one of convention is only to raise, in a more open way, very similar questions about dramatic action and its relation to reality. For a convention is not just a method: an arbitrary and voluntary technical choice. It embodies in itself those emphases, omissions, valuations, interests, indifferences, which compose a way of seeing life, and drama as part of life. Certainly we have to insist that the masked actors and chorus in the Theatre of Dionysus at Athens were not less real than the costumed actors on the furnished set of *Caste* at the Prince of Wales's Theatre, London. But we have then also to recognize that the reality, in each case, depends on a whole set of other interests, responses and assumptions; in fact on that selection of interests and values that we call a particular culture.

This point bears both ways. It is useful as a defence against rigid assumptions, about the 'true nature' of drama, or 'effective theatre', in any particular period. As we have seen, the real range of dramatic method, in writing and in performance, is immense. But this does not mean that the whole of this range is available to anyone wishing to use it. On the contrary, a method can be effectively rooted in experience only when it connects with ways of seeing and responding that are more than 'methods'; when it connects with real interests and possible ways of seeing.

One lesson that we then have to draw is that some of the major drama of the past, which we can see to be superbly fashioned for its own purposes, is, while always available as art (the art of another period, to be consciously looked at) not at all available, in the same way, as a basis for new work. In practice, always, an apparent use of some older dramatic method is a substantial change of it, in a new context. Where it is simply transplanted (as in Eliot's drawing-room Eumenides) it is neither old nor new, and no effective convention is discoverable. And where, as has happened, an older method is wholly reworked – as in Brecht's reworking of direct address, from what had become localized as exposition, soliloquy and aside – it begins to operate in a new structure of feeling, and to have quite different implications and effects.

The magnificent design of a play like Sophocles' *Antigone* depends, that is to say, on an idea of design which is no longer generally dramatically available. The same is true of *Everyman*, where the willingness to see and respond in that way is a critical feature of the success of the method. Such ideas of design are widely variable, as is already obvious between the *Antigone* and *Everyman*. The essential design of *Antony and Cleopatra* – its responses to space and power, to love and death – is similarly particular. And I think we have to go on to recognize that 'design', in these senses, is radically different from 'representation', in its modern senses. There is a critical and revolutionary change from dramatic production of a design to the dramatic reproduction of a different and more locally human order of experience. The naturalist revolution has been very long; some of its elements appear, already, in the transition from medieval to Elizabethan drama. But it was only when it was almost complete that we could see its full implications, which, were basically that human experience can be understood in solely human terms, and that what has to be dramatized is this human action, however local it may seem, rather than the setting of this human action in a version of divine or cosmic reality.

Certain essential changes of convention were made necessary by this new emphasis. These were part of the major and irreversible change from feudal to bourgeois societies: a movement away from intrinsic design, hierarchy, and a perspective that reached beyond man. But the bourgeois revolt was itself very complicated. At one obvious level, which seems to culminate in *Caste* and its innumerable successors, the emphasis was on man wholly visible in society, which then allowed a method of dramatic representation, almost literally reproduction, that had its own internal consistencies but also, obviously, its limits. Within this movement, and eventually declaring itself as its enemy, was an emphasis on man, on his private and social experience, which was simultaneously an emphasis on his complexity, on his lack of transparency, and so on the inadequacy of his ordinary external representations. This is the basis of the distinction we have already made between 'the naturalist habit' and 'naturalism', but it is also the basis of a very important connection between naturalism, in this full sense, and its successors, in turn its enemies, which, in expressionism, symbolism and the absurd, created methods which directly rather than indirectly dramatized the complex, the opaque and the internal experience.

This connection further allows us to see a point of great significance in any contemporary consideration of dramatic action: that these later experimental forms shared with high naturalism an unusual fixity and stasis, for which, in the naturalist habit (from the indicated pictures of *The London Merchant* to the picture-frame stage of *Caste*) the theatres were already prepared. The structure of the *Antigone*, it is true, had been built on moments of achieved stasis: the indications, the sculptured scenes, that we noted. But there the design, in the open theatre as in the detailed experience of the writing, referred the audience outwards, to an accessible order. The simpler *Everyman* could build this order, with God on his scaffold, as the dramatic locale. It was only in *Antony and Cleopatra*, and, significantly, in the whole drama of that period, that movement itself, the direct dramatization of historical action, could be made the basis of a dramatic method. And this is above all an action in which men are making their immediate history, rather than reacting to a history which is determined or being made outside them. But in the deadlock of high naturalism, and in the enclosed, static actions of the counter-naturalist forms which succeeded it, there has been, especially in the theatre, a progressive immobility, in most serious work. The stasis of *Waiting for Godot* is in that sense a true culmination. The first form of this stasis was the stage as a room: not just the triumph of theatrical carpentry, but the conviction that important reality occurred in rooms – the rooms of private houses – to which report was carried, from which people looked and went out, but where the central interest – what was called 'what happened, not to society, but to people' – was played through. Experiment, within naturalism, was then largely a series of indications, by atmosphere, visual devices, descriptions, insets, of what went on and what existed, beyond both the room and the stage. The second form of this stasis was indeed a clearing of the room from the stage, but its replacement by the drama of a single mind, in which, so to say, those men staring from the windows of a naturalist room, feeling trapped and baffled as they looked out at the world, were replaced by a dramatic form in which the stare from the window was the essential viewpoint on reality, and what was seen, in the action, was one man's version of his world, within which he created figures to enact it.

What is then interesting is that the film and television camera, which so radically extended the possible range of dramatic methods, could be used for any of these underlying conventions. They could look into the room, with greater subtlety of detail in this face, this hand, this object, and they could solve, technically, many of the problems of inset, extension, visual device. In a majority of cases, they have done no more; the essential conventions are still of the stage as a room, with some mechanically extending movements beyond it. Or, in a different convention, the camera could be, more powerfully than on the stages of expressionism, symbolism and the absurd, a watching and shaping eye, which made a version of the world, and composed figures within it.

These seem, now, the serious uses, but we have to remember how deep was that element of the high bourgeois drama in which reaction rather than action was selected for emphasis. It is one thing to react when there is an order to react to: as in the quite different dramatic designs of Greek, medieval, neo-classical and some Renaissance drama. It is quite another matter, in our kind of world, to exclude decisive action – direct intervention, open conflict, the acts of building and destroying – from the dramatic version of reality as a whole.

The mind seems to move, at this point. For it is of course true that in part of the dramatic tradition, from the duel in *Hamlet* to the poisoning at Solhoug and its many equivalents and successors, action, of an apparently direct kind, has been constantly dramatized and has been popular. What we have to ask, I think, is why that sort of action has been so commonly relegated to the less serious levels of drama: 'blood-and-thunder', 'epic', 'all action and no experience'. It is true that most of it has been self-sufficient and enclosed. The fight or the chase comes up with a predictability, at certain points in the action, which makes certain that however we respond to it at the time we have usually not seen or learned anything that we would want to remember: that no dramatic experience, in the full sense, as opposed to a temporarily exciting activity, has been created. But it does not follow that the mere exclusion of that kind of action – and so the resolution of all conflicts within the room or within the mind – is any greater guarantee of dramatic seriousness. The assumption that it is so has more to do with certain habits of our culture than with the intrinsic possibilities of drama. What seems to matter, as we begin to look at it in this way, is why that kind of action was separated from serious dramatic experience, until to go beyond the room, or beyond the observing mind, was not to go into the streets, the workplaces, the assemblies, but into what seemed merely noisy, busy and external. In the popular drama, we have stayed with the dramatization of crime, of historical actions, of adventure and exploration: significantly often in other places and other times, from the costume epic to the Western, but often, also, in our own places and times, where the action is visible and where it can be said to be, as in that regular metaphor, dramatic.

Action and writing

The problem of the theatre returns to haunt us. For it is the equation of drama with theatre that is now our most evident difficulty. In many theatres of the past, action of the most open kind could be written and played. But steadily, the walls were built: around the action, and around the whole performance. A moving and open art became relatively static and framed, and a quite different 'art of the theatre' was developed within these voluntary limits. A division occurred, between writing and action, which has become more apparent in each successive phase of this culture. One of the sources of this division was print: the attachment of writing to this static form, away from the human voices and movements to which it stood in a merely abstract relation. Another source, of a deeper kind, was a revaluation of action within the society. Certain 'representative' modes of dramatic writing seem to have developed, hand in hand, with certain 'representative' institutions for political action and decision. Near their most serious interests, most men learned to give up the idea of intervention, participation, direct action, even as a possibility, in favour of indirect, conventional and reacting forms. The desire for action was not lost, but was specialized to certain areas, away from central concerns. It seems paradoxical to say that the drama has lost the secret of action when Drury Lane, in the nineteenth century, could put on its stage a huge tank for a naval battle or lines for a train crash, or when commercial television, in our own period, shows every night, in careful detail, a bank robbery, a murder, a fight between spies, a running battle across a plain. But the truth is that *these* things can be enacted, because they belong in the margins of the society and the mind. Other things can be discussed, reacted to, but only rarely shown. In particular, any decisive action, in which men in general try to change their condition, is unconsciously ruled out. The social like the spiritual crisis is resolved by adjustment, in which the world can be rearranged in the mind, or presented in a singular distortion, but not, in the dramatic action, fully engaged with, struggled against, altered. This deep lack in the society has been the source of the dramatic crisis as of so much else. Our enclosed theatres, in which the acts of adjustment grow constantly in refinement, can be seen as its temples. Film and television, inherently more open and active forms, repeated this essential process, in a majority of cases: whether as marginal spectacle or as enclosed adjustment. Briefly, in the Romantic drama, after the French Revolution, action was forced back into dramatic writing, but this drama never found its adequate theatre. In our own time, as in some parts of the world some deadlocks have been broken, the cinema has dramatized direct action, not just as spectacle – the Drury Lane tank swollen to a giant set – but as contemporary reality, in which men move and decide, on their most serious experiences. Here, undoubtedly, is the point of growth of any drama of our century: to go where reality is being formed, at work, in the streets, in assemblies, and to engage at those points with the human needs to which the actions relate.

Writing a dramatic action

Drama is always so central an element of the life of a society that a change in its methods cannot be isolated from much wider changes. While people's feelings, essentially, are shut up in rooms, the drama will stay with them. While action is only interesting, because distanced and uninvolving, in crime and sensation or in distant places and times, the majority forms will go on serving those interests. While society is generalized, and separated from the life of the individual, drama will pursue contemporary reality not as a human need but as a general report, as in the rise of documentary as a method. The important changes will come together or not at all, but this is not to say that they will all come at once, in some sudden transformation. They will come here and there, as possible new actions and methods.

And it is then worth considering the problems of the dramatist, in this kind of change. At a certain point, as we have seen, dramatists stopped writing actions, in any whole sense, and either wrote a pattern of response, which the new arts of stage-management, naturalist acting and production built into a performance, or sketched a general action – what is still sometimes called a scenario – which they would punctuate with directions, exclamations and the necessary minimum of information, the real action being staged by someone other than the writer, usually the spectacular producer or director. Plays became scripts: stories which others adapted for performance, whether of a naturalist or spectacular kind. And this convention, now, has been deeply learned; it is what is asked for; what writers exist to provide.

In the enclosed conditions of the theatres, a dramatist who goes in and learns the accepted rules can write a work which goes with the grain, and is in that sense complete. But the major difficulty is still that these rules are not just the facts of performance; they are the expression of a particular structure of feeling, a set of interests, valuations and indifferences. In some ways this is now breaking down, and there is an evident restlessness. Certain kinds of action can still be written there, especially when what is ordinarily an inert and conventional self-consciousness, inherent in recent theatre history, can be actively used, as in some of Brecht, as an experience rather than a method: an awareness of presence, challenge, alternative ways of seeing, participation, breaking the line between audience and stage.

But it is in a different direction from that of the majority forms, in cinema and television. There the drama can move beyond representation and mime, to direct production. For the enclosed sensibility, this is a loss of the meaning of theatre. For the newly open and mobile experience, it is an unparalleled opportunity, and the dramatist can, in new ways, write his action directly. Live performance, of course, is given up, and this is some loss, especially in terms of existing kinds of performance. But what is gained is the possibility of control, in the essential continuity of creation and production. A dramatic action can be composed, in its final form, in a way much more satisfactory than the apparent finality of print, which, as we have seen, turns out, in performance, to need radical reworking to become drama, unless, as in certain situations in the past, the conventions are so settled that the creation and the performance can be essentially written in a single text. Those settled conditions are unlikely to recur; they belonged with particular and now unavailable societies; only permanent companies, in this place and that, can offer, locally, any comparable integrity.

A dramatic action can then be composed, in its final form, by the use of the camera, in television and film. But in practice this is still very difficult, because of the transfer of habits from the theatres, and because of the quite new problems of writing which the dramatist encounters. To write an action, for this means of performance, is not simply to write a report of an action, or even its detailed description; it is also to write the movements as they are to be made, and simultaneously the ways in which the movements are to be seen. To write a 'scene', again, is not to write a general description, and of course not one or two static settings, but to integrate all that is to be seen with the primary writing of movements and viewpoints. What had been separated, as actors' movements and settings, must now be written in a single form. Speech, similarly, and any associated sound, must be written within this form, and yet, in another way, must contain this form: not words in front of a background, nor words accompanying movement, but words, scene and movement in a single dimension of writing.

The difficulties are enormous. As Bergman noted, some of the essential notation does not yet exist. And it is then possible for writers to retreat to 'the story which others adapt for performance', or for the writer-director, more often in practice the director-writer, to emerge as the dominant figure. The writer who is not a technician can then run for the theatres, and leave the new forms alone. The major expense of this kind of production, and the commercial or bureaucratic pressures which can bear so heavily, have already made an atmosphere from which many people involved have wanted to run.

The opportunities, however, remain. Not only in methods, but in the existence of audiences, not simply larger but of a different kind: untrained to existing theatrical conventions, and sometimes surprisingly open to new dramatic experience: to new relations, in fact, between dramatists and audiences, of a more open and public kind. Some of the essential writing has to be done in forms moving away from print: in writing and recording voices – not only local rhythms but more general rhythms and sequences – and in stills and in actual work at the place of production. This co-operative work has to be consciously learned by a writer. It is often avoided because of the fear of 'creation by committee', but it need not be always like this, and in some actual cases has not been like it. In a slowly and consciously assembled form, very similar in that respect to writing, co-operation can be very different from what is possible in a relatively sudden and separate performance. In these conditions the new methods can in practice be made.

Conclusion

I have taken the argument this far, from account and classification to criticism and recommendation, because a serious interest in drama in performance must always, in the end, move to what is now actually happening. The practical details belong to specific work: not methods but experiences: actual texts in performance. What begins, though, as a practical problem in writing needs to go, sometimes, into history and theory: as a way of clearing the mind and of beginning a discussion.

What I hope this essay has done, in its several practical examples of plays in performance, and then in argument, is to show, by the facts of variation, not only the rigidity of existing orthodox formulas, but also the openings, the possibilities, and of course the restraints, in the existing situation. For any dramatic writer, the problem of the relation between text and performance is what he takes, repeatedly, to his table; what he has been taking, in such differing circumstances, for more than two thousand years. For any actor, designer and director, the same kind of problem – of moving the writing through to an actual production – is permanent, though in its very permanence, as for the writer, various, experimental, changing. And for readers and audiences, these varying activities and relations, though they may not directly work on them, are there all the time, so that what happens between text and performance is a continuing concern, in all that major area of writing and acting that is our traditional and our living drama.

■　■　■

Source

Williams, R. (1954, 1968, 1972) 'Argument: Text and Performance', *Drama in Performance*, Harmondsworth: Penguin: 170–188.

First published in 1954, revised and 'recast' version published in revised and extended version of *Drama in Performance* (1968) published by C. A. Watts.

Raymond Williams (1921–92)

Probably the major UK cultural theorist of our time, and certainly the first major British critic to consider the practice of performance as a necessary and integral part of the study of theatre. In his early book on *Drama from Ibsen to Eliot* (1952; later expanded to include Brecht, 1968), followed by *Modern Tragedy* (1966), he sought to put forward a critical and analytical overview of drama as a major European forum of ideas, but in *Drama and Performance* (1954) he broke new ground with a study of the relation between the script of a play and the physical performance of it. After a series of seminal books on the relationship between culture and society, all of which examined drama as a socio-cultural form, he returned to theatre in some of his last essays and lectures collected together in *The Politics of Modernism* (1989). Even so, it is only in *Drama and Performance* that he examines theatre as practice, and focuses on a series of key examples of dramatic literature from the Greek to the 'experimental', where he creates imaginative reconstructions of historical performances. In this analysis he departs from both the literary and the sociological approaches that inform the rest of his work.

This final essay from the book draws together the threads of his argument, namely that there is a changing relationship between what we call a text, and the performance of that text, which depends to a greater degree on the understanding of conventions by the audience. As such the essay is both historically and ideologically important to the development of theatre theory in our time.

Reader cross-references

Barthes – a semiological, critical approach to text
Benjamin – an earlier, Marxist approach
Brecht – a view of the importance of engaging the audience
Schechner – for more recent ideas on text

Further reading

Williams, R. (1968, 1969) *Drama from Ibsen to Brecht*, London: Chatto & Windus.
Williams, R. (1976, 1983) *Keywords: A Vocabulary of Culture and Society*, revised and expanded edition, London: Methuen.
Williams, R. (1989) *The Politics of Modernism*, London: Verso.

Chapter 42

Robert Wilson

INTERVIEW

You've just returned from Paris where you produced Great Day in the Morning, *an evening of Negro spirituals, with the celebrated American soprano Jessye Norman. In the summer of 1984, Norman will also be appearing in your staging of* Civil Wars. *How did this ongoing collaboration come about?*

About five years ago I was performing in Paris and Jessye was there singing at the same time. She's a big, big star in France, much bigger than she is in America. Various people had told me that I would like what she was doing so I went to one of her performances and I was overwhelmed by her – by the way she walked on stage, the way she stood and, of course, the way she sang. With the least amount of effort she can fill an enormous hall. That's Jessye's genius. She can sing the quietest, softest sound with her back to the audience and that sound will touch the back wall of the theater. So I was overwhelmed and I went backstage and stood in line and said, 'Hello, my name is Bob Wilson. You're absolutely fantastic and I would love to work with you.' She didn't know who I was and asked, 'What is it that you do?' 'Well, I'm a theatre director and artist. I make works for the theater.' 'Well,' she said, 'Thank you very much' and that was it. Then about eight months later I was in Texas visiting my family and I read in a Dallas paper that she was appearing at Tanglewood. I was coming back to New York anyway so I decided to go straight to Tanglewood and hear her sing. Again, I was over-whelmed. I went backstage and stood in a long line and finally when my turn came, she turned and said, 'Oh, Hello, Mr Wilson, it's nice to see you again.' She has a phenomenal memory. Anyway, we had lunch the next day and I told her about a new piece that I was going to do in Berlin (*Death, Destruction and Detroit*). I made some drawings for her and tried to explain how I work. Then I told her that when I do the piece I would like her to come and see it. And she did come. Soon after that I began to make sketches and work on an idea for her. This was about three years ago. I showed her a diagram and said, 'Here's a possible structure for a two act work for you. What do you think the music should be? Should we find a composer to write for you?' And she said, 'Well, I've been thinking of doing something with Negro spirituals, the songs of the slaves, and I think these would be appropriate settings. And the idea interested me because it didn't have anything to do with slavery necessarily, it wouldn't have to be an illustration of the music – you know, a black person in a field of cotton. So Jessye and I began talking and thinking about what songs to use and how they should be fitted together. We began a collaboration. Over the last two years we'd get together from time to time and rehearse and gradually we found what the piece was about. It was a very close collaboration. I really think I work best when I can build and create a work with someone.

How would you characterize the relationship between the songs and your own visual presentation?

I just picked settings that I thought were appropriate in some way for this music as a group of pictures or tableaux but which didn't necessarily illustrate the music. And everything had to be in scale to Jessye. There were certain moods in the landscapes that helped in deciding what songs to use but the songs are not meant to illustrate the background. The background is like a picture book that makes sense on its own. In *Great Day*, the visual is as important as what we hear. I think it helps us hear and the singing helps us see. I think what I disliked about opera when I first went was that I couldn't hear I was so visually distracted. I heard best when I shut my eyes. It's very difficult to see and hear at the same time and mostly we do one or the other. What I try to do in all my work is make a balance between what you hear and what you see, so that perhaps you can do both at the same time.

These days your productions are usually greeted with instantaneous acclaim, but Great
Day *created something of a furor at its première in Paris. In fact, you were vigor-*
ously booed by a large faction of the audience at the end of the performance. I imagine
the presence of Jessye Norman might have attracted a somewhat different audience
than usually attends your productions, perhaps one unprepared for the kind of work
you do.

I think it's an audience that tends to go to concerts, recitals and opera, not
necessarily my audience. She had sung many times at that theater and so a
lot of people came expecting the kind of thing they had heard in the past.
They also didn't understand what spirituals are. These songs are religious in
nature, they're all from the Bible which was the only book the slaves had to
read. They're not songs of anger; they're songs of nobility and dignity, the
songs of an oppressed race. The problems resulted from a misunderstanding
– audiences not knowing what the spirituals are, not knowing how the music
came about or the way it was sung or simply the way it *was*, which was to
some extent the way we presented it. They were frustrated and confused.
The staging and designs responded to the religious nature of the music and
the way the songs were sung. They were sung as a way of life – you heard
singing as you woke up in the morning and dressed, you sang as you went
through the day, it was the way you closed the day. Jessye said she always
remembered hearing her grandmother sing all day long. Her mother too.
The slaves grew up singing as part of life. It was not something they did for
entertainment, it was a way of life. It was natural, like breathing. There was
song all day long.

And that's actually the form of Great Day. *It's a kind of progression through the*
day.

Right, that's it. It's a great day and a woman begins the morning singing. It
starts early in the morning with the sunrise and it ends with the morning
again. Singing is heard through the course of the day. I show various things
that people would do every day. You see someone contemplating and someone
walking in a forest.
   You see someone waking up in bed and someone sleeping in the middle
of the night. I made this room with a huge window.
   It's not a specific room or even a window necessarily. It could be 1840
or 2040.

Perhaps you could describe the scene on the lake, which drew both praise from critics
and scornful laughter from some members of the audience. It seems to embody the
spiritual nature of the work and the meditative qualities you were seeking to capture.

There's a dock out in the lake and it's midnight.

There are stars in the sky and the moonlight is reflecting on the water. Jessye walks out in a blue robe and sings a song she wrote herself, a song based on a slave poem that's sung a cappella. There's a simple white chair at the end of the dock. She walks over to it and begins to sing 'Sometimes I Feel Like a Motherless Child.' A little golden light falls down on her as she sits in the white chair improvising the song. She's written a part for a cello and as it's played a grey Canadian goose moves across the sky, its wings slowly flapping. But she doesn't see it, her focus is turned inward. She has two or three very simple gestures that are counted and carefully lit. After sitting there for ten minutes or so, humming and singing, she stands up and begins to walk off. Just before she gets to the edge of the stage she kneels down and takes a handful of water from the lake and washes her face. And she begins to sing again. Then she turns and walks offstage in profile, humming the same music. And that's how we did these songs. We didn't present them like gospel numbers, adding tambourines and banjos and making an entertainment – all that came later. And so when Jessye was humming a song for ten minutes or sitting in silence the audience became very restless. But it would have been very inappropriate to present this music any other way and that was completely misunderstood – though not by the serious writers of the French press who did understand for the most part. I must say that I was surprised by the incredible reaction at the end, the bursts of boos and bravos. Some of the press wrote that it was an occasion similar to the première of *The Rite of Spring*, which had its first performance in the same theater over sixty years before. After that, there was no way of ever getting away from the idea of a controversy because audiences came expecting a controversial event and they acted controversial.

Great Day in the Morning *was to have been presented at the Brooklyn Academy of Music this winter but a few months ago performances were postponed. Was* Great Day *withdrawn so you could do some more work on it, as some have suggested, or was it once again a matter of financing?*

Financing and time. There wasn't enough time to mount it properly. The work is in a finished state though I do intend to make a few changes. It will be performed in the future, possibly at Covent Garden and La Scala. It may also go to Africa and Moscow.

During the past year you also produced The Golden Windows *at the Munich Kammerspiele, a new work featuring one of your own texts.*

Yes. My text. I also designed, directed and lit it. It's a smaller scale work. I built a little house.

It's early evening. There's a door that opens – light streams from the doorway. Then midnight.

The house is in the center. Then the early morning.

The house is now at the left side of the stage. Those three perspectives.

The title of the work and perhaps a few of its images were suggested by a story in a now forgotten book of homiletic fables by the American writer Laura E. Richards (1903). What was the attraction of this obscure story book?

It was a fairy tale I heard as a child. I just remembered the story. Actually I had written the play before I thought of the title. The title didn't have anything to do with the play necessarily, but then it became part of it.

In the story a little boy gazes at a house on a distant hill which seems to have windows of gold and diamonds. One day he travels to the neighboring hill only to find a common farmhouse with ordinary glass windows. At the end of the story another house with golden windows appears to him in the distance. It is his own house, transfigured by the light of the setting sun. While *The Golden Windows* isn't based on this story, or even directly related to it, the two works do share the image of a house on a hill – a house whose appearance changes according to the time of day it is viewed – and most importantly, a sense of the transforming power of light.

Light plays an integral role in the work. It's like an actor. Mainly, though, I just liked the title.

The play was performed in German and you worked with actors of the Kammerspiele.

Yes. I used members of their repertory company. Brilliant, brilliant actors. I think it's the most difficult thing for actors of the Schaubühne or the Kammerspiele to perform my texts because they don't tell a story. That's what all their training is aimed at – telling a story, interpreting a text, psychological theater. And if you do that with my works the audience gets confused. You have to be able to say the text in a way that one can think about many sorts of things. If you say it in such a way that you must pay attention to every word you'll go crazy because one thought doesn't follow another thought logically. One thought can set off many thoughts. You have to sort of float with the situation.

Do you think this work will ever be seen in America?

There's a possibility that *The Golden Windows* could come to the United States in the summer or autumn of 1985. That will be the first time I have any time to stage it because I'm scheduled to do other things.

American audiences have not seen a major Wilson work since Einstein on the Beach *was presented here in 1976. Money is invariably given as the reason so few of your productions reach this country. Is it solely a matter of financing or are other factors involved?*

Financing has a lot to do with it. The other problem is where do you put it. Where do you put a work like *The Golden Windows*? In Munich I'm at the Kammerspiele, a municipal theater where I'm seen by a subscription audience. I have a poster from the Kammerspiele. Look at their season – they have plays by Chekhov, Shakespeare, they have *Medea*, a Sean O'Casey play, Goethe's *Tasso* and they have my work. Where in this city would you find a program like that?

The resident theaters in this country might conceivably be a place where your work could be seen. Have you approached them?

They haven't approached me, you can put it that way. Yes, I have gone to them on occasion but I don't have time to now. I have too many other things to do.

What about the Metropolitan Opera? There was discussion at one point about an operatic version of Death, Destruction and Detroit.

Well, we had talked about it, I guess. I'm not a popular person at the Met.

You've also reached a stage in your career where you no longer have to accept compromise. You're in demand at subsidized European state theaters and festivals, organizations far better equipped to meet your exacting standards. Theater in this country usually means compromising in terms of just getting a play on.

Entirely true. The Met is a very well-organized house and the labor is probably the best in the world for working with time. Still, they don't light a show the way I do. They don't rehearse the way I rehearse. There's not the same attention placed on detail. Lighting is an important part of my work. I usually spend years on my drawings and days setting light cues. Over here they light a show in eight hours. It's very hard to do the kind of work I do in structures in this country, it really needs a festival structure. And again there's the cost. *Civil Wars* in Los Angeles will be two and a half million dollars for three performances and that doesn't even include artists' fees. It's insane. Budgets, unions. *Einstein on the Beach* at the Metropolitan Opera cost $90,000 per performance. Just to run a show that was already created.

The technical demands of your works also present certain difficulties. A Robert Wilson play can no longer be staged just anywhere.

My work is unique, it means big houses. I work best in a large scale.

You don't plan to produce your own shows in this country as you sometimes did in the past?

I can't, though really in some way I do. Contracts with houses and unions. It's a whole profession. As a producer I'm not knowledgeable.

In the past you've spoken with some bitterness of this country's lack of support for your work. Now that you're so busy creating works for the leading theaters and opera houses of Europe is this still such a concern with you?

It's . . . a frustration. I don't want to be an expatriot but that's the way it is – I'm leaving this January and I don't come back to America until the very end of 1984.

In a recent interview you announced your intention to do more interpretive work in the coming years. Great Day in the Morning, *the first piece you've created to existing texts, represents a step in that direction. What was behind this decision?*

The creation of new works is what I do best but I also think it's important to do other things, and so I want to interpret other people's work. I'm doing a new opera with Gavin Bryars, an English composer, which is based on Euripides' *Medea*. It will be performed at the opera house in Lyon and then will come to the Paris Opera.

What attracted you to this classic text?

I don't know. I just read the play and was fascinated by it. I liked the architecture of the story. It was very different from my work and yet similar in some ways.

Your Medea *began life as a play with music. It's now a full-scale opera. What was the reason for this transformation?*

I'd just rather hear words sung than spoken, I think. I'll also be doing another version of *Medea* in Lyon, a baroque opera by Charpentier which has never been performed. Then I'm doing *Four Saints in Three Acts*, the Gertrude Stein-Virgil Thompson opera, in Stuttgart in May of 1985. I also plan to do *Parsifal* in 1986 or 87, then a *King Lear*, yes to Shakespeare's text, and maybe later I'll do some contemporary works.

From time to time your work is described as a modern equivalent of Wagner's Gesamtkunstwerk. *Now you are planning to produce several of the Wagnerian music dramas. I would be interested in knowing when you first encountered Wagner's music and at what point you contemplated staging his operas?*

The Wagner family came to Spoletto when I did *A Letter for Queen Victoria* in 1974 and they said, 'Oh, Mr Wilson, it's so beautiful. You're the perfect one to do Wagner.' Well, at that time I barely knew who Wagner was. So I said, 'Thank you very much. I'm flattered.' They asked me if I would be interested in coming to Bayreuth to direct something and I answered, 'Well, possibly, but do you ever do new works because I'm really interested in creating *new* works.' Gian Carlo Menotti was sitting next to me and he started kicking me under the table. 'No, no, we don't do new operas, Mr Wilson. We only do Wagner.' 'Well,' I said, 'I'm really not interested just now.' Then they asked me a couple of years later and I actually went to the festival. Finally they came when I did *Edison* – Wolfgang Wagner and his wife – and they said, 'We're going to do a new *Parsifal* and we want to talk to you about that,' and I said I was very interested in doing it. They said, 'Well, Mr Levine has already been contracted to conduct it. Could you work with him?' And I said, 'Yes.'

After so many years as a German (even a family) institution, Bayreuth has begun seeking outside talent. There was a French team (Chéreau and Boulez) for the centennial Ring. *This summer's cycle will be essentially an English production (Hall, Solti and designer William Dudley). And you and Levine would have logically consituted an American team.*

But Levine refused to work with me and he had already been contracted. It's sad. It was the hundredth anniversary. I mean, I don't particularly like Levine though there are some things he does conduct quite well, still I agreed to work with him because the best place to do *Parsifal* is, of course, Bayreuth.

Later you were commissioned to create a Parsifal *for the State Opera in Kassel, West Germany. Although this production was eventually canceled, I know you devoted a considerable amount of time to the project. I'd be interested in hearing how you set about approaching this monumental work, which would seem an ideal vehicle for you, resonating as it does so many of the themes and concerns of your own work.*

Well, everyone always said *Parsifal* would be the work to do so I started to listen to the music and I hired Annette Michelson, a writer and scholar, to work with me for a number of months on a concept. I looked at various productions and found out what other people had done with the opera. There's a beautiful one that Appia designed and the one Wieland Wagner did in the fifties was really great, beautifully proportioned. I tried to find what Wagner was attempting to do musically and also what he was trying to say with the text. I'll only do one *Parsifal* in my life and I want this to be one of the great ones. So I thought about the text and the music and the most complicated problem to solve was how to present a work that's very religious – it's very close to what I just did with Jessye – with a sincere religious attitude. It never seemed right to me to have this fake church service with these knights standing around singing and passing this holy grail. It was somehow sacreligious, everything the work was supposed not to be. When I listen to the music here it's a religious experience but when I go to the theater and see this temple-church-whatever and these klutzy knights walking around with this cup, it's ridiculous, it's disturbing and it's all wrong. So that's one problem to solve. Then there's the idea that Parsifal is the innocent fool. How is that portrayed? Christopher Knowles would have been the perfect actor for me but someone like Manfred Jung playing this innocent fool is no good – in one sense, in another sense I guess it's o.k. You know when Levine does *Parsifal* at the Met there's a time in the third act when I feel I'm going to scream if he doesn't stop or he doesn't go faster. It's interminable. Yet it can be done in such a way that you say to yourself, 'I can listen to this for the rest of my life.' That's what's so fascinating about *Parsifal*. It can be unbearably long or it can be . . . forever. Here, I can show you the designs. They're all finished.

There's no house curtain. Instead there's a curtain of light.

Then a wall of water with the beams of light coming vertically across. Eventually a lake appears at the back and that's the prelude.

The whole piece is in blue. Gurnemanz appears here at the downstage edge of the lake.

Just before Parsifal enters I have this enormous white swan, the swan that he's just shot, falling very slowly into the lake.

For the transformation scene – 'Time becomes space here' – I have a great disk of light that moves on stage from the side and an iceberg floating upstage.

Eventually the disk of light settles in the center of the lake. Parsifal stands downstage watching with his back to the audience the way the audience watches it.

I don't have the knights or any of that. Amfortas is carried out in his litter and he goes into the iceberg and takes out an Egyptian box. Inside is a clear glass chalice which is shaped like an X.

He holds it up and then he disappears. At the end, Gurnemanz comes into the ring of light and asks Parsifal, 'What have you seen?' And there's just the light, the whiteness. The idea is to make this mysterious temple of light. It's as if one were to see this big ring of light floating out here in the middle of the Hudson. It's all about light. And that's the first act. The second act starts the same way with the vertical beams of light crossing the water. We're still at the lake but now it's night and a metal tower rises out of the water.

It's like a fairy tale. That's where Chéreau missed the boat for me. His *Ring* is beautiful looking, gorgeous, but it's so serious and heavy. And it's fantastic to have an opera with giants and a dragon, it's stories for children. Klingsor appears in a window in the tower and he's a bad guy almost the way Ivan the Terrible is in the movie. Kundry is next to him – and I want to do it with Jessye – and her hair falls out of the tower. After their scene, the doors close and the tower sinks beneath the waves. Then we go underwater for the flower garden scene.

There are ferns and painted flowers that open. They're all flat with lights inside them, only the rocks are dimensional. The flower garden is all in color. It's like Chinese flowers that open in the water. At the end of the act Klingsor throws his spear at Parsifal. Here it's a rod of light. The scene is all back painted and at the moment Parsifal picks up the glowing rod, we turn on all the lights from behind and everything appears in cold black and white like a skeleton. Parsifal takes the rod of light and draws the outline of the chalice in light, and that's the end of the second act. The third act begins the same way as the first except that I've put the singers on the other side of the stage. For springtime (the Good Friday scene), I've created an enormous tulip that's lowered into the lake, like the big swan you saw in the first act.

I also bring all the chorus onstage for one brief moment when they're trying to convince Amfortas to perform the grail ceremony. We have him lying in his litter and they rush on and form a huge wall of bodies downstage.

The ring of light comes back on. It's now a black disk, which slowly falls into the lake, turning white when Parsifal stands on it. He takes the chalice from the Egyptian box in the iceberg and holds it up. The iceberg disappears.

At the end he leaves the stage. No one is on stage. Fire comes out of the ring of light and stars appear in the sky.

In a sense what you've done is create your own mysteries within Wagner's larger ones. Your scenario also seems to have purged the opera of what many feel is mock Christianity. What interests me even more is how you will approach the work's complex psychological characterizations. How will you deal with Wagner's characters and the acting requirements of the piece?

I can only tell you that it won't be psychological acting. It will be the opposite of what Chéreau did with the *Ring*. I never understood why they called that naturalistic acting. It's the most artificial, unnatural way of behaving on stage that I've ever seen in my life. But they all said that Chéreau has reinvented naturalistic acting. It's just too much for me. I'm not interested in that kind of thing.

While your Parsifal *will be produced at some future date, it's regrettable you were denied the chance to stage the Bayreuth centennial production. The occasion demanded some kind of great event — either a radical re-evaluation of the work or a personal commentary by a major contemporary artist, or at least a fresh sensibility. Certainly it provided an unparalleled opportunity in terms of visibility and critical attention. All things considered you probably would have been an ideal person for the job.*

I would have been the ideal person, yeah.

Götz Friederich was eventually chosen to direct the centennial production, I believe at a relatively late date.

You know why? Because Friederich can come in and do it in two days. I saw a new production of *Tristan* he did two years ago in Stuttgart. It was the third *Tristan* he had done that year. I was there the night before the last general rehearsal and he still hadn't decided where the singers were going to be. It never *was* decided. In the second act he never even told them where to go. Now, how on this earth do you do that? They had one big vulgar spot that followed the singers wherever they went, and of course, they went where they normally go anyway. It's ridiculous. So that's why it went to Friederich. It's perfect for Levine and the way he thinks and the way they run a house and the way they make art. And did you hear anything about the performances? No one even *mentioned* the *Parsifal* last summer. No one talked about it. The hundredth anniversary!

It's been rumored that you will be staging Tristan *at Bayreuth some time in the future, possibly with Jessye Norman as Isolde.*

Well, I would like to do it. I was asked. La Scala also asked me to do the *Parsifal* and I will if I get the rehearsal time I need. I would like Abbado to conduct, if he will work with me.

You're one of the few American directors who works regularly with a dramaturg, a fixture of the German state theater system. Was the concept of a dramaturg new to you when you went to Berlin in 1979 to stage Death, Destruction and Detroit *for the Schaubühne?*

That's right. I always had various people around when I was working before – advisors, people who did research – but I never really had the concept of a dramaturg in mind. When they first gave me one in Berlin I said, 'This is ridiculous.' I walk in and there's a staff of twenty people. What are they all going to do? 'A dramaturg?' I said, 'I wrote the play! How is he going to tell me what I'm doing with this crazy American language and all?' But they were very, very helpful – I learned so much about what I was doing and about the possibilities of what could be done. I've since learned to work very closely with dramaturgs and now I think it's almost essential to have one because I'm not scholarly, I don't have a strong background in history or a lot of formal or classical education and, anyway, it's very helpful to have someone like that to talk to. In Germany they've also translated my texts so they have to be writers as well as scholars because my texts are difficult to translate – there's slang and puns and things not immediately translatable. At the Schaubühne I worked with Peter Krumme who was excellent.

Was he involved with the day to day rehearsals?

Yes, he was there all the time and was directly involved with the actors and their interpretations. We worked as a team. When I produced *The Golden Windows* in Munich, again a fantasy thing with the kind of crazy texts I do, I worked very closely with Michael Wachsmann. He's brilliant but he doesn't say very much. 'Maybe this word should be over there' or 'Take that out' or 'Maybe there should be a slight hesitation in the middle of this word.' I work with what they tell me, with what they feel is correct. It's very much a collaboration. I really like working with a dramaturg and I think they're underestimated – in terms of my work anyway.

While you've spent most of the last few years in Europe creating new works, you recently performed in Japan and will be returning there in the near future to produce several segments of Civil Wars. *I'd think the Japanese would be an ideal audience, especially since the stylization, formality and durational qualities of their own theater forms logically prepare them for the imaginative demands of your work.*

That's what everyone has said and I was very nervous about it. I did the prologue to the fourth act of *Deafman Glance*, which is a murder scene, with a beautiful Japanese actress (Chizuko Sugiura). It was actually one of the first things I ever made for the theater. They were a wonderful audience and it was very well received. There was a scholar who came and wrote a piece saying that the work was timeless but it happened in this century. In some ways the play is very modern but he saw that it was timeless, it could have happened any time. And that's the Japanese, they live with such an awareness of tradition and the past. They're very contemporary, very modern but they're still building houses with bamboo and paper.

You've made a number of video works in the last couple of years, some of which have been seen in this country. Are you planning to devote more time to media projects in the future?

I think T.V. is the future. To be very honest with you I don't watch it because it doesn't interest me, but at the same time I'm fascinated by the possibilities of the medium and am already planning more works with T.V. I went to see Martha Graham's company when I was rehearsing an opera in Washington some time ago and I noticed that a work she had created in 1946 was listed in the program as having been copyrighted in 1977. I was told that she filmed it in 1977 and that established the copyright. That's what I want to do with my works. People are asking about *Einstein* in particular, and I will do it again some place and film it.

Your works tend to play to a select, somewhat narrow audience made up of fans, theater people, writers, artists and art patrons. You've spoken in the past of wanting to attract new audiences to your work.

Right.

Are you still actively seeking a larger audience?

Absolutely. I think that's what I'm trying to do with *Civil Wars*. It's on the scale of larger popular theater. That's how I intended it. It's an event, a large popular event. It's meant to be the way rock con-certs are. I was in Rome a few weeks ago and Syberberg's film of *Parsifal*, which is four and a half hours long, was shown before three thousand people in a large open air space. It was fantastic. It was a big event. There was something exciting about being there, just like at a rock concert. I saw this *Napoleon* film at Radio City Music Hall and it was very exciting. It was in Japan when I was there. Everywhere it's been, it's been something special. It's an event and I think that's great. When I first went to hear a rock concert about fifteen years ago I thought, 'Gee, this is really the great opera of our time.' I don't think that when I go to the Metropolitan Opera. Maybe I do if I go to see Patrice

Chéreau's *Lulu* at the Paris Opera. That's a great cultural event, but I don't go expecting such an experience at the Met. I mean, who's going to fly from Paris to see something at the Met? Chéreau just did *Peer Gynt* in Paris and people came from all over Europe. People went to Berlin for Peter Stein's *Oresteia*. That's an event. People come from all over Europe to see *The Golden Windows* in Munich. Who comes to Broadway to see *Sweeney Todd*? Who goes to see another John Dexter production at the Metropolitan Opera? Nobody! Nobody is interested. That's what's so *dull* about this city. No one comes here to see anything. People come from New Jersey to see Broadway musicals. It's all for a suburban audience.

What about dance and avant garde theater?

Well, if I want to see the avant garde of America I'll go to Europe. You can't see it here. Richard Foreman is working at the Paris Opera. I just saw his new piece at the Festival of Autumn. I go to Europe to see that kind of thing, not America. Maybe people will go to the Village to see Joe Papp's work if there's something special about it but Joe presents his work for an audience that is very select, very narrow. He calls it a public theater, a popular theater, but I don't think it's that at all.

Do you think you can attract a popular audience as such to The Civil Wars?

I hope so. I hope we get it done.

■   ■   ■

Source

Wilson, R. (1983) 'Robert Wilson: Current Projects. Interview with Laurence Shyrer', *Theater*, Summer/Fall 1983: 84–91.

Robert Wilson (1944–)

One of the most important examples in our time of the director as total scenographer. He is an artist who uses the stage as a three-dimensional and aural palette, working with sound, gesture, movement, light, and time, to produce theatre pieces which are often epic and concerned with the symbols and poetics of our century. The titles of some of these – *The Life and Times of Joseph Stalin* (1973), *Einstein on the Beach* (1976), *Death, Destruction, and Detroit* (1979), and *CIVIL* warS (1984) – show his interest in deconstructing twentieth-century myths and reconstituting them as elements in a total theatre piece – a 'Gesamtkunstwerk' in the Wagnerian sense. He works with major choreographers such as Lucinda Childs, and composers such as Philip Glass and Gavin Bryars, all of whose work helps to create a sense of material which is constantly re-interpreting ourselves and our preoccupations. Wilson's work is often long, visually simple, and full of contrasts and contradictions which force the spectator to attend. His techniques owe much to modern technology – the freeze-frame, slow motion, playback – and his interest in the relationship between the mental and the physical has led him to examine the effects of dislocation on our perceptions of the world.

In this interview Wilson's mode of thinking and perceiving is exposed by the way in which he speaks, carefully choosing words as he carefully chooses images for his work, currently moving through a phase of approaching classic texts from European literature.

Reader cross-references

Anderson, Appia, Craig and **Schlemmer** – other visual approaches to theatre
Bausch – performances that juxtapose the unexpected
Brecht – theatrical contrasts
Cunningham – American antecedents
Glass and **Müller** – two of his major collaborators
Kantor – another approach to non-linear theatre
LeCompte – another deconstructive approach to narrative
Lepage – a parallel scope
Meyerhold – a much earlier view of total theatre
Piscator – an earlier view of visual staging

Further reading

Donker, J. (1985) *The President of Paradise*, Amsterdam: International Theatre Bookshop.
Williams, D. and Bradby, D. (1988) *Directors Theatre*, London: Macmillan.
Witts, N. (1986) 'Robert Wilson and Gavin Bryars' Medea', *Forty Years of Mise en Scène 1945–1985*, Dundee: Lochee Publications.

A Chronology of Texts

A Bibliography of Twentieth-Century Performance

The following bibliography is a contribution to defining the field of performance. It lists texts that in one way or another address over-arching performance concerns, those which are definitive in their field, and those that the editors have found to be especially useful. It there-fore lists some of the full publications from which this book's forty-two texts are drawn, but not others.

(Source details for each of the forty-two main texts can be found in their accompanying contextual summaries, along with further refer-ences, specific to individual artists or authors.)

Adair, C. (1992) *Women and Dance: Sylphs and Sirens*, London: Macmillan.

Adshead, J. and Layson, J. (eds) (1988) *Dance Analysis*, London: Dance Books.

Adshead-Lansdale, J. and Layson, J. (eds) (1994) *Dance History: An Introduction*, London: Routledge.

Artaud, A. (1938, 1964, 1970) *The Theatre and Its Double*, trans. V. Corti, London: Calder & Boyars.

Au, S. (1988) *Ballet and Modern Dance*, London: Thames & Hudson.

Austin, W. (1966) *Music in the 20th Century*, London: Norton.

Baer, N. Van N. (ed.) (1991) *Theatre in Revolution: Russian Avant-Garde Stage Design 1913–1935*, London: Thames & Hudson.

Banes, S. (1981) *Democracy's Body: Judson Dance Theatre 1962–1964*, Ann Arbor, Mich.: UMI Research Press.

—— (1987) *Terpsichore in Sneakers: Post-Modern Dance*, 2nd edition, Middletown: Conn.: Wesleyan University Press.

—— (1994) *Greenwich Village 1963: Avant-Garde Performance and the Effervescent Body*, Durham, N. C.: Duke University Press.

—— (1994) *Writing Dancing in the Age of Postmodernism*, Middletown, Conn.: Wesleyan University Press.

Barba, E. (1979) *The Floating Islands: Reflections with Odin Teatret*, trans. J. Barba, F. Pardeilhan, J.C. Rodesch, S. Shapiro, J. Varley, Denmark: Thomsens Bogtrykheri.

Barba, E. and Savarese, N. (1991) *A Dictionary of Theatre Anthropology: The Secret Art of the Performer*, London: Routledge.

Barthes, R. (1968, 1977) `The Death of the Author', *Image-Music-Text*, trans. and ed. S. Heath, London: Fontana: 142–148.

—— (1972) *Mythologies*, trans. A. Lavers, London: Jonathan Cape.

—— (1972, 1977) *Image-Music-Text*, trans. and ed. S. Heath, London: Fontana.

Battcock, G. (ed.) (1968) *Minimal Art: A Critical Anthology*, New York: Dutton.

Beacham, R.C. (ed.) (1993) *Adolphe Appia: Texts on Theatre*, London: Routledge.

Beck, J. (1972) *The Life of the Theatre: The Relation of the Artist to the Struggle of the People*, San Francisco: City Lights Books.

Benjamin, W. (1973a) *Illuminations*, trans. H. Zohn, London: Fontana.

—— (1973b) *Understanding Brecht*, trans. A. Bostock, London: NLB.

Bentley, E. (1968) *The Theory of the Modern Stage*, Harmondsworth: Penguin.

Berger, J. (1972) *Ways of Seeing*, Harmondsworth: Penguin.

Bharucha, R. (1993) *Theatre and the World*, London: Routledge.

Boal, A. (1974, 1979) *Theatre of the Oppressed*, trans. C. A. and M.O.L. McBride, London: Pluto.

—— (1992) *Games For Actors and Non-Actors*, trans. A. Jackson, London: Routledge.

Bradbury, M. and MacFarlane, J. (eds) (1976) *Modernism 1890–1930*, Harmondsworth: Penguin.

Bradby, D. and Williams, D. (1988) *Directors' Theatre*, London: Macmillan.

Braun, E. (trans. and ed.) (1969) *Meyerhold on Theatre*, New York: Hill & Wang.

Brecht, S. (1978) *The Theatre of Visions: Robert Wilson*, Frankfurt am Main: Suhrkamp.

Brinson, P. and van Praagh, P. (1963) *The Choreographic Art*, London: A & C Black.

Brockett, O.G. and Findlay, R.R. (1973) *Century of Innovation*, Englewood Cliffs, N.J.: Prentice-Hall.

Brook, P. (1968, 1990) *The Empty Space*, Harmondsworth: Penguin.

Brown, J.M. (ed.) (1979, 1980) *The Vision of Modern Dance*, London: Dance Books.

Brown, M.W. (1988) *The Story of the Armory Show*, New York: Abbeville.

Burbank, R. (1984) *Twentieth Century Music*, New York: Facts on File.

Burt, R. (1995) *The Male Dancer: Bodies, Spectacle, Sexualities*, London: Routledge.

Cage, J. (1961, 1973) *Silence*, Middletown, Conn.: Wesleyan University Press.

Case, S.-E. (1988) *Feminism and Theatre*, New York: Methuen.

Clément, C. (1989) *Opera or the Undoing of Women*, London: Verso.

Cohen, S.J. (ed.) (1974, 1992) *Dance as a Theatre Art: Source Readings from 1581 to the Present*, 2nd edition, New York: Dance Horizons/Princeton Book Company.

Copeland, R. and Cohen, M. (eds) (1983) *What is Dance? Readings in Theory and Criticism*, New York: Oxford University Press.

Couzen-Hoy, D. (ed.) (1992) *Foucault: A Critical Reader*, Oxford: Basil Blackwell.

Craig, E.G. (1911, 1956) *On the Art of the Theatre*, New York: Theatre Arts Books.

Derrida, J. (1993) *Writing and Difference*, London: Routledge.

Drain, R. (ed.) (1995) *Twentieth-Century Theatre: A Sourcebook*, London: Routledge.

Dreier, R. (1986) `Minimal Music', *The New Grove Dictionary of American Music*, ed. H.W. Hitchcock and S. Sadie, New York: Macmillan.

Duncan, I. (1928) *The Art of the Dance*, New York: Theatre Arts Books.

Dürrenmatt, F. (1976) *Writings on Theatre and Drama*, London: Cape.

Elam, K. (1980) *The Semiotics of Theatre and Drama*, London: Methuen.

Fabre, G. (1983) *Drum Beats, Mask and Metaphor: Contemporary Afro-American Theatre*, Harvard: Harvard University Press.

Foster, H. (ed.) (1983) *Postmodern Culture*, London: Pluto.

Foster, S.L. (1986) *Reading Dancing*, Berkeley: University of California Press.

Gablick, S. (1984) *Has Modernism Failed?*, London: Thames & Hudson.

Garvin, H.R. (ed.) (1980) *Romanticism, Modernism, Postmodernism*, London: Associated University Presses.

Goldberg, R. (1979, 1988) *Performance Art from Futurism to the Present*, London: Thames and Hudson.

Griffiths, P. (1978) *A Concise History of Modern Music from Debussy to Boulez*, London: Thames & Hudson.

Gropius, W. and Wensinger, A. (1961) *The Theater of the Bauhaus*, Middletown, Conn.: Wesleyan University Press.

Grotowski, J. (1968, 1969) *Towards a Poor Theatre*, trans. M. Buszewicz and J. Barba, ed. E. Barba, London: Methuen.

Harris, M.E. (1987) *The Arts at Black Mountain College*, Cambridge, Mass.: MIT Press.

Hayman, R. (1977) *Artaud and After*, Oxford: Oxford University Press.

Hewison, R. (1990) *Future Tense: A New Art for the Nineties*, London: Methuen.

Hilton, J. (1987) *Performance*, London: Macmillan.

Horst, L. and Russell, C. (1961, 1963) *Modern Dance Forms*, New York: Dance Horizons.

Humphrey, D. (1959) *The Art of Making Dances*, New York: Grove.

Huyssen, A. (1986) *After the Great Divide: Modernism, Mass Culture, Postmodernism*, London: Macmillan.

Innes, C. (1993) *Avant Garde Theatre 1892–1992*, London: Routledge.

Jencks, C. (1977) *The Language of Post-Modern Architecture*, New York: Rizzoli.

—— (1987) *What is Post-Modernism?*, London: Academy Editions.

Kaprow, A. (1966) *Assemblage, Environments and Happenings*, New York: Abrams.

Kaye, N. (1994) *Postmodernism and Performance*, London: Macmillan.

—— (1995) *Art into Theatre*, London: Macmillan.

Kirby, M. (1966) *Happenings*, New York: Dutton.

—— (1969) *Total Theatre*, New York: Dutton.

—— (1971) *Futurist Performance*, New York: Dutton.

—— (ed.) (1974) *The New Theatre: Performance Documentation*, The Drama Review Series, New York: New York University Press.

Kobialka, M. (trans. and ed.) (1993) *A Journey Through Other Spaces: Essays and Manifestos by Tadeusz Kantor*, Berkeley, Calif.: University of California Press.

Koegler, H. (1977, 1982) *The Concise Oxford Dictionary of Ballet*, Oxford: Oxford University Press.

Kostelanetz, R. (1968, 1980) *The Theatre of Mixed Means*, New York: Archae Editions.

—— (ed.) (1993) *Dictionary of the Avant-Gardes*, New York: a cappella books.

Kriegsman, S.A. (1981) *Modern Dance in America: The Bennington Years*, Boston, Mass.: G.K. Hall.

Livet, A. (ed.) (1978) *Contemporary Dance*, New York: Abbeville.

Lyotard, J.-F. (1979, 1984) *The Postmodern Condition: A Report on Knowledge*, trans. G. Bennington and B. Massumi, Manchester: Manchester University Press.

Martin, J. (1933, 1965) *The Modern Dance*, New York: Dance Horizons.

Masson-Sekine, N. (ed.) (1988) *Butoh: Shades of Darkness*, Tokyo: Shufonotomo.

McClary, S. (1991) *Feminine Endings: Music, Gender and Sexuality*, Minnesota: University of Minnesota Press.

McLuhan, M. (1964) *Understanding Media: The Extensions of Man*, London: Routledge.

Mitter, S. (1992) *Systems of Rehearsal*, London: Routledge.

Moi, T. (ed.) (1986) *The Kristeva Reader*, London: Blackwell.

Morton, B. and Collins, P. (eds) (1992) *Contemporary Composers*, Chicago and London: St James.

Nairne, S. (1987) *State of the Art: Ideas and Images in the 1980s*, London: Chatto & Windus.

Nattiez, J.-J. (1990) *Music and Discourse: Toward a Semiology of Music*, New Jersey: Princeton University Press.

Norris, C. (1993) *Deconstruction: Theory and Practice*, London: Routledge.

Nyman, M. (1974) *Experimental Music, Cage and Beyond*, London: Studio Vista.

Ortolani, B. (ed.) (1994) *International Bibliography of Theatre 1990–1991*, Theatre Research Data Centre.

Park, J. (ed.) (1991) *Cultural Icons*, London: Bloomsbury.

Patterson, M. (1981) *The Revolution in German Theatre 1900–1933*, London: Routledge.

Pavis, P. (1992) *Theatre at the Crossroads of Culture*, London: Routledge.

Percival, J. (1971) *Experimental Dance*, London: Studio Vista.

Piscator, E. (1929, 1980) *The Political Theatre*, trans. H. Rorrison, London: Eyre Methuen.

Rainer, Y. (1974) *Work 1961–73*, Halifax, Nova Scotia: The Press of the Nova Scotia College of Art and Design.

Read, A. (1993) *Theatre and Everyday Life*, London: Routledge.

Reinelt, J.G. and Roach, J.R. (eds) (1992) *Critical Theory and Performance*, Ann Arbor, Mich.: University of Michigan Press.

Richards, T. (1995) *At Work with Grotowski on Physical Action*, London: Routledge.

Richter, H. (1964, 1965) *Dada: Art and Anti-Art*, trans. D. Britt, London: Thames & Hudson.

Roose-Evans, J. (1970) *Experimental Theatre from Stanislavsky to Brecht*, London: Studio Vista.

Sadie, S. (ed.) (1988) *The New Grove Twentieth Century American Masters*, London: Macmillan.

Savran, D. (1988) *Breaking the Rules*, New York: Theatre Communications Group.

Sayre, H.M. (1989) *The Object of Performance: The American Avant-Garde since 1970*, Chicago: University of Chicago Press.

Schechner, R. (1988) *Performance Theory*, London: Routledge.

—— (1993) *The Future of Ritual: Writings on Culture and Performance*, London: Routledge.

Schutzman, M. and Cohen-Cruz, J. (eds) (1994) *Playing Boal*, London: Routledge.

Senelick, L. (1992) *Gender and Performance*, Hanover: University Press of New England.

Shank, T. (1982) *American Alternative Theatre*, New York: Grove Press.

Shaw, S. and Allen, K. (eds) (1994) *Make Space*, London: Theatre Design Umbrella and Society of British Theatre Designers.

Silverman, H. (1990) *Post-Modernism, Philosophy and the Arts*, London: Routledge.

Slonimsky, N. (1971) *Music since 1900*, New York: Scribners.

—— (1992) *Baker's Biographical Dictionary of Musicians*, 8th edition, New York: Schirmer.

Sontag, S. (1966) *Against Interpretation and Other Essays*, New York: Farrar, Straus and Giroux.

Stangos, N. (ed.) (1974, 1981) *Concepts of Modern Art*, London: Thames & Hudson.

Stanislavski, K. (1950) *Building a Character*, trans. E.R. Hapgood, London: Max Reinhardt.

Steinberg, C. (ed.) (1980) *The Dance Anthology*, New York: New American Library.

Thomas, H. (ed.) (1993) *Dance, Gender and Culture*, London: Macmillan.

Watson, I. (1995) *Towards a Third Theatre*, London: Routledge.

Willett, J. (ed.) (1964) *Brecht on Theatre: The Development of an Aesthetic*, New York: Hill & Wang.

—— (1978) *The New Sobriety 1917–1933: Art and Politics in the Weimar Period*, London: Thames & Hudson.

—— (1984) *The Weimar Years: A Culture Cut Short*, London: Thames & Hudson.

Williams, R. (1954, 1968, 1972) *Drama in Performance*, Harmondsworth: Penguin.

—— (1968, 1969) *Drama from Ibsen to Brecht*, London: Chatto & Windus.

—— (1983) *Keywords: A Vocabulary of Culture and Society*, revised and expanded edition, London: Methuen.

—— (1989) *The Politics of Modernism*, London: Verso.

Wolff, J. (1981) *The Social Production of Art*, London: Macmillan.

Yarrow, R. (ed.) (1992) *European Theatre 1960–1990: Cross-Cultural Perspectives*, London: Routledge.

Yates, P. (1978) *20th Century Music*, London: Allen & Unwin.

Index

Titles of works in *italics*